G0-CBU-089

The Economics of Taxation

The Economics of Taxation

SIMON JAMES

University of Exeter

CHRISTOPHER NOBES

University of Strathclyde

SECOND EDITION

Philip Allan

First published 1978 by

PHILIP ALLAN PUBLISHERS LIMITED
Market Place
Deddington
Oxford OX5 4SE

Second edition 1983

British Library Cataloguing in Publication Data

James, Simon, 1952-
The economics of taxation.–2nd ed.
1. Taxation—Great Britain
I. Title II. Nobes, Christopher
336.2′00941 HJ2619

ISBN 0-86003-051-2
ISBN 0-86003-145-4 Pbk

Typeset by *Sunrise Setting*, Torquay
Printed at Billing and Sons Limited, Worcester

Contents

List of Tables and Figures

Tables

Figures

Preface

Preface to the Second Edition

The basic structure of the book remains the same in the second edition, but we have taken the opportunity to rewrite the chapter on stabilisation, the two chapters on corporation tax and parts of most of the other chapters. We have also added references to statute and case law and, of course, up-dated the text where appropriate.

The separate *Workbook* has proved useful and a revised version will be available from 1984 onwards.

We are grateful to a number of people for helpful comments on the first edition and to Marion Bradford, Elvy Ibbotson and Vi Palfrey for secretarial help.

February 1983

Simon James
University of Exeter
Christopher Nobes
University of Strathclyde

A Note on the Finance Act 1983

The rates of tax for 1983/84 shown in this book are those which were proposed by the Chancellor in his Budget of March 1983. Normally, these would have been accepted by Parliament and passed into law.

However, in May 1983, while *The Economics of Taxation* was in press, the Conservative Government announced the date of the general election. In order to rush the Finance Bill through before Parliament was dissolved, the Government made a number of concessions to the Labour Opposition. In all probability further tax changes will be made after the election, and perhaps the original proposals will be reinstated. Nevertheless, the latest Finance Act compares with the Budget proposals as follows. The allowances shown in Table 8A were accepted. The thresholds for higher rates of tax (Table 8B) and the increase in the threshold for investment income surcharge were not accepted. The limit on mortgage interest relief remained at £25,000. The proposals for the rates of capital transfer tax were not accepted, but under the provisions of the Finance Act 1982, the thresholds were increased in line with the increase in the retail prices index in 1982. These thresholds are shown in Table 8C.

Preface to the First Edition

This book sets out to provide an introduction to the economic theory of taxation, together with an account and discussion of the tax system operating in the United Kingdom. The book assumes that the reader has some background in economics, but not necessarily a great deal; perhaps a first year university course or equivalent. It is to be hoped, therefore, that the book will be of interest to students studying taxation, whether their main discipline is economics, accountancy, law, politics or social administration. A separate *Workbook* containing questions and exercises on the material and some more detailed technical matter excluded from the book is also available.

In the field of taxation, generalisations are always subject to qualification (including, no doubt, this one!). Some of the analysis in this volume is subject to detailed qualifications that are the proper province of the theoretical economist. We have not tried to include all these qualifications and special cases since this would have resulted in a much more theoretical and lengthy book than we thought appropriate. We have, however, tried to indicate where these finer points exist, and to provide sufficient references for those interested in pursuing them.

On the more practical side, most of the examples in the text have used the actual tax rates in force in 1977/8. No doubt the rates will, as in the past, be subject to change, but this in itself will not normally affect the points illustrated by the examples.

In order to avoid distracting the reader with footnotes to references, we have used the system whereby only the name of the author and the date of publication, e.g. Johnson (1971) appears in the text itself. The full reference is then given at the end of the chapter.

Our first debt in writing this book must be to the many students whose interest in the subject has encouraged us tremendously. Their differing approaches have presented many stimulating challenges. We are also very grateful to Professor J. Black, Dr F.A. Cowell and Professor D. Walker who each made many helpful comments and suggestions on the whole of the first draft; and to Mr R.T. Bartlett, Mr J.F. Bradley, Dr I.G. Bulkley, Mr G. Channon, Mr L.J. Field, Mr A.G. Mahoney and Mr E.D. Murray who each provided many useful comments on substantial parts of it. Needless to say, remaining errors and obscurities are our own. Last, but by no means least, we are very grateful to Mrs Marion Bradford and Mrs I. Holland for secretarial assistance.

SIMON JAMES
CHRISTOPHER NOBES
University of Exeter

March 1978

1

General Introduction

'And it came to pass in those days, that there went out a decree from Caesar Augustus, that all the world should be taxed' (St. Luke ii I). And it was. In fact, the world has been 'rendering unto Caesar' ever since!

Taxation has been associated with many historical developments other than the Christmas story. A very early example is reported by Dowell (1884); it appears that taxes were one of the causes of the revolt of the Iceni, and were referred to as oppressive in the harangue of Boadicea to her forces before the battle with Suetonius. Taxation has played a part in many other revolts. The demands of King John for 'scutage' (an early form of taxation) advanced the crisis of 1215 which led to John's submission and the issue of *Magna Carta.* In the seventeenth century, the King's need for money from taxation resulted in the recall of Parliament and was a factor leading to the Civil War and the execution of Charles I. The importance of taxation as one of the causes of the French and American Revolutions is also well known.

In addition, taxation has contributed to major administrative developments. As we shall see in Chapter 10, the census in ancient Rome was used to record the property of each citizen for the purposes of taxation. The Domesday Book was compiled to meet the necessities of a new government in difficult times, and formed the basis of taxation for several centuries. Taxation also had an immense influence on the development of Parliament in the United Kingdom.

In modern Britain, the importance of taxation is clear from its sheer volume alone. Some idea of the magnitude of modern tax revenues may be gained by comparing it with gross domestic product. In 1982, GDP at factor cost in the United Kingdom amounted to nearly £230 billion. In that year, the Inland Revenue, Customs and Excise and other departments collected over £100 billion in revenue. Looked at in a different way, the average level of taxation in 1982 was over £1,700 per head of population.

As we shall see, the effects of taxation percolate throughout the economy via changes in prices, output and incomes. In this way, even individuals who are not direct taxpayers are affected by the tax system. The authors tried very hard to imagine circumstances in which an individual would be immune from the effects of taxation, but without success.

The Structure of the Book

In examining the subject of taxation, it appeared logical to divide the book into two parts. The first part is concerned almost entirely with analysis. It begins with a chapter on the need for taxation, and the classification of taxes. The effects of taxation on different aspects of economic life are then dealt with in turn. Chapter 3 examines the effects of taxation on the efficient (or inefficient) operation of a market economy. Chapter 4 deals with the effects on incentives, in particular incentives to work; and Chapter 5 with equity considerations. The final chapter in Part I discusses fiscal policy and the aggregate level of economic activity, together with the rate of inflation.

There is, without doubt, some overlap in the subject matter in each of these chapters. Any tax will almost certainly have effects in each of the four areas described.

Furthermore, a tax designed to meet the requirements of one area may well conflict with the requirements of another. A tax designed to provide incentives to work and save, for example, may be considered for other reasons to be an inequitable tax.

Alternatively, a tax system designed to be equitable may impede the efficient operation of the economy.

It follows that the first six chapters have very little to say overall about the sort of tax system society *should* have. Society may, perfectly rationally, prefer an equitable tax system to an efficient one, or *vice versa*. The first part of the book simply sets out to show some of the effects of such decisions.

Part I is also concerned with the general principles of taxation, without close reference to institutional arrangements. It is to be hoped, therefore, that many of the results will be applicable to the actual tax system operating at any particular time in any particular country.

Part II, on the other hand, is much more closely concerned with the operation of the tax system in the United Kingdom. Attempts are made to assess the advantages and disadvantages of particular institutional arrangements in the light of the principles discussed in the first part of the book and, in some cases, in the light of overseas tax systems.

Part II begins with a comparison of different taxes within the United Kingdom and of taxation in different countries. Chapter 8 then closely scrutinises income tax. The process is taken further in Chapter 9, where some possible reforms of the British system are presented. Chapter 10 turns to the taxation of wealth, and in particular the arguments for and against a wealth tax. Chapter 11 is concerned with indirect taxation, and Chapters 12 and 13 deal with corporation tax systems in general, and with the UK corporation tax in particular.

Reference

Dowell S. (1884), *A History of Taxation and Taxes in England*, Longmans, Vol. 1, p.6.

Part I

PRINCIPLES OF TAXATION

Taxes, after all, are the dues that we pay for the privileges of membership in an organised society.

FRANKLIN D. ROOSEVELT, in a speech at Worcester, Mass., Oct. 21 1936

The art of taxation consists in so plucking the goose as to obtain the largest possible amount of feathers with the smallest possible amount of hissing.

JEAN BAPTISTE COLBERT (attributed) c. 1665

2

Introduction to Part I

Before dealing with the theory of taxation in detail, there are two areas which should be discussed. The first of these areas concerns the purpose of taxation, and the second covers the definition and classification of taxes.

2.1 The Need for Taxation

It has been said that 'what the government gives it must first take away'. The economic resources available to society are limited, and so an increase in government expenditure normally means a reduction in private spending. Taxation is one method of transferring resources from the private to the public sector, but there are others. One of these alternative methods is the debasement of the currency through the production of too much money. The government simply creates more money and uses it to purchase goods and services. This technique has been tried many times over the centuries and was, for example, vehemently condemned in the fourteenth century by Nicholas Oresme (c. 1360). The main problem is that it leads to inflation. As the value of money falls, purchasing power is transferred from the holders of money to the government. This process has therefore been described as an 'inflation tax' by Johnson

(1971), Friedman and Friedman (1980) and others.

Another possibility is for the government to charge for the goods and services it provides. This is quite straightforward where the government operates like a commercial business. However, it would be very difficult, or even impossible, to charge individuals directly on the basis of the use they make of many government services. Particular examples include defence and law enforcement. A further method of raising money is to borrow it. Governments can borrow either from their own citizens or from overseas, but there are limits to the amounts that people are prepared to lend, even to governments.

Taxation has its limits as well, but they considerably exceed the amounts that can be raised by resorting to the printing press, charging consumers directly, or borrowing. So while governments often use all four methods of raising resources, taxation is usually by far the most important source of government revenue.

According to Musgrave (1959), the economic functions of government may be divided into three main categories. The first is to overcome the inefficiencies of the market system in the allocation of economic resources. The second is the redistribution of income and wealth in order to move towards the distribution that society considers to be 'just' or 'equitable'. Third, there may be a role for government in smoothing out cyclical fluctuations in the economy and ensuring a high level of employment and price stability. As we shall see in Part I, taxation has an important role to play in each of these functions of government.

Market Failure

Under certain circumstances, the market mechanism is able to supply goods and services efficiently. The concept of efficiency is discussed in Section 3.1 so there is no need for duplication here. Suffice it to say that market efficiency requires the following:

Individuals can be excluded from consuming goods if they do not pay for them.
There are no external effects.
The market is perfectly competitive.

Under these conditions, the market will tend to conform to consumer preferences. If, for example, consumers suddenly wanted more of a particular good, its price would rise and more would be produced. The market would also tend to use the methods of production which cost least.

In other circumstances, however, the market may operate inefficiently. It may be worth looking briefly at four of these circumstances: public goods, merit goods, externalities and imperfect competition.

The existence of public goods was described early on by Adam Smith (1776). He acknowledged that the government has the

> duty of erecting and maintaining certain public works and certain public institutions, which it can never be for the interest of any individual or small number of individuals, to erect and maintain; because the profit could never repay the expense to any individual or small number of individuals, though it may frequently do much more than repay it to a great society. (Book IV, Ch. IX, p. 185)

The characteristics of a public good are found in varying degrees in a wide range of goods and services. It is possible to isolate these characteristics by looking at a 'pure' public good which has two important features. First of all, individuals cannot be excluded from consuming a pure public good, even if they do not pay for it. This means that firms would have great difficulty in charging individuals for any public goods they produced. The market, if left to itself, would therefore tend to under-produce public goods. For example, suppose a firm set up in business to provide national defence. It would find it very difficult to charge individuals, because they could benefit from the firm's activities whether they paid or not.

The second feature of a pure public good is that consumption by one individual does not prevent anyone else from consuming the good. For example, if one more person is born and benefits from national defence, this does not stop anyone else from benefiting. This is quite different from a private good, for example a meal, when, if one person consumes the good, no one else can.

If extra individuals can benefit from a public good at no cost to anyone else, it is inefficient to exclude them (if this can be done) just because they do not pay. For example, up to capacity, extra individuals can use a particular bridge without preventing anyone else from crossing. To exclude them from doing so would therefore be wasteful.

So, for two reasons, the market may be an inefficient method of providing public goods. There is scope, therefore, for a non-market method of provision in which the government provides the good, and finds the money by raising taxes.

In addition, the government often supplies, or encourages the supply of, goods and services which have little in common with public goods, but are perhaps considered to have some 'merit' in their own right. Examples of these 'merit goods' include performances of opera and free school meals. By the same token, the government also discourages goods that are considered to be undesirable. These 'de-merit' goods include alcohol, tobacco and other drugs.

Such policies may be considered by some to be paternalistic. Indeed, in order to justify such action on purely economic grounds, one might want to show that the government acts more in the consumer's interests than the consumer himself does. However, we do not need to concern ourselves too much here with whether or not governments are justified in encouraging consumption of some goods and discouraging others (this is discussed further, for example, in Musgrave and Musgrave (1980), pp. 83–6). We simply need to acknowledge that they do. It can then be seen that taxation is a useful source of finance for merit goods; it is also a handy method of discouraging the consumption of de-merit goods.

External effects can also provide a role for government. There are two possibilities here — external benefits and external costs. Where there are external benefits associated with the production of a particular good, the private sector is likely to produce too little because firms do not take into account the benefit to individuals other than their customers. With external costs, the same line of reasoning suggests over-production. There are several possible policy solutions for external effects. For instance, the production of goods with external benefits could be subsidised so that production increases. Again, this may be paid for out of tax revenue. With external costs, one solution might be to impose a tax — as we shall see in Section 3.5.

Imperfect competition provides a different set of implications for the tax system. For example, basic economic theory suggests that an industry which becomes monopolised may supply its product in smaller quantities and at a higher price than when the industry was competitive. This may imply the need for a regulating body, such as the Monopolies Commission, which would require public funds for its support.

Distribution

A distribution of income and wealth that is solely determined by the market is unlikely to be the distribution most desired by society. In the market system, an individual's income is determined by the factors of production he owns and the price which those factors will fetch in the market. Society may not consider this to be a proper way of distributing its resources among its members. In an extreme case, for example, where an individual did not own any factors of production (that is, he had no capital or land and was unable to work), the individual would receive no income. If the community decides to influence the distribution of income and wealth, it is likely that the tax system will be one of the main methods employed.

Stabilisation

The third function of government is that of stabilising the economy at a high level of employment while simultaneously stabilising prices. As Chapter 6 shows, there has been some debate on the role of government in this area. What is not in dispute, however, is that the tax system is a powerful method of influencing the level of activity, should the government wish to use it.

2.2 Definitions and Classifications

A tax is a compulsory levy made by public authorities for which nothing is received *directly* in return. We have seen that the levy is partly used to provide public goods in return, but that its size is also determined by many other factors. Taxes are, therefore, transfers of money to the public sector, but they exclude loan transactions and direct payments for publicly produced goods and services.

Some problems are encountered when trying to draw the line between those payments which are taxes and those which are not. For example, it might be argued that National Insurance contributions are directly paid in order to receive subsequent benefits, and that, therefore, they do not constitute a tax. However, they have other characteristics which are sufficiently like those of taxes that they are reasonably considered to be a tax — the payments are compulsory and are charged on a basis which does not take into account factors which a normal insurance scheme would include, but which does consider an individual's income. In addition, the payments do not cover the whole cost of the system, and increases in contributions are often for macroeconomic fiscal reasons, irrespective of whether the National Insurance Fund is running short.

Other borderline cases are such payments as those for passports or television licences, which exhibit some features which are like taxes and some which are not. Our main concern in this book will be with payments which are very obviously taxes, like income tax and value added tax. These are compulsory and are not directly related to benefits received by taxpayers. However, although both these payments are taxes, they are clearly different types of taxes. This realisation leads us into a discussion of classification or taxonomy (pun gently intended).

It is possible to classify taxes in many different ways. A fairly straightforward, though detailed, classification is that used by the Organisation for Economic Cooperation and Development (OECD 1976). Taxes are grouped into those on goods and services, those on income, profits and capital gains, those on net wealth, and so on, and each group is further sub-divided (Table 2A). When comparing taxes from one country to another, such a classification is very useful, but it avoids a number of important problems about the real economic nature of different taxes. As a means of understanding taxes, the following ways of classifying them by their characteristics may be more illuminating.

Direct or Indirect

This split depends upon the nature of the past and present administrative arrangements for assessment and collection of the tax. If the tax is actually assessed on and collected from the individuals who are intended to bear it, it is called a *direct* tax. For example, capital gains tax is assessed on an individual who realises a capital gain. The tax is paid by personal cheque from the individual to the Inland Revenue. On the other hand, value added tax is collected from all the businesses involved in the production and distribution of a good for a final consumer. To a large extent, the tax will cause the price to the consumer to rise (see Chapter 5). Therefore, this tax on consumers is collected from businesses: it is an *indirect* tax. The way in which the burden of taxes is distributed throughout the economy is examined in Chapter 5. Taxes were originally classified as direct or indirect at a time when it was thought that direct taxes were not shifted at all (i.e. the taxpayer bore the tax fully), and indirect taxes were shifted completely. Modern opinion is rather more sophisticated, but the original labels are still used.

Income tax on earned income is, in most cases, deducted from the wages or salaries of employees by their employers. The employer then pays the income tax to the Inland Revenue (see Chapter 8). However, the individual deals with the Revenue personally on any matters that are not straightforward, and there are many other sources of income on which the assessment and payment of income tax is completely direct. Therefore, income tax is said to be a direct tax.

A feature that direct taxes share is that the amount of tax can be related to individual circumstances, for example, the taxpayer's commitments or family size. Indirect taxes cannot take individual circumstances into account. Manipulation of the average rate of tax borne by different individuals is also possible with direct taxation, as mentioned below. Direct taxes include income tax, corporation tax, capital gains tax, capital transfer tax and any future wealth tax. Indirect taxes include value added tax and excise duties.

Tax Base

Taxes may also be classified by tax base. Taxes may be based on a stock of something (capital taxes), or on a flow of something (current taxes). However, here there is ample room for definitional problems. Income tax and corporation tax are current taxes on income. In principle, capital gains tax is also a form of tax on current income, despite the confusion that its name might lead to. The tax base of capital gains tax is the increase in value which accrues to an investment over time. This 'income' is not taxed until it is realised, at the time of the sale of the investment. Therefore, it might be called a postponed current tax.

Value added tax and excise duties are current taxes on

Table 2A

1000 *Taxes on goods and services*
- 1100 Taxes on the production, sale, transfer, leasing and delivery of goods and rendering of services
  - 1110 General taxes
  - 1120 Taxes on specific goods and services
    - 1121 Excises
    - 1122 Fiscal monopolies
    - 1123 Customs and import duties
    - 1124 Taxes on exports
    - 1125 Taxes on specific services
    - 1126 Other taxes

- 1200 Taxes in respect of ownership and use of, or permission to use, goods or to perform activities
  - 1210 Recurrent taxes
    - 1211 Paid by households in respect of motor vehicles
    - 1212 Paid by others in respect of motor vehicles
    - 1213 Paid in respect of other goods
    - 1220 Other taxes

2000 *Taxes on Income, Profits and Capital Gains*
- 2100 Paid by households and institutions
  - 2110 On income and profits
  - 2120 On capital gains
- 2200 Paid by corporate enterprises
  - 2210 On income and profits
  - 2220 On capital gains

expenditure. Capital transfer tax is really a tax on capital, although it has a facet which reminds one of a tax on income, in that the tax is only borne when the capital moves. Wealth taxes are purer examples of capital taxes.

It would be possible to divide current taxes further, into those on sources of income and those on uses of it. Income tax and capital gains tax are examples of the former; valued added tax is an example of the latter.

The OECD Classification

3000 *Social Security Contributions*
- 3100 Paid by employees
- 3200 Paid by employers
- 3300 Paid by self-employed or non-employed persons

4000 *Taxes on employers based on payroll or manpower*

5000 *Taxes on net wealth and immovable property*
- 5100 Recurrent taxes on net wealth
  - 5110 Paid by households and institutions
  - 5120 Paid by corporate enterprises
- 5200 Recurrent taxes on immovable property
  - 5210 Paid by households
  - 5220 Paid by enterprises
  - 5230 Paid by institutions, etc.
- 5300 Non-recurrent taxes on net wealth and immovable property
  - 5310 On net wealth
  - 5320 On immovable property

6000 *Taxes and stamp duties on gifts, inheritances and on capital and financial transactions*
- 6100 On gifts and inheritances
  - 6110 Gifts
  - 6120 Inheritances
- 6200 On capital and financial transactions

7000 *Other taxes*
- 7100 Paid solely by enterprises
- 7200 Other

Specific and Ad Valorem Taxes

Taxes may be divided up on the basis of the relationship of the amount of tax to the size of the tax base. A tax whose size bore no relationship to any tax base except the existence of the taxpayer would be a poll tax, for example a tax of £10 per head throughout the population. Taxes which are based on the weight or size of the tax base are called 'specific' or 'unit' taxes: for example, an excise duty of £1 per bottle of whisky or £200 per ton of tobacco. Taxes which are based on values are called *ad valorem* taxes. Value added tax and all the direct taxes we have met are examples of these.

Rate Structure

Since direct taxes are assessed on individuals, it is possible to arrange for the marginal and average rates of a tax to change according to the size of an individual's tax base. Taxes can be classified according to the way the rate varies with income. Taxes which take an increasing proportion of an income as the income rises are called *progressive*. Those which continue to take the same proportion (though an increasing absolute amount, of course) are called *proportional*. Those which take a decreasing proportion of income are called *regressive*.

As an example, suppose that there is a system of income tax which taxes individuals on the following basis. Income up to £1000 per year is exempt from tax, extra income between £1000 and £2000 per year is taxed at 30 per cent, and income above £2000 per year is taxed at 50 per cent. Let us look at the tax paid by four individuals on incomes of £1200, £1800, £2200 and £2800 respectively. These results are shown in Table 2B.

We can see that the proportion taken in tax (the average tax rate) is rising as income rises. Another identifying feature of progressive systems is that the marginal rate of tax will always be above the average rate of tax. It is this fact which causes the average rate to rise.

Capital transfer tax and wealth taxes have increasing average rates. If these taxes are to be called 'progressive', we must be clear that they are progressive to increasing wealth rather than, necessarily, to increasing income. Value added tax and excise duties, being indirect, cannot operate on the basis of a changing rate for those who spend different amounts. However, they can be progressive or regressive, as income changes, by applying different rates of tax to different goods. If the goods that tend to be bought by those with higher incomes bear a higher rate of tax, the indirect tax may be progressive: on average, a higher proportion of higher incomes would be paid in tax.

Table 2B A Progressive System

	£	£	£	£
Income	1200	1800	2200	2800
Exempt income	1000	1000	1000	1000
Remainder	200	800	1200	1800
Tax at 30%	60	240	300	300
Tax at 50%	–	–	100	400
Total tax	60	240	400	700
Average tax rate $\frac{\text{total tax}}{\text{income}}$ % :	5.0	13.3	18.2	25.0
Marginal rate % :	30.0	30.0	50.0	50.0

Good or Bad?

It would also be possible to analyse taxes as to whether they are good or bad according to certain criteria. For example, Adam Smith (1776) proposed four canons of taxation:

(i) equity, i.e. fairness with respect to the tax contributions of different individuals;
(ii) certainty, i.e. a lack of arbitrariness or uncertainty about tax liabilities, or the tax effects of particular actions;
(iii) convenience, with respect to the timing and manner of payment;
(iv) efficiency, i.e. a small cost of collection as a proportion of the revenue raised, and the avoidance of distortionary effects on the behaviour of taxpayers (i.e. the principle of neutrality).

Each of these canons, and other criteria for judging taxes, are referred to frequently throughout this book.

Avoidance and Evasion

It is worth defining avoidance and evasion here because they are mentioned in several places throughout the book. Avoidance is the manipulation of one's affairs, within the law, so as to reduce tax liability. Evasion is illegal manipulation to reduce tax liability. Section 5.8 deals with this in greater detail.

These classifications and definitions will be used and developed throughout this book, particularly in Part I. The important taxes that will be met are shown in Figure 2A. Since there are several ways of classifying taxes, as we have seen, a large number of alternative tables would be possible.

Further Reading

For those interested in the need for taxation and the economics of the public sector there is no shortage of reading. Peston (1972), for example, deals with public goods and external effects. Many more issues are raised by the two Musgraves (1980) and by Musgrave (1959). There is also plenty of controversy. Seldon (1977), for instance, argues that a large amount of taxation should be replaced by a system of charges.

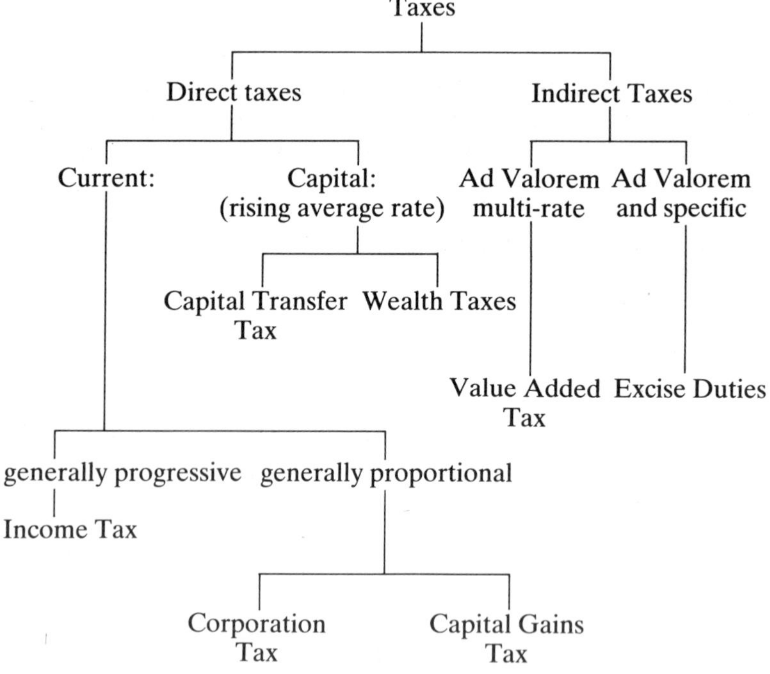

Figure 2A *Classification of Some Important Taxes*

References

Friedman M. and Friedman R. (1980), *Free to Choose,* Secker and Warburg, pp. 267–70.

Johnson H.G. (1971), *Macroeconomics and Monetary Theory,* Gray-Mills, p.152.

Musgrave R.A. (1959), *The Theory of Public Finance*, McGraw-Hill.

Musgrave R.A. and Musgrave P.B. (1980), *Public Finance in Theory and Practice,* 3rd edn, McGraw-Hill International edn.

OECD (1976), *Revenue Statistics,* OECD, Paris, Part II.

Oresme N. (c.1360), *De Origine, Natura, Jure et Mutationibus Monetarum.*

Peston M. (1972), *Public Goods and The Public Sector,* Macmillan.

Seldon A. (1977), *Charge,* Temple Smith.

Smith A. (1776), *The Wealth of Nations,* Cannan edn, Methuen, 1950.

3

Taxation and Efficiency

Adam Smith's fourth canon of taxation was that: 'every tax ought to be so contrived as both to take out and to keep out of the pockets of the people as little as possible, over and above what it brings into the public treasury of the state'. He then went on to describe four ways by which taxes could fail to meet this requirement (Smith, 1776, Book V, Ch. II). A 'great number of officers' may be needed to levy the tax; it may 'obstruct the industry of the people'; penalties may be inflicted on individuals attempting to evade the tax; and finally, taxpayers may be subject to 'frequent visits and the odious examination of the tax-gatherers'. And so, he concluded 'it is in some one or other of these four different ways that taxes are frequently so much more burdensome to the people than they are beneficial to the sovereign'.

For the purposes of this and the following chapters, we shall reclassify these burdens of taxation into three groups. The first category, known in modern literature as the *excess burden of taxation*, develops Smith's point about the impediment of taxation to production, but extends it to include the distortion of consumer choice between goods that are actually produced. The second, *administrative costs,* covers the burden to the public sector of administering taxes. It corresponds to Smith's 'great number of officers' required to levy the tax. The third group covers those costs incurred by the private sector in complying (or not complying) with the requirements of the tax system; that is, *compliance costs*. It includes both Smith's frequent visitations from tax-gatherers and his penalties for evasion, but in this modern age we can also add in the 'great number of officers' employed by firms and individuals in the private sector to look after their tax affairs.

In this chapter, we shall look first at the concept of economic efficiency and examine the excess burden of various taxes in the light of efficiency criteria. Then we shall consider administrative and compliance costs, and finally describe and comment on the phenomenon of 'tax expenditure'.

Throughout the chapter we shall concentrate on the *use* of existing resources within an economic system. We shall proceed therefore on the assumption that there is a given *supply* of resources: that is, a given total amount of labour looking for employment, and a given amount of capital and enterprise. Questions concerning the effects of taxation on the supply of these factors will be postponed to Chapter 4.

3.1 Economic Efficiency

The first task is to describe the meaning of economic efficiency. It is occasionally suggested that the conditions required for efficiency are unlikely to be found in what is referred to as 'the real world'. Yet, in order to make any significant analytical progress, it is necessary to have a clear idea of efficiency and how an 'optimal allocation of resources' may be defined. It is then possible to use such criteria to judge how taxes might interfere with the efficient functioning of an economy. It is also possible to recognise those circumstances in which different taxes may be used to encourage an economy to move towards a more 'desirable' allocation of resources than that currently prevailing.

The simplest form of economic efficiency can be seen by imagining an economy with a single consumer: a Robinson Crusoe society. This one individual has a given supply of resources which he can use to produce various goods. He also has a set of preferences regarding the products he would like to consume. It may be said that in such a one-man economy, the consumer behaves efficiently if he uses these resources to produce that combination of goods which maximises the benefit he can derive from the resources available to him.

In a society with many consumers, the issue becomes more complicated as the output of the economy can be distributed between individuals in many different ways. To keep our discussion reasonably straightforward, we shall defer our treatment of the more controversial issue of the distribution of income to Chapter 5 and confine ourselves here to the narrower issue of resource allocation.

Pareto Efficiency

To examine the issue of resource allocation the concept of 'Pareto efficiency' is especially useful. A particular allocation of resources is said to be Pareto-efficient if no rearrangement of resources could make one person better off without making someone else worse off. Or, to put it the other way round, if it is possible to change the methods of production, or the type of goods produced, so that one person can be made better off without others being made worse off, then the existing allocation of resources is sub-optimal and the efficiency of the economy can be increased by making the change.

In practice, of course, because most economic changes make some people better off and some people worse off, the concept of efficiency may be modified so that the requirement is that the gainers gain more than the losers lose. In other words, efficiency would be enhanced if, as a result of a change, the gainers were able to compensate the losers by the amount of their loss, and still be better off. Whether or not the losers are actually compensated is a question of distribution, and so again will be left for Chapter 5.

Ideal Output

The private sector may achieve a Pareto-optimal output through the market mechanism if two conditions prevail: the presence of perfect competition and the absence of economic effects external to the market. The conditions of perfect competition imply that each firm faces a perfectly elastic demand curve for its output and a perfectly elastic supply curve for its inputs. In other words, no firm is large enough to be able to influence the market prices at which it sells its produce or purchases its inputs. If firms wish to maximise their profits under these circumstances they will attempt to supply the level of output where the price (marginal revenue) of the good is just equal to the marginal cost of producing it. The owners of factors of production would be at an optimum position if they provided the services of their factors up to the point where the price equals the marginal cost of provision. Consumers would also be at an optimum position if they allocated their expenditure to maximise the benefits they received from it. In this situation, no one (consumers, owners of factor services, or owners of firms) could be made better off without someone else being made worse off. It can be seen from this brief description of perfect competition that the private sector can achieve an efficient level and pattern of output through the market, provided there are no effects external to the market.

The essential characteristic of external effects is that private costs and benefits differ from social costs and benefits. For example, an external cost would exist where an industrial firm imposed costs on the surrounding community in the form of noise, pollution and congestion for which the firm did not have to pay. As the firm is not facing all of its costs, over-production will result if the market is left to itself.

An example of an external benefit is refuse collection in an urban area. The benefits of refuse collection to the community as a whole are normally greater than the benefits accruing to the individuals whose refuse is actually collected. Where the production of a particular good confers external benefits on the community, the market would tend to supply a level of output below the optimum since the external benefits would not be taken into account.

So, for the unregulated private sector to be able to produce an optimum output, the conditions of perfect competition must prevail and there must be no external effects. The concepts of efficiency and optimality may now be used to illustrate the concept of excess burden.

3.2 The Excess Burden of Taxation

Clearly, taxes transfer spending power from the taxpayer to the government. In addition to this transfer of resources, taxes may distort consumers' choices between goods, or producers' choices between factors, and so impose an additional burden on the taxpaying community. This point can be made more explicit by distinguishing between the *income* effects of a tax and the *substitution* effects. These effects are discussed further in Section 4.1, but it is also worth introducing them here.

The income effects arise because, when a tax is imposed or increased, the taxpayer's spending power is reduced. Income effects do not in themselves result in economic inefficiency. They simply represent the transfer of resources from the taxpayer to the government.

Substitution effects arise when a tax affects relative prices and so leads individuals to substitute one form of consumption or activity for another. For example, suppose that a tax were placed on margarine, but not on butter. Consumers might then substitute butter for margarine even when, in the absence of the tax, they would have preferred the latter. The substitution effects of taxes can, therefore, lead to economic inefficiency because they interfere with consumer choice.

As a second example, it may be noted that after 1747 many taxpayers decided to avoid the window tax by bricking up their windows. (Before stricter powers were introduced in 1747, the normal method of avoiding the tax was by stopping up the windows before the assessor arrived, and re-opening them after he had left!) The lack of amenity arising from the blocking of windows was clearly a cost of the window tax; but although it was a cost to the taxpayer, it was of no benefit to the government. This type of cost may be described as the *excess burden* of taxation.

Excess burden may be analysed further by looking at the effects of imposing a specific tax on a single commodity, X. Suppose that the conditions of supply and demand for X are described in Figure 3A. If there are no external effects and the market is working perfectly, the supply schedule SS will reflect the social opportunity cost of producing X. On the other side of the market, DD indicates the benefits received by individuals from consuming X (as demonstrated by the amount they are willing to pay for it). If the market is working perfectly, the level of output will move towards an equilibrium point of Q_1. At this point the marginal cost of producing X is just equal to the marginal benefit of consuming it. By the above definition, the ideal level of output is Q_1 and any other

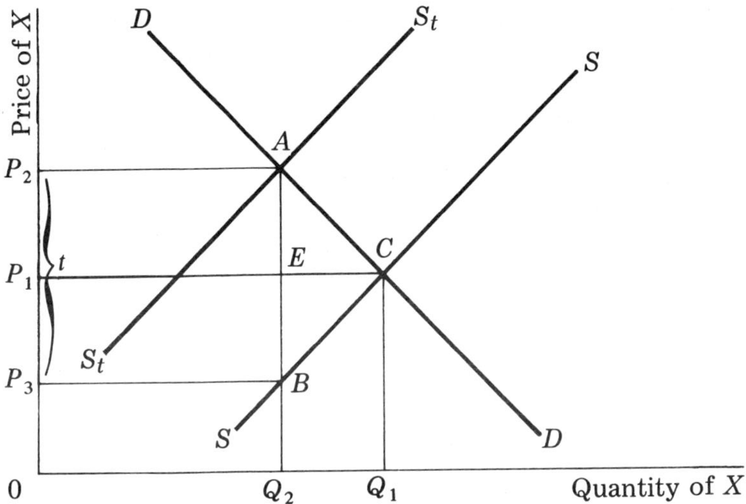

Figure 3A *Imposition of a Tax t on Good X*

level of output must be inferior. If more X were produced, the cost of the extra units would exceed the benefit; if less were produced, the lost units would reduce consumer benefit by more than they reduced producer cost.

Clearly, at the margin, the last unit of *X* produced confers little or no net benefit on the community, as the cost of production is just equal to the benefit of consumption. Equally clearly, all the other units produced confer a greater benefit than their cost. This extra benefit may be divided into two parts. First of all, there is the *consumer surplus* which is the benefit (as shown by the demand curve *DD*) received from the consumption of units of *X*, minus the price the consumer has to pay (P_1). In other words, it is the benefit the consumer gets but does not have to pay for. (Strictly speaking, it is an approximation to net consumer benefit: for further discussion see, for example, Hicks (1939), Note to Chapter 2). Secondly, there is the concept of *producer surplus* which is the price (P_1) that the producer receives less the cost of production. The concept is not quite as straightforward as consumer surplus, but it remains useful for our purposes and so it will be retained.

Now suppose that a tax of value *t* is imposed on every unit of *X* produced. In this example it may be assumed that it is the supplier rather than the consumer who is responsible for paying the tax to the authorities. As a result, the tax increases the cost of producing X by an amount t, and so the supply curve shifts upwards to S_tS_t. The market price consequently rises to P_2. However, the supplier, who hands over the tax, only keeps an amount P_3 per unit, which is the market price P_2 minus the tax t. Following the rise in the market price to P_2, the equilibrium level of output falls from Q_1 to Q_2.

The revenue paid by the taxpayers and received by the government is t times the number of units sold, and is shown in Figure 3A as the area P_3P_2AB. As a result of the price rise the consumers are worse off by an amount P_1P_2AC. Yet the government receives only P_1P_2AE of this, leaving a net loss of consumer surplus of AEC. Similarly there is a net loss of producer surplus of ECB. The excess burden of the tax is therefore shown by the area ABC.

A slightly different way of looking at this loss of economic welfare is to notice that the tax has resulted in a drop in production from Q_1 to Q_2. It is clear that these lost units of X would confer greater benefit (shown by DD) on the community than their cost (shown by SS). The tax has obstructed opportunities for profitable trade, and the loss is again described by the triangle ABC. The way in which the costs of the tax are distributed between the producers and the consumers is left for Chapter 5, but it is fairly easy to see from Figure 3A that it depends on the price elasticities of supply and demand.

We shall see that, in nearly all circumstances, all taxes have some effect on the allocation of resources. The only tax which it could be claimed was neutral with respect to the working of the price mechanism is a lump sum tax on each person — that is, a poll tax. Because such a tax does not vary with different forms of economic behaviour, it might be said that it is unlikely to affect that behaviour and so to impose an excess burden. Yet even with a poll tax it is possible to visualise an excess burden. A poll tax imposed on all heads, including children, may have some effect on taxpayers' plans regarding family size. Certainly, tax systems have been used to influence family size; a particular example is the French *quotient familial* system (see Barr, James and Prest (1977), p. 123). Even a poll tax, therefore, would only be completely neutral in the unlikely event that it came as a complete surprise.

In practice, the regressive nature of poll taxes precludes their

imposition on any scale in a modern s
concept of a lump sum tax will be useful i
characteristics of other taxes. To avoid dist
changes in government expenditure, our m
will be to compare taxes of equal yield, supp
expenditure remains the same, both in size an
the best 'dummy' taxes for this purpose is the

Some of the implications of excess burden
now be explored. A useful illustration is the tim ... ed debate
over the relative merits of income and excise taxes.

3.3 Income Taxes *Versus* Excise Taxes

An early proposition put forward by Hicks (1939) and by Joseph (1939) held that income taxes impose a lower excess burden than taxes on specific goods, as income taxes do not distort consumers' choices between goods. We shall first examine this argument, and then go on to consider the circumstances in which income taxes also impose an excess burden on taxpayers.

To isolate the basic proposition, it will be assumed that several other variables remain constant. These assumptions will be withdrawn later to see how the argument is likely to be modified in practice. It will be supposed to begin with that perfect competition prevails, that there are no external effects and that a Pareto-efficient allocation of resources exists before either tax is imposed. We will assume that the supply of factors of production is fixed, and that these factors are fully employed both before and after either the income tax or the excise tax is imposed. To abstract the analysis from distributional considerations, each individual will be assumed to be the same, that is to have the same income, tastes and so on. At this stage we shall also suppose that neither tax involves any administrative or compliance costs. We further suppose that the same amount of revenue has to be raised by whichever tax is used, and that the pattern of government spending is the same in both cases. The taxes will be applied to a simple two-good (X and Y) model. Finally, let us suppose that the choice of tax is between a commodity tax, which is levied on good X, but not on good Y, and a proportional income tax which is levied on all incomes. We begin with a 'partial' approach to the problem, that is an approach

...self to the effects of the taxes on the choice which a ... consumer makes between the two goods, and then proceed ... more general analysis of a simple economic system.

Partial Approach

Figure 3B represents the position of a typical individual with a choice of consuming different combinations of *X* and *Y*. Before either tax is imposed, and with a given money income, the individual faces a budget constraint *AB*, which shows that he could consume a maximum of *B* of *X*, or *A* of *Y*, or some combination of *X* and *Y*. The slope of *AB* reveals the relative prices of *X* and *Y*. Next, our consumer's preferences are represented by a set of indifference curves, each of which is a locus of the combinations of *X* and *Y* between which the individual is indifferent. If the consumer wishes to maximise the benefits he derives from consumption, he will

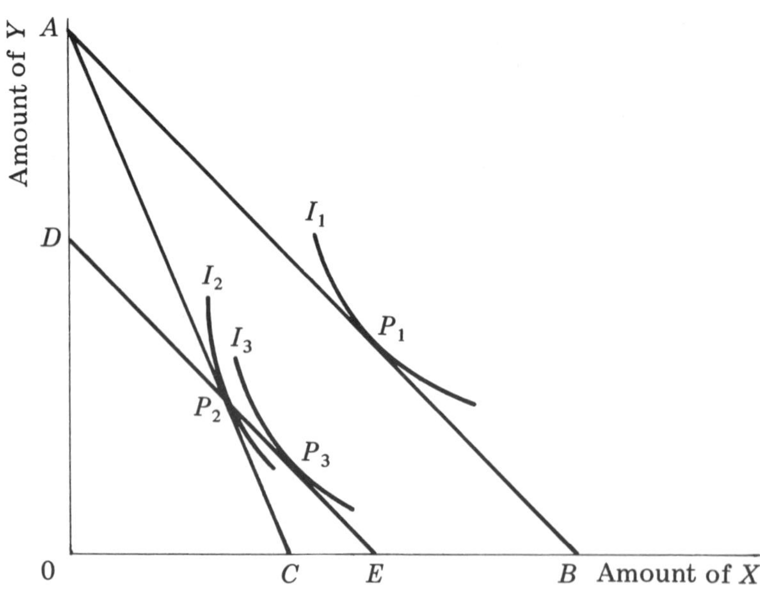

Figure 3B *Income Tax versus a Specific Excise Tax*

choose that combination of *X* and *Y* which enables him to reach his highest possible indifference curve, given his budget constraint. Without either tax the highest attainable indifference curve is I_1, and so our individual will consume at point P_1.

A specific excise tax levied on commodity *X* has the effect of shifting the consumer's budget constraint from *AB* to *AC*. It must swivel in this way because, if our individual consumed only *Y*, he would be able to buy the same amount as before. The increase in the slope of the budget constraint signifies an increase in the relative price of *X*. Given a budget constraint of *AC*, the highest attainable indifference curve is now I_2. The difference between the levels of benefit derived at P_1 on indifference curve I_1 and at P_2 on indifference curve I_2 represents the amount the consumer is worse off as a result of the tax.

If an income tax is imposed instead, the effect is also to shift the budget constraint inwards. The income tax does not distort the consumer's choice between *X* and *Y*, and so their relative prices must remain the same. Therefore, the new budget constraint *DE* must be parallel to *AB*. The tax simply reduces his income so that he can afford less of both. As the income tax is required to raise the same revenue as the excise tax, *DE* will pass through P_2, so that the individual is left with sufficient income to be able to buy the same combination of goods, irrespective of the tax to which he is subjected. However, with a budget constraint of *DE* he can attain the higher indifference curve of I_3. Clearly he is better off on I_3 that on I_2. On the assumptions listed above, therefore, an income tax inflicts less excess burden on the taxpayer than does a specific tax of equal yield. It does so simply because it interferes less with consumer choice and the allocation of resources.

Note that the argument depends on the indirect tax being imposed on *X* but not on *Y*. If the tax were levied on both goods, the analysis would be the same as that for an income tax. The crucial point is that the excess burden of a tax depends on the extent to which that tax distorts the price mechanism. This result suggests that a tax system with a broad tax base is likely to impose less excess burden than one with a narrow base. If the collection of tax is spread over a large number of goods and activities, then generally it will interfere less with consumer choice than if taxes were concentrated on a smaller area of the economy. This simple model, however, is not the end of the story because it cannot be used to examine the total effects on the economy as a whole. We shall, therefore, now turn to a more general approach.

The General Approach

The general approach is not (as the partial approach is) limited to the consumption side of the economy: it also includes the production of goods. Again, we keep to a simple two-commodity model with goods *X* and *Y*. We continue to assume that each individual is the same and has the same income, expenditure patterns and so on. The position of the community can then be described, on a much smaller scale, by the position of any one of its individual members.

This is done in Figure 3C. *TT* represents a microcosm of the production possibility frontier and shows the combinations of *X* and *Y* which can be produced. It is concave to the origin because the

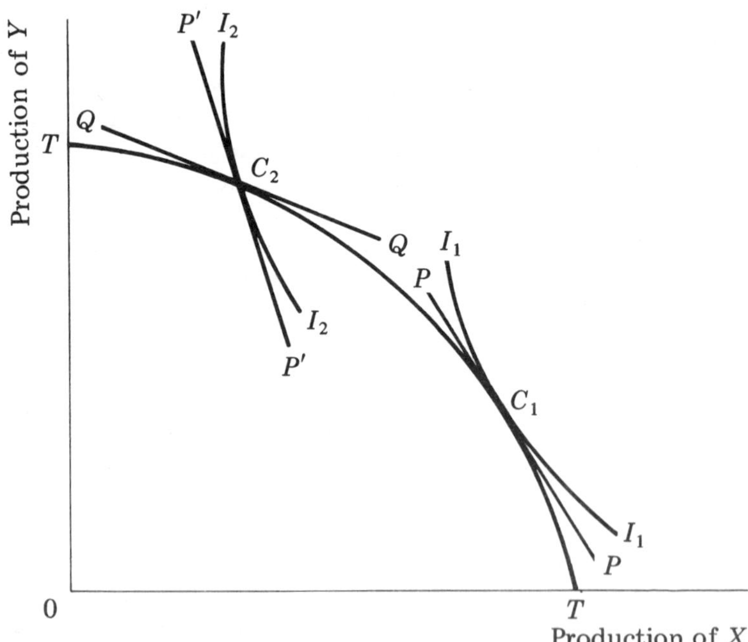

Figure 3C *General Approach*

production of X and Y is subject to diminishing returns. The slope of TT at any point represents the social opportunity cost of producing each good in terms of the other. The highest indifference curve attainable by our representative individual is I_1I_1, which means that his most preferred combination of X and Y is the point C_1. This is also the point which maximises profit for producers and is economically efficient in the way described earlier in this chapter. At C_1, the tangent to both TT and I_1I_1 is the line PP, the slope of which represents the initial relative price of X and Y in terms of each other. This same price ratio initially faces both producers and consumers. Finally, as an additional simplifying assumption, suppose that the tax revenue raised is shared out equally among the taxpayers.

If a specific tax is imposed on X, its price will rise, and the relative price ratio will become steeper as shown, for example, by $P'P'$. As a result, consumers buy less X but more Y. Because the tax revenue is redistributed among consumers, our representative individual is not forced inside the production frontier. However, given the new relative price ratio, the highest attainable indifference curve is now I_2I_2. Producers still face the real opportunity cost of producing Y in terms of X. This is shown by the price ratio represented by the slope of QQ. It is only the prices between producers and consumers that have been distorted. However, in a similar fashion to the situation described by Figure 3A, a wedge has been driven between the price paid by the consumer for X and that received by the producer. Again, consumers have substituted away from consuming X as though the higher price were the result of a higher social opportunity cost of production, whereas it is only a result of the tax. Because the tax revenue is redistributed to taxpayers, the difference in benefit between I_1I_1 and I_2I_2 is the excess burden of the specific tax.

Contrast this result with that of an income tax. Under the previous assumptions such a tax would not affect the relative prices facing consumers. Also, because the tax is returned to taxpayers, our representative individual could continue to attain I_1I_1. It follows, therefore, that in these circumstances the income tax imposes no excess burden.

So from both the partial and general approaches it is possible to examine the proposition that a specific indirect tax has a greater excess burden than an income tax. The time has now come to withdraw some of the assumptions and see if the proposition still holds in other circumstances. We begin by withdrawing the assumption that a state of Pareto-optimality existed before either tax was imposed.

A Sub-Optimal Economy

The question now is whether a Pareto-optimal allocation of resources (C_1 in Figure 3C) is the most appropriate starting point for the analysis. If either of our earlier assumptions of perfect competition or no external effects does not hold, then private marginal costs will diverge from price and the economy will tend to move away from an efficient allocation of resources. For example, if competition were restricted in an industry, from the extreme case of a monopoly to situations with a large number of sellers, we should expect the price of the goods produced by that industry to exceed the marginal cost of production. The greater the difference between price and marginal cost, the more encouragement there is for resources to be pushed away from the non-competitive industry. Hence in Figure 3C, if the X industry were to be monopolised, the output of X would tend to fall, the production of Y to rise and the economy to move from C_1 to C_2.

With an economy starting at a sub-optimal position, it can easily be seen that the relative merits of an income tax and a specific tax might be reversed. If our economy is at C_2, an income tax will not alter this misallocation of resources for the reasons described above. On the other hand, an excise tax on Y will tend to re-adjust the relative price ratio of X and Y and push the economy back towards C_1. Despite the surprising implication that the output of the more competitive industry should be taxed in such circumstances, we can see that an indirect tax may have superior allocative effects over a direct tax. It could be said that an indirect tax may even have a 'negative excess burden' in such a situation, in that the value of the revenue received is greater than the costs imposed on taxpayers. A similar result occurs where there are external effects. Discussion of these circumstances, however, will be saved for Section 3.5 on indirect taxes.

Supply of Labour

Although detailed consideration of the effects of taxation on the supply of resources is reserved for Chapter 4, we should show here how the withdrawal of the assumption of a fixed supply of labour affects the preceding analysis. In these circumstances, it is clear that income tax can also be a distorting factor. Rather than distorting the choice between different goods, it can distort the choice between goods and leisure. This was shown convincingly by Little (1951).

Suppose we have a simple three-good model consisting of food, clothing and leisure. Suppose also that labour is the only factor of production. If an excise tax were introduced on clothing, but not on food, it would distort the choice between food and clothing and also the choice between clothing and leisure. It would, however, leave the choice between food and leisure as before. A similar analysis applies for an excise tax on food, but not on clothing.

If an income tax were introduced it would also create distortions. It would distort the choice between food and leisure, and the choice between clothing and leisure. It would not, however, distort the choice between food and clothing. The two excise taxes and the income tax each distort two choices, but not the third. The relative merits of income and excise taxes depend, therefore, on how far each would actually distort particular choices. This in turn depends on a number of practical considerations, and we come now to the first of these, which is how direct taxes are actually operated in practice.

3.4 Direct Taxes

There is no income tax in the world which taxes all incomes in the same way, as assumed above. An income tax which discriminates between incomes is likely to influence the allocation of resources and, as a result, may impose an excess burden on the community. One of the best ways of examining these influences is to compare the effects of an income tax with those of a poll tax of equal yield.

Income in Kind

The first type of income that is difficult to tax is income in kind. This is income in the form of goods and services rather than cash, for example fringe benefits given by employers. This type of income is often not taxed adequately, or even not taxed at all, mainly because it is simply too difficult to measure or administer. The result is that there is a tendency for income to be taken in kind rather than in cash. It is not hard to show that this is economically inefficient. If an individual is paid for his services partly by the provision of, say, a new company car, he has to keep it unless he is allowed to sell it. If he were paid the cash equivalent he could buy the car if that were his first choice, but if he preferred anything else, he could use the cash to obtain it and so be better off. A likely preference might be to buy an older and cheaper car and to use the rest of the money for other purposes. Clearly, the greater the difference in tax liability between income paid in cash and income paid in kind, the greater the incentive for employees to demand (and employers to make) payment in kind rather than in cash. It is a curious effect of modern income tax that it may be encouraging the economy back towards a system of barter from which it took our impoverished ancestors an age to escape.

Examples of income in kind are abundant and the system appears to be thriving. For instance, nearly all forms of 'do-it- yourself' work fall into this category. If a man paints his own home, he does not pay income tax on his own services. In contrast, if he paid someone else to paint his house (or if he painted someone else's for cash) income tax is imposed on the transaction. The result is an incentive towards do-it-yourself work, even where it may be more efficient for individuals to specialise in the occupations at which they have a comparative advantage. Another example is the exemption from tax of the implicit income which individuals who own their homes receive from living in them. In contrast, the rent a tenant pays his landlord is taxed. The result may be an incentive to buy one's own home, even when it might otherwise be economically more efficient to rent, especially for the many people who have to move house from time to time.

It is interesting to speculate about how far income tax is responsible for the modern trend towards self-sufficiency simply because it fails to tax income in kind. Picture a modern income tax payer. Not only does he (or she) own and maintain his house, but he is his own chauffeur, mechanic, handyman, electrician, plumber and window-cleaner. Sundays are devoted to washing the car and gardening. He produces his own wine and serves himself at the local supermarket. It has even been suggested that he should assess his own income tax liability! (Barr *et al.* 1977). Without pushing speculation too far, it is clear that an income tax which exempts most income in kind will encourage individuals towards self-sufficiency and trade by barter more than an equi-yield poll tax would. Some evidence on the extent of the distortion towards 'household labour' was provided by Boskin (1975) using US data for 1972. Boskin estimated that the annual cost of this distortion to the US economy was of the order of \$20–\$40 billion.

Evasion

Apart from the lack of tax on income in kind, some incomes escape tax by evasion, even though they are received in cash. Although by the very nature of the subject very little is (officially) known about it, 'casual empiricism' suggests that evasion is fairly widespread, particularly in categories such as landlords, small businessmen and shopkeepers, and certain forms of casual employment. There have been various estimates. For example, in 1979 Sir William Pile, then Chairman of the Board of Inland Revenue, stated that it was 'not implausible' that incomes not declared for tax purposes could amount to $7\frac{1}{2}$ per cent of gross domestic product: a view endorsed in 1980 by his successor as Chairman (Inland Revenue, 1981). The importance of this is due to the likely effects on the allocation of labour, since occupations which afford opportunities to evade tax are likely to be more attractive than those which do not. There are, of course, also administrative and non-compliance costs, both in the efforts of individuals to evade tax, and in the efforts of the Inland Revenue to prevent such evasion.

Administration

Administrative considerations may result effectively in tax being levied at different rates on different incomes. For instance, in practice more deductions are available to the self-employed than to employees (see Section 8.5 for the UK arrangements, and Long (1982) for an analysis of the position in the USA). In effect, this can mean that self-employment income is taxed at lower rates. The result again may be a reallocation of resources. In this case, individuals may seek to become self-employed, even though from an economic viewpoint it might be more efficient for them to work as employees.

Spending patterns are almost certain to be affected when particular items of expenditure are allowable against income for particular political purposes. The tax treatment of mortgage interest payments and qualifying life assurance contributions are two examples (see Chapter 8). It may well be that society considers itself to be better off by encouraging particular forms of expenditure in this way, but it should be realised that it may involve a loss of economic efficiency. We shall have more to say about these tax deductions in Section 3.7 below.

Allocation of Factors of Production

Income taxes (as opposed to, say, a poll tax) may also affect the allocation of factors of production between different industries. Again, to allow us to concentrate on the allocation of resources, discussion of the overall supply of factors will be deferred to the following chapter. We can begin here with the allocation of labour.

One of the reasons why different occupations are associated with different wage rates is because some jobs are more demanding than others. A particular job may involve more effort, risk, discomfort, or training than other occupations. The less attractive aspects of the job have therefore to be compensated for in money, so that a sufficient number of individuals are prepared to undertake it. North Sea diving is a good example. Other jobs may be more pleasant, even enjoyable, and so require less pecuniary compensation: teaching, for instance. In the development of economic thought these divergences in wages were known as 'equalising differences', because they tended to equalise the net benefit (pecuniary and non-pecuniary) of different occupations for similar individuals.

A proportional income tax, as opposed to a poll tax, can influence these 'equalising differences' where different jobs require different levels of pecuniary remuneration. Imagine, for instance, a simple economy where workers are exactly the same in the sense that they have the same abilities, attitudes, preferences and so on, and that there are two types of job.

The first job, which is rather a pleasant occupation, can attract the required number of workers with a wage of £6,000 per year. The second job is less pleasant and, to persuade enough workers to come forward, requires a further premium of £4,000 per annum making £10,000 in all. Suppose now that a certain level of government revenue has to be raised, either by a proportional income tax, or by a poll tax. Suppose that the required level of the poll tax would be £4,000 per person, and that to raise the same revenue (after allowing for any effects resulting from the imposition of the tax) the proportional income tax rate would have to be set at 50 per cent of income. Finally, suppose for simplicity that neither tax affects gross wages.

It can be seen at once that the poll tax would not change the wage differential between the two jobs:

	No tax wage £	*Net wage with a £4000 poll tax* £	*Net wage with a 50% income tax* £
Pleasant job	6000	2000	3000
Unpleasant job	10,000	6000	5000
Differential	4000	4000	2000

A proportional income tax, however, may have such a result, as it reduces the differential between the two jobs, in this case by half. We may, therefore, expect a flow of labour away from those jobs which require pecuniary compensation for their unpopular characteristics, and towards jobs that are more congenial. A progressive income tax will have even more pronounced effects.

Progressive income taxes may also discriminate against occupations with fluctuating earnings, because each tax year is usually considered separately from every other tax year. For example, take two occupations which yield the same income over the lifetime of the worker. The first job yields the same amount of income each year, and consequently incurs the same tax liability in each year. The second job has a lower income in some years and a higher income in others. Over a lifetime, the job with the fluctuating income will incur a higher tax liability because the progressive tax structure pushes the worker into higher tax brackets in the high income years. Examples of jobs like this include authors and actors. Also, this applies to those occupations where incomes rise over a person's working life.

In principle, the adverse treatment of incomes that rise or fall (or both) could be avoided by appropriate averaging provisions. In other words, an individual's tax liability in any one year could be determined with reference to his income in other years. There are some such provisions in a number of countries, but their potential complexity prevents their widespread adoption. For instance, in the United Kingdom authors are permitted to spread their income, but this concession is not extended to most occupations. So we may conclude, therefore, that a progressive income tax is likely to discriminate against those occupations where the remuneration changes from year to year.

In a similar fashion, it can be shown that a progressive income tax may affect the allocation of capital between different industries more than a proportional income tax or a poll tax would. The important features in this case are the risk involved in different types of investments and how individuals react to this risk. A further influence is the extent to which individuals are permitted to offset their losses against their gains for tax purposes. These will not, however, be examined closely in this chapter, though a parallel discussion appears in Chapter 4, concerning the overall supply of capital.

3.5 Indirect Taxes

In Section 3.3 it was suggested that, in certain circumstances, indirect taxes could improve economic welfare. This section will explore these circumstances in more detail, and then go on to examine the welfare losses associated with indirect taxes in other circumstances.

Possible Welfare Gains

In looking at the effects of indirect taxes on the efficient operation of an economy, let us first consider the case where a tax might actually increase economic welfare. As we have seen in Section 3.3, this may occur where there are external effects.

The traditional example of an external cost is a factory polluting the surrounding environment. If the owners of the factory do not remove the effects of the pollution, a cost is clearly imposed on the community. Another example concerns congestion costs. If a large firm moves into a crowded city it will increase the congestion suffered by the inhabitants, yet only a small part of the increase in inconvenience will apply to the firm itself. This point is explored by Mishan (1967).

Turning to a more general example, suppose an industry in the process of producing a good X, inflicts external costs on the community at large. In Figure 3D the demand for X is represented by the demand curve DD. The total cost to society of producing X is shown by S_sS_s. However, because there are external costs, the

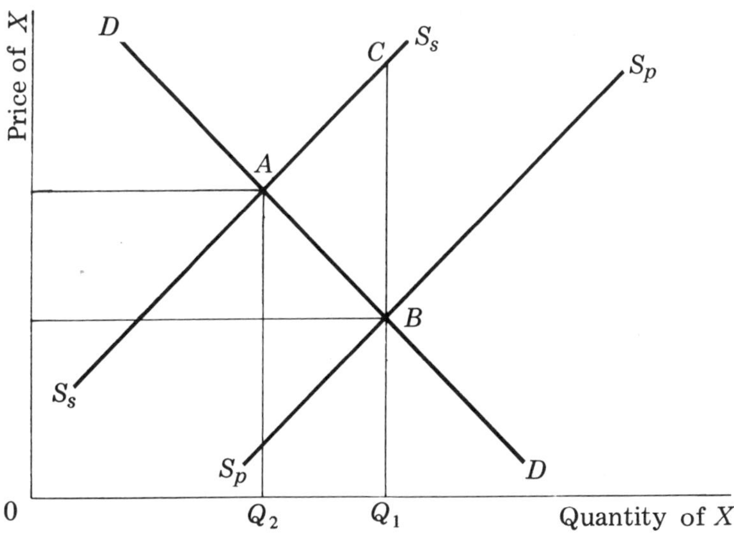

Figure 3D *An Excise Tax and External Effects*

private costs of production (that is, those costs borne by the industry itself) are less than S_sS_s, and are represented by S_pS_p. If the market is competitive, the industry will tend to produce an amount Q_1, which is the level at which private costs are just equal to the price. Yet by the definition in Section 3.1, the optimum level of production is the lower amount Q_2. At levels of output in excess of Q_2, the total costs to society of the extra production exceed the benefits.

Clearly, there are a number of ways by which the industry could be encouraged to cut back production, for example by regulation. However, it may be possible to retain the benefits of the market mechanism by imposing an excise tax on X to represent the external costs inflicted by the industry on the community. If the tax accurately reflected the external costs, the industry's supply curve would become S_sS_s, and production would tend to fall back to Q_2. Such a tax would therefore have a beneficial effect on economic welfare, that is a negative excess burden. By similar reasoning to that in Section 3.3, this welfare gain is given by the triangle ABC.

A similar result may occur where a consumer does not act in his own best interest. For instance, it is possible (nay, all too easy) to imagine an individual who does not take full account of the future results of some of his actions, and who smokes or drinks (or both) to excess. In the words of Pigou (1932), 'it follows that the aggregate amount of economic satisfaction which people in fact enjoy is much less than it would be if their telescopic faculty were not perverted'. If it is true in some instances that the government knows better than individuals what is in their best interests (and is prepared to act in those interests), then there is an economic case for public sector intervention to discourage excess consumption of certain goods. One way of doing this is to impose an excise tax on the goods.

Minimising Welfare Losses

If more revenue is needed after having used all the taxes which have beneficial effects on economic welfare, we must turn to those taxes which impose least excess burden. In order to find these, the normal approach is to examine the price elasticities of demand and supply for various commodities. To begin with, let us suppose that the elasticities of supply of different commodities are the same. It is then possible to show that for any given level of indirect taxation, excess burden will be minimised if the tax is imposed on the goods with the lowest elasticities of demand.

In Figure 3E it is assumed for simplicity that here is a perfectly elastic supply schedule (S_1S_1) for good G. It is also supposed that there are two possible demand curves for G; the first is D_1D_1 and the second, a more elastic schedule, D_2D_2. A specific tax on G will result in the supply schedule rising to S_tS_t. The tax will raise the same amount of revenue whichever demand schedule applies. However, it can be seen that, if the relevant demand curve were D_2D_2, the loss of the consumer surplus as a result of the tax would be the area ABC. However, if the demand curve were the less elastic D_1D_1, the welfare loss would be the smaller triangle ADC.

The moral of this story is that if a tax is imposed on a good and if all other things are equal, then the lower the price elasticity of demand is for a particular good, the lower will be the welfare loss. This point may also be seen intuitively from Figure 3E, by noticing that the output of G would be less affected by the tax if D_1D_1 (the less elastic schedule) applied.

It can also be shown that, if all other things are equal (including

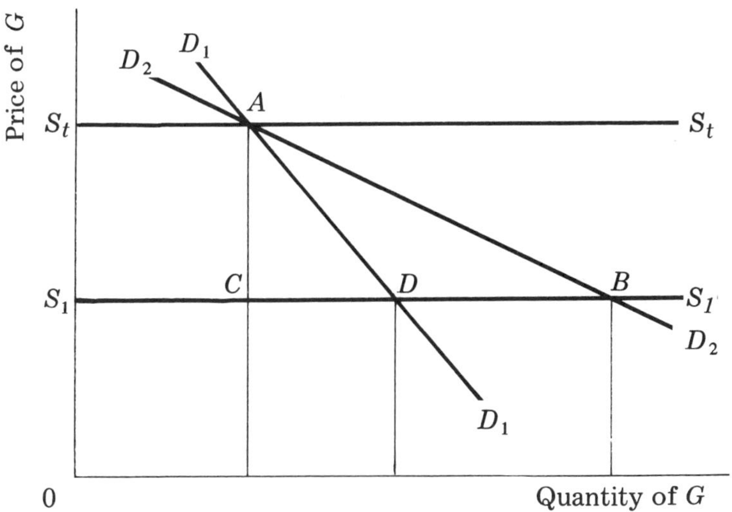

Figure 3E *Excess Burden and Price Elasticity*

the elasticity of demand), then with the imposition of a tax, lower welfare losses will be associated with lower elasticities of supply. An extreme case would be a zero elasticity of supply, as shown in Figure 3F. Here an excise tax lower than an amount *OR* (for example, a tax of *RT*) would affect neither the amount produced nor the price at which it was sold. As we shall see in Chapter 5, the entire burden in such cases will be borne by the supplier. It is interesting to note that this is one of the traditional arguments in favour of taxing land; on the assumption that land is in fixed supply, taxing the rent will not reduce the amount of land available for production. In the words of Henry George (1882), 'it is not necessary to confiscate the land; it is only necessary to confiscate rent'. It should be added that, in a number of senses, the supply of land as a factor of production is not inelastic in supply — see for example Prest (1981).

3.6 Administrative and Compliance Costs

Excess burden is not the only characteristic which should be considered in judging the relative merits of various taxes. There are also the direct costs of actually running a tax system. Earlier, we described the costs to the public sector as administrative costs, and those to the private sector as compliance costs.

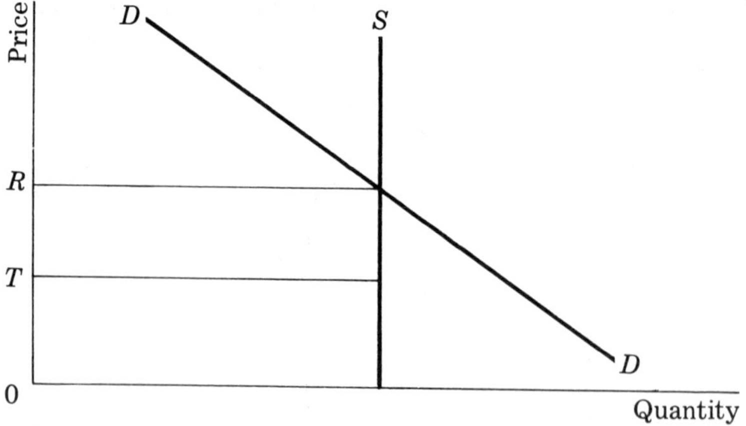

Figure 3F *Zero Elasticity of Supply*

Some costs can be imposed on either the private or the public sectors. The process of assessment, for example, may be undertaken by the revenue service, or taxpayers can be made to assess themselves; see Barr *et al.* (1977). More generally, however, those features of a tax that impose costs on one sector also tend to impose costs on the other. The most important of these features, the degree of complexity, clearly influences administrative and compliance costs in the same direction.

It is relatively easy to isolate some of the more detailed factors that determine the costs of a tax to both sectors. These include the amount of work required to determine liability, the frequency of payment, and the number of 'tax points' or taxpayers from whom revenue has to be collected. Attempts at avoidance and evasion involve both compliance (or 'non-compliance') costs to the private sector in taking advantage of these opportunities, and administrative costs to the public sector in trying to hinder the process.

Change is also expensive. When the administration of an existing tax is changed, or a new tax is introduced, both the taxpayers and the authorities face costs of adaptation to the new system. Yet, although administrative and compliance costs have many things in common, it is worthwhile taking a look at each in turn.

Administrative Costs

In comparison with the excess burden of taxes and with compliance costs, administrative costs are easy to measure. Administrative costs should, of course, include the full resource cost to the public sector of operating each tax. They should therefore include not only the wages and salaries of staff, and the full cost of the accommodation and materials used by the staff, but also the services received but not paid for from other departments.

The most useful way of presenting these costs is as a percentage of the revenue collected. It is then possible to compare the costs of collecting different taxes, and to see how these costs have been changing over time. For example, Table 3A indicates that the percentage cost of collecting VAT is high relative to the administrative costs of collecting car tax and the duties on oil and tobacco. It also indicates that the costs of collecting customs duties

Table 3A Administrative Costs of the Customs and Excise in Collecting Different Taxes

	Revenue	*Cost*	*Cost as a Percentage of Revenue*
	£m	*£m*	%
VAT	10,966.6	128.8	1.2
Car Tax	483.6	1.2	0.2
Hydrocarbon oil	3,576.4	7.2	0.2
Alcoholic drink	2,601.0	26.4	1.0
Tobacco	2,820.6	3.2	0.1
Betting & Gaming	459.6	4.7	1.0
Matches/mechanical lighters	9.6	0.2	2.0
Customs duties	817.0	45.8	5.6
CAP work	292.9	4.2	1.4
(Preventive & Fraud)	–	62.7	–
	22,027.5	299.7	1.36

Source: Commissioners of H.M. Customs and Excise, *72nd Report* for year ended 31 March 1981, Cmnd. 8521, HMSO, 1982.

is unusually high. Presenting these costs as a percentage of revenue is also a very useful way of comparing the costs of revenue authorities in different countries.

Compliance Costs

Compliance costs are very much more difficult to calculate. The costs of complying with the requirements of a tax include not only money spent on accountants and tax guides, but also taxpayers' time spent in completing returns. The mental costs to taxpayers of any anxiety suffered as a result of the operation of the tax must also be included. Although this is not a direct pecuniary expense, it is 'certainly equivalent to the expense at which every man would be willing to redeem himself from it' (Smith, 1776, Book V, Ch. II). Then there are the costs to third parties, such as friends and relatives who are asked to assist taxpayers with their returns, and the costs to firms and other institutions of acting as tax collectors, for example in withholding their employees' tax and accounting for it to the Inland Revenue.

Clearly, compliance costs, or the 'hidden costs of taxation' in the words of Sandford, are very much harder to calculate than administrative costs. Such estimates as there are of compliance costs suggest that they can be substantial. For example, Sandford (1973, p. 44) estimated that the measurable compliance costs of direct personal taxes in England and Wales in 1970 were somewhere between 2.5 and 4.4 per cent of the revenue collected. So, in considering the costs of various taxes, one has to include not only the excess burden of the taxes and public sector administrative costs, but also the private sector's costs of compliance.

The Allocation of Costs

Where administrative functions can be carried out either by the private sector or by the public sector, the question arises as to which should perform these tasks. It has been suggested by Sandford (1973, p. 160) that, all other things being equal, there are three reasons for preferring public administrative costs to private compliance costs.

First, administrative costs are met out of general tax revenue which is extracted from the taxpaying community in line with the government's concept of equity and general tax policy. Compliance costs, on the other hand, fall unevenly on private taxpayers (and some non-taxpayers) and can be surprisingly regressive in their incidence; see Sandford (1973). Second, compliance costs may lead to more taxpayer resentment and reluctance to comply with the tax system than would equivalent administrative costs. Third, we have seen that compliance costs are very much harder to calculate than administrative costs. This may lead to a tendency for tax policy makers to be less concerned about rising compliance costs than about rising administrative costs.

However, in some cases it might be cheaper for particular tasks to be done in the private sector. For example, the Pay-As-You-Earn scheme uses employers as tax collectors and is almost certainly cheaper than any method by which the Inland Revenue could undertake equivalent work. In addition, it could be argued that a competitive private market sector is more likely than the public sector to find and develop the most efficient methods of carrying out such work.

3.7 Tax Expenditure

A separate topic, but nevertheless one relevant to discussion of taxation and efficiency, is the subject of *tax expenditure*. This occurs when some fiscal advantage is conferred on a group of individuals, or a particular activity, by reducing tax liability rather than by direct cash subsidy. Examples include the tax treatment of mortgage interest and qualifying life assurance premiums. Clearly, both tax concessions and cash subsidies have much in common. They allow the government to favour certain groups or activities, and they both require the level of taxation on others to be higher, or public expenditure on alternative projects to be lower, than would otherwise be the case. But the use of tax expenditure to achieve these aims may be less efficient than an equivalent system of cash payments.

The first difficulty is that subsidies through a tax expenditure programme are relatively hidden. When the government provides cash aid, the figures are widely known, and are scrutinised carefully by the executive and by Parliament both in debate and in committees such as the Treasury and Civil Service Committee. Direct subsidies are therefore open to review, debate and possible alteration at regular intervals. This is not so for tax concessions. Although deductions against tax liabilities are costs to government in the same way as cash payments or provisions in kind, they remain comparatively hidden and secure from scrutiny. Hence, it is even more likely than with outright subsidies that tax deductions may remain even when the case for them has diminished or even disappeared.

An example of this is the treatment of mortgage interest payments. Before 1963, the imputed income that an owner-occupier received from living in his own home was liable to tax under Schedule A of the income tax code. Naturally, the costs of owning that home, including mortgage interest payments, were deductible in computing taxable income. However, when the taxation of income imputed to home ownership was abolished by the 1963 Finance Act, the mortgage interest deduction remained. Since 1983–84, the tax adjustments have generally been made by the mortgagors, rather than by the Inland Revenue.

There are difficulties in calculating the level of tax expenditure. The net revenue loss of any one allowance depends on the marginal tax rates of the taxpayers concerned. This in turn depends on what other allowances are received by the relevant taxpayers. It also, of course, depends on their incomes. A list of direct tax allowances and reliefs now appears at the end of the Government's expenditure plans, but it is clear that tax expenditure still receives far less attention than cash expenditure does.

A second and related difficulty is that the 'tax expenditure budget', being relatively hidden, is not methodically co-ordinated with the regular government Budget. The results can be quite curious. The 1972 Green Paper, *Proposals for a Tax-Credit System,* for example, looked at the interaction of the then current tax allowances and cash payments for children. It found that the overlap formed 'a serious problem. The combination of the full tax allowances and family allowances alone results in nine different rates. Nor can it really be said that the differing amounts have a logical connection with one another' (para. 3).

A third problem is that allowances against tax are not worth the same amounts to different people. The most obvious example is that people who do not receive a sufficiently high income to render them liable to tax do not gain any benefit from deductions against tax. Furthermore, the benefit in tax saved is greater for individuals subject to higher rates of tax.

A fourth difficulty is that tax expenditures complicate the tax system itself. Increased complexity inevitably increases administrative and compliance costs and, given the other problems, it seems reasonable to suggest that a convincing case ought to be made before aid for a particular cause is given through tax expenditure rather than by explicit subsidy.

The actual size of the tax expenditure budget in the United Kingdom is hard to determine. For the United States, Surrey (1973) reports a tax expenditure budget of between $60 billion and $65 billion, a sum equal to one-quarter of the regular Budget. In the United Kingdom, no such overall figure is yet available on a regular basis, though the position was investigated by Willis and Hardwick (1978). However, to continue with the example of mortgage interest relief, the estimated cost of this deduction in 1982–83 was as much as £2,180 million (*Hansard*, 23 April 1982, col. 155).

The question why tax expenditure rather than direct subsidy is used to dispense aid is interesting. Apart from any historical reasons, it might be that politicians would prefer not to be seen spending public money, and so they hide behind the veil of taxation. For the same sorts of reasons, those in receipt of benefits from the state may well prefer a tax concession to a cash handout. It might be that the pervasiveness of the modern tax system is such that tax expenditure is a convenient tool for those wishing to manipulate the economy. Whatever the reasons, it is clear that the subject of tax expenditure deserves more attention than it has received to date.

3.8 Summary

Apart from the revenue actually raised, taxation imposes economic costs on society. These costs may be classified into three groups: the excess burden of taxation, compliance costs, and administrative costs.

The excess burden of a particular tax depends on its effects on the working of the price mechanism. In practice, the actual burden is determined by a large number of factors, such as the rates and coverage of particular taxes. In some circumstances, where the market is not working efficiently, it is possible that some taxes can be used to improve economic welfare.

Administrative and compliance costs are the costs of operating a tax system imposed on the public and private sectors respectively. The evidence suggests that these costs can be considerable, and vary significantly between different taxes.

'Tax expenditure' is used to provide assistance to particular groups, or for particular causes, through reductions in tax liability rather than the more direct method of cash payments. There are a number of possible disadvantages associated with the use of tax expenditure.

Further Reading

The relative merits of direct and indirect taxes are considered further in

Little (1951), Friedman (1952), Walker (1955), Harberger (1974) and Atkinson (1977). Compliance costs are discussed in Sandford (1973 and 1976) and in Meade *et al.* (1978, Appendix 22.1). Tax expenditure is covered by Surrey (1973), Willis and Hardwick (1978) and Aaron and Boskin (1980, Part II). Much of the material in this and the following three chapters is treated in greater detail by Prest and Barr (1979) and Musgrave and Musgrave (1980).

References

Aaron H.J. and Boskin M.J. (1980), *The Economics of Taxation*, Brookings Institution.

Atkinson A.B. (1977), 'Optimal taxation and the direct versus indirect tax controversy', *Canadian Journal of Economics*, Vol. 10, pp. 590–606.

Barr N.A., James S.R. and Prest A.R. (1977), *Self-Assessment for Income Tax*, Heinemann Educational Books.

Boskin M.J. (1975), 'Efficiency aspects of the differential tax treatment of Market and Household Economic Activity', *Journal of Public Economics*, Vol. 4, pp. 1–25.

Friedman M. (1952), 'The 'welfare' effects of an income tax and an excise tax', *Journal of Political Economy*, pp. 25–33, plus a revision in pp. 332–6.

George H. (1882), *Progress and Poverty*, Kegan Paul, Trench & Co., p. 364.

Harberger A.C. (1974), *Taxation and Welfare*, Little Brown.

Hicks J.R. (1939), *Value and Capital*, Oxford University Press.

Inland Revenue (1981), *123rd Report*, (for the year ended 31st March 1980).

Joseph M.F.W. (1939), 'The excess burden of indirect taxation', *Review of Economic Studies*, Vol. 6, No. 3. pp. 226–31.

Little I.M.D. (1951), 'Direct versus indirect taxes', *Economic Journal*, Vol. 61, pp. 577–84.

Long J.E. (1982), 'The income tax and self employment', *National Tax Journal*, Vol. XXXV, pp. 31–42.

Meade J.E. *et al.* (1978), *The Structure and Reform of Direct Taxation*, Institute for Fiscal Studies.

Mishan E.J. (1967), *The Costs of Economic Growth*, Penguin Books.

Musgrave R.A. and Musgrave P.B. (1980), *Public Finance in Theory and Practice*, 3rd edn., McGraw-Hill.

Pigou A.C. (1932), *The Economics of Welfare*, 4th edn, Macmillan, p. 26.

Prest A.R. (1981), *The Taxation of Urban Land*, Manchester University Press.

Prest A.R. and Barr N.A. (1979), *Public Finance in Theory and Practice*, 6th edn, Weidenfeld and Nicolson.

Proposals for a Tax-Credit System, Cmnd. 5116, HMSO, 1972.

Sandford C.T. (1973), *Hidden Costs of Taxation*, Institute for Fiscal Studies.

Sandford C.T. (1976), 'Tax compliance costs matter: Chancellor please note', *British Tax Review*, No. 4.

Smith A. (1776), *The Wealth of Nations*, Cannan edn, Methuen, 1950.

Surrey S.S. (1973), *Pathways to Tax Reform*, Harvard University Press.

Walker D. (1955), 'The direct and indirect tax problem: fifteen years of controversy', *Public Finance*, Vol. 10, pp. 153–76.

Willis J.R.M. and Hardwick P.J.W. (1978), *Tax Expenditures in the United Kingdom*, Institute for Fiscal Studies.

4

Taxation and Incentives

It is regularly asserted that taxation provides a disincentive to people to undertake economic activity. The frequency and vigour of these statements is perhaps understandable. As a popular political issue, the subject is capable of generating a fair amount of heat but, it seems, very little light. The purpose of this chapter, therefore, is to examine the theory of the effects of taxation on incentives, and to look briefly at some of the empirical work that has been carried out. We shall deal in turn with the effects of taxation on work effort, on saving and on enterprise.

4.1 Effects of Income Tax on Work Effort

The question that should be tackled first is why one should wish to examine the effects of taxation on work effort. Economic welfare consists not only of the material income from work, but also the psychic benefit individuals receive from leisure. Man does not live by GNP alone! Individuals will maximise their welfare in this respect if they work up to the point where the benefit from a small amount of extra work is just equal to the benefit of taking the same amount of time as leisure. Below that level the marginal benefits from work exceed those from leisure, and above that level the reverse is true.

Therefore, the problem is not simply maximising the number of hours people spend at work. The role of economics here is to see if the effects of various taxes on work effort can be predicted and, if they can, whether or not they are likely to influence adversely individuals' choices between work and leisure. For example, individuals may work less than the ideal amount because part of the benefit from working is taxed away.

One other preliminary point should be made at this stage. The total supply of labour is determined by both the average amount that individuals work, and the overall size of the population. However, for three reasons, we shall not concern ourselves here with the effects of taxes on population growth. First, it is not clear what the optimum population for any given area is. Second, it seems unlikely that any normal tax system would have a major effect on the birth rate (though this is possible: see the end of Section 3.2); and such effect as there is on work effort would clearly occur only in the very long run. Third, even if the total supply of labour were increasing as a result of population growth, there would still be concern about the *per capita* level of income, and therefore concern about the work effort of existing individuals. So we shall confine ourselves here to the examination of the work effort of the existing population.

Initially we shall look at the effects of taxation in the context of the supply curve of labour, and then go on to analyse these effects in more detail.

Supply Curve of Labour

Examining the supply curve of labour is perhaps the simplest way of tackling this issue. To concentrate on the essential points we shall make some simplifying assumptions which will be relaxed towards the end of this section. We shall assume that individuals can vary their hours of work; that there are no non-pecuniary benefits from work; and that all earnings are taxable. Let us further suppose that each hour of work is equally productive; that there is only one wage rate and that the demand for labour is perfectly elastic. The tax

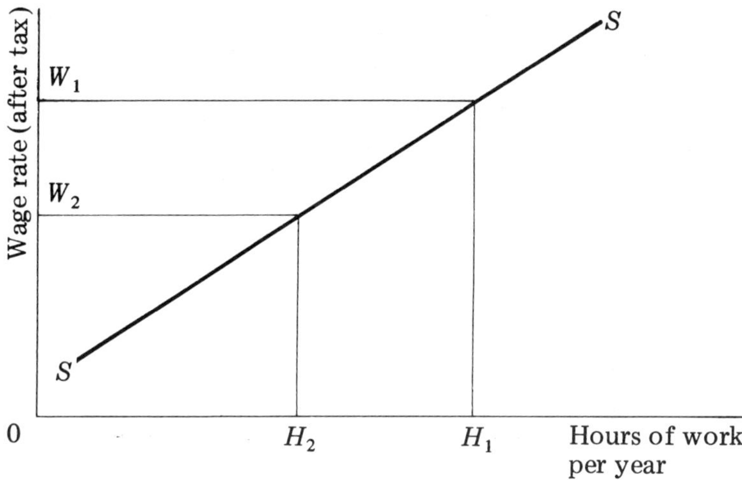

Figure 4A *The Supply Curve of Labour*

imposed is a proportional income tax, and the revenue raised by it is spent on something that does not affect the workforce.

If the supply curve of labour is upward sloping (like *SS* in Figure 4A), it follows that an increase in income tax will reduce the number of hours worked. This can be seen by imagining the pre-increase net wage rate to be W_1 and the hours worked to be H_1. An increase in income tax would reduce the net wage rate to, say, W_2 and the hours of work to H_2. However, while it is true that in these circumstances an income tax is a disincentive to work effort, in other circumstances it may result in more work.

Suppose now that the supply curve of labour bends back on itself, as in figure 4B. This simply means that if wage rates rise beyond a certain point people will choose to work less. This may be interpreted as individuals choosing to enjoy part of their increased prosperity in the form of more leisure. Historically, in industrialised countries hours of work have fallen as wage rates have risen, and some further evidence for the existence of a backward-bending supply curve is discussed in Section 4.2.

In these circumstances, a similar increase in income tax will result in more hours worked. In Figure 4B, a drop in the after-tax wage

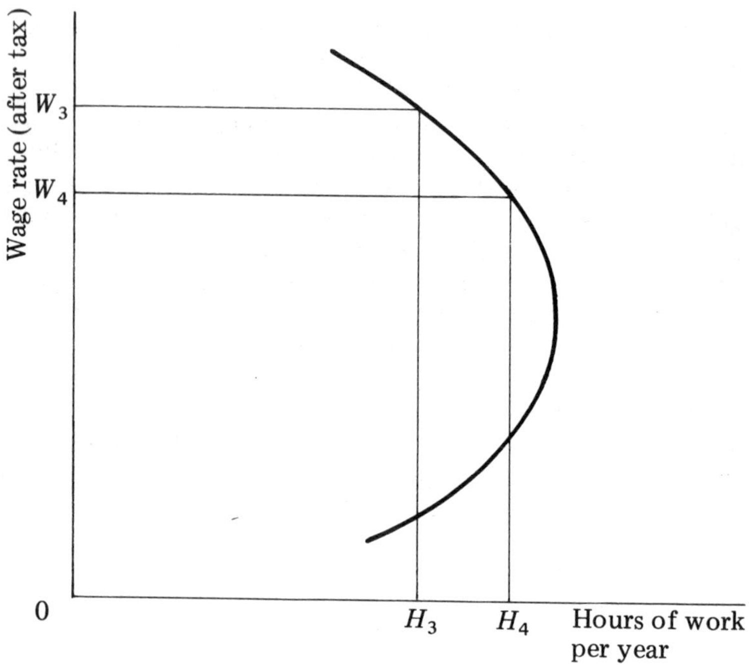

Figure 4B *The Backward-Bending Supply Curve of Labour*

rate from W_3 to W_4 will result in an increase in hours worked from H_3 to H_4. So it can be seen that the effects of taxation are not as straightforward as might appear at first sight. We shall now take the analysis a little further.

Income and Substitution Effects

We can distinguish between two quite separate influences on work effort when a tax is imposed or increased. The first is the *income effect*, which results from the taxpayer being made worse off than he would be without the extra tax. Normally, when a tax is imposed we should expect the income effect to encourage the taxpayer to work harder. The reason is that, as the tax makes him poorer, he can afford less of all things, including leisure. The extent of the income effect is determined by the proportion of an individual's gross income which goes in tax, that is the *average* rate of tax.

The second influence is the *substitution effect*. In economic theory the substitution effect describes the relationship between a change in relative prices and any resulting change in a person's expenditure pattern. In other words, it describes the extent to which an individual substitutes goods for each other as their prices rise or fall. In the context of taxation, the substitution effect describes the effect on a person's choice between work and leisure as the marginal benefit from either or both alters. For example, if the rate of income tax rises so that the marginal benefit from work falls, a person may choose to substitute some leisure for some of his working time. A tax which reduces the marginal benefit from work will normally have a substitution effect which discourages work effort. In the case of an income tax, the extent of the substitution effect is determined by the *marginal* rate of tax.

The theory, therefore, leaves us unable to predict the overall effect of a tax change on the supply of labour, as the income and substitution effects usually work in opposite directions. The two effects can also be shown by using indifference curve analysis and this method has the advantage of enabling us to compare the work effects of different taxes. It will still not be possible to predict the overall effects of the taxes, but it can be shown how different taxes are likely to have different effects on work incentives.

The analysis is similar to that used in the partial approach in Section 3.3, except that instead of two goods X and Y, the individual is faced in Figure 4C with a choice between work (represented by earnings) on the vertical axis, and leisure on the horizontal axis. To avoid unnecessary complexity the assumptions made for the analysis of the supply curve of labour will be retained for the time being. In addition, it will be assumed that both leisure and consumption are superior goods; in other words that the demand for both rises as income rises. On the supposition that the individual can vary his hours of work, his choice between work and leisure is represented by AB in Figure 4C. Given some set of individual preferences, his highest attainable indifference curve before any taxes are imposed is I_1 and he will choose to spend OL_1 hours of leisure, leaving time to earn OE_1.

If a proportional income tax is now imposed on all earnings, the individual's 'budget constraint' will swivel inwards to CB. The line

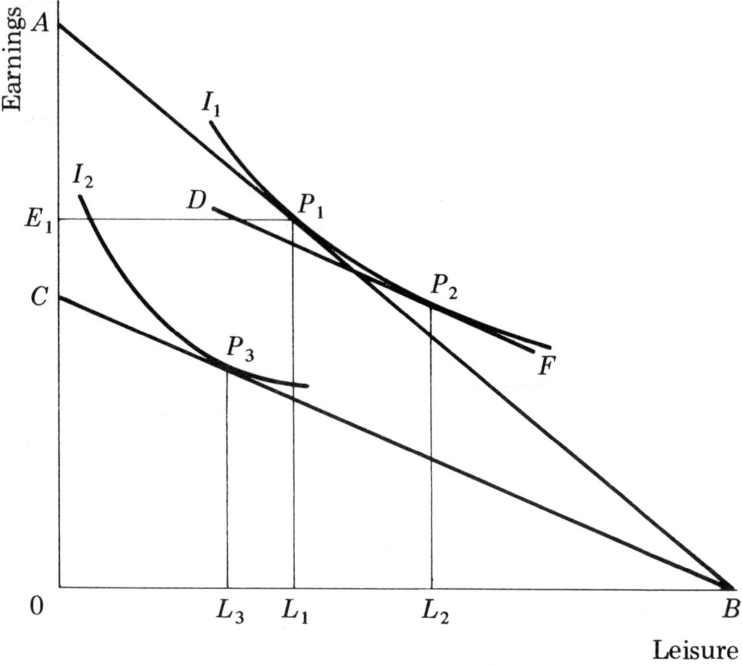

Figure 4C *The Choice between Work and Leisure*

still terminates at point B, as an individual choosing no income in these circumstances would still not pay any tax. The flatter slope of CB shows that the individual's earnings/leisure trade-off has altered; that is, to earn the same amount of income after tax, the individual has now to give up more leisure. We shall look first at the situation where the individual works harder as a result of the tax. Suppose, therefore, that he moves to point P_3 and takes a reduced amount of leisure OL_3.

The income and substitution effects may be observed separately as follows. The income effect can be removed by compensating the individual with an amount just sufficient to make him as well off as he would have been without the tax. In other words, his income would have to be increased so that he could just attain his former indifference curve I_1. This can be done by shifting the new budget constraint BC outwards until it is at a tangent to I_1. This is shown by

DF. The line *DF* must be parallel to *CB* because we wish to retain the post-tax trade-off between earnings and leisure and so preserve the substitution effect.

The substitution effect alone can now be seen as the movement from P_1 to P_2, round the indifference curve, as the individual substitutes more leisure for less work. In the diagram, the individual (if the income effect were zero) would take an amount OL_2 of leisure after the tax was imposed, rather than OL_1.

The income effect can be seen as the remaining effect of the tax. This effect is operating in the opposite direction and encourages the individual to work harder. The combination of the two effects results in the taxpayer taking OL_3 of leisure rather than OL_2. It should be pointed out that this result depends on the assumption that leisure is a superior good. If it were an inferior good, then the demand for leisure would be inversely related to the level of income, and the income effect would work in the same direction as the substitution effect. This seems to be an unlikely possibility. It would imply, for example, that when an individual's investment income rose (his marginal wage rate remaining the same), he would spend more time at work. We shall continue, therefore, to assume that leisure is a superior good, and that the income effect of a tax increase encourages people to work harder.

In the case described in Figure 4C, the income effect outweighs the substitution effect with the overall result that the individual works harder. This is not the only possible result. The two effects could cancel out, or the substitution effect could predominate, in which case the tax would lead to less work. This is the same result as before, but we now have the tools to compare the effects on work of different taxes. The first comparison presented will be between a proportional income tax and a poll tax, followed by a comparison of considerable importance to a modern British fiscal policy, that is between proportional and progressive income taxes.

Poll Tax versus Proportional Income Tax

The basic proposition here is that although the overall effect of either tax cannot be predicted by theory alone, it can be shown that a poll tax will have a more favourable (or less unfavourable) effect on work effort than a proportional income tax of equal yield. This is

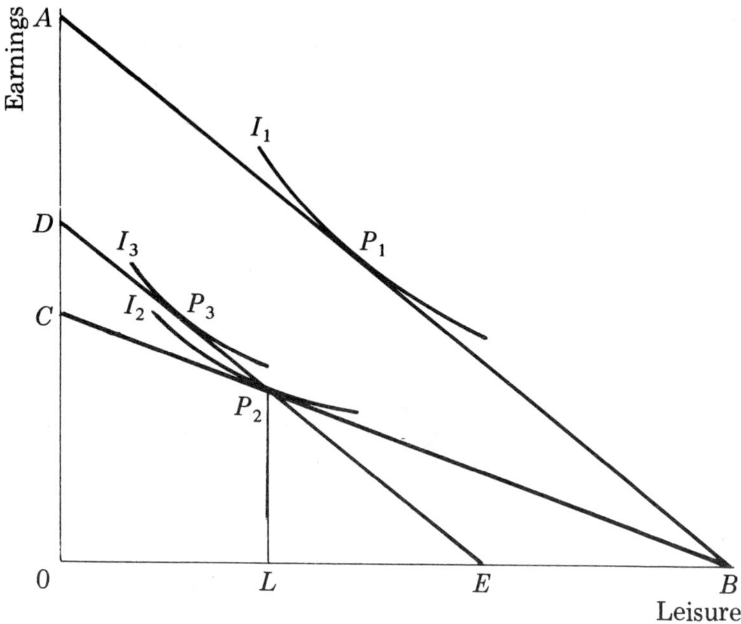

Figure 4D *Poll Tax versus Proportional Income Tax*

shown in Figure 4D. The line *AB* represents the individual's budget constraint when neither tax is imposed, and *CB* represents the constraint when the proportional income tax has been imposed. Confronted with the income tax, our individual chooses point P_2 and takes *OL* hours of leisure.

When the poll tax is imposed, the budget constraint is represented by *DE*. This line is parallel to *AB* because a poll tax does not vary with the amount of income earned and so does not distort the trade-off between earnings and leisure (that is, the slope of the budget constraint). As the two taxes yield the same amount of revenue, *DE* must pass through the point P_2.

It can now be seen that, faced with a poll tax, the individual can attain the higher indifference curve I_3, which leads him to take less leisure than he would if faced with the income tax. This result occurs because the income effect is the same for the two taxes as they absorb the same amount of income. The income tax, however, has a substitution effect adverse to work effort because it distorts the trade-off between earnings and leisure. The poll tax does not have this effect and so provides less of a disincentive to work.

Proportional versus Progressive Income Taxes

This type of analysis can be extended to show that a proportional income tax has a more favourable (or less unfavourable) effect on individual work effort than does a progressive income tax of equal yield. This may be explained as follows. The definition of a proportional income tax is that the marginal and average rates are equal. With progressive income tax, the marginal rate exceeds the average rate of tax. Since the comparison is between taxes of equal yield, we should expect the income effect to be the same in both cases. However, the progressive tax involves a higher *marginal* rate. This means that the progressive tax has a stronger substitution effect and therefore is likely to be more adverse to work effort than a proportional tax. (An exception is where the substitution effect is zero: that is, the individual will work the same number of hours regardless of his after-tax wage rate.)

The same analysis can also be applied in the opposite direction to show that a regressive tax is more likely to be favourable to work effort than a proportional tax. The income effect of a regressive tax will be much the same as the income effect of a proportional tax of equal yield. But the regressive tax will have a lower marginal rate and therefore a weaker substitution effect than the progressive tax.

Progressive Taxation and the Community

The comparison between the effects of proportional and progressive taxes on the community as a whole is a little more complex. Clearly, as the income tax becomes more progressive, people on lower incomes pay less, and people on higher incomes pay more. For convenience we will divide the community into five groups according to their level of income and the comparative effects of a proportional and a progressive tax. The groups range from group I with the lowest incomes up to group V with the highest incomes, though the actual division is based more on analytical convenience than any attempt to reflect the distribution of income precisely. Using these groups, we shall compare a proportional and a progressive tax which each extract the same revenue yield from the community as a whole, but not from each group or individual.

As we have seen, a proportional income tax is one that is levied at the same rate on all income, so that the marginal rate is always equal to the average rate of tax. Each income group, therefore, will be subject to the same rates. This is illustrated in Figure 4E. Under an alternative progressive tax each group is treated differently. We might arrange that the first income group would be exempt from tax altogether. The second group would be subject to lower marginal and average rates than in the proportional case. The third group would face the same marginal rate with both types of tax, but a lower average rate under a progressive system. For the fourth group the marginal rate would be higher but the average rate lower with the progressive tax. The fifth group would suffer both higher marginal and higher average rates under the progressive tax. The position of each of these groups can be seen from Table 4A (although the table itself is designed to illustrate the more general case of any increase in the progressivity of income tax).

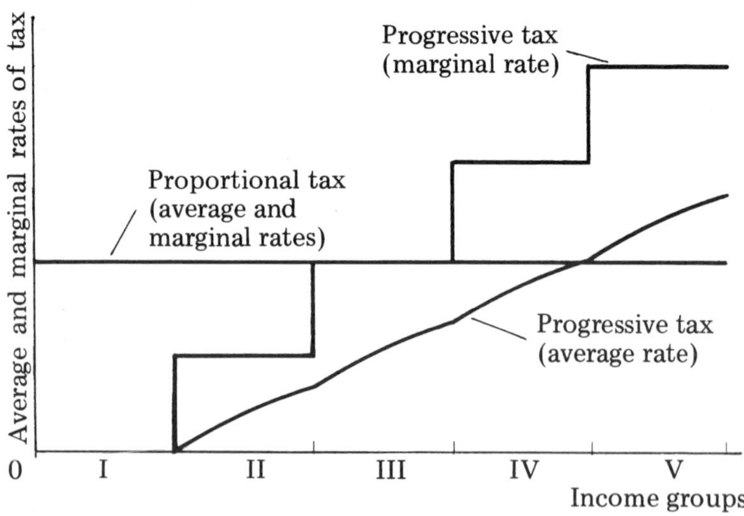

Figure 4E *Progressive and Proportional Taxes*

Table 4A Work Effects of an Increase in the Progressivity of Income Tax

Income group	*Change in average rate of tax*	*Change in marginal rate of tax*	*Work effects*			
			Income effect	*Substitution effect*		*Net effect*
I	–	–	D	I	=	?
II	–	–	D	I	=	?
III	–	O	D	O	=	D
IV	–	+	D	D	=	D
V	+	+	I	D	=	?

Key: + Increase in the rate of tax; – decrease in the rate of tax;
I incentive effect; D disincentive effect; ? uncertain effect;
O no effect.

We have already examined the effects of changes in the marginal and average rates of tax, but it is useful to summarise the argument at this stage:

(a) An increase in the marginal rate of tax results in a substitution effect which normally provides a disincentive to work.
(b) A decrease in the marginal rate produces the opposite result — an incentive to work.
(c) An increase in the average rate of tax results in an income effect which is usually associated with an incentive to greater work effort.
(d) A decrease in the average rate of tax produces the opposite result.

Referring to Table 4A, the comparative effects of a proportional and a progressive tax on each of the five groups can now be traced through. Beginning with the first and second income groups, it can be seen that an increase in the progressivity of income taxes has two opposing effects. The lower average rates of the more progressive tax imply income effects that are unfavourable to work effort. However, the lower marginal tax rates imply offsetting substitution effects which are favourable to increased work effort. We cannot say, therefore, *a priori*, what the net effect of increasing progressivity would be on low income groups.

Nevertheless, it may be noted that a particular area of disincentive effects exists at and just beyond the threshold of the progressive tax. At this point, the marginal rate of tax is significant (and unfavourable to work), but the average rate and its associated income effect are very small. This point has special relevance for the income tax system in the United Kingdom with its unusually high starting rate (see Section 8.2).

The outcome for the next two groups is more certain — a net disincentive effect. For the third group, the marginal rate of tax is the same in both cases, but under a more progressive tax the average rate is lower, suggesting an income effect with an adverse effect on work. The fourth group also faces greater disincentive with the progressive tax, but this time from both income and substitution effects. This arises from the higher marginal but lower average rate of tax under the progressive tax. The net effect on the fifth group is uncertain.

So it is not possible to predict on purely theoretical grounds what the overall effects of a more progressive tax would be on the work effort of the groups I, II and V. It cannot be predicted, therefore, what the fiscal effect on the total supply of labour would be. It would depend on the strength of the opposing income and substitution effects, and the number of people, in each group. However, under the assumptions made above, it can be said that the effects on the groups III and IV are unambiguously adverse to work effort.

Complications

The analysis so far has ignored many of the practical considerations which may influence the amount of work done under different taxes. Our conclusions may be modified, for example, if there are non-pecuniary benefits from work which are not taxed, or not taxed as heavily as money income. One particular consideration which should be dealt with here is whether or not individuals have any choice over the number of hours they work. It might be argued that individuals must either work the standard week or not work at all.

At first sight, this line of argument appears quite convincing, especially in the short term. Yet there must be considerable doubt about its importance in the longer term. The first response is that, if the labour market is at all competitive, employers have an incentive to conform to the wishes of the workers. If, for example, workers suddenly decide they want a shorter working week, employers who offer it will gain an advantage over employers who do not. Those employers who provide popular working conditions are likely to find it easier to attract suitable employees than those employers who provide unpopular working arrangements. Even if the labour market is not competitive, working conditions may be altered as a result of workers' preferences being expressed through union pressure, or government activity, or both.

In addition, there is often scope for absenteeism, overtime working, or 'moonlighting' on a second job. Furthermore, some individuals can choose to leave the job market through early retirement, or to delay joining it by remaining in further education. Housewives are often in a position where they can choose whether or not to work. On top of this, the standard working week is very different in different occupations, so workers can usually choose the job that comes closest to satisfying their preferred working arrangements. It seems safe to conclude, therefore, that the existence of a standard working week is unlikely to prevent changes in taxation from influencing the supply of labour.

A second practical consideration is the quality of the work done. The discussion so far has assumed that each hour of work is equally productive. It is quite possible that adjustment in the labour market comes through changes in the quality of the labour supplied, rather than the quantity. In other words, if the tax system provided a disincentive to work, people might still work the same number of hours, but choose more congenial or easier jobs, even though these jobs involved relatively low wages.

There are several ways by which taxation can influence the level of productivity. Taxation might affect the willingness of individuals to go to the trouble and expense of acquiring more productive skills, or of moving to a more productive job. It might also affect their willingness to work in more difficult jobs, or to strive for promotion. In addition, it is conceivable that taxation might influence the amount of encouragement parents give to their children to acquire skills, and so on.

As a final complication in this context, Brown and Dawson (1969, p. 90) have pointed out that misconceptions of the tax system may also influence incentives. If people *think* that tax rates are higher or lower than they really are, then this in itself can affect their work effort. Enlightening them may also affect it.

Income Taxes versus Excise Taxes

The question here is whether an income tax has the same effects on work effort as a system of excise taxes covering all goods and services. Clearly, a fair comparison requires the excise taxes to be arranged so that they are equally progressive and raise the same revenue as the alternative income tax. The requirement of an equal degree of progressivity raises difficulties, because the only feasible method of increasing the progressivity of excise taxes is by taxing goods consumed by the rich more heavily than the goods consumed by the poor. But this is a very rough and ready way of influencing progressivity, since individuals' tastes differ. Some of the rich may purchase large amounts of goods normally consumed by the poor. Some of the poor may consume goods normally considered the province of the rich. Income taxes, on the other hand, can (evasion apart) be levied precisely in accordance with each individual's income.

Nevertheless, in order to carry our reasoning a little further, let us suppose it is possible to compare an income tax with a system of excise taxes of equal yield and progressivity. Under these circumstances, it might be thought that the two tax systems would have the same effects on the supply of labour. However, this may not be true for two reasons.

The first is that many goods and services may be complementary to (or substitutes for) work or leisure. An increase in tax on goods or services consumed during leisure time may reduce the incentives to take time off work. Relevant examples include mid-week sports activities such as cricket, tennis and football; holiday accommodation; and 'leisure goods' such as sailing boats, camping equipment and alcohol. Similarly, more work may be encouraged by a reduction in taxes on items complementary to work, for example tools and transport for commuters.

The second reason is that excise taxes may be more 'hidden' than income taxes. Indirect taxes which increase prices also reduce the real net wage rate. However, excise taxes may not be shown separately in the prices of goods and services on which they are imposed, whereas income taxes may appear more obvious and direct, especially on weekly or monthly payslips. But it is not possible to predict whether income taxes have more of a disincentive effect than excise taxes. It would depend on whether a more 'hidden' tax has different substitution and income effects than a more obvious tax.

There is a further point here in relation to Musgrave's 'spite effect' (Musgrave (1959), p. 240). Individuals may work less as a result of a tax increase in order to satisfy some need for revenge on the government, or perhaps to strengthen the case for tax cuts. The effect may be strengthened if the taxes are considered to be unfair. If such a spite effect is significant, it seems reasonable to suppose that it will be stronger the more obvious the tax.

It is clear from the discussion so far, that economic theory cannot predict the actual effects of a change in taxation on work effort. It depends on the relative strengths of the income and substitution effects. It also depends on a number of practical considerations. We turn now, therefore, to look at some of the empirical work that has been undertaken in this area.

4.2 Empirical Evidence

Many attempts have been made to assess the effects of taxation on the supply of labour. Surveys of this work can be found in Godfrey (1975) and in Brown (1980). There are two main sources of empirical evidence: econometric studies of observed labour market behaviour, and a large number of surveys into taxpayers' attitudes and their perceived behaviour. There is also some experimental evidence which is discussed under negative income tax in Section 9.1.

Econometric Evidence

Following a pioneering study by Douglas (1934), there has been a large number of attempts to estimate the relationship between the supply of labour and real wage rates. Many of these studies have been summarised by Break (1953 and 1974), in Cain and Watts (1973) and by Brown (1980).

One fairly general, and not unexpected, result is that the effects on the work effort of married women are very different from the effects on men. Generally, it appears that a change in wage rates has a large and positive effect on the number of hours of paid employment which married women undertake. In addition Ashenfelter and Heckman (1974) and Greenhalgh (1977) found that the effect of the *husband's* wage rate on the *wife's* labour supply was large and negative. In other words, it seems that an increase in the wife's net wage is likely to encourage her to work more, but that an increase in her husband's wage may have the opposite effect.

The effects of wage changes on male working hours appear to be much smaller. Much of the work that has been done has also supported the hypothesis of a backward-bending supply curve of labour for men. This result appears to apply over a wide range of earnings.

One American example is the econometric study by Owen (1971). The data employed were for non-student male employees in the private non-agricultural sector of the United States in the period 1960–61. The results suggested that most of the increase in leisure time was associated with increases in the real hourly wage rate. An additional finding provided further support for the backward-bending hypothesis. It appeared that the effect on the demand for leisure of changes in real income (the income effect) was stronger than the effect of changes in the relative price of leisure (the substitution effect).

An econometric study based on United Kingdom data was undertaken by Metcalfe, Nickell and Richardson (1976). The study analysed the structure of hours of work and hourly earnings between different industries. It was based on 1966 data from 96 manufacturing industries in Britain. Again, evidence was found that the labour supply curve bends backwards.

The authors of this study also pointed out an interesting implication of a backward-bending labour supply curve. Such a curve provides one of the few examples of a policy for greater equality which may be consistent with a policy encouraging work effort. In the authors' own words:

> A compression of the wage structure, if desired on equity grounds, would *not* have the kind of work disincentive effects popularly associated with such a move. If anything it would actually *raise* hours supplied.
>
> (p. 300)

Although many studies have reached broadly similar conclusions they should, nevertheless, be interpreted with some care. There are some practical difficulties associated with the use of econometric methods in this context and they are discussed in Godfrey (1975), Atkinson and Stiglitz (1980), and in Brown (1980 and 1981). In recent years, several investigators have tackled an increasing number of these difficulties. While they have had a great deal of success, it is clear that much remains to be done and that the estimates calculated so far should be considered provisional.

Other Evidence

The other main source of evidence of the effects of taxation on work effort are the many surveys which have been carried out. Once more there are methodological difficulties, many of which are discussed, for example, in Moser and Kalton (1971).

The essential problem is, of course, how to extract information which is both accurate and relevant. Individuals may not give accurate replies in response to a survey for a number of reasons. The respondents may not be aware of the real answers, or there may be other reasons why they wish to give an impression of their behaviour which is not wholly consistent with the facts. A traditional example here is surveys of alcohol consumption! It is also possible that respondents may be influenced by the interviewer, or by the layout of the questionnaire.

The questions themselves are also important. Vague questions are likely to lead to vague answers. However, more detailed questions may put ideas into respondents' minds and so affect their replies. Finally, sample surveys present a number of well-known difficulties in terms of obtaining respondents who are representative of the population as a whole.

While the problems of survey methodology can be serious and should be kept in mind, they do not mean that the evidence unearthed by various surveys can be ignored. There is not, however, sufficient space here to present the full results of all the surveys and how they coped with the various methodological problems. All that will be attempted is a description of some of the main results.

Break (1957) undertook a survey of 306 self-employed solicitors and accountants in England in 1956. Considerable care was taken to avoid influencing the respondents. For example, the subject of taxation was not raised by the interviewer until the person interviewed had had a full opportunity to describe the reasons for doing the amount of work he was doing. On the basis of his findings Break concluded that: 'The chorus of complaints, vehement and eloquent, against "penal" taxation, echoed by the great majority of respondents interviewed for the present study, was surprisingly infrequently translated into action. It was almost a commonplace for respondents to state categorically that taxes were removing all their incentives; but when the facts were assembled, about as many actually were working harder as were working less.'

Barlow, Brazer and Morgan (1966) undertook personal interviews in the United States in 1964 with 957 individuals whose incomes in 1961 were $10,000 or higher. Only one-eighth of the sample reported that they had reduced their work effort as a result of progressive income tax, though many of these respondents still continued to work 60 or more hours a week. Barlow, Brazer and Morgan concluded that: 'It is clear that there are many more powerful motives affecting the working behaviour of high-income people than the marginal income tax rates. People are aware of taxes and do not enjoy paying them, but other considerations are far more important to them in deciding how long to work.'

Chatterjee and Robinson (1969) surveyed a sample of 103 'professionals' (accountants, lawyers and insurance agents) and 266 'non-professionals' from the Kitchener-Waterloo metropolitan area in Canada. Their results appear to indicate that taxation had more effect on the work effort of the non-professionals than that of the professionals. Although Chatterjee and Robinson gave no estimate of the quantitative effects of taxation, they did conclude that 'generally ... taxation influences in the aggregate supply of effort seem to be relatively negligible'.

In a survey of low income recipients, Brown and Levin (1974) studied the effects of tax on overtime undertaken by weekly paid workers in 1971. Over 2,000 individuals were interviewed. They were first asked a large number of questions about their work and at this stage, tax was not mentioned by the interviewer. They were then asked if tax made any difference to the amount of overtime they worked. Brown and Levin were then able to eliminate those replies which were inconsistent with earlier statements. They also deleted those who claimed that tax had no effect on their overtime, either because they were not regular taxpayers, or because they could not vary their hours of work. The conclusion was that: 'The evidence clearly suggests ... that the aggregate effect of tax on overtime is small; it may perhaps add about 1 per cent to the total hours worked, since on balance tax has made people work more, rather than less overtime. The only evidence which is not consistent with this is that the number of women claiming to work less is greater than the number claiming to work more.'

Fields and Stanbury (1970 and 1971) repeated the earlier study undertaken by Break (1957). They did this to see if the effects of taxation had varied over time, and also to provide an additional test of the various hypotheses regarding work incentives. The results appear to show that there had been little change in the effects of taxation on incentives, except that there had been some increase in the number of respondents experiencing disincentives.

The studies carried out have covered many different groups of taxpayers in different countries and at different times. Yet the results do give a general impression of the effects of taxation on work incentives. An important result is that there appears to be no substantial disincentive effect from taxation. Instead, it appears that there are both small incentive and small disincentive effects which tend, of course, to offset each other, so that the net effect of taxation on the supply of labour is likely to be small. So far as males are concerned, this is consistent with the econometric evidence described briefly above. However, the econometric studies also suggest more clearly that there is a greater effect on the work effort of married women.

4.3 Effects of Taxation on Saving and Capital Formation

Saving is important for a number of reasons. When people save part of their income, economic resources are released which may be invested in various projects. In the long run, therefore, the level of saving may influence the rate of economic growth. Changes in the level of savings can also affect the level of economic activity in the short term. However, discussion of the problems of stabilisation policy are reserved for Chapter 6. What will be attempted here is a comparison between the likely effects of different taxes on the level of saving. The traditional comparison is between taxes on income and taxes on expenditure. The taxes on expenditure could take the form of the indirect taxes we have already come across.

Alternatively, the comparison is often between an income tax and a *personal* expenditure tax. The latter is discussed in greater detail in Chapter 9.

There are two main areas of interest here, which again may be classified into income and substitution effects. The substitution effects operate on the rates of return to saving under different taxes. The income effects mainly involve the relative burden of different taxes on different sections of the community.

The Substitution Effect

The substitution effect has often been discussed in terms of the 'double taxation of savings' by an income tax. The argument is that an income tax is imposed on both the income when it is first received, and any interest paid when the income is saved. A tax on expenditure on the other hand, only taxes the savings once — when they are spent. An expenditure tax therefore allows a more favourable return to saving, as interest can be received on the gross amount of any income saved.

This may be illustrated with an example. Suppose that an individual receives £1000 which he intends to save for one year and then spend, together with the interest received. Suppose also that the current rate of interest is 10 per cent and that the individual can either be subject to an income tax or to an expenditure tax. To keep things straightforward, it will be assumed that both taxes are levied on a 'gross' basis; that is, the amount inclusive of tax itself. (In practice, of course, taxes on expenditure are normally applied to the value net of tax, though the Swedish value added tax is levied on the gross amount).

The differential effects of the two taxes are shown in Table 4B. With the 50 per cent income tax, £500 is extracted in tax, leaving £500 to be saved. The interest after one year amounts to £50, but half of this is taxed as well, leaving a total of £525 to be spent.

With the expenditure tax there is no liability when the money is received. This means that the entire £1000 can be saved, and that a higher amount (£100) is received in interest after a year. As the interest is not taxed when it is paid out, this makes a total amount of £1100. When this is spent, the 50 per cent expenditure tax on the gross figure accounts for £550 leaving a spending power of £550.

The benefit to saving under an expenditure tax arises because the tax liability on income that is saved is deferred until the savings are spent. It follows that the comparative gain to saving under an expenditure tax will be equal to the after-tax yield on the postponed tax. In our example, £500 of tax is deferred with the expenditure tax and the post-tax interest on the £500 is £25. It can therefore be seen that an expenditure tax results in a higher return to saving than an income tax. If the higher return encourages a higher level of saving, then an expenditure tax is likely to be more favourable to saving than an income tax imposed at the same rate.

It follows that, all other things being equal, a tax on expenditure will favour those who save rather than those who spend. If the rich save a larger proportion of their incomes than the poor, then taxes on expenditure may attract criticism on equity grounds.

One particular qualification should be made to the example. The revenue of the expenditure tax is usually worth less than the revenue from the income tax. This may sound surprising as it can be seen from Table 4B that the income tax raises £525 in revenue, whereas the expenditure tax raises £550. The reason is that the effect of an expenditure tax (as opposed to an income tax) is to delay the actual payment of tax when saving is undertaken. Provided society discounts the future, receipts from the expenditure tax will tend to be worth less than receipts from income tax.

This can be easily demonstrated using the example in Table 4B. Suppose that society discounts the future at a rate of 10 per cent per

Table 4B An Income Tax, an Expenditure Tax and Saving

	Income tax			*Expenditure tax*		
	Gross amount	*Tax*	*Net amount saved*	*Gross amount*	*Tax*	*Net amount saved*
Money received	1000	500	500	1000	0	1000
Interest after one year	50	25	25	100	0	100
Money spent	525	0	525	1100	550	550

annum. In the first year, the present value of the income tax yield would be £523 [500 plus £25/(1 + 0.1)]. The present value of the expenditure tax, on the other hand, would be only £500 [550/(1 + 0.1)]. It is true that, in this example, a substantially lower discount rate would reverse this result. However, in practice this would be unlikely, since a lower discount rate would also imply a lower real rate of interest. It is fairly safe to conclude, therefore, that the real value of the expenditure tax will usually be lower than that of an income tax levied at the same 'gross' rate. The same result holds during inflationary periods. Because the expenditure tax results in payment being postponed, the tax can be paid in depreciated currency.

A second qualification to this comparison arises with the possibility that the community as a whole could run down the level of its savings. In other words, the community might spend more than it received for a period. In this case, the yield of a tax on spending (expenditure tax) would exceed that of an income tax. This possibility, however, is unlikely to be important for any lengthy period.

The next point concerns how to make a fair comparison between an income tax and an expenditure tax. We could, as before, compare taxes of equal yield. This would mean that the expenditure tax would normally have to be levied at a higher gross rate to raise the same amount of revenue as an income tax. Nevertheless, even a higher rate expenditure tax would still be more likely to favour saving than an equal yield income tax.

However, it might be argued in this particular case that the right comparison is not between taxes of equal yield, but between taxes which reduce private expenditure equally. If the introduction of an expenditure tax actually led to an increase in private saving, then this in itself would release resources which could be used to support a higher level of government expenditure. This means that it is not necessarily true that an expenditure tax would have to be levied at a higher rate than an equivalent income tax.

Income Effects

The income effects of taxation with respect to saving should also be examined. A comparison between taxes will be affected if different taxes fall more heavily on different sections of the community. The 'double taxation' of saving feature of the income tax also has income effects in that the income tax will have a greater impact than an equivalent expenditure tax on those who save.

A separate and more important factor with income effects is the degree of progressivity of different taxes. A progressive tax will fall more heavily than a less progressive tax on prosperous members of society. As the rich save a larger proportion of their incomes than the poor, a more progressive tax may be considered as falling more heavily on savings.

The crucial factor is the *marginal* propensity to consume, rather than the average propensity to consume — see Lubell (1947). If the marginal propensity to consume is the same for each income group, then an extra £1 of tax will have the same effect on saving wherever the burden falls. For example, suppose that the marginal propensity to consume is 0.75 throughout the income scale; suppose also that an extra £1 in tax is imposed on the rich and the proceeds redistributed to the poor. The aggregate levels of consumption and saving will remain the same. All that happens is that 25p of saving by the rich is replaced by 25p of saving by the poor.

If, however, the marginal propensity to consume falls as income rises, the degree of progressivity of a tax will influence the level of saving. Suppose, by way of example, that the rich all have a marginal propensity to consume of 0.5, and the poor a propensity of 0.9. If £1 is now redistributed from the rich to the poor, the aggregate level of saving will fall. The rich would save 50p less, but the poor would save only 10p more.

So if the marginal propensity to consume declines as income rises, savings will generally be discouraged more by a highly progressive tax than by a less progressive tax of equal yield. On this basis, it could be said that the income tax, which is levied at progressive rates, falls more heavily on savings than indirect taxes do. As we shall see in Section 11.5, indirect taxes are slightly regressive overall.

For two reasons, therefore, savings are more likely to be adversely affected by income taxes than by taxes on expenditure. The substitution effect means that there is a lower rate of return to saving under an income tax. Secondly, the income tax is generally more progressive than taxes on expenditure are. The result is that the income tax is more often paid out of income that would otherwise be saved.

Qualifications

The first qualification is that income taxes can be designed to favour saving. An income tax that exempted investment income would avoid the 'double taxation of savings' characteristic discussed above. As we shall see from Section 8.2, the income tax in the United Kingdom favours some of the main methods of saving. Particularly important is the tax treatment of mortgage interest, contributions to superannuation schemes and life assurance premiums. On the other hand, the investment income surcharge further reduces the return to saving by taxing some of the income from savings at higher rates than those on other forms of income (Section 8.2).

A second qualification is that, in some cases, the level of saving may be determined by some target rather than by the rate of return. For example, some individuals may wish to achieve a certain capital sum for their retirement or some other purpose. In these cases, factors such as the 'double taxation' of saving under an income tax will not necessarily reduce the amount saved.

Empirical Evidence

As perhaps might be expected, there are difficulties involved in isolating the effects of taxation on saving. Many other factors, such as demographic and other social changes and the existence of state pension schemes, are likely to affect personal savings. Corporations and government also undertake saving, and the extent to which they do so can be influenced by other factors again. Furthermore, personal, corporate and, quite probably, government savings are related. On the question of the relationship between the rate of return and the level of saving, different investigators have found different results: see, for instance, the paper by Howrey and Hymans and the following discussion in Pechman (1980). To take three examples, a study by Blinder (1975) implied a very low savings elasticity. Wright (1969) found that there was a relationship between saving and the rate of interest, but that the relationship was not very strong. Boskin (1978) found a much stronger relationship. As with the empirical research on labour supply, a great deal remains to be done and further research will hopefully add considerably to our knowledge of this topic.

With regard to the marginal propensity to consume, the empirical evidence has also sometimes led to conflicting conclusions. Nevertheless, there is evidence suggesting that the marginal propensity to consume declines as income rises. Husby (1971), for example, using both cross-sectional and time series data, obtained results which implied that, 'in the short run, the marginal propensity to consume of high income families is lower than that of low income families'. Further empirical studies on the effects of taxation on saving are given in Break (1974).

4.4 Effects of Taxation on Enterprise and Risk-Taking

It was pointed out in the previous section that saving releases economic resources for investment. In this context, investment refers to individuals and companies investing both directly in capital goods and other inputs, and indirectly by buying shares or bonds issued by enterprises. Both types of investment are normally expected to yield a return. However, both also carry a risk that losses rather than profits will be made. The question here, then, concerns the effects of taxation on the willingness of individuals to make investments involving an element of risk.

Why do people take risks? It is quite plausible that some people enjoy taking risks. This would provide one possible explanation for gambling. Nevertheless, more generally, there is evidence to suppose that individuals would prefer to avoid risk, all other things being equal. This preference helps to account for the popularity of insurance, which is a method of pooling risks, thereby reducing the amount of risk faced by each individual. In the investment field itself, unit and investment trusts are popular methods of investing in a large number of companies, thereby spreading the risk of loss.

If people are generally averse to taking risks, it is reasonable to suppose that they will only be induced to do so if they expect to receive some sort of return. Clearly, taxation will affect these returns and therefore the level of investment.

To examine these effects, one may begin with a proportional income tax that does not allow losses to be offset against gains in the calculation of taxable income. In other words, the government shares in the profits of enterprise, but not the loses. The result is that the tax lowers the expected return to risky investments by more than it would reduce the return to a 'safe' investment such as National Savings Certificates. It also reduces the expected return of investments with a high level of risk by more than it does for investments associated with lower levels of risk. It follows that such a tax provides more of a disincentive to undertake risk than, for example, a poll tax of equal expected yield would.

What happens if losses *are* allowed to be set off against profits? In these circumstances, the government would share in the losses as well as the profits, in that when losses are incurred, tax revenue falls. In a sense, the government then becomes a sleeping partner in enterprises. When enterprises make profits, the government, through taxation, takes a share, but it also shares in the risk through loss-offsets. For individual investors, a loss-offset system which works perfectly would remove the disincentive effect mentioned in the previous case. It is true that the income tax would still reduce the expected return to investment, but with loss-offsets it would also reduce the risks associated with that return.

In this situation it was shown by Domar and Musgrave (1944) that the overall amount of risk-taking could actually increase following an increase in income tax. When an income tax is imposed or increased, the individual finds that both his expected (after-tax) return and the level of risk he faces diminish. As a result, he may decide to increase his income from investment. He can do this either by increasing his investment, or transferring his investment to projects or shares which offer a higher return but are more risky. As the individual increases the amount of risk he faces, the government as well has to accept more risk through the tax system. The combined effect on society as a whole, therefore, may be to increase the amount of risk-taking.

Qualifications

There are, as usual, some qualifications to the analysis. The most important is that even with loss-offsets, the expected rate of return on risky investment may still be reduced by taxation. There are three main reasons for this.

First, there may be nothing to set the losses against. This may occur where a firm goes out of business before it has time to make a profit.

Second, the losses may have to be carried forward to be set against future profits. This may happen either because no profits were made previously, or because the tax system limits the extent to which losses may be carried backwards. For example, in the United Kingdom losses can usually be carried forwards, but normally cannot be carried back further than the previous year. As people discount the future, it can be seen that losses carried forward to be set against future income are worth less than the amount actually lost. Inflation will normally increase the difference.

Third, personal income tax (unlike corporation tax) is levied at progressive rates. As the income tax does not have adequate provisions to average out income over the years, loss-offsets cannot be fully effective. The reason is that losses may be set off against income in years when an individual's marginal rate of tax is relatively low. So, loss-offsets may not work fully, and income tax may still lower the rate of return on high risk as opposed to low risk assets.

We have seen in this section that it is not necessarily true that income tax decreases risk. It is possible that the effect of an income tax may be to increase the amount of risky investment undertaken by society as a whole. However, if losses are not fully set off against income, the rate of return on risky investments will be lowered.

4.5 Optimal Taxation

Although a great deal of the work that has been undertaken on 'optimal taxation' is beyond the scope of this book, it seems worthwhile to provide a (very) brief summary of such work and to indicate to those interested where a start could be made on the literature.

Using the criterion of economic efficiency, a good tax system is one which minimises the excess burden (including the effects on the supply of factors of production) at a given level of tax revenue. A more complete approach from the efficiency viewpoint would also take account of administrative and compliance costs. However, a tax system can also be evaluated in terms of how fair or equitable it is perceived to be (and this topic is discussed in the following chapter). The literature on optimal taxation has been concerned with the integration of both efficiency and equity criteria. The main difficulty is the trade-off which often exists between efficiency and incentives on the one hand, and equity on the other. For example, it may be that society considers a highly progressive tax to be equitable, but that such a tax might damage incentives to work. The problem in this case is therefore to find the tax rates which give the best trade-off between incentives and equity.

While almost all the literature on optimal taxation tends to be highly mathematical, a brief non-technical account of optimal income taxation appears in the Meade Committee (1978, Chapter 14). The committee concluded (on page 316) that:

> as a general principle i) *average* rates of tax should be high on high incomes and low on low incomes, but at the same time ii) *marginal* rates of tax should be exceptionally low at both the bottom and the top ends of the income scale.

For example, the argument for low marginal (but not average) rates of tax at the top end of the scale may be summarised as follows. There are relatively few taxpayers at the top end, so a reduction in marginal rates would not cost very much in forgone tax revenue, even if no extra work were forthcoming. However, it is the substitution effect associated with the marginal rate which provides the disincentive, so a reduction may increase work effort and therefore possibly also increase tax revenue.

Although the optimal tax literature is now voluminous, there are several useful surveys, such as that by Bradford and Rozen (1976). Sandmo (1976) provides an introductory survey of optimal commodity taxation, and Atkinson (1977) reveiws the issue with respect to the direct *versus* indirect tax controversy. A more general, but also more technical, discussion appears in Atkinson and Stiglitz (1980).

The work undertaken to date on optimal taxation has attracted some criticism. For instance, Brennan and Buchanan (1977, p. 255) went so far as to describe it as institutionally vacuous, and Ricketts (1981, p. 44) concluded that, 'the literature on tax policy ... is almost exclusively concerned with factors which are entirely missing from models of optimal taxation'. There is also an amusing article by Broome (1975). The criticism that the analysis has neglected several important aspects such as horizontal equity, evasion, administration and taxpayer preferences between different taxes is largely accurate. However, this does not, of course, prevent such aspects from being incorporated into future work.

A second criticism has been that the conclusions of optimal tax analysis could have been reached by intuitive argument, without the need for extensive mathematical analysis. While this is true of a number of results, it does not apply to some others. A third point, acknowledged by Atkinson and Stiglitz, is that the analysis does not lead to unambiguous policy conclusions and that the results depend on economic relationships about which there is little empirical evidence. Nevertheless, the analysis of optimal taxation has yielded a substantial amount of insight into various arguments. At the risk of some apparent repetition, it can safely be asserted that this is a third area in this chapter in which we can expect future work to extend knowledge of taxation considerably.

4.6 Summary

This chapter has examined the effects of taxation on work effort, saving and risk-taking. It has shown that an increase in income tax does not necessarily provide a disincentive to work. On the contrary, it is quite possible that an increase in taxation could spur the working population to greater efforts.

Even though we cannot say on theoretical grounds alone whether or not taxes influence the amount of work done, we can compare the effects of different taxes. Thus, for example, we would expect a poll tax to have a more favourable (or less unfavourable) effect on work effort than a proportional income tax of equal yield. Similarly, we would expect a proportional income tax to provide more of an incentive (or less of a disincentive) to work than a progressive income tax of equal yield.

It is also possible to compare the effects of different taxes on the level of saving. Generally, it is likely that income taxes will provide more of a disincentive to saving than expenditure taxes of equal yield. This is for two reasons. First, the 'double taxation of savings' feature of an income tax lowers the rate of return to saving by more than a tax on expenditure would. Second, if income taxes are more progressive than indirect taxes, it is more likely that they will be paid out of income that would otherwise have been saved.

Taxation may also affect the level of enterprise in the community. However, the effect of a tax system which allows losses to be set off against gains in the computation of taxable income is that the government shares in both the return and the risk involved in investment. In these circumstances, the amount of risk undertaken within the community may rise when a tax is imposed or increased.

Further Reading

A more theoretical treatment of the material in this chapter appears in Musgrave (1959) and Atkinson and Stiglitz (1980). Taxation and the labour supply is dealt with in Brown (1980 and 1981) and the argument with respect to risk-taking is examined further by Mossin (1968).

References

Ashenfelter O. and Heckman J. (1974), 'The estimation of income and substitution effects in a model of family labour supply', *Econometrica*, Vol. 42, pp. 73–85.

Atkinson A.B. (1977), 'Optimal taxation and the direct versus indirect tax controversy', *Canadian Journal of Economics*, Vol. 10, pp. 590–606.

Atkinson A.B. and Stiglitz J.E. (1980), *Lectures on Public Economics*, McGraw-Hill.

Barlow R., Brazer H.E. and Morgan J.N. (1966), *Economic Behaviour of the Affluent*, Brookings Institution.

Blinder A.S. (1975), 'Distribution effects and the aggregate consumption function', *Journal of Political Economy*, Vol. 83, pp. 447–75.

Boskin M.J. (1978), 'Taxation, saving and the rate of interest', *Journal of Political Economy*, Vol. 86, pp. S3–S27.

Bradford D.F. and Rozen H.S. (1976), 'The optimal taxation of commodities and income', *American Economic Review*, Papers and Proceedings, Vol. 66, pp. 94–101.

Break G.F. (1953), 'Income taxes, wage rates and the incentive to supply labour services', *National Tax Journal*, Vol. 6.

Break G.F. (1957), 'Income taxes and the incentive to work: an empirical study', *American Economic Review*, Vol. 47, pp. 529–49.

Break G.F. (1974), 'The evidence and economic effects of taxation', in A. Blinder *et al.*, *The Economics of Public Finance*, Brookings Institution.

Brennan G. and Buchanan J.M. (1977), 'Towards a tax constitution for Leviathan', *Journal of Public Economics*, Vol. 8, pp. 255–74.

Broome J. (1975), 'An important theorem on income tax', *Review of Economic Studies*, Vol. 42, pp. 649–52.

Brown C.V. (1980), *Taxation and the Incentive to Work*, Oxford University Press.

Brown C.V. (ed) (1981), *Taxation and Labour Supply*, Allen & Unwin.

Brown C.V. and Dawson D.A. (1969), *Personal Taxation Incentives and Tax Reform*, PEP Broadsheet, No. 506, London.

Brown C.V. and Levin E. (1974), 'The effects of income taxation on overtime: the results of a national survey', *Economic Journal*, Vol. 84, pp. 833–48.

Cain G.G. and Watts H.W. (1973), *Income Maintenance and Labour Supply*, Rand McNally.

Chatterjee A. and Robinson J. (1969), 'Effects of personal income tax on work effort: a sample survey', *Canadian Tax Journal*, May/June.

Domar E.D. and Musgrave R.A. (1944), 'Proportional income tax and risk-taking', *Quarterly Journal of Economics*, Vol. 58, pp. 388–422.

Douglas P.H. (1934), *The Theory of Wages*, Macmillan.

Fields D.B. and Stanbury W.T. (1970), 'Incentives, disincentives and the income tax: further empirical evidence', *Public Finance*, Vol. 25, pp. 381–415.

Fields D.B. and Stanbury W.T. (1971), 'Income taxes and incentives to work: some additional empirical evidence', *American Economic Review*, Vol. 61, pp. 435–43.

Godfrey L. (1975), *Theoretical and Empirical Aspects of the Effects of Taxation on the Supply of Labour*, OECD.

Greenhalgh C. (1977), 'A labour supply function for married women in Great Britain', *Economica,* Vol. 44, pp. 249–65.

Howrey E.P. and Hymans S.H. (1980), 'The measurement and determination of loanable-funds saving', in Pechman (ed.) (1980) *op. cit.*

Husby R.D. (1971), 'A nonlinear consumption function estimated from time-series and cross-section data', *Review of Economics and Statistics*, Vol. 53, pp. 76–9.

Lubell H. (1947), 'Effects of redistribution of income on consumers' expenditure', *American Economic Review*, Vol. 37, pp. 157–170.

Meade Committee (1978), *The Structure and Reform of Direct Taxation*, Institute for Fiscal Studies.

Metcalfe D., Nickell S. and Richardson R. (1976), 'The structure of hours and earnings in British manufacturing industry' *Oxford Economic Papers*, Vol. 28, pp. 284–303.

Moser C.A. and Kalton G. (1971), *Survey Methods in Social Investigation*, 2nd edn, Heinemann Educational Books.

Mossin J.(1968), 'Taxation and risk-taking: an expected utility approach', *Economica*, Vol. 35, pp. 74–82.

Musgrave R.A. (1959), *The Theory of Public Finance*, McGraw-Hill.

Owen J.D. (1971), 'The demand for leisure', *Journal of Political Economy*, Vol. 79, pp. 56–76.

Pechman J.A. (ed) (1980), *What Should be Taxed: Income or Expenditure?*, Brookings Institution.

Ricketts M. (1981), 'Tax theory and tax policy', in A. Peacock and F. Forte, *The Political Economy of Taxation*, Basil Blackwell.

Sandmo A. (1976), 'Optimal taxation: An introduction to the literature', *Journal of Public Economics*, Vol. 6, pp. 37–54.

Wright C. (1969), 'Saving and the rate of interest', in A.C. Harberger and M.J. Bailey (eds), *The Taxation of Income From Capital*, Brookings Institution.

5

Taxation and Equity

This chapter attempts to introduce and to summarise some of the facts and theories relating to a very broad subject. The reader should be aware that here we can only scratch the skin of this fascinating corpus of knowledge.

In the first section we will look briefly at the importance of being fair and at some definitional matters. Then, in the next two sections, equity criteria are examined in greater detail and the ability-to-pay approach in particular is explored further. Sections 5.4 and 5.5 look at the distributional effects of different taxes, and redistribution in the UK since 1938. Then, there are sections on the effects of inflation on equity, and the importance of administrative fairness. Finally, there is a section on avoidance and evasion.

5.1 The Importance of Being Fair

Among the considerations which Adam Smith thought that a tax should include was that, 'the subjects of every state ought to contribute towards the support of the government as nearly as possible in proportion to their respective abilities; that is in proportion to the revenue which they respectively enjoy under the protection of the state' (Smith, 1776, Book V, Ch. II, Part II, p. 310) or, possibly, for the rich: 'something more than in proportion' (p. 327). This first canon of taxation is concerned with equity between taxpayers.

The importance of fairness in taxation rests particularly in the natural desire of the governors and governed for justice. This may seem a somewhat circular argument. However, this is not the place for a rigorous philosophical analysis of the concept of justice. What is clear is that practical problems arise if the taxation system is perceived to be unjust. At the extremes, such cataclysmic events as the French and American Revolutions were partly due to perceived inequity in taxation. Less dramatic, but nevertheless important, is the tendency for evasion and other forms of taxpayer resistance to increase under systems which are perceived to be seriously unfair (see Section 5.8).

The most obvious requirement of equity or fairness is to treat equal people in equal circumstances in an equal way. This is called preserving 'horizontal equity'. If there is a reason for not discriminating between equals, then this suggests that there *should be* discrimination between those who are not equal. Such different treatment of people in different circumstances would be used to preserve 'vertical equity'.

There are, of course, great problems in deciding who is equal to whom. Does equality mean equality of income, expenditure, wealth, total utility, benefit gained from the expenditure of the tax-raising authority, or some combination of these and other factors? We will look at this question in the next two sections.

Economists are trained from an early age to steer clear of normative arguments, and consequently are inclined to leave the definition of equity to others. In practice, decisions about the redistribution of income via progressive taxation and transfer payments to the poor, for example, are based on widely held feelings that this is equitable. We will try to get as far as we can in examining the reasonableness of these feelings within the limitations of our knowledge, the space available here and the desire to remain 'positive.'

It is important, also, to recognise that it is not enough to ask whether a tax is equitable *in vacuo*. It is necessary to know whether the pre-tax distribution of income, and other benefits which might be considered to have a bearing on equity, is satisfactory in the context of our criteria of fairness. If it *is*, then an equitable tax would have to raise money without altering the balance between the members of the population. If it is not, and if redistribution is to be an aim of the tax, a quite different tax structure will be necessary.

We will wait until Section 5.4 to look at the distributional effects of taxes. As an introduction to this and to the sections immediately following, we must now consider alternative criteria for judging whether a distribution is fair.

One possibility is to use *endowment-based* criteria. These assume that an individual has an innate right to the fruits of his own labour. The inequalities in ability between individuals are recognised and allowed for. The resulting 'natural' distribution of income is deemed to be fair. Clearly, this basis has a long history in our civilisation and we do not have to look further than nineteenth-century Britain to find an approximate example. Reliance on endowment-based criteria will lead to *laissez-faire* government. It is possible to modify this approach by allowing for adjustments to the distribution to take account of the 'unfair' benefits of monopoly power, or of inherited, married or gifted wealth, or of superior education or status.

A second basis for criteria about the fairness of distribution is that which seeks the *greatest utility* or the greatest happiness for the greatest number. This does not necessarily mean that all men must be made equal; this only becomes an inevitable result if everyone's marginal utility curves are the same, as we will see in Section 5.3.

A third set of criteria are those which are *equity-based*. At one extreme this means that, since each individual is of equal worth, he must be allowed equal welfare. However, there are more moderate interpretations as we will see soon. From now on, this chapter concerns itself with these equity-based criteria.

A good example of the use of equity arguments for the introduction of a tax arose in 1964 when the then-Chancellor, James Callaghan, was introducing capital gains tax in the Commons. He said that, 'Capital gains confer much the same kind of benefit on the recipient as taxed *earnings* more hardly won. Yet earnings pay full tax while capital gains go free. This is unfair to the wage and salary earner' (Hansard, vol. 710, col. 245). We will investigate this particular case further in Section 5.6 on equity and inflation.

5.2 Equity Criteria

The Benefit Approach

One idea for equity which was discussed by early thinkers and political economists like Smith, Locke, Rousseau, Bentham and Mill was that the tax burden should be split up according to the benefits gained from the government expenditures which are funded by the taxation. These benefits are not directly traceable to individual recipients because of the nature of government expenditures. It is partly true today, and was largely true in the days of the above philosophers, that government expenditure consisted of the provision of public goods like defence, justice, and law and order. Although the benefits of these goods cannot be traced, it is possible to theorise about which groups in society receive the most 'protection'. Some theorists said that the rich benefited most from this protection and would clearly be prepared to pay most for it, whereas others said that the weak and poor benefited more. This latter argument would require a fair tax to take a larger proportion of low incomes than of high incomes, that is to be regressive.

This problem, about who benefits most, makes it very difficult to use the benefit approach to equity. There are other problems too, which contribute to its lack of applicability. For example, there are types of government expenditure which are designed to be fairly straightforward redistributions of income towards those in need. Family Income Supplement, Supplementary Benefit and old age pensions are examples of such 'transfer payments'. It would be clearly absurd to try to operate the benefit principle when it came to deciding who should bear the taxes that pay for these.

The benefit approach is only seen in action in several special cases like television licences and motor taxation. Its main attraction is that it can include both the taxation and the resulting government expenditure. If it were considered equitable that a tax should be distributionally neutral then, under the benefit approach, an equitable tax should leave everyone with the same net benefit, which takes account of both the tax and the benefits.

Other approaches to equity, which we are about to examine, are less satisfactory in this respect for they consider only the effects of raising the tax. However, it is possible to solve this problem of estimating the effects of a new tax by supposing that there is a distributionally neutral equal reduction in another tax or equal increase in government expenditure.

The Ability-to-Pay Approach

Before examining whether the ability-to-pay approach requires that taxpayers should be taxed until they are left equal, or until they have made an equal sacrifice, or until some other criterion is met, we will discuss what attributes give a taxpayer *any* ability-to-pay, that is in what his taxable capacity rests.

Possible candidates include income, expenditure and wealth. At first sight, an increase in any of these suggests an increase in ability-to-pay. Income is perhaps the most obvious, but considerable problems of definition exist. One is whether income includes capital gains, gifts received and gambling wins. If it does, ways must be found to include these in the tax base if equity is to be maintained between earners with different mixes of income. A further problem is to decide the extent to which a person's ability-to-pay is altered by his circumstances. Has a single person an equal ability-to-pay to a person with an equal income who is married and who maintains his mother-in-law? It seems clear that the latter has a lower ability-to-pay and, on this reasoning, income taxation is based on a net income after the deduction of a formalised series of allowances for expenditure.

Criticisms are made against using income as the basis, on the grounds that expenditure would be a more satisfactory basis. First, expenditure out of income from capital gains, gifts, gambling winnings and even the cashing-in of wealth is automatically included. Second it has been suggested that income tax represents a double taxation on saving: once by reducing the amount that can be saved and then by taxing the returns to saving. On the other hand, it might be argued that the income from savings constitutes extra ability-to-pay and that a sales tax would lead to under-taxation of savings by postponing tax temporarily or indefinitely, depending on expenditure plans. This was discussed in Section 4.3.

A further criticism of income as a basis can be traced back to the *Leviathan* of Hobbes in which saving and investment are regarded as beneficial, whereas consumption is anti-social. Therefore, taxation should be based on consumption (what people take out of the common pool), not income (what people put in). This is really another argument for the lighter treatment of saving, which is the difference between income and consumption. However, it does not recognise that saving is just a decision to postpone consumption on economic grounds (such as the ruling rate of interest) and that benefits of status, economic power and security are gained by building up capital, in addition to the return on it.

An additional practical advantage which might be claimed for the income basis is that it is much easier to build progressiveness into income taxation than into sales taxation, because only the former is a direct tax based on the individual. However, this need not be the case if an expenditure tax is used as proposed particularly by Professor Kaldor (1955) and the Meade Committee (1978).

An expenditure tax would involve personal assessment based on an individual's expenditure. This could be deduced from his income of all kinds, his saving and his dis-saving. Certain types of expenditure could be exempted if necessary, and adjustments could be made for the extent to which expenditure on durable goods was seen to be other than current expenditure. This form of taxation is looked at in more detail in Chapter 9.

In practice, despite very considerable arguments in favour of an expenditure tax, the net income concept has remained the prime basis for taxation based on ability-to-pay.

There remains the question whether wealth represents a separate ability-to-pay. This is examined in some detail in Chapter 10, but will be briefly discussed here. There are really two cases. One concerns wealth which arises from an individual's savings out of income, the other concerns wealth arising in other ways like inheritance, marriage, gifts and gambling.

Leaving aside for the moment the opportunity to dis-save in order to spend more than one's income allows, it is clear that the possession of wealth provides advantages such as security and status in both the above cases. This suggests that, just on these grounds, there may be a case for the taxation of wealth. The further fact that an individual with wealth can dis-save to increase his expenditure suggests, for example, that an individual with a certain income and two Rembrandt paintings has a greater ability-to-pay than another with an equal income and no Rembrandts. The former may at worst sell one Rembrandt to pay a wealth tax on them both, and he is still left with one Rembrandt more than his fellow.

However, on grounds of equity, we need to look separately at the two different cases mentioned above, relating to the source of the wealth. In the former case, in which the individual's wealth comes from his own saving, if we hold to the *income basis* for ability-to-pay, it will be inequitable to tax first the income out of which savings were made, then the return to the savings and then the accumulated savings themselves.

A wealth tax of 2 per cent each year is equivalent to an income tax of 20 per cent when the return on capital is 10 per cent each year. To tax both capital and the income from the capital is inequitable when the capital has been accumulated out of taxed income which would otherwise have been spent without further direct taxation. Any expenditure taxes will merely be postponed by building up the capital, assuming that the intention in saving is to postpone consumption. If the intention is to build up security, status and economic power, we are back to the argument previously raised, which may provide an equitable basis for the taxation of wealth even when it has been accumulated by an individual from taxed income.

The second case, that of wealth from other sources, much more obviously suggests an extra taxable capacity. It seems fair to regard the wealth as representing a separate ability-to-pay. However, assuming that the taxation on inheritance and gifts (that is, capital transfer tax) has been set at an appropriate level, wealth tax would seem to be a double taxation even in this case.

We have argued, then, that income is the most usual basis for the ability-to-pay approach, and that the ability-to-pay approach is the most useful basis for a consideration of equity. In practice, decisions about how to raise taxes are usually taken out of the context of the effects of the resultant expeditures, because there is seldom the possibility of tracing a tax to a type of expenditure. Consequently, although there are theoretical reservations about the one-sidedness of the ability-to-pay approach, at least these reservations are not problems for the analysis of real taxes.

5.3 Income and Utility

If equity considerations are to be based mainly on ability-to-pay which is to be measured by income, we next need to establish the quantitative relationship between ability-to-pay and income. It should be noted that a similar analysis to that below could be applied for a 'direct' lifetime expenditure tax. It has already been mentioned that some form of net income will be used so as to take account of the individual's circumstances. Does twice as much net income mean twice the ability-to-pay? In order to answer this question, we will first make a recourse to the traditional theory of sacrifice of utility as discussed by such economists as Mill, Sidgwick, Edgeworth and Pigou.

The assumptions of the sacrifice approach are that it is possible to correlate units of income with units of utility, that everyone has the same utility function which slopes downwards, and that the expenditure effects of the taxation can be ignored by making other distributionally neutral adjustments, as mentioned before. The assumption of a downward-sloping utility curve is another way of saying that there is diminishing marginal utility for money and the goods that it can buy. These assumptions will be challenged later, but can first be maintained while we look at three suggestions as to what an equitable split of the total sacrifice due to taxation would be.

The first suggestion is that it would be equitable if all income earners were to make an equal sacrifice of utility. The assumption has been made that the marginal utility curve slopes downwards. In other words, each extra unit of money brings with it less utility than the last, or the loss of a unit of money is less of a sacrifice of utility for the individual with a higher income. Clearly, then, to achieve an equal sacrifice of utility on these assumptions, a higher income must yield a higher amount of tax. However, depending on the slope of the marginal utility curve, the proportion of income paid in tax may not rise. It is possible for the appropriate tax system to be regressive, proportional or progressive.

An alternative suggestion is that each income earner should make an equi-proportional sacrifice of utility. On our present assumptions, since marginal utility declines with extra income, the greater an individual's income the larger proportion of it he would have to give up in order to lose a certain proportion of his total utility. This means that income taxation needs to be progressive in this case.

A third suggestion is that there should be the least aggregate sacrifice of total utility. This would maximise the total utility throughout the population. It means that having paid the taxation, each member's marginal utility for money would be the same. There would be no way of taking a unit of money from any taxpayer and giving it to another that would increase total utility. On our assumption of identical utility schedules, this means that everyone must end up with the same post-tax income. This needs a taxation system which would involve 100 per cent marginal rates.

At this point it may be useful to refer to Figure 5A which gives a diagrammatic representation of the various approaches to equity. There have been more complex suggestions about equity in this context. For example, society might give priority to improving the position of the least advantaged (Rawls, 1972). Such matters must be left to more specialised books.

On the above assumptions, each of these utility sacrifice suggestions satisfies the simplest of the criteria for equity: that people with the same income will pay the same amount of tax. It is also clear that people with different incomes will pay different amounts in tax. In each case a higher income will bear a higher amount of tax. The second suggestion, of equi-proportional sacrifice, may seem particularly reasonable and a useful justification for a progressive system of income tax. It was important in early arguments in favour of progression (Pigou, 1932). Unfortunately, the assumptions we have used are rather difficult to substantiate.

Let us reconsider the assumption that everyone has the same downward-sloping marginal utility curve. This would mean that one person's utility *curve* would remain the same as his income increased, and that two people with different incomes would also both be on the same utility curve. It does seem reasonable to suggest that someone who has not yet satisfied the basic needs of life (like food, clothing and shelter) will gain more utility from an extra unit of money than someone who has. However, it is certainly possible to produce reasons that might lead to *upward*-sloping parts of the marginal utility curve. For example, it may be that appetites for some goods are stimulated by consumption. Also, some types of consumption which yield great utility may only be possible once a certain threshold has been reached.

This inconclusiveness is confirmed when one adds in the importance of individual personality, background and expectations. These must affect individual relationships between income and

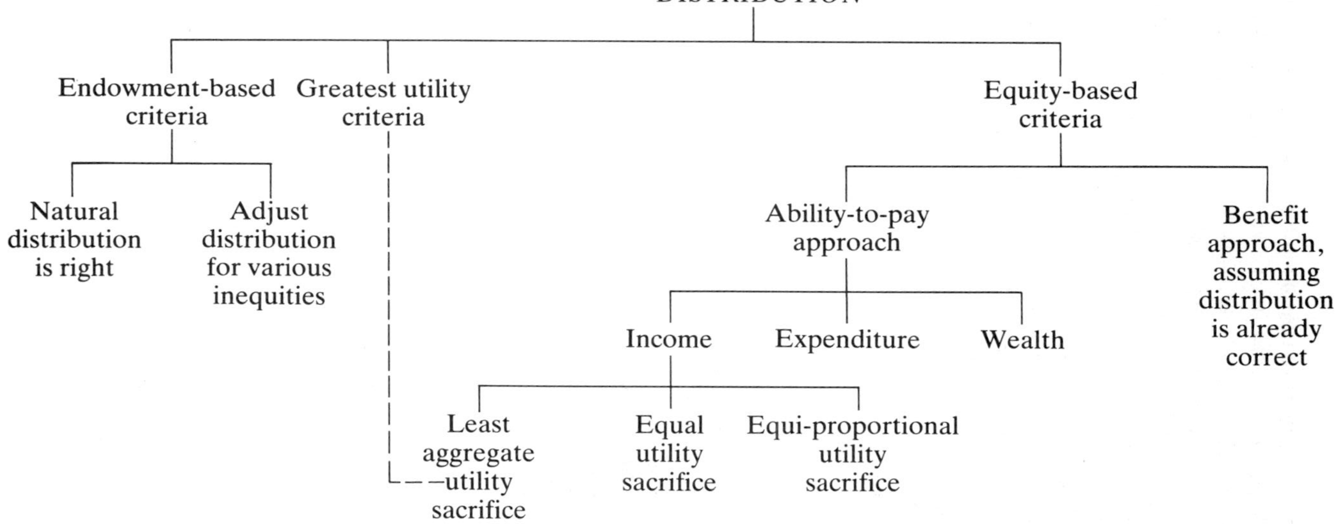

Figure 5A *Approaches for a Fair Distribution*

utility. It may be that different people are not on different parts of the *same* utility curve. Consider C who has been used to drinking cider, living in a bed-sitter and taking holidays in Skegness; and D who drinks claret, lives in a substantial villa and takes holidays in the Caribbean in the winter and at St Tropez in the summer. Both individuals are reasonably content, although C would like to be able to afford D's life-style. However, D would similarly like to afford the much grander ways of E. These would seem to C like wealth beyond the wildest dreams of avarice.

It appears implausible to suggest that we would hurt D much less by causing him to sacrifice some part of his accustomed way of life than we would hurt C. Consequently, it appears unreasonable to suggest that D is on the same utility curve as C (though further along it). The other requirement of the initial assumption, that as C's income moved towards D's, his marginal utility would continue to fall, is only slightly more plausible. This topic is dealt with in much greater depth by other writers (Musgrave, 1959; Simons, 1970).

Difficulties like these which are met when dealing with the treatment of people in different circumstances make it impossible to construct a sound theoretical case for progressive taxation based on such manifestly reasonable propositions as equi-proportional sacrifice of utility. However, we observe that decisions *are* made about tax rates, poverty definitions and welfare programmes, and they seem to be based in the long-run on what society considers to be equitable. We find the Royal Commission on Taxation (1954) saying that 'not merely progressive taxation, but a steep gradient of taxation, is needed in order to conform with the notions of equitable distribution that are widely, almost universally accepted'.

This is, of course, a highly unsatisfactory, begging-the-question basis for progression (Blum and Kalven 1953). However, as we will see in Section 5.5, the British income tax system, and especially the total taxation system, is much less progressive than we are sometimes led to believe. Before this, let us look at the redistributional effects of direct and indirect taxes.

5.4 Distributional Effects of Taxes

If it can be decided what a fair distribution of income,wealth and so on would be, and if plans for particular types of taxes to achieve this are to be made, we must know in greater detail what the effects of such taxes as a progressive income tax will be. Despite our theoretical rejection of an expenditure base for the ability-to-pay approach, would it be more effective to institute a high rate of VAT on luxury goods than to have a progressive income tax, if we wished to take money from high income-earners and not from low income-earners?

The effects of progressive income taxes on individuals have been examined in the previous chapter. The direct and immediate effects on the distribution of income will clearly be towards reducing the disparity of income. However, there are many indirect effects. For example, the total amount to be distibuted may fall as a result of efficiency costs and extra leisure taken by high earners (see Chapter 4). The resulting reduced hours of work may lead to a rise in the return of labour which will raise prices for consumers. The way in which the burden of tax eventually falls is called the 'effective' or 'economic' incidence. In this example we can see that it is the *consumers* who would suffer part of the economic incidence of the progessive income tax which had statutory incidence on the high income earners.

Expenditure taxes also have this difference in incidence which is called 'shifting'. The taxes are levied on producers, but borne to some extent by consumers. This is why such taxation is called indirect. In the long-run, of course, the incidence of all taxes is on individuals. The reactions between individuals and companies to taxation will include the adjustment of sales and purchases in such a way that prices or wages or profits may suffer most, but eventually each is felt fully by individuals. The distributional effects are due to the fact that the various prices, wages, profits and so on are of different relative importance to different people.

Let us look at the distributional effects of indirect taxes in a little more detail, asssuming a general sales tax on all consumption goods. The tax enters as a wedge between net and gross prices. Assuming that there are no effects on money wages or costs of production, this will mean that there is a real income effect. As there is no tax on saving or on capital goods, the burden on a particular household will depend upon the split of its income between consumption and saving. If it is true that the ratio of consumption expenditure to incomes falls as income increases, then the proposed sales tax will be regressive.

In the long run, however, it is not so clear that there is a diminishing average propensity to consume as suggested above. Over a person's lifetime income may be saved in order to be spent later, in which case the general sales tax is merely being postponed. Traditionally, this has been said to be an advantage, because paying now is worse than paying later. However, during times when inflation rates are higher than interest rates, this is no longer so. Nevertheless, the administrative difficulties of running a lifetime sales tax would be enormous. We should at least realise that, over a lifetime, the regressiveness of a general sales tax would be much less than a cross-sectional study at one point in time would suggest.

A *selective* sales tax on good Y only would lead to a rise in the price of Y. The size of this price rise depends on the price elasticities of demand and supply for Y. This was illustrated in Chapter 3 using a diagram similar to Figure 5B, which shows that, under certain elasticities of supply and demand, both the supplier and the consumer bear some of the tax. The price rises from P_1 to P_2, but the suppliers' receipts fall from P_1 to P_3 for each unit.

On the other hand, if demand is perfectly elastic, the suppliers suffer all the price fall and hence the whole burden of the tax. If the demand is perfectly inelastic, the consumers suffer fully. These cases are illustrated in Figure 5C.

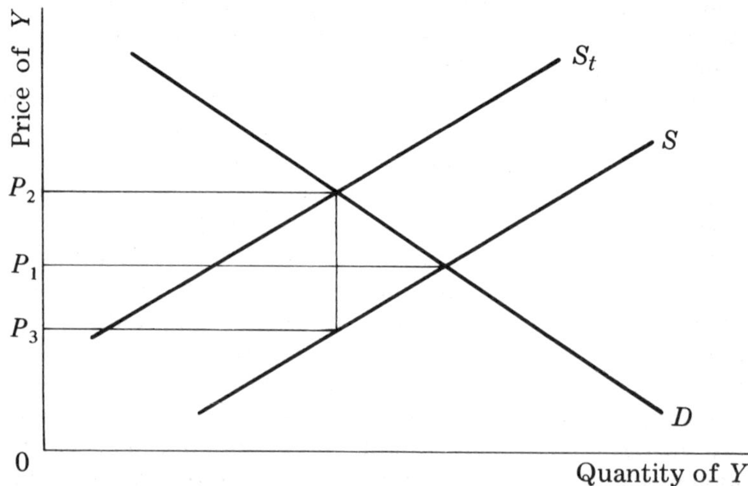

Figure 5B *The Imposition of a Sales Tax*

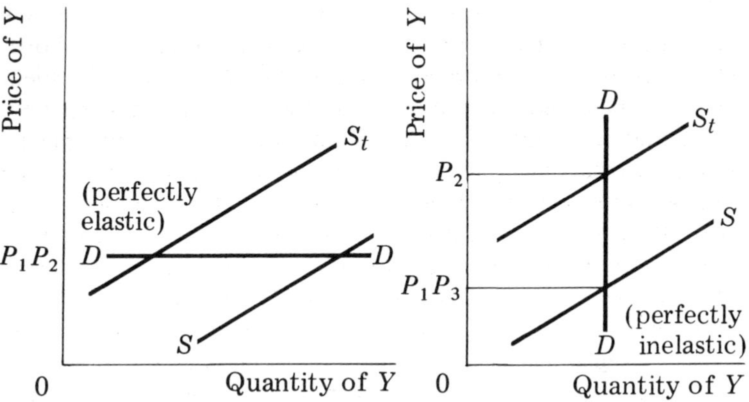

Figure 5C *Sales Tax with Polar Demand Conditions*

Similarly, it could be shown that a tax on goods in perfectly elastic supply will be borne by consumers, and a tax on goods in perfectly inelastic supply will be borne by producers.

We may expect that most goods will not be in perfectly inelastic supply or perfectly elastic demand, therefore some immediate burden will be borne by consumers. Depending upon the nature of good *Y*, and therefore upon what categories of households tend to buy it, the imposition of a selective sales tax may be regressive, proportional, or progressive. If the goods bearing high rates of sales tax constitute a higher proportion of the budgets of low income households than they do of high income households, the tax will be regressive. This is examined in more detail using real taxes in Section 11.5. As an indication of the lengths to which it may be necessary to take this analysis, the effects on employment should be noted. If the goods consumed by the rich are produced by particularly labour-intensive industries which employ the poor, then a sales tax designed to affect consumption by the rich would also affect the incomes of the poor if employment or wages were lower than they would otherwise have been.

A further indirect tax should be mentioned and that is a payroll tax. In competitive markets with a fairly inelastic total labour supply, a general payroll tax cannot be avoided by moving to tax-free employment, and it should be borne by wage earners whether the employer or the employee actually pays it (Musgrave and Musgrave, 1980). However, many markets are not competitive, and unions may not accept a reduction in wages when an employer has to pay increased contributions for national insurance, for example. Therefore, either prices must go up, in which case the wage earner shares the burden with others, or prices cannot be raised, in which case the employer bears the tax.

Tax Capitalisation

Taxes can also affect the capital value of assets. This happens because the value of an asset reflects the income (both pecuniary and non-pecuniary) that the asset is expected to yield. As an illustration of this relationship it can be mentioned that the prices of securities usually fluctuate so that their expected yields stay (roughly) in line with interest rates generally. If a tax changes the expected yield of an asset, then it will also change its market price. In other words, the tax has been capitalised.

As a simple example, consider the value of an undated government bond which yields £10 per year. Suppose also that to begin with there is no taxation on income from investments. If interest rates generally were, say, 10 per cent, the market price of the bond would tend towards £100. The reason is that at £100 the yield on the bond would also be 10 per cent and therefore in line with interest rates elsewhere. If the price of the bond were higher, then its yield would be lower than that of alternative investments. Its price would tend to fall since investors could gain by selling their stock and investing elsewhere. The opposite tendency would occur if the price were lower than £100.

Suppose now that a tax of 50 per cent were imposed on the income from this particular bond only. Suppose also that this new tax was expected to be permanent. If interest rates generally remained at 10 per cent, the price of the bond would fall to £50. This would restore the next yield to 10 per cent, again in line with that available from other assets. Even though the tax was imposed on the *income* from the asset, the burden, in the form of a *capital* loss, would have been suffered by the holders of the bond at the time the tax was introduced. Anyone who invested in the bond later would avoid this capital loss and yet still receive a 10 per cent return.

In practice, of course, the effects of tax capitalisation may be less dramatic. For instance, the prices of redeemable bonds will tend to move slowly towards their repayment price.

Nevertheless, tax capitalisation remains an important part of tax incidence and adds complexity to tax policy generally and equity in particular. To take one of a number of possible cases — mortgage interest relief. It is sometimes suggested that this relief should be retained in order to help individuals buy their own homes. However, the concession has increased the demand and therefore the price of housing. In other words, the concession has been capitalised, and the beneficiaries were those who already owned houses when the relief was introduced, rather than those who sought to purchase them. This example also illustrates the point that once a certain tax feature has been introduced and capitalised, removing it can have further inequitable effects. If the tax relief on mortgage interest were withdrawn, those who had bought at the relief-inflated price would suffer a capital loss. Indeed, this happened in 1974 when the relief was restricted to that on a loan of £25,000. Following this restriction the prices of more expensive houses generally fell (Kay and King 1980, p. 13).

Conclusion

In order to operate an effective redistributional package of taxes, the economic incidence of each tax must be known. As we have seen, the variety of taxes that may be used is considerable. There may be taxes on labour income or capital income or both, and there is the opportunity to be selective by geographical area or type of industry. In addition, there can be expenditure taxes on all goods, or certain types of goods.

Having identified the types of individuals that we wish to bear most tax and those who should bear the least, a suitable package may be assembled. Equal attention must be paid to the sources of income and to the uses. As long as we are content with a fairly broad approach to equity rather than one which identifies individuals, we can rely on the general relationships between the level of income and the types of sources and uses of it. For example, the contribution to income made by capital sources, and the proportion of income spent on champagne, both rise as income rises. Making sure that the economic incidence has been taken into account, these may be areas towards which to aim taxation if we wish the tax system to be progressive. For further detail, see Keller (1980).

5.5 Redistribution and The British Tax System

An immense amount of ink has flowed on the subject of the distribution of wealth and income. Some of these writings are referred to in this section and in suggestions for further reading at the end of this chapter. There is space here for an introduction only.

Measures of Distribution and Redistribution

Distribution of income is often examined by measuring the proportion of the total income that is received by the top percentile of recipients, the next percentile down, and so on. This approach can then be repeated over many years to see how distribution is changing. If such information is arranged cumulatively, that is showing the top percentile, then the top two percentiles together and so on (see Table 5A), Lorenz curves can be drawn to compare different years. An example is shown in Figure 5D.

A statistical measure of the inequality that this information reveals can be calculated. This is called the *Gini coefficient*. It relies

Table 5A Percentage Distribution of Incomes After Income Tax and Surtax

Group of income-recipients	*1949* %	*1957* %	*1960* %	*1963* %	*1967* %	*1970–71* %	*1976–77* %
Top 1%	6.4	5.0	5.1	5.2	4.9	4.5	3.5
2%–5%	11.3	9.9	10.5	10.5	9.9	10.0	9.4
6%–10%	9.4	9.1	9.4	9.5	9.5	9.4	9.5
11%–40%	37.0	38.5	39.8	39.5	39.2	40.4	40.6
41%–70%	21.3	24.0	23.5	23.5	24.5	23.8	24.1
Bottom 30%	14.6	13.4	11.7	11.8	12.0	11.8	12.9

Source: Diamond Commission (1979), Table 2.3.

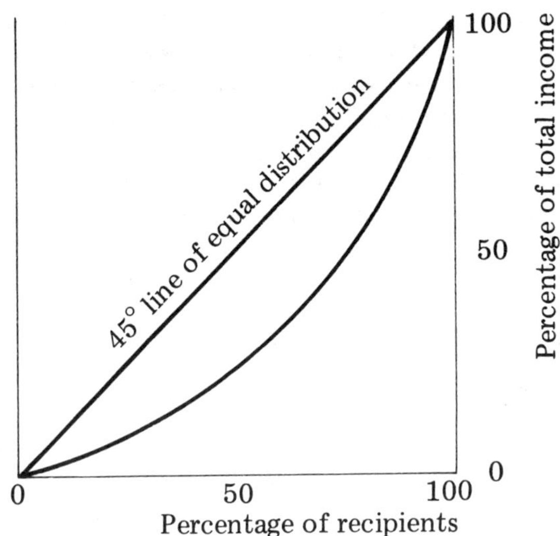

Figure 5D *A Lorenz Curve*

on the fact that an equal distribution would produce a straight line and that, the greater the area between the straight line and the Lorenz curve, the greater the inequality. The Gini coefficient measures this area graphically (from a Lorenz curve) or statistically. There are some problems with Gini coefficients, but these need not concern us here (Cowell, 1977).

These techniques can be used to compare distributions of pre-tax or post-tax income over different years (or different countries, for other purposes), or of pre-tax income with post-tax income. This latter comparison will provide a measure of the redistributional effectiveness of the tax system. The distribution of *wealth* can be examined in a similar way.

An alternative measure of redistribution looks at the way in which the excess of traceable taxes over traceable benefits is split up by type of household. This is a measure of what should be *causing* redistribution, whereas the previous measures are of *how much* redistribution has been caused.

All these measures, which are used in the following pages, take the 'household' as the unit of comparison because of the great difficulties of separating the population into individuals for these purposes. One important problem concerns the 'income' of dependent children who would nearly all appear to be at the bottom of the table for the distribution of income using normal definitions. Clearly, such a result would be highly misleading when income is being used, at least partly, as a proxy for welfare. The majority of children do not have standards of living which can be sensibly related to their measurable incomes. For a discussion on measures of tax progression, see Formby *et al.* (1981).

The Distribution of Income from 1938

There have been several surveys of the distribution of income. Those of F.W. Paish from 1938 to 1955 (Paish, 1957) and H.F. Lydall from 1938 to 1957 (Lydall, 1959) show that the concentration of income in the hands of the top 5 per cent of income-earners was reduced and was reducing at an accelerating rate from 1938 to the mid-1950s.

A later survey by R.J. Nicholson from 1949 to 1957 (Nicholson, 1973) shows that the growth rate of pre-tax incomes was faster in the lower income bands than in the higher bands. During this period there were rising prices and increasing employment, and earned income was rising faster than other types of income. For these reasons, the distribution moved towards equality in those years.

From 1957 onwards these effects were counteracted by an increase in the number of salaried employments, the rewards of which were larger and were growing faster than wages; by an increase in the levels of professional self-employed incomes; and by a large increase in the values of rents, dividends and interest. These counter-influences meant that the distribution of pre-tax incomes remained fairly stable for the decade to the mid-1960s. In the 1970s, the slight trend towards equality continued. The early 1970s saw large pay rises and then limits on rises, especially for the better paid.

There have been considerable changes in the proportions of personal income that went in income taxation and national insurance contributions: for example, from 14.9 per cent of personal income in 1963 to 23.4 per cent in 1975. There was, however, a fall in taxes on expenditure from 13.2 per cent to 11.3 per cent in this period (Table 3 of Diamond Commission, 1976).

The distributional effects of all these changes can be seen in Table

Table 5B Distribution of Personal Income

	1949	*1959*	*1964*	*1967*	*1972–73*	*1976–77*
Pre-tax income of top 10%	33.2	29.4	29.1	28.0	26.9	25.8
Post-tax income of top 10%	27.1	25.2	25.9	24.3	23.6	22.4
Pre-tax Gini	41.1	39.8	39.9	38.2	37.4	36.5
Post-tax Gini	35.5	36.0	36.6	33.5	33.1	31.5

Source: Diamond Commission (1976), Table 3 and (1979), pp. 16 and 24.

5B. This shows the changes in the shares of income of the top ten percentiles of earners and the Gini coefficients for the whole distributions. There was a gradual movement towards equality of pre-tax incomes, which was then accentuated by the effects of taxation. The changes to the income tax system in 1973 and 1979 benefited those on moderately high incomes, but it was still very

Table 5C Progressiveness in 1975–76

Quantile Group of Income before Tax	*Tax as Percentage of Income before Tax*
Top 1 per cent	46.1
2–5 per cent	27.0
6–10 per cent	22.9
Top 10 per cent	29.6
11–20 per cent	21.0
Top 20 per cent	26.4
21–40 per cent	19.1
41–60 per cent	16.8
61–80 per cent	8.8
81–100 per cent	1.5
All groups	19.7

Source: Diamond Commission (1979), Table 2.7.

clearly the case in 1975–76 that the income tax system was progressive, that is, tax became a successively higher proportion of pre-tax income at successively higher levels of income. This is illustrated in Table 5C.

An alternative way of measuring the direction and comparative size of distributional effects of taxation was mentioned at the beginning of this section. This relies on measuring the excess of taxes over transfer benefits by types of household. A study of this showed that the excess was greater for rich families and small families; thus this method suggests that redistribution of income towards poor and large families should have occurred (Nicholson and Britton, 1976). Similar information is also available in the Diamond Commission (1979, Chapter 3). For example, see Table 5D.

Table 5D Direct Taxes as Percentages of Income, 1977

Household Type	*Tax as % of Income*
One non-pensioner	18.8
Two non-pensioners	20.4
Two non-pensioners + two children	18.7
Two non-pensioners + four children	14.8
One pensioner	0.1
Two pensioners	0.2

Source: Diamond Commission (1979), Table 3.8.

Criticisms

Partly due to the impact of inflation, some serious effects became particularly noticeable in the late 1970s. First, there are large numbers of people at the bottom end of the income scale whose implicit marginal rates of taxation are in excess of 100 per cent (Field *et al.*, 1977). This is due to the interaction of the systems of income tax, National Insurance, Family Income Supplement (FIS) and Supplementary Benefit (SB). The poverty levels as defined by FIS and SB are both above the level at which income tax begins to operate.

Even at higher levels, if one includes the $8\frac{3}{4}$ per cent National

Insurance contributions (which in 1982–83 were not levied on slices of income above £220 per week), the system is not seriously progressive except at the bottom end, as shown in Table 5E. In 1982–83 a very large majority of earners fell into the £0–£12,800 bands of taxable income — that is, income after allowances. The only change in marginal rates as income rises within these bands is a *fall* from 38.75 per cent to 30.00 per cent.

Further, the allowances, which are supposed to benefit low earners by removing them from the tax net, turn out to be of proportionally greater benefit to higher rate taxpayers. This can be seen from Table 15 of the Diamond Commission (1976).

Despite these detailed criticisms (that certain aspects of the system are not at all progressive), we have seen that there has been a slight but continuous movement towards equality of income. This was assisted by the total effect of the taxation system. Nevertheless, the progressive nature of the tax system is much less severe than a simple look at income tax rates would suggest.

The Distribution of Wealth

There are very great difficulties in defining and measuring personal wealth. The Diamond Commission Report (1976, Table 29 and 1979, Table 4.4) contains considerable information on the subject, includ-

Table 5E Marginal Tax Rates, 1982–83

*Taxable Income (£)**	Marginal Rate (Tax and NI) (%)
Up to 0	8.75
0–7,000	38.75
7,001–12,800	30.00
12,801–15,100	40.00
15,101–19,100	45.00
19,101–25,300	50.00
25,301–31,500	55.00
31,501 +	60.00

Note: * This represents income after allowances. The marginal NI contribution ceases above £11,000 per year. This has been taken to be a taxable income of £7,000, allowing for married allowance and mortgage interest payments.

ing a Gini coefficient calculation suggesting a gradual move towards greater equality, in the years from 1960 to 1976. The distribution of wealth is very susceptible to high rates of wage inflation, stock market falls and other factors unconnected with tax, some of which may be reversible; therefore measures from year to year are rather less reliable than long-term trends, which certainly suggest a movement towards equality. We discuss this topic further in Chapter 10.

5.6 The Effects of Inflation on Equity

This section examines the different effect that inflation has on different taxes. Because of these differential effects, if the mix of taxes had been equitable in the mid-sixties when inflation was low, it could not have been equitable by the mid-seventies and afterwards when inflation was much higher.

If there is a general price inflation during which all prices rise to the same extent, the equity of *ad valorem* taxes on expenditure will not be directly affected, even if there are several rates of tax. However, if there are relative price changes and the goods concerned bear atypical tax rates, there will be equity effects. For example, if luxury goods rise more in price than other goods and if they bear a higher tax, the expenditure tax system will become more progressive than it was intended to be. Nevertheless, in practice, the major problems arise with *direct* taxation. We will look at the effects of inflation on earned income, and on two types of unearned income: capital gains and interest.

Earned Income

Under inflation, the equity aspects of the taxation of earned income will be affected, unless either the income tax system is proportional or adjustments are made to it to counter the effects of inflation. Without such adjustments to a progressive rate structure, inflation pushes earners into higher rate bands without increasing their real gross incomes. Let us postulate a progressive system which exempts the first £1000 of income each year, taxes the next £4000 at 30 per cent and any extra income at 50 per cent. Let us now suppose that F starts with an income of £1500 and G with £6000. Their taxation will appear thus:

	F	*G*
Income	1,500	6,000
Allowances	1,000	1,000
Taxable Income	500	5,000
Tax at 30%, 50%	150	1,700
Average tax rate	10.0%	28.3%

Suppose that, after a few years, inflation has run to a cumulative total of 100 per cent and has affected incomes and prices identically. The position now becomes:

	F	*G*
Income	3,000	12,000
Allowances	1,000	1,000
Taxable Income	2,000	11,000
Tax at 30%, 50%	600	4,700
Average tax rate	20.0%	39.2%

If the previous system is thought to have been equitable, there will now be an inequity between high and low earners and between income taxpayers and expenditure taxpayers, whose average rate will have stayed the same. As usual, it has been assumed that the extra tax would result only in distributionally neutral adjustments in either government expenditures or other taxes. For an application of this to the UK income tax, see Nobes (1977).

Fortunately for income taxpayers, the allowances are raised from time to time and the taxable income levels at which higher marginal rates apply are also occasionally raised. Indeed in 1977, rather against the will of the Chancellor and the Treasury, Parliament decided that there would in future be a presumption in favour of automatic indexation of allowances to the rate of inflation at each yearly Budget. (This was called the Rooker–Wise Amendment after the two MPs who proposed it.) Despite this, governments have since persuaded Parliament to vote for some Finance Bills which do not fully adjust allowances. Nevertheless, the UK income tax system is partially indexed, and the disturbing effects on average rates (referred to above) have not come to pass.

For a general review of the problem of indexation, see Brinner (1976).

Capital Gains

Capital gains tax is a rather more complex case because, whereas income tax is a tax on the current returns to current toil, capital gains tax works on gains which accrue over time. This is because capital gains tax, which is charged at a 30 per cent rate, only becomes due when an asset is sold and the gain is realised (see Section 8.3 for more details). It means that both the real gain and an inflationary or monetary gain are brought in to charge to tax. In inflationary times it is clear that, since gains evolve over a long period, the comparison of purchase money with sales money is not performed in sensibly comparable units. Consequently, real tax rates are much higher than nominal tax rates. If, for example, one adjusted purchase money of 1974 to a date for sale in 1984, after 10 per cent per annum inflation, the calculation below would occur. £1 in 1974 is equivalent to £2.5937 in 1984, making the simplifying assumption that the factor $(1 + \text{rate})^{10}$ can be used.

	1974 pounds	*1984 pounds*
Original purchase	10,000	25,937
5% real growth over 10 years	6,289	16,312
Final value	16,289	42,249
less Original purchase	−10,000	
Tax based on		32,249
Tax at 30%		9,675
Effective rate (9,675 ÷ 16,312)		59.3%

Further similar calculations produce the following table of real rates under different inflation and growth assumptions:

Rates of inflation	*0%*	*10%*	*20%*
5% real growth	30%	59%	70%
10% real growth	30%	42%	46%

These rates apply to the whole ten years' gain. The fact that they are deferred is not relevant in our analysis of the effects of inflation, because they are deferred whether or not there is inflation. These very high real rates of taxation which are caused by the taxation of money gains have unfortunate effects. First, they may involve a disincentive to save. Secondly, since the taxation only comes into effect when an asset is realised, there is a 'locked-in' effect. That is, there is an incentive to leave one's investment where it is despite more attractive pre-tax opportunities. This is economically inefficient. The 'locked-in' effect would exist even without inflation, but is worsened by it.

Thus, there seem to be arguments for the indexation of capital gains tax. These include an equity argument based on a comparison with income tax which is approximately indexed. However, despite the fact, mentioned in Section 5.1, that capital gains tax was introduced by the Commons as a necessity for equity when compared with the taxation of *earned* income, a more relevant and closer comparison would be with other types of *unearned* income, like interest. Therefore, before firmly accepting the above conclusion about the indexation of capital gains tax, we must examine the effects of inflation on other unearned income.

Fixed-Interest Securities

The effects of inflation on the returns of fixed-interest securities are very severe. Not only does the interest get less valuable year by year in real terms, but also the original investment loses value cumulatively. Both effects are included in the formula:

$$(1 + r) = \frac{(1 + n)}{(1 + i)}$$

where r equals real rate of interest, n is the quoted nominal rate of interest and i is the rate of inflation. When the rate of inflation exceeds the nominal rate of interest, the real rate of interest on

Table 5F An Example of Real Post-Tax Returns Over a 10 Year Period

Rates of inflation	*0%*	*10%*	*20%*
8% debentures after basic tax	100	(−57)	(−119)
8% debentures after higher tax	100	(−131)	(−220)
5% growth paintings after basic tax	100	79	72
5% growth paintings after higher tax	100	58	43

capital can be seen to be negative.

The effects of this can be seen in Table 5F, in which the post-tax returns over ten years on debentures and such assets as paintings are expressed as percentages of the returns under no inflation. This is taken from Nobes (1977) which assumed tax rates ruling at the time. However, later tax rates would give broadly similar results; it is assumed that there is no indexation of capital gains tax, but that marginal rates of income tax are adjusted.

The figures in Table 5F suggest that real post-tax returns on fixed-interest securities suffer much more seriously than those on investment to which capital gains accrue, even if there was no indexation of capital gains tax.

In the 1982 Finance Act a form of indexation of capital gains tax was introduced (see Section 8.3). This does not allow the creation or augmentation of losses. Thus, it does not solve the problem for fixed-interest securities. Consequently, equity would appear to have worsened between the two forms of unearned 'income' considered here, as a result of indexation of capital gains tax.

The issue of certain index-linked National Savings Certificates is an example of an attempt to provide some assistance in this area.

Corporation Tax

The effects of inflation on corporation tax will be considered in Section 13.6.

5.7 Administrative Fairness

It is of great assistance to the smooth running of the tax system and to the reduction of evasion if the government and revenue authorities can build administrative fairness into the system. Taking a broad view of what might be included under this heading, this section discusses several examples.

The general attitude of the Inland Revenue in its dealings with the public by letter, telephone and face-to-face is important. In the experience of the authors (and there seems to be no more objective evidence available at present), although written contact is extremely formal, contact by telephone or face-to-face seems to be pleasant and helpful. In general, the Revenue operates a 10.00 a.m. to 4.00 p.m. walk-in enquiry service in decentralised tax offices throughout the country. If a person's tax is not dealt with locally, the local office is prepared to send for the file and deal with the case locally. Indeed, in London, where these problems occur most frequently, PAYE enquiry bureaux have been set up.

A further example of the willingness of the Inland Revenue to try to answer questions in a helpful way is the extensive enquiry service at the East Kilbride Computer Centre. This service was greatly expanded to deal with the unexpectedly large flow of personal enquiries. Although it seems unrealistic to expect that the Revenue will ever be popular, this willingness to discuss and explain the rules and individual assessments is gratifying.

Also, there is a very large number of explanatory leaflets available. In general they are fairly easy to understand. An analysis of the complexity of such information has been carried out, using a 'fog index' which relies on the length of words and sentences. Many of the leaflets were found to be easier to read than 'quality' daily newspapers (James and Lewis, 1977).

The existence of an appeals system is a further example of administrative fairness. This is reinforced by the involvement of independent Commissioners (see Chapter 8). There is also some provision for postponement or cancellation of assessments when this would reduce trivial transactions or allow the process of appeal or relieve hardship. Such a detail as rounding in favour of the taxpayer when performing calculations is also an endearing trait.

These examples of practical administrative fairness work within a system which has some properties which are generally regarded as equitable, at least in theory. Many of these have already been discussed, like progressiveness. This has the side-effect that, since it implies a system based on marginal rates, it is usually the case that the absurd situation of receiving an increase in income but suffering an even larger increase in tax is avoided. Unfortunately, there are nevertheless some examples of such implicit rates in excess of 100 per cent (See Section 9.1).

Another factor which is perceived to be equitable is the favourable treatment of earned income as opposed to unearned income. This idea that those who toil should be more lightly taxed than those who sit back and count the takings is called 'differentiation' (see Chapter 8). It was given practical effect by a Liberal administration in 1907. A further example is the use of *net* income which takes account of family and other commitments.

Although a theoretical argument was put forward for the use of income as the basis for an ability-to-pay approach to equity, we saw that, because of the problems of economic incidence and because of practical difficulties of bringing all income into tax, a package of taxes of various sorts which operated on both sources and uses of income might be the best way to work towards an equitable distribution. When one looks at the mix of taxes in use in the UK at present, it is clear that they have no main and consistent purpose of accomplishing an equitable distribution. Nevertheless, it is a tenable opinion that, given a lack of consistent and sound theory, it is fairer to tax everything relatively lightly than to tax one thing very heavily, be it unearned income, luxury goods, inherited wealth, or whatever. This is a rare illustration of the compatibility of equity and efficiency, as it was mentioned in Section 3.3 that a tax with a broad base is likely to impose less excess burden than one with a narrow base. As will be seen in the next section, the perception by taxpayers of general fairness in the whole tax system is important in the control of avoidance and evasion.

5.8 Avoidance and Evasion

Definitions

As we have seen, *avoidance* is an individual's manipulation of his afffairs within the law so as to reduce his tax liability. *Evasion* is illegal manipulation to reduce tax liability. Accountants refer to avoidance as 'tax planning' or 'tax mitigation', which emphasises its legality. In order to enable a more precise discussion of avoidance in this section, we need to look a little more closely at its definition.

It could be said using the above definition that, if an individual reduced his consumption of gin and increased his consumption of tonic water when a tax on spirits was imposed, he was avoiding tax. Similarly, if an individual buys a larger house with a larger mortgage and gets married, he could be said to be avoiding tax (but at what cost!). Clearly, the usefulness of the term 'avoidance' is reduced if these examples are included within it.

Following Professor Sandford's suggestion (Sandford, 1973), avoidance will be used to mean something which is contrary to the spirit of the law and which accomplishes the pre-tax objective. For example, if an individual splits up his estate in various ways and into various sorts of property solely in order to pass on as much wealth as possible to his heirs, he is attempting to accomplish the objective he had before capital transfer tax was introduced, and he is operating against the spirit of the law. On the other hand, in the previous examples the intention of the law may have been to discourage drinking and to encourage owner-occupation, and at least to have been neutral about marriage.

Prevalence

Not surprisingly, information about avoidance and evasion is sparse. There are no accurate quantitative estimates of their importance. It is clear, however, that the Inland Revenue is continually worried by the problem and has produced high estimates of the level of evasion (see Section 3.4). Also, a survey of accountants (Sandford, 1973) has shown that they are keen that their clients should take advantage of the possibilities for avoidance, though many of them draw the line at complex artificial schemes. Their clients also dislike complex means of avoidance. However, the search for loopholes continues and if there has been any reduction in avoidance it is probably due to the closing of loopholes rather than restraint by taxpayers. The replacement of estate duty by capital transfer tax has removed the most fruitful source of avoidance schemes (see Chapter 10).

The survey was not informative about evasion, except to reveal that some clients of accountants did not know the difference between avoidance and evasion, and to record the feeling of accountants that evasion may be on the increase and is particularly popular with the self-employed.

Causes

The causes of avoidance and evasion include high tax rates, imprecise laws, insufficient penalties, and inequity.

Avoidance and evasion become more rewarding as rates of tax become higher. Therefore, it is worth spending more money on advice, performing more complex manoeuvres and taking greater risks.

Imprecise laws neither make the letter of the law tight, nor the spirit of the law clear. It is obviously very difficult to legislate with great precision and foresight for the steadily more complex taxes which we now face. However, the speed with which the professional accountants and others find loopholes is alarming. Another improvement would be gained if it became clear that loopholes would be speedily closed once discovered. This would reduce both the incentive for expending effort in finding them and the number of cases that got through them. Adam Smith's canon on 'certainty' relates to this. He wrote that 'the tax which each individual is bound to pay ought to be certain and not arbitrary' (Smith, 1776). The increasing legal complexity which is necessary to maintain equity and to reduce avoidance has the unfortunate side effect of reducing comprehensibility. A survey of the length of Income Tax Acts has shown that, if this is any proxy for complexity, there has been a great increase in complexity over the last century. Table 5G is drawn from this survey (Grout and Sabine, 1976).

If the penalties available to the Revenue and the Courts were unimportant compared to the benefits, evasion would increase. In the UK it is more the case that the penalties *imposed* may be inadequate, and that the Revenue may err too much towards giving hints that evasion has been detected, rather than treating it more seriously. It is often the case now that minor forms of evasion are 'punished' merely by charging interest on the tax that should have been paid earlier. This interest may even be less than the benefit the

Table 5G Length of Income Tax Acts

Date	*No. of pages*
1842	135
1918	180
1952	510
1970	1200
1976	1600

taxpayer has gained from the use of the unpaid money.

In the UK, the social penalties of evasion are probably greater than in the USA, for example, where evasion is regarded as a national sport, or in Italy where it is regarded as a moral duty! If an atmosphere could be created to the effect that evasion was not only illegal but also morally wrong and socially inequitable, this might be very effective in controlling it. A survey of taxpayers in European countries (including Britain) indicates that a positive attitude by taxpayers towards the tax system, and a negative attitude towards offenders can contribute to the control of evasion (Strümpel, 1969).

If the system is commonly regarded as being inequitable, this will lead to an increased desire to avoid or evade tax, and these activities will become increasingly socially acceptable. We have looked at equity in some detail in this chapter. One other obvious inequity would be the ease of avoidance and evasion. In addition to the suggestion that one could get away with paying less tax there would be the feeling that one did not want to pay more tax just because other people were allowed to be successful at avoidance and evasion.

One commentator on the ease of avoidance of the old estate duty writes that 'where those with good tax advisers — and perhaps fewer scruples — can pay little tax while others pay tax at rates of up to 75 per cent, there can be little respect for the equity of taxation' (Atkinson, 1974). A survey in the United States has provided evidence that there is a relationship between inequity and evasion (Spicer, 1975).

Effects

Finally, let us look at the costs and other disadvantages of avoidance and evasion. Both forms of reducing taxation involve the taxpayer's time and the consequent adjustment to his affairs which may run counter to commercial or economic logic except for the tax advantages. Avoidance, and sometimes evasion, also involves the time and resources of expert advisers. The costs in terms of reduced economic welfare of all this effort and re-arrangement must be considerable. In addition, there are the rather more subtle mental costs created by having to draw up complex wills early in life, or by having to pass property before one would most like to, or by general anxiety. At the extremes, there are the mental and physical costs of leaving one's country for tax reasons.

The disadvantageous effects on distribution are of the most obvious concern in this chapter. Some forms of avoidance and evasion may render particular redistributional plans completely ineffective. Clearly, the old estate duty was intended to redistribute wealth, but was much less effective than it might have been because of the ease of avoidance through lifetime gifts. When planning such a tax, estimates need to be made of the possible re-arrangements that might follow its introduction, and the sort of people who would thereby avoid the redistributional effects.

Income and wealth are redistibuted towards those who successfully commit avoidance and evasion, and away from those who do not. This comes about not only because the avoiders and evaders pay less than they otherwise would, but also because the rates of taxation have to be increased in order to raise a predetermined amount of revenue from other taxpayers. This is clearly inequitable and, as has already been mentioned, the perception of this will lead to further avoidance and evasion. All these costs and disadvantages suggest that effective effort put into the reduction of avoidance and evasion would be well worthwhile. This will be so up to the point at which the extra policing, complexity and other costs outweigh the benefit to society as a whole of the reduction in avoidance and evasion.

5.9 Summary

This chapter began by looking at the philosophical and practical benefits of fairness in taxation. Equal treatment of equals must be the most basic of requirements, but even this involves a series of assumptions and definitional problems. These problems are as nothing compared with those of satisfactorily treating those who are not equal.

The benefit approach to equity turns out to be of little practical value because it is difficult to trace benefits to individuals or groups; because it breaks down when considering transfer payments, for example; and because taxes and expenditure are not usually directly linked. The ability-to-pay approach usually relies upon an income basis. Its assumptions are not strong enough for us to rely upon the argument for progressiveness that it appears to provide.

Turning to the distributional effects of taxes, we see that the incidence of taxes is usually *shifted* to some extent from the point of assessment. The indirect effects of an income tax may involve hours worked and prices charged. The degree to which consumers suffer directly from sales taxes depends on elasticities of demand and supply. Studies of distributional effects need to include the effective incidence of taxes and the dispersal of benefits of government expenditure. This is likely to be very complicated.

The British income tax system has been mildly redistributive since 1938. However, it is less progressive than a simple look at income tax rates might suggest.

The effects of inflation on equity are important and unintentional. Earned income fares reasonably well because of its current nature and because effort is put into correcting for inflation. Capital gains suffer increasingly high real rates in inflationary conditions. However, calls for indexation of capital gains taxation seem inappropriate unless there is also indexation of fixed interest securities which suffer even more under inflation.

The chapter concluded with considerations of the various elements of the tax system that may contribute to equity, and a discussion of the causes and costs of avoidance and evasion.

Further Reading

General reading on the subject matter of this chapter might include Atkinson (1980), Musgrave and Musgrave (1980, Chapters 5, 11, 12 and 13), Kay and King (1980), Prest and Barr (1979, Chapter 5) and Kincaid (1973, Chapters 5 and 6). For measures of equality, refer to Cowell (1977) and Sen (1973). The effects of inflation are dealt with by Brinner (1976) and the OECD (1976).

References

Atkinson A.B. (1974), *Unequal Shares,* Pelican Books, p. 128.

Atkinson A.B. (1975), *The Economics of Inequality,* Clarendon Press.

Atkinson A.B. (1980), *Wealth, Income and Inequality*, Oxford University Press.

Blum W.J. and Kalven H. (1953), *The Uneasy Case for Progressive Taxation,* University of Chicago Press.

Brinner A.B. (1976), 'Inflation and the definition of taxable personal income', in H.J. Aaron (ed.) *Inflation and the Income Tax*, Brookings Institution, Washington, DC.

Cowell F. (1977), *Measuring Inequality*, Philip Allan, Chapter 2.

Diamond Commission (1976), *The Royal Commission on the Distribution of Income and Wealth*, Report No. 4, Cmnd. 6626, HMSO.

Diamond Commission (1979), *Report No. 7*, Cmnd. 7595, HMSO.

Field F., Meacher M. and Pond C. (1977), *To Him Who Hath*, Pelican Books, Chapter 3.

Formby J.P., Seaks T.G. and Smith W.J. (1981), 'A comparison of two measures of progressivity', *The Economic Journal*, December.

Grout V. and Sabine B. (1976), 'The first hundred years of tax cases', *British Tax Review*, No. 2.

James S.R. and Lewis A. (1977), 'Fiscal fog', *British Tax Review*, No. 6.

Kaldor N. (1955), *An Expenditure Tax*, Unwin University Books.

Kay J.A. and King M.A. (1980), *The British Tax System*, Oxford University Press.

Keller W.J. (1980), *Tax Incidence: A General Equilibrium Approach*, North-Holland.

Kincaid J.C. (1973), *Poverty and Equality in Britain* , Pelican Books.

Lydall H.F. (1959), 'The long term trend in the size distribution of income', *Journal of the Royal Statistical Society,* Series A, 122, Part 1.

Meade Committee (1978), *The Structure and Reform of Direct Taxation*, Institute for Fiscal Studies (IFS), Allen and Unwin.

Musgrave R.A. (1959), *The Theory of Public Finance,* McGraw-Hill, Chapter 5.

Musgrave R.A. and Musgrave P.B. (1980), *Public Finance in Theory and Practice*, McGraw-Hill, pp. 410–13.

Nicholson R.J. (1973), 'The distribution of personal income', in A.B. Atkinson (ed.) *Wealth, Income and Inequality*, Penguin Books.

Nicholson J.L. and Britton A.J.C. (1976), 'The redistribution of income', in A.B. Atkinson (ed.) *The Personal Distribution of Incomes*, Allen and Unwin.

Nobes C.W. (1977), 'Capital gains tax and inflation', *British Tax Review*, No. 3.

OECD (1976), *The Adjustment of Personal Income Tax Systems for Inflation*.

Paish F.W. (1957) 'The real incidence of personal taxation', *Lloyds Bank Review*, Vol. 43.

Pigou A.C. (1932), *The Economics of Welfare*, 4th edn, Macmillan, Part 4,

Chapter 9.
Prest A.R. and Barr N.A. (1979), *Public Finance*, Weidenfeld and Nicolson.
Rawls, J. (1972), *A Theory of Justice*, Oxford University Press.
Royal Commission on the Taxation of Profits and Income Second Report (1954), Cmnd. 9105, HMSO, p. 33.
Sandford C.T. (1973), *Hidden Costs of Taxation*, Institute for Fiscal Studies, Chapter 8.
Sen A.K. (1973), *On Economic Inequality*, Clarendon Press.
Simons H.C. (1970), 'The case for progressive taxation', in R.W. Houghton (ed.), *Public Finance*, Penguin Books.
Smith A. (1776), *The Wealth of Nations*, edited by E. Cannan, Methuen, 1950.
Spicer M. (1975), 'New approaches to the problem of tax evasion', *British Tax Review*, N. 3.
Strümpel B. (1969), 'Contribution of survey research to public finance', in A. Peacock (ed.), *Quantitative Analysis in Public Finance*, Praeger, p. 26.

6

Taxation and Stabilisation

Unemployment and inflation are two of the major problems facing modern economies. They also present two interrelated issues. The first is that economies may, indeed have, appeared to develop secular trends towards higher levels of unemployment or inflation and, sometimes, both. In addition to any such trends, the level of economic activity has fluctuated over time. This has been described as the business cycle and consists of a continuing series of so called 'booms' and 'slumps'. The practical implication of these problems is a policy (or policies) designed to smooth out the cyclical fluctuations and to minimise the levels of unemployment and inflation.

In this chapter we begin with the basic issue of the role of the state in achieving these aims. No doubt controversy over this issue will continue for ever, but most of the main points of current contention are described. This is followed by a discussion of fiscal policy, and the chapter ends on the relative merits of different taxes as instruments of stabilisation policy.

6.1 The Role of the State

There has been an enormous range of views as to the extent to which the state ought to intervene in economic life. For instance, the 'mercantilist' theories generally held that the state had a major role to play in promoting economic welfare. In particular, it was considered that there should be intervention to build up and maintain a favourable balance of trade with other countries. This involved state regulation and protection in the form of tariffs and embargoes on imports. For example, the famous Navigation Acts (the first of which was passed in 1650) were designed to promote British shipping. Mercantilism also implied policies designed to encourage industries which exported goods and industries which could produce substitutes for imported goods. These views were widely held from the sixteenth to eighteenth centuries (and, it may be suggested, are still thriving in certain quarters!).

The succeeding doctrine of *laissez-faire* took the opposite view: that economic wealth was best produced by self-interested individuals directed by the 'invisible hand' of free markets, rather than by the government. In the words of Adam Smith (1776):

> The uniform, constant and uninterrupted effort of every man to better his condition, the principle from which public and national, as well as private opulence is originally derived, is frequently powerful enough to maintain the natural progress of things toward improvement, in spite both of the extravagance of government, and of the greatest errors of administration. Like the unknown principle of animal life, it frequently restores health and vigour to the constitution, in spite, not only of the disease, but of the absurd prescriptions of the doctor.

The influence of *laissez-faire* was extensive in the nineteenth century.

In the twentieth century the arguments over the proper role of government have continued, of course, at least as vigorously. However, a new dimension of the debate has concentrated on the relative merits of the different methods by which any given level of government intervention should be conducted.

In particular, there are two major types of policy which the government can use to influence the level of economic activity: fiscal policy and monetary policy. *Fiscal policy* refers to changes in government spending or income including, of course, taxation. As its name suggests, *monetary policy* is mainly conducted through measures designed to influence the supply of money or the level of interest rates. There is a considerable overlap between fiscal and monetary policy. A change in fiscal policy will usually affect the monetary side of the economy, and this in turn will affect the results of the original change in fiscal policy. For example, suppose that the government pursues an expansionary fiscal policy which results in an increase in the budget deficit. This increase in the deficit has to be financed one way or another. It can be done by borrowing, or it can be done by increasing the money supply. Either way, such changes will influence the effects of the expansionary fiscal policy.

Despite the interdependence of fiscal and monetary policies, there has been a vigorous controversy as to which of the two is the more effective. The debate is often described as being between the 'Keynesians' on the one hand and the 'monetarists' on the other. This is very much a crude view of the discussion, but it does provide a useful way of presenting many of the issues involved in stabilisation policy.

The 'Keynesian' Approach

The term 'Keynesian' is used here to indicate a range of views, rather than solely the work of John Maynard Keynes. Keynes was certainly one of the most prominent expounders of these views in the 1930s, but he was by no means the only economist to pursue them. It should also be added that a number of propositions which are often included under the general heading of 'Keynesian' are quite different from the thinking of Keynes himself (see, for example, Leijonhufvud, 1968). Indeed, Sir Austin Robinson (1977) reports that Keynes himself, after dining with the Washington Keynesian economists in 1944, commented that 'I was the only non-Keynesian there'. Also, Colin Clark (1970) relates that, in 1946, Keynes explained to Abba Lerner: 'You see, I am not a Keynesian'. And, just to round it off, Samuelson (1970, p. 193) has quoted Milton Friedman, who is perhaps the most widely known prophet of monetarism, as saying 'we are all Keynesians now!'

Despite this daunting background, it is possible to present a stylised version of the 'Keynesian' approach, though perhaps with some trepidation. The initial contrast is with the preceding view of *laissez-faire*. As we have seen, that view suggested that markets were best left to themselves. In particular, involuntary unemployment was not seen as a fundamental problem. (Involuntary unemployment here refers to individuals who are willing to work at prevailing wage rates, or for less, but are unable to find employment.) In support of this proposition was 'Say's Law' (Say, 1803) which held that supply creates its own demand. In other words, 'demand is only limited by production. No man produces, but with a view to consume or sell, and he never sells, but with an intention to purchase some other commodity' (Ricardo, 1821, chapter XXI). Therefore, there cannot be a lack of aggregate demand and, so the argument runs, if there is unemployment, it is caused by obstacles to the efficient operation of the market, such as trades unions or custom or whatever, keeping wage rates at an artificially high level.

Although the mass unemployment and misery of the Great Depression concentrated minds wonderfully on the validity of this line of argument, it had encountered opposition much earlier. Malthus, perhaps best known for his views on population, expressed concern that 'effective demand' might be insufficient as he explained, for example, in a letter to Ricardo on 7 July 1821. It might be noted that Keynes' opinion was that, 'If only Malthus, instead of Ricardo, had been the parent stem from which nineteenth century economics proceeded, what a much wiser and richer place the world would be today!' (Keynes, 1933). It was also soon pointed out that whereas Say's Law must be true for a barter economy (where buying and selling necessarily occur simultaneously), this does not have to happen in a monetary economy (Mill, 1844), though at the time this was not widely recognised as a major problem.

It was not until the 'Keynesian revolution' that the problem was placed firmly on the academic agenda. In particular, Keynes' *General Theory of Employment, Interest and Money* (1936) provided a powerful focus for the following debate. Perhaps it is of interest to note that Keynes himself, in a letter dated 1 January, 1935 to George Bernard Shaw, wrote: 'I believe myself to be writing a book on economic theory which will largely revolutionise – not, I suppose, at once but in the course of the next ten years – the way the world thinks about economic problems' (quoted in Harrod, 1951, Chapter 11).

In this book, Keynes provided a general theory for the economic system which suggested that the economy may move to a position involving involuntary unemployment, and would not then tend back towards full employment. For instance, a drop in investment would reduce aggregate demand, which in turn would reduce employment and national income. Furthermore, the drop in national income could be greater than the original fall in investment through the operation of the multiplier. This simply describes the process where a fall in the income of one group will cause them to spend less, which will reduce the income of others, who in turn will reduce their expenditure and so on. It might be possible to reduce the resulting unemployment through an expansionary monetary policy, but some Keynesians thought that it might not prove effective. For example, it may not be possible to reduce interest rates sufficiently to stimulate the required level of aggregate demand.

The answer then seemed to be an expansionary fiscal policy whereby the government increased spending or reduced taxation or both. Again, the multiplier may increase the changes in national income. The following unusual illustration from the *General Theory* gives something of the flavour of the argument:

> If the Treasury were to fill old bottles with bank notes, bury them at suitable depths in disused coalmines which are then filled up to the surface with town rubbish, and leave it to private enterprise on well-tried principles of *laissez-faire* to dig the notes up again ... there need be no more unemployment and, with the help of the repercussions, the real income of the community, and its capital wealth also, would probably become a good deal greater than it actually is.
>
> (Keynes, 1936, Book III, Chapter 10).

So the argument is that government is able to reduce unemployment, and can then maintain full employment by manipulating aggregate demand — a policy sometimes known as 'fine-tuning'. Beyond that, markets can be left to allocate resources more or less efficiently.

Such Keynesian principles exerted a very strong influence on UK macroeconomic policy in the 1950s and 1960s. However, increasingly, concern was aroused about whether full employment could be maintained at the same time as price stability. Both unemployment and inflation can be affected by the level of aggregate demand. This led to a further development in 'Keynesian' thought — the Phillips curve (Phillips, 1958; Lipsey, 1960). Phillips' view was that, as the pressure of aggregate demand rose, so the rate of increase of wages would rise. Also, the level of aggregate demand would be indicated by the level of unemployment. Phillips examined the wage and unemployment rates of nearly a century, and suggested that there was an inverse relationship between the two. As wages have a strong influence on prices, the analysis appeared to show that there was a trade-off between inflation and unemployment. It seemed that there was a whole range of possible combinations of these two variables, with high rates of inflation being compatible with low levels of unemployment, and lower rates of inflation being compatible with higher levels of unemployment. It was then only a small step to suggest that the government could 'choose' which combination it wished to aim at, by controlling the level of aggregate demand.

There is a further strand in 'Keynesian' thought which has become known as disequilibrium analysis. This view also places considerable importance on the role of markets in the economy. However, it has stressed the possibility that prices may not always respond flexibly to economic pressures. Market adjustment may then occur through the *quantities* bought and sold, as well as, or instead of, through prices. This line of thought recognises the role of government intervention through fiscal and monetary policy, but perhaps with the assistance of some form of prices and incomes policy.

One other feature of the Keynesian approach contrasts with much of the pre-Keynesian thought and has been particularly evident in discussions of economic policy. In the nineteenth and early twentieth centuries a great emphasis was often placed on long-term considerations. Considerations such as involuntary unemployment sometimes received less attention, since it was supposed that in the longer term, markets were capable of dealing with them. Although a great deal of the 'Keynesian' stress on 'short-term' issues comes from Keynesians rather than Keynes, a clear lead in this came from Keynes himself. As Joan Robinson (1971) put it, Keynes 'brought the argument down from timeless stationary states into the present, here and now, when the past cannot be changed and the future cannot be known'. And as Keynes put it in an earlier work:

> This *long-run* is a misleading guide to current affairs. *In the long run* we are all dead. Economists set themselves too easy, too useless a task if in

> tempestuous seasons they can only tell us that when the storm is long past the ocean is flat again.
>
> (Keynes, 1924)

It is difficult to summarise the 'Keynesian' approach in a short space. For our purposes, perhaps it is sufficient to say that it presumes that national income is determined by real, rather than monetary, magnitudes; and that government can intervene successfully, particularly through fiscal policy, to reduce unemployment and inflation. Therefore, the government should do so.

The 'Monetarist' Approach

The Keynesian approach to macroeconomic policy has provoked criticism from various quarters, perhaps most noticeably from individuals belonging to the 'monetarist' school of thought. Like Keynesianism, monetarism means different things to different people. For instance, in the UK in political circles, it has been used to describe a belief in *laissez-faire*, and as a term of abuse. Michael Foot (1983), as a Leader of the Opposition, was quoted as saying that 'monetarism is a world-wide disease'.

On a less dramatic note, the term monetarism covers a range of views which emphasise the role of money in the operation of the economic system. It therefore provides a considerable contrast to Keynesianism which has tended to play down the importance of money and monetary policy, relative to fiscal policy. We shall not attempt a full account of monetarism here, though descriptions can be found in Chrystal (1979), and Vane and Thompson (1979). Rather we shall summarise particular areas of debate and some of these will be discussed further, later in the chapter.

The first point is that monetarists have suggested that most of the instability in modern economies is monetary in origin. For example, from their study of the monetary history of the United States between 1867 and 1960, Friedman and Schwartz (1963) have argued that all major American recessions have been caused by a contraction of the money supply. Equally, Friedman (1970) has also argued that 'inflation is always and everywhere a monetary phenomenon'.

Secondly, the effectiveness of fiscal policy on its own may in any case be very low. For example, suppose an expansionary fiscal policy were undertaken in order to increase national income. Suppose also that monetary policy were neglected and the money supply remained the same. The fiscal policy would put pressure on the money supply and interest rates would tend to rise. This in turn would tend to reduce private expenditure and so reduce the effectiveness of the original expansionary policy.

A third attack on the 'Keynesian' position is that attempts to 'fine-tune' the economy are unlikely to be accurate. In extreme cases, the results may even be perverse. The argument is that there are significant and variable time lags in the operation of both fiscal and monetary policy (see Section 6.2). By the time policy action actually influences the economy, circumstances may have changed, so that the action is inappropriate, or even working in the wrong direction.

Fourthly, there may be other reasons why fiscal policy is unsuitable for stabilisation policy, principally because of the efficiency costs of expanding and contracting public expenditure for this reason only. Instead, it has been argued, fiscal policy has a more appropriate role in other areas. Again, according to Friedman (1948), the level of government spending should be determined on the basis of the 'community's desire, need and willingness to pay for public services', and not by the cyclical fluctuations of the economy.

A fifth onslaught has centred around the possible trade-off between unemployment and inflation as illustrated by the Phillips curve. Whatever the accuracy of the Phillips curve in earlier years, by the end of the 1960s it was quite clear that both inflation and unemployment were rising to alarming heights simultaneously. Several commentators, including Friedman (1968) and Phelps (1968) suggested that the trade-off disappears when people have adjusted to the new rates of inflation. In other words, the Phillips curve would appear to suggest only a short-run relationship between inflation and unemployment. In the long run, the 'curve' becomes vertical at the 'natural rate of unemployment'. Such a rate of unemployment can be changed by microeconomic techniques, such as improving the efficiency of the labour market. The monetarist point is that macroeconomic policies designed to reduce unemployment below the natural rate are unlikely to be successful in the long run.

This analysis has been further extended by work on the ways in which individuals and firms adjust to changes in the economy. In particular, there is the 'rational expectations' approach which supposes that economic decisions will be made rationally and in the light of all available information including, of course, anticipated government stabilisation policies. Such decision-making may well frustrate such policies, though the extent to which this can happen is very much a matter of debate (for example, see Peel, 1981).

Again, like Keynesianism, monetarism is difficult to summarise briefly. Perhaps it is sufficient here to say that it places far more importance on the influence of money on the economic system. However, given the various problems of stabilisation policy, such as lags, it also casts doubt on the effectiveness of attempts to fine-tune the economy. This has led to suggestions that perhaps the best the government can do is to stabilise its own activity in order to avoid increasing instability in the rest of the economy.

What can we conclude from this brief account? Clearly, the role of the public sector here will continue to be the subject of strenuous argument. It seems reasonable to conclude that fiscal policy is not an omnipotent instrument of economic policy. Yet it clearly has economic effects and therefore it is unlikely that governments will refrain for long from using it as an instrument of macroeconomic policy. Indeed, they have used it extensively in the past. It is therefore important to look further at fiscal policy and some of its implications, and this is done in the rest of the chapter.

6.2 Fiscal Policy

Although fiscal policy includes both the revenue and expenditure sides of government activity, we shall be concerned here almost exclusively with taxation. As in earlier chapters we shall initially avoid a number of distracting complications, by making certain assumptions. The sort of problems these complications cause can then be discussed as the assumptions are withdrawn later.

It will be assumed that any tax change has an instantaneous effect on the economy, and does not affect the distribution of income; also, that the supply of money is sufficiently elastic to prevent any change in interest rates and that there is a certain level of unemployment. Furthermore, suppose the economy is closed, i.e. there are no exports or imports. In addition, it is assumed that the tax system does not affect the efficiency of the economy, or the supply of factors of production and that it consists only of a lump sum tax of T.

We shall also make the 'Keynesian' assumption that the level of national income (Y) is determined by the amount which people wish to consume (C), invest (I) and the level of government expenditure (G). Hence:

$$Y = C + I + G \tag{1}$$

The amounts of investment and government expenditure are fixed. Another assumption is that there is a Keynesian consumption function which suggests that consumption consists of two elements. The first is a, which is the amount consumed regardless of the level of income. However, it is also suggested that as income rises, so consumption will rise, but not by as much. Thus, the second element is bYd, where b is the marginal propensity to consume and has a value between 0 and 1; and Yd is the level of disposable income. Hence:

$$C = a + bYd \tag{2}$$

Disposable income, Yd, is simply gross income Y minus the lump sum tax T.

$$Yd = Y - T \tag{3}$$

The term Yd in equation (2) can now be replaced by $Y - T$ and the new equation (2) substituted into (1) giving:

$$Y = a + b(Y - T) + I + G$$

This can be simplified by grouping the Y terms on the left-hand side and factoring out the Ys so that:

$$(1 - b)Y = a - bT + I + G$$

The next stage is to divide through by $1 - b$. This gives:

$$Y = \frac{a - bT + I + G}{1 - b}$$

from which the familiar multiplier is derived. From this we can also derive a tax multiplier:

$$\frac{-b}{1 - b}$$

which shows, in this simple model, the relationship between changes in taxation and changes in national income. If we now pick some plausible, but hypothetical, value for the marginal propensity to consume, say 0.8, the value of the tax multiplier becomes −4. This means that an increase or decrease in taxation would change national income by four times the original change — which is quite impressive!

Qualifications

The reason why the tax multiplier is so powerful in this model is, of course, that the only alternative to spending on domestic goods and services is saving. If some of the assumptions are relaxed, other alternatives become available and so the value of the multiplier is drastically reduced. In an open economy, such as that of the UK, a large amount of any change in expenditure will be absorbed by changes in imports. Also, the tax system does not consist of lump sum taxes. Not only do different taxes have different and usually more complex tax multipliers, but most taxes are related to income or expenditure, which further reduces the value of tax multipliers as a whole. The effect is further reinforced by the existence of many income-related benefits, which are discussed in Section 9.1.

The Government Budget

A further assumption was that government expenditure remained the same. Suppose now that the government wished, say, to increase taxation and its expenditure by the same amount. What then would be the value of this 'balanced budget' multiplier? Referring back to the simple model embodied in equations (1) to (3), it can be seen that the value depends on the type of additional government expenditure. If it consists of goods and services, then the normal multiplier applies, which added to the tax multiplier gives a value of 1:

$$\frac{1}{1-b} + \frac{-b}{1-b} = \frac{1-b}{1-b} = 1$$

In other words, if an increase of £1 in tax revenue were accompanied by an increase in government expenditure of £1, the result would be a final increase of £1 in national income. The reason for the rise is that in this case the government has a 'higher marginal propensity to consume' than the taxpayers. However, if the government expenditure consisted of an increase in transfer payments, there would be no increase in national income. The reason is that the taxpayers will reduce their consumption in line with the marginal propensity to consume and the recipients of the transfer payments will do the opposite, which might well leave no net result. An example of this is given in Section 4.3 under 'income effects'.

Crowding-Out

'Crowding-out' refers to the possibility that an expansion of the public sector may result in a lower increase in national income because it displaces some private expenditure. If the economy were operating at full capacity (including full employment), then any increase in public expenditure must necessarily crowd-out at least the same amount of private expenditure.

However, this is not the real concern in this context. The problem is that if the government is trying to reduce unemployment (of all factors of production) by expanding public expenditure, any gains made will be offset by any resulting losses of employment in the private sector. This can be shown if the earlier assumption, that the money supply is sufficiently elastic to prevent any change in interest rates, is relaxed. We can also introduce the likely possibilities that private consusmption and investment expenditure are influenced by interest rates. An expansionary fiscal policy will increase the demand for money for transactions purposes and, other things being equal, increase interest rates and so reduce private expenditure. A similar effect might occur if the expansionary policy led to increased prices.

As far as taxation is concerned, this is meant to crowd-out private expenditure. However, there are still some implications. For example, in certain circumstances described above, the balanced budget multiplier was shown to be equal to one. Crowding-out will result in a value of less than one.

Lags

One of the major assumptions made above was that any tax change had an instantaneous effect on the economy. Clearly, in practice, fiscal policy, and for that matter monetary policy, usually encounter a number of delays in their operation. The importance of lags in stabilisation has been stressed by Friedman (1947 and 1948). Since 1948 the nature of these delays has been much explored, but the basic classification still remains useful. This classification recognises three types of lag: the recognition lag, the implementation lag, and the response lag.

The *recognition lag* is the delay from the time the need for action arises until that need is actually recognised by the government. Or, as Prest puts it: 'It may be that the authorities are too slow to recognise the onset of slump or boom, either because no storm signals are flying or else because their vision is defective' (Prest, 1975, p. 102). It may also take time to come to a decision.

Much of the recognition lag exists because of the time taken to collect and analyse economic data. The delay could be very small or even negative if it were possible to forecast future levels of economic activity. However, economic forecasting has its limitations; perhaps best summarised by Denis Healey as Chancellor of the Exchequer:

> The numbers contained in the forecasts — specific to $\frac{1}{2}$ per cent in every case — give a spurious impression of certainty. But their origin lies in the extrapolation from a partially known past, through an unknown present, to an unknowable future according to theories about the causal relationships between certain economic variables which are hotly disputed by academic economists, and may well in fact change from country to country or from decade to decade.
>
> (Healey, 1974)

The *implementation lag* is the delay between the decision to take action and the implementation of that action. The delay occurs because, naturally, it takes time to carry out policy changes. It may be wise for the Chancellor to wait for the next Budget, or the most appropriate time to hold a 'mini-Budget'. It then takes time for the Inland Revenue or Customs and Excise to put the changes into operation.

The *response lag* (sometimes known as the 'outside lag') refers to the time between the implementation of a policy measure and the time it finally influences the economy. For example, when income tax rates are increased, it may take many months for taxpayers to adjust the level of their expenditure.

Clearly, the existence of lags limits the effectiveness of stabilisation policy and, in some circumstances, can result in greater instability. For instance, suppose that without any government intervention, the economy would follow the path *AB* shown in Figure 6A. Suppose also that the government intends to pursue a policy of stabilisation. As the economy approaches point *D* this would imply an expansionary policy.

However, depending on the length of the lags, the expansionary policy would not take effect until conditions had changed. If it took effect around, say, point *E*, then it would add to existing inflationary pressures. At this point, the government may be tempted to pursue a contractionary policy which, because of lags, may serve only to worsen the following recession. So it can be seen that lags, together with an inability to forecast the future level of economic activity accurately, can lead to a 'stabilisation' policy which actually contributes to instability. In these circumstances, the economy may follow a path such as *AC* in Figure 6A.

The second major argument against discretionary change is that its very existence might contribute to economic instability. In using its discretionary powers, it is conceivable that the government may

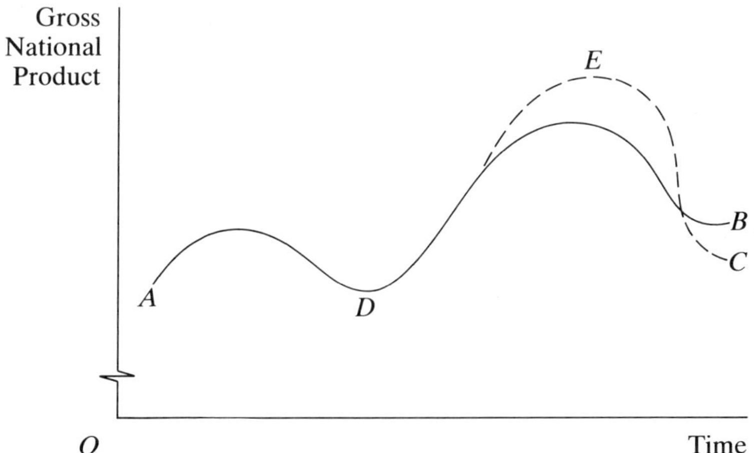

Figure 6A *Stabilisation Policy and Lags*

be influenced more by the proximity of the next election than by the interests of long-term economic stability. It might be possible for a government to increase its electoral popularity by inflating the economy a year or so before the election. Following the election, the effects of the inflationary policy could be seen by the government to be undesirable, with the result that the pre-election policy could be reversed. If voters do not realise what is going on, or discount the future, the 'political business cycle' could continue indefinitely to provide a destabilising influence on the economy.

An early theory of the political business cycle was put forward by Kalecki (1943). He argued that, if the government were faced with a slump, it would expand the economy to avoid large-scale unemployment. However, in the subsequent boom, political pressure for a cutback would develop. Particular pressure would come from 'big business' because it would be more difficult to control the workforce when there was full employment. This pressure would cause the government to reduce its budget deficit and a 'slump would follow in which government spending policy would come again into its own' (p. 330).

More recently, the subject was examined by Nordhaus (1975). He looked at the implications of the short-run Phillips curve trade-off between inflation and unemployment within a political framework. Some of the historical evidence was also considered. One of Nordhaus' conclusions was that 'within an incumbent's term of office there is a predictable pattern of policy, starting with relative austerity in early years and ending with the potlatch right before elections' (p. 187: A potlatch is an occasion when members of some Indian tribes of the American North-West consume large quantities of food and present generous gifts to each other. They also destroy valuable goods as a sort of conspicuous consumption). Further work along these lines has also been done; for example, by Lindbeck (1976), Frey (1978) and Frey and Schneider (1978). Although UK evidence does not appear to support the conclusion that governments systematically manipulate the economy for electoral purposes, it is possible that they may sometimes be tempted to do so.

Automatic versus Discretionary Intervention

A possible method of reducing such temptations to governments, and also some of the lags in policy effects, is to design a system of government finance which responds *automatically* to changes in the level of economic activity. This is in contrast to a more 'discretionary' policy which refers to deliberate adjustments made by the government as part of its day-to-day management of the economy. An increase in tax rates is therefore an example of discretionary policy. Automatic change, on the other hand, refers to potential changes which are *built-in* to the system in some way — either into the tax structure itself, or as a set of rules determining the action to be taken in various situations.

For the tax system, this implies that tax revenue should rise and fall as national income rises and falls. So, for example, as an economy moves into a recession, the fall in national income should be partially offset by a fall in tax *receipts*. This feature of the tax system is sometimes referred to as 'built-in flexibility'.

The most important example of built-in flexibility is the progressivity of the income tax system. Progressivity means that income tax receipts change proportionately more than any original change in national income. For example, if all wages and prices in the economy doubled, then, all other things being equal, income tax revenue would more than double. Clearly this effect will be greater, the greater the progressivity of the tax. With the introduction of provisions indexing the income tax to changes in the price level (see Chapter 8), tax revenue no longer changes as a result of inflationary changes. However, it still responds to changes in real incomes, so that for example, in a recession, income tax receipts in real terms can still be expected to fall proportionately more than the original fall in real national income.

One of the main advantages of built-in flexibility is that it avoids the recognition lag altogether. It might also avoid at least part of the implementation lag, though this depends on the type of tax. For instance, delays in the collection of a particular tax (for example, see Section 8.5) will postpone changes in the level of tax receipts.

Nonetheless, built-in flexibility has its limitations as a stabilising device. First of all, it cannot cope with large exogenous changes. The fourfold increase in the price of oil in 1974, for instance, created a deflationary effect in Western countries that could not possibly be offset by built-in flexibility alone.

Secondly, built-in flexibility cannot eliminate cycles; it can only reduce them. This is because it requires an initial change in the level of national income before tax receipts can change. Unless the rates of tax were set at 100 per cent (or more!) one would not expect the initial change to be completely offset.

The third limitation is that, while built-in flexibility undoubtedly cushions the effects of economic depression, it also impedes recovery. As the economy picks up, part of the additional national income is siphoned off in taxes. Clearly, the greater the degree of built-in flexibility, the more such economic recovery will be impeded.

Fiscal Drag

'Fiscal drag' refers to the effect that, as nominal incomes rise over time, a progressive tax system will take an increasing proportion of national income. It occurs whether the rise in nominal income results from inflation (in the absence of indexation), or from an increase in real output per head, or both. The element of fiscal drag arising from real changes could also be roughly offset by using an index of average earnings (though changes in the proportion of national income which accrue as profit, interest or rent would modify the process).

Fiscal drag becomes a less important phenomenon after the indexation of income tax. However, the problem with indexation is that it greatly reduces the effectiveness of the tax system in automatically stabilising the economy. Yet there is still likely to be some small element of built-in flexibility. For example, suppose that (in the case of income tax) the tax threshold and rate bands were linked to average earnings. Suppose also that when the economy moves into recession, most of the fall in national income is reflected in a decrease in the number employed rather than a decrease in the average wage of those still at work. Under these circumstances, one may still expect a drop in national income to be partially offset by a fall in tax receipts. As a second example, if the index-linked adjustment took place once a year, there would still be a small stabilising effect within the tax year, though not from one year to the next.

Nevertheless, despite these examples, indexation tends to neutralise the built-in flexibility of a progressive tax system. It seems reasonable to conclude, therefore, that however attractive a system of automatic stabilisers may appear, discretionary policy is almost certain to remain an essential element of macroeconomic policy.

6.3 The Relative Merits of Different Taxes

Taxes differ considerably in their suitability as instruments of stabilisation policy. Some taxes have only indirect effects on the level of national income, other taxes affect income directly, but sometimes only after a considerable delay; and the revenue from some taxes is too small to make much impact on the overall economy. We shall deal with each of these points in turn.

Appropriate and Inappropriate Taxes

Given that the intention is to influence aggregate demand, taxes on various forms of expenditure play a useful part in fiscal policy. An increase in value added tax, for example, has a direct effect on spending in the economy. It is also useful for stabilisation purposes if the indirect taxes with the highest rates are imposed on goods for which the demand fluctuates considerably over the trade cycle. In other words, for this purpose tax should be imposed on the goods with the highest income elasticities of demand.

Income tax is also appropriate in this respect as changes in after-tax income must influence the level of expenditure. This should be qualified, however, as spending habits may not adjust quickly to changes in income. Friedman's permanent income hypothesis (Friedman, 1957), for example, suggests that consumers ignore short-run fluctuations in income when planning their consumption. Instead, consumers take into account their 'normal' or 'permanent' level of income. One implication of this is that a tax change which is regarded as only a short-term measure is unlikely to influence consumption significantly.

Taxes on corporate income (corporation tax) could also be useful stabilisers. A particular advantage is that company profits are likely to fluctuate more than the average form of income over the business cycle.

Taxes on wealth, or the movement of wealth, are very much less appropriate than either indirect taxes or income taxes. Levies such as capital transfer tax or a wealth tax will obviously have some effect on individuals' spending plans, but only indirect effects. They are therefore unsuitable for use as instruments of stabilisation policy.

A different point arises when the government's primary aim is to reduce unemployment or to reduce inflation, but not both equally. Some taxes are more appropriate for the first of these two targets than for the second. For example, suppose that the main aim is the reduction of inflation. It is true that an increase in, say, value added tax would have a deflationary effect. Yet it is possible for the price increases resulting from an increase in VAT to impede a policy of reducing inflation. The VAT-induced price increases may be interpreted as inflationary and so support expectations of future inflation. The increases may trigger wage and further price increases elsewhere in the economy. So, while VAT may be an effective stabiliser as far as output is concerned, it may be less effective where inflation is the main problem.

Speed of Adjustment

The next consideration is the time it takes for the stabilising influence of a particular tax to take effect. We saw in the previous section that lags can easily reduce the effectiveness of an adjustment in taxation. We also saw that the first lag (the recognition lag) could be avoided if the revenue of a particular tax reacted automatically to a change in national income. The income tax has an advantage in this respect because of its progressivity.

It should be remembered that the UK income tax *is* progressive despite its long basic rate band (see Sections 2.2 and 8.2). The reason is that, for the great majority of taxpayers, the first part of their income is exempt from tax. The proportion of their income going in tax therefore rises as their income rises. In addition, of course, if a person becomes unemployed he (or she) will usually cease to pay income tax (and national insurance contributions, but not indirect taxes).

Indirect taxes and corporation tax are less advantageous in this respect because they are not generally progressive, as Section 11.5 shows. Some indirect taxes are also based on quantity rather than value: for example, the excise duties on alcoholic drinks which are charged at fixed rates per gallon. The result is that the yield of these taxes does not respond automatically to changes in prices.

Indirect taxes are better with respect to the second category of lag (the implementation lag), as changes in tax rates can be put into force fairly quickly. In some ways, income tax can also be adjusted quickly. For example, it is posible to increase personal allowances during the tax year and the Pay-As-You-Earn system will automatically adjust the amount of tax withheld from employees' pay. However, as we shall see in Chapter 8, it is not quite so easy to *reduce* the value of allowances in the middle of the tax year, because of the cumulative feature of PAYE.

On the third type of lag (the response lag), income tax scores highly because the PAYE system ensures that tax payments are kept up to date with tax liability. There is an exception with Schedule D income (that is, income from self-employment). Most Schedule D income is assessed on a preceding year basis. As we shall see in Section 8.5, this means that *changes* in the amount of tax paid can occur anything up to two years after the original change in income.

However, this is only a small drawback of the income tax as most income tax is collected under Schedule E on a current year basis. Corporation tax as a whole suffers more from delay because much of the revenue is collected in arrears. But the amount of revenue from mainstream corporation tax is unimportant compared to that from income tax.

The Size of the Tax Base

If the yield of a tax is very small, it can have only a small effect on aggregate demand, regardless of its advantages in other respects. No doubt every little helps, but the main instruments of stabilisation policy must raise substantial amounts of tax in order to be effective.

Under this criterion, income tax must emerge as the most important single tax. In 1980–81 some £24,300 million was raised in income tax. The tax with the next largest revenue was value added tax, which raised a rather more modest £11,443 million in 1980–81.

A related aspect is the width of the tax base. If a tax has a reasonably broad coverage, such as income tax or value added tax, its stabilising effects are likely to be felt fairly evenly throughout the economy. In contrast, a tax on a narrow range of goods, such as the car tax, is likely to have a concentrated effect on a small part of the economy. If such a tax were used to stabilise the economy as a whole, it might decrease stability in the sector of the economy to which it was applied. In addition, as we have seen in earlier chapters, such a tax may also have undesirable implications for efficiency and equity.

So what can we conclude regarding the relative merits of different taxes as potential stabilising devices? The only tax which scores well on each of the three criteria put forward in this chapter is the income tax. Some other taxes may also be useful. Value added tax, for example, has a wide base. In addition, the Treasury has the power to vary the rate of VAT by up to 25 per cent during the year for the purposes of economic management. This avoids the need to wait for the annual Budget or having to arrange an extra one.

6.4 Summary

In this chapter we have discussed some of the arguments for and against government intervention to stabilise the level of economic activity. Whether or not the government should intervene, it has been tempted to do so in the past and no doubt will do so in the future. It therefore becomes necessary to examine the implications of stabilisation policy. Using a simple model, it was shown that fiscal policy can have powerful effects, but these effects will vary considerably under different circumstances. In considering the relative merits of different taxes it soon becomes clear that the income tax is the major weapon in the stabilisation armoury.

Further Reading

Issues of stabilisation policy are discussed further in Cook and Jackson (1979), Musgrave and Musgrave (1980) and Peacock and Shaw (1976). For evidence on the stability or otherwise of British fiscal policy, a useful start can be made with Boltho (1981).

References

Boltho A. (1981), 'British fiscal policy 1955–71 — stabilising or destabilising?', *Oxford Bulletin of Economics and Statistics*, Vol. 43, pp. 357–62.

Chrystal K.A. (1979), *Controversies in British Macroeconomics*, Philip Allan.

Clark C. (1970), *Taxmanship*, Institute of Economic Affairs.

Cook S.T. and Jackson P.M. (1979), *Current Issues in Fiscal Policy*, Martin Robertson.

Foot M. (1983), 'Sayings of the week', *The Observer*, 13 February.

Frey B.S. (1978), *Modern Political Economy*, Martin Robertson.

Frey B.S. and Schneider F. (1978), 'A politico-economic model of the United Kingdom', *Economic Journal*, Vol. 88, pp. 243–53.

Friedman M. (1947), 'Lerner on the economics of control', *Journal of Political Economy*, Vol. 55, pp. 405–16.

Friedman M. (1948), 'A monetary and fiscal framework for economic stability', *American Economic Review*, Vol. 38, pp. 245–64.

Friedman M. (1957), *A Theory of the Consumption Function*, National Bureau of Economic Research.

Friedman M. (1968), 'The role of monetary policy', *American Economic Review*, Vol. 58, pp. 1–17.

Friedman M. (1970), *The Counter-Revolution in Monetary Theory*, Institute of Economic Affairs.

Friedman M. and Schwartz A.J. (1963), *A Monetary History of the United States, 1867–1960*, Princeton University Press.

Harrod R.F. (1951) *The Life of John Maynard Keynes*, Macmillan.

Healey D. (1974), Budget Statement, 12 November, *Hansard*, Vol. 881, Cols. 252, 253.

Kalecki M. (1943), 'Political aspects of full employment', *Political Quarterly*, Vol. 14, pp. 322–31.

Keynes J.M. (1924), *A Tract on Monetary Reform*, Macmillan, p. 80.

Keynes J.M. (1933), *Essays in Biography*, 'Thomas Robert Malthus', Macmillan.

Keynes J.M. (1936), *The General Theory of Employment, Interest and Money*, Macmillan.

Leijonhufvud A. (1968), *On Keynesian Economics and the Economics of Keynes*, Oxford University Press.

Lindbeck A. (1976), 'Stabilisation policy in small open economies with endogenous politicians', *American Economic Review: Papers and Proceedings*, Vol. 66, pp. 1–19.

Lipsey R.G. (1960), 'The relationship between unemployment and the rate of change of money wage rates in the United Kingdom, 1862–1957, *Economica*, Vol. 27, pp. 1–31.

Mill J.S. (1844), *Essays on some Unsettled Questions of Political Economy*, Longman.

Musgrave R.A. and Musgrave P.B. (1980), *Public Finance in Theory and*

Practice, 3rd edn., McGraw-Hill.
Nordhaus W.D. (1975), 'The political business cycle', *The Review of Economic Studies*, Vol. 42, pp. 169–90.
Peacock A. and Shaw G.K. (1976), *The Economic Theory of Fiscal Policy*, revised edition, Allen and Unwin.
Peel D.A. (1981), 'On fiscal and monetary stabilisation policy under rational expectations', *Public Finance*, Vol. 26, pp. 290–96.
Phelps E.S. (1968), 'Money wage dynamics and labour market equilibrium', *Journal of Political Economy*, July/August.
Phillips A.W. (1958), 'The relation between unemployment and the rate of change of money wage rates, 1861–1957, *Economica*, Vol. 25, pp. 283–99.
Prest A.R. (1975), *Public Finance in Theory and Practice*, 5th edn., Weidenfeld and Nicolson.
Ricardo D. (1821), *The Principles of Political Economy and Taxation*, Everyman edition, 1969.
Robinson Sir Austin (1977), 'Comment', in T.W. Hutchison, *Keynes v. the 'Keynesians' ...?*, Institute of Economic Affairs.
Robinson J. (1971), *Economic Heresies*, Macmillan.
Samuelson P.A. (1970), *Economics*, 8th edn., McGraw-Hill.
Say Jean Baptiste (1803), *Traité d'économie politique*.
Vane H.R. and Thompson J.L. (1979), *Monetarism: Theory, Evidence and Policy*, Martin Robertson.

Part II

TAXATION POLICY AND PRACTICE

The schoolboy whips his taxed top; the beardless youth manages his taxed horse, with a taxed bridle, on a taxed road; and the dying Englishman, pouring his medicine, which has paid seven per cent, into a spoon that has paid fifteen per cent — flings himself back upon his chintz bed, which has paid twenty-two per cent — and expires in the arms of an apothecary who has paid a licence of a hundred pounds for the privilege of putting him to death.

REV. SIDNEY SMITH, *Words* (1859) vol. i., 'Review of Seybert's Statistical Annals of the United States'

The Income Tax has made more Liars out of the American people than golf has.

WILL ROGERS, 'Helping the Girls with Their Income Taxes', *The Illiterate Digest,* (1924)

7

Introduction to Part II

In Part I there was an examination of various theoretical problems relating to taxation in general. Particular taxes were used as illustrations from time to time, but there was no systematic description and analysis of present taxes in the United Kingdom. Part II contains such a description of present taxes, analysis of their strengths and weaknesses, and discussion of alternatives and possible reforms. There are three chapters on direct personal taxation, a chapter on indirect taxation and two chapters on corporate taxation.

Many of the characteristics of the taxes are illustrated numerically. However, more complex calculations are omitted, but can be found in the *Workbook* associated with this volume.

This chapter itself sets the scene for Part II by discussing the relative importance of the various United Kingdom taxes, and then drawing some broad international comparisons.

7.1 The Relative Importance of United Kingdom Taxes

This section provides a broad summary of the importance in terms of receipts of the main United Kingdom taxes. Table 7A provides information on this subject. In some cases, two similar taxes have

Table 7A Important Taxes, Receipts (£m)

INLAND REVENUE

	Income Tax	*Corporation Tax (incl. ACT)*	*Petroleum Revenue Tax*	*Capital Gains Tax*	*Capital Transfer Tax*	*Stamp Duties*
1978–79	18763	3940	183	353	323	434
1979–80	20610	4646	1436	431	403	622
1980–81	24300	4645	2410	508	425	641
1981–82	28724	4926	2391	526	480	796

CUSTOMS AND EXCISE

	Alcohol	*Tobacco*	*Betting & Gaming*	*Hydro-Carbons*	*Customs Duties*	*VAT (incl. cars)*
1978–79	2336	2445	339	2467	735	5212
1979–80	2442	2579	406	2928	937	8695
1980–81	2599	2816	460	3576	816	11443

OTHER

	Rates	*Motor Duties*	*Employers' NI Surcharge*	*GDP (market prices) (for comparison)*	
1978–79	5793	1124	1910	(1978)	164916
1979–80	6750	1147	3014	(1979)	192343
1980–81	8859	1358	3585	(1980)	224949

Sources: *Financial Statistics,* HMSO, June 1982, Tables 3.2, 3.3, 3.4 and 4.1. *Monthly Digest of Statistics,* HMSO, May 1982, Table 1.1.

been added together, as the table shows. Greater detail is provided in later chapters, for example in Table 11A for indirect taxes.

It can be seen that income tax is by far the largest source of revenue. Consequently, it is described in considerable detail in Chapters 8 and 9, with substantial attention being paid to possibilities of reform. Corporation tax and value added tax are also important sources of revenue, and are studied in some detail. It is interesting to note that despite the volume of discussion and complaint that one hears about capital transfer tax and capital gains tax, these taxes each raise less than 2 per cent of the revenue of income tax.

The information in Table 7A can be combined by collection agency. This is shown in Table 7B.

Table 7B Tax Collecting Agencies (£m)

	Inland Revenue	*Customs and Excise*
1978–79	24055	13764
1979–80	28207	18337
1980–81	32983	21933

Source: *Financial Statistics*, HMSO, July 1982, Tables 3.2 and 3.3.
Note: These totals include some items not included in Table 7A.

7.2 Taxation in Different Countries

According to popular mythology, the United Kingdom has one of the highest levels of taxation in the world. Although the UK tax system has many unusual features, it is fairly easy to show that the level of taxation is not exceptionally high.

The Level of Taxation

One of the conventional ways of comparing taxation in different countries is to compare their total tax revenue as a percentage of GDP. This method has its limitations. For example, if a country changes from a policy of giving financial assistance to its citizens in the form of tax relief, to a policy of giving cash payments, its tax/GDP ratio will rise. This happened in the United Kingdom when payments of child benefit replaced the old income tax allowances.

Nevertheless, such a comparison does provide a rough picture of the tax position in different countries. Table 7C presents the figures for total tax revenue as a percentage of GDP in 23 member countries of the Organisation for Economic Co-operation and Development (OECD). If social security contributions are excluded, it can be seen that the United Kingdom had the twelfth highest tax/GDP ratio in 1979. On this basis, it is not all that clear that, 'the United Kingdom is unequivocally a high-tax country' (Bracewell-Milnes, 1976). The shift from direct to indirect taxation in the 1979 Finance Act would presumably move us further down the table for later years (see, for example, Table 7A, or Section 11.4).

Further, there are several reasons why social security

Table 7C Total Tax Revenue as a Percentage of GNP in 1979

	Including Social Security contributions	*Excluding Social Security contributions*
Sweden	50.27 (1)	36.64 (3)
Netherlands	47.42 (2)	29.36 (9)
Luxembourg	46.17 (3)	32.51 (4)
Norway	46.06 (4)	38.18 (2)
Belgium	44.69 (5)	31.52 (6)
Denmark	44.09 (6)	43.42 (1)
Austria	41.36 (7)	28.63(11)
France	41.16 (8)	23.56(15)
Germany	37.34 (9)	24.62(14)
Finland	35.03(10)	31.73 (5)
United Kingdom	34.02(11)	28.12(12)
Ireland	33.82(12)	28.97(10)
United States	31.32(13)	23.37(16)
New Zealand	31.18(14)	31.18 (7)
Switzerland	31.12(15)	21.47(17)
Canada	31.01(16)	27.59(13)
Italy	30.09(17)	19.04(20)
Australia	29.82(18)	29.82 (8)
Greece	27.69(19)	19.28(19)
Portugal	25.82(20)	18.87(21)
Japan	24.77(21)	17.52(22)
Spain	23.27(22)	11.59(23)
Turkey	20.84(23)	19.52(18)

Source: OECD (1981), p. 78.

Note: Figures in brackets indicate country positions.

contibutions should also be considered. Australia and New Zealand finance their social security systems entirely from general taxation revenue, and the social security systems in many other countries, such as Denmark and Ireland, are mainly financed in this way. On the other hand, several countries, such as France, the Federal Republic of Germany and the Netherlands largely finance their systems from social security contributions. Such contributions are usually compulsory and have much in common with more conventional forms of taxation. (The position in the United

Kingdom is discussed in Section 8.2.)

When social security contributions are included, the picture changes significantly. For example, the Netherlands increases its position from 9th to 2nd, and Australia drops from 8th place to 18th. The United Kingdom moves from 12th to 11th place — still half way up the table. With a tax/GDP ratio of 34.02 per cent, the United Kingdom is considerably lower than countries such as Sweden (50.27), Luxembourg (46.17) and Norway (46.06). It seems reasonable to conclude that in terms of total tax revenue, the United

Table 7D Source of Tax Revenue as a Percentage of Total Tax Revenues in 1979

	Goods and services	*Income and profits*	*Social security*
Australia	31.71	54.63	–
Austria	31.88	26.48	30.78
Belgium	26.03	41.71	29.48
Canada	32.16	45.32	11.02
Denmark	38.94	53.43	1.53
Finland	40.84	47.53	9.44
France	31.27	17.30	42.77
Germany	26.91	34.95	34.07
Greece	45.07	15.56	30.37
Ireland	43.67	35.84	14.34
Italy	26.49	31.49	36.74
Japan	17.48	39.89	25.27
Luxembourg	18.09	45.72	25.58
Netherlands	25.09	32.43	38.08
New Zealand	22.94	68.49	–
Norway	38.61	43.83	17.10
Portugal	37.05	25.19	26.91
Spain	20.98	23.82	50.19
Sweden	23.93	45.49	27.11
Switzerland	20.30	41.28	31.03
Turkey	33.18	54.56	6.34
United Kingdom	26.92	38.96	17.35
United States	16.53	47.60	25.39

Source: OECD (1981), p. 81, 83 and 87.

Kingdom is not among the more highly taxed countries.

The Sources of Taxation

The United Kingdom is not particularly unusual in the sources of its revenue either. Table 7D shows that in 1979, 38.96 per cent of United Kingdom tax revenue came from taxes on income and profits. This is a substantially higher percentage than that for countries such as Italy (31.49) and France (17.30). On the other hand, the figure is very much lower than in countries such as New Zealand (68.49), Denmark (53.43) and Australia (54.63).

It should be pointed out again that, if social security contributions are counted as direct taxes, the picture is modified. The relative proportion of revenue from direct taxation then rises for France and Italy, but falls back for Australia, Denmark and New Zealand.

So, once more, the United Kingdom does not appear to have any special claim to fame in the fiscal league. However, in the structure of particular taxes, most especially the income tax, the United Kingdom has some very unusual characteristics indeed. Detailed discussion of these features is presented in Chapters 8 and 9.

Reference

Bracewell-Milnes B. (1976), *The Camel's Back*, Centre for Policy Studies, p. 11.

8

Personal Income Tax

'It is a vile, Jacobin, jumped up Jack-in-office piece of impertinence – is a true Briton to have no privacy? Are the fruits of his labour and toil to be picked over, farthing by farthing, by the pimply minions of Bureaucracy?' (quoted in Sabine 1965, p. 31). Income tax has never been popular in the United Kingdom as illustrated by the above reaction from a member of the navy to its introduction in 1799. Yet, as the coverage of the tax has grown wider and wider, the British seem to have learned to live with it.

However, the British income tax has many curious characteristics. Indeed, with the exception of the Irish system, there is nothing else quite like it in the world. In this chapter we shall try to describe the system. This will involve looking in turn at the development of the system, the current tax structure, the Pay-As-You-Earn machinery and the treatment of business income. In the following chapter we shall look at some of the proposals for reforming the British system.

8.1 Historical Aspects of Income Tax

Like many other taxes, income tax began as a war tax. It was first introduced in 1799 to finance the war with Napoleon. When peace came in 1802 the tax was withdrawn, but re-imposed when hostilities recommenced in 1803. It was abolished once more when peace was achieved in 1815. The tax was reintroduced in 1842 and has remained in force ever since.

In its development the British tax system shares a number of characteristics with overseas systems. This includes its transformation from a primitive tax imposed at low rates on the few citizens who had relatively high incomes, to a modern sophisticated tax which is imposed at high rates on the many citizens, including those who have relatively low incomes. As with many other taxes it has also become an immensely complicated tax.

However, as we shall see, the British tax system differs from its overseas equivalents in two main ways. The first is that the tax is raised under a system of schedules. The second is that it has developed the art of witholding tax at source to a very sophisticated degree.

Complexity

The administration of income tax has always been complicated. In 1799, income in excess of £60 a year was subject to a graduated scale of rates rising to a maximum of 10 per cent on income over £200. In calculating taxable income there was a wide range of deductions for dependents, life assurance premiums, debt interest and so on. The original Act (an amending Act was passed only three months later) was a complex document of some 152 pages in length, and the government felt it necessary to produce a guide entitled 'A Plain, Short and Easy Description of the Different Clauses of the Income Tax so as to render it Familiar to the Meanest Capacity' (Farnsworth, 1951, p. 15).

Nevertheless, compared to the modern income tax, the original version was simplicity itself. It could afford to be, as tax rates were comparatively low and were applied to only a small proportion of the population. The present tax is much more complicated for a number of reasons.

First, with rates of tax of up to 75 per cent in 1983–84, a rough and ready system is inadequate. Because there is so much less room for manoeuvre with high rates of tax, the tax must be sufficiently sophisticated to take into account a large number of individual circumstances.

Second, again because of high rates of tax, evasion and avoidance become very much more rewarding pursuits. If an individual is suffering tax at 75 pence in his marginal pound of income, it is clearly worth his while to spend up to 75 pence to save that pound from tax. And it is not simply the prerogative of the rich. With a basic rate of 30 per cent in 1983–84 (plus the National Insurance contributions discussed below), the incentive to reduce liability is widespread. There is also a similar incentive for the Inland Revenue and the government to spend resources on preventing such evasion and avoidance.

Third, as the tax system has affected more and more people in more ways, there has been a temptation for governments to use it for purposes other than raising revenue. This inevitably means complexity. We have already seen in Section 3.7 that there is a good reason for lobby groups to believe that they may be better off if they demand government aid in the form of a tax concession rather than a direct cash subsidy.

A fourth factor is well described by Sabine (1965) at the end of his fascinating account of the history of the British income tax:

> One consistent feature of direct taxation has been its extraordinary sensitivity to criticism and its extreme flexibility and adaptability to accommodating such criticism. (p. 254)

This feature is not, of course, consistent with simplicity.

The System of Schedules

An early complication, introduced in 1803, was the division of the tax into five schedules — A, B, C, D and E. Under the previous system, a return of total income had been required and this proved highly unpopular, being considered as a serious infringement of privacy. With the 1803 system, taxpayers would declare income received under each schedule separately and so avoid the need for any official to know a taxpayer's total income. In fact, from 1803, returns of total income were not required on a wide scale until the introduction of super-tax in 1909.

With some modifications, the system of schedules survives to this day as one of the particular characteristics of the British income tax. The two most important schedules are Schedule E which covers income from employment, and Schedule D which includes income from trades, professions, businesses, property and other annual profits. Much less important, in terms of revenue, are Schedule A (some types of income from property), Schedule B (income from commercial woodlands) and Schedule C (interest and annuities payable out of public revenue). A sixth heading, Schedule F, was introduced in 1965 to cover the taxation of dividends subject to rates of tax higher than the basic rate.

Withholding at Source

A further feature contributing to complexity, and one very much pioneered in the United Kingdom, is the extensive withholding of tax from incomes at their source. The principle of the withholding of tax in fact preceded the income tax by many years. For example, an Act of 1657 allowed certain tenants to deduct tax from their rent payments.

Withholding at source has since developed into a fine art, and in the modern British income tax it takes three main forms. The first is withholding from wages and salaries through the sophisticated and uniquely British Pay-As-You-Earn system discussed in Section 8.4. The second is withholding from interest payments which is achieved using several methods, also discussed below. The third concerns dividends and the imputation system of corporation tax discussed in Section 12.3. Withholding at source does not take place as such on dividends, but the effect of the imputation system is that there is no outstanding income tax liability at the basic rate.

8.2 The Income Tax Structure in 1983–84

One of the most noticeable characteristics of the British Tax system is that it is subject to continual change. Writing about it is very much like trying to hit a moving target. This section describes the tax structure proposed in the Finance Bill 1983. This involves discussion of allowances and expenses, the rates of tax, National Insurance contributions and the treatment of married couples.

The basic rules for income tax are to be found in the 1970 Income and Corporation Taxes Act and in subsequent yearly Finance Acts, which are preceded by Budget statements and Finance Bills. These statutes are supplemented by case law which interprets some of the finer points. There are references to these sources at various points in this chapter.

Allowances and Expenses

For the individual taxpayer, the process of income tax assessment begins with the calculation of his total income. The next stage is to calculate his *taxable income*, which is total income minus any allowances and expenses the individual is entitled to claim. For the purposes of our discussion it is useful to distinguish between allowances and expenses.

Allowances refer to income that is tax-free regardless of the individual's pattern of expenditure or the source of his income. They therefore include the personal allowances shown in Table 8A. These were originally granted in an attempt to reduce taxable income by the extent that an individual had his income pre-empted by responsibilities like a wife or children. It would appear to enhance equity if tax was thus based more closely on disposable income rather than total income. However, it is now fairly clear that the sizes of the allowances have lost all resemblance to the real costs they were supposed to be related to. The most controversial matter connected with this is the taxation of husbands and wives. This is dealt with in a separate section below. Perhaps the most obvious reason for continuing some form of allowances is that they act as a zero-rate band of income, which takes large numbers of potential taxpayers out of the 'tax net', and contributes to the progressivity of the tax (see Sections 2.2 and 5.6).

Although the value of the personal allowances has been eroded by inflation over the years, after 1981–82 the main ones are to be increased annually in line with the increase in the retail prices index for the previous calendar year. These allowances are the single and married allowances, wife's earned income allowance, age allowance, additional personal allowance and widow's bereavement allowance. Despite these provisions for indexation, lower increases can be made, of course, provided Parliament approves. Indeed, no increases at all were made for 1981–82, though extra increases were made in 1982–83 and 1983–84.

Table 8A Allowances Against Gross Income in 1982–83 and 1983–84

	1982–83 £	*1983–84* £
Single person's allowance	1,565	1,785
Married allowance	2,445	2,795
Wife's earned income allowance	1,565	1,785
Age allowance — single person	2,070	2,360
Age allowance — married couple	3,295	3,755
Additional personal allowance	880	1,010
Widow's bereavement allowance	880	1,010
Dependent relative allowance,	100	100
except if the claimant is a woman other than a married woman living with her husband	145	145
Housekeeper allowance	100	100
Son or daughter's services	55	55
Blind person's allowance (each)	360	360

Note: On 15 March 1983, while this book was in press, the Chancellor presented his budget. His proposed allowances are shown above, but they have to be accepted by Parliament before they pass into law.

The single, married and wife's earned income allowances are discussed below, but some of the others merit a brief description here. Age allowance is granted instead of the ordinary single and married persons' allowances to single people aged 65 years or more and to married couples if either partner is aged 65 or over. However, the allowance is restricted if income exceeds a certain amount. For 1983–84 it was reduced by £2 for every £3 by which the income exceeds £7,600 until it is worth the same as the appropriate personal allowances for those under 65. For example, if a married couple with at least one of the partners aged 65 or more has a combined income of £7,900, their age allowance for 1983–4 would be 3,555 (i.e. £3,755 – 2/3 × £300 excess). The additional personal allowance is given in respect of a child or children dependent on a person who does not qualify for the married allowance. It may also be claimed by a married man whose wife is totally incapacitated, but in all cases the amount of the allowance is the same regardless of the number of children. Before 1979–80 there was a general system of tax allowances for children, the rates of which depended on the age of the child. There was also a taxable social security family allowance which was paid for all children except the first. Both these arrangements have now been replaced by tax-free payments of child benefit which is paid at a flat rate for each child. The widow's bereavement allowance was introduced in 1980 and applies only to the tax year in which the husband dies and the following tax year. In addition, this allowance is granted only if the husband was entitled to claim the married allowance — ignoring the effect of separate assessment (described below).

In addition to the allowances, there are also some *expenses* which are affected by income tax. In the past, both mortgage interest payments and insurance premium payments have led to allowable deductions against income tax. However, in order to burden the private sector rather than the Inland Revenue with the administration of this, both matters have now been substantially taken out of the income tax system. From 1979–80, insurance companies had to reduce their premiums or increase benefits to reflect the implicit tax deductibility. They can claim the 'tax' from the Inland Revenue. From 1983–84, mortgagors must operate a similar system. The mortgage relief applies to loans used for the purchase and improvement of an individual's main or only residence. In 1983–84, interest relating to loans of up to £30,000 was 'deductible', and was previously £25,000.

As with allowances, one justification for this implicit deductibility of mortgage interest and insurance premiums is that such payments reduce disposable income and thus ability to pay the income tax. However, it is not clear that this is a tremendously strong argument, since the individual has chosen to reduce his disposable income in this way. Further, in the case of interest, he receives untaxed benefits from owning the house, like the avoidance of rental payments and the capital gains (the latter are untaxed on a main residence). Nevertheless, governments have deemed it desirable to encourage home ownership, and this is an obvious way of doing so. However, this method has the drawbacks associated with tax expenditure (see Section 3.7) and may have been capitalised in an unintended way (See Section 5.4).

Some types of expenses may be claimed only against specific

sources of income. For example, the expenses incurred in running a business cannot be deducted from an individual's employment income. More details on allowable expenses are given in Section 8.5.

The Rates of Tax

Before April 1973, income tax was imposed at a single 'standard' rate. In addition, a separate 'surtax' was levied at a series of progressive rates on higher incomes. The computation of the two taxes was on a slightly different basis, and income tax was assessed by decentralised tax offices whereas surtax was dealt with centrally by the Surtax Office. One other important feature of the pre-1973 system was the 'earned income relief' which consisted of a deduction of two-ninths of earned income, so that only seven-ninths of earnings were subject to tax.

From 1973–74 income tax and surtax were combined, with the standard rate becoming known as the basic rate and surtax as 'higher rates' of tax. The new 'unified' tax is dealt with in local tax offices. The earned income relief was abolished, and tax rates reduced, but a new levy called 'investment income surcharge' was introduced instead.

Both before and after 1973, one of the more unusual characteristics of the tax structure has been that most taxpayers have been subject to tax at the same marginal rate. In 1983–84 the very long basic rate band applied to the first £14,600 of taxable income. The rather uneven steps in the rates of tax which result can be seen from Table 8B and even more clearly in Figure 8A.

The long basic rate band has the administrative advantage discussed in Section 8.4 that tax can be withheld accurately at source from many types of income. There may also be some advantage in that taxpayers are more likely to know the marginal rate of tax they pay. This would, of course, be harder to establish if the first £14,600 of taxable income were subject to a graduated rate scale rather than the single basic rate.

However, the long basic rate band has some unfortunate implications for equity between taxpayers. It means that individuals on very low incomes pay tax at a high marginal rate (30 per cent in 1983–84). It also means, of course, that the same marginal rate

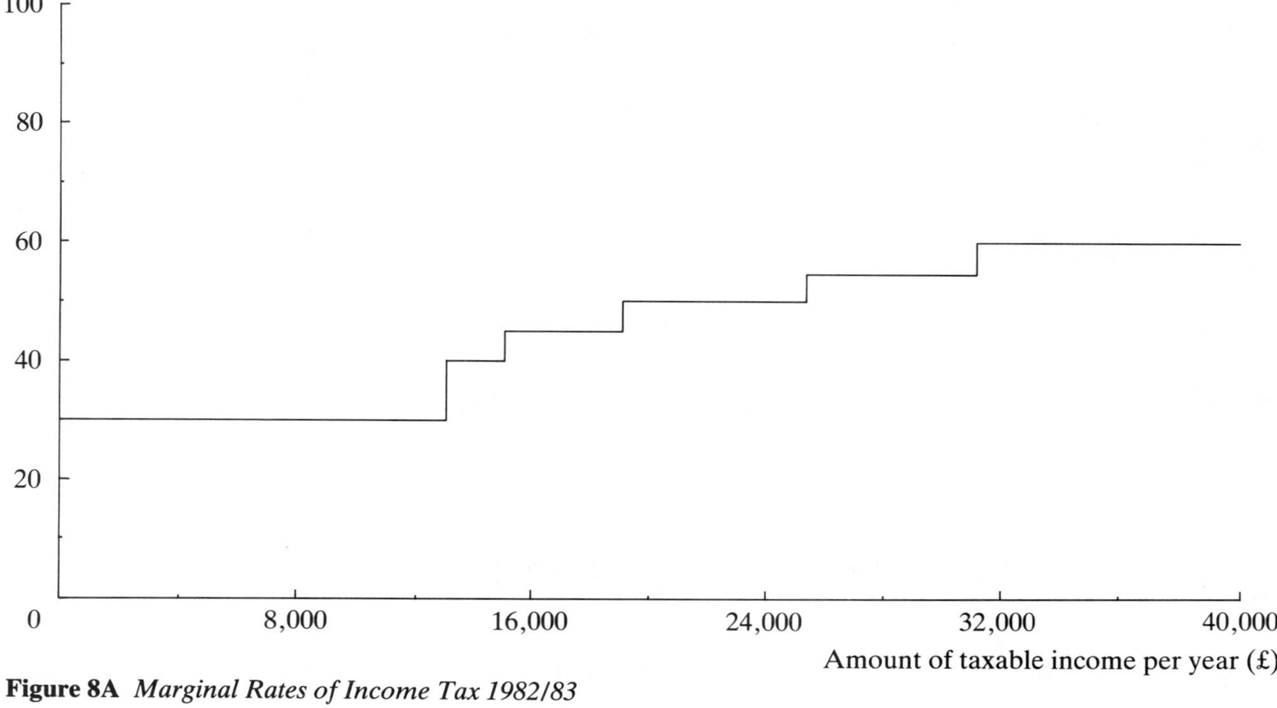

Figure 8A *Marginal Rates of Income Tax 1982/83*

Table 8B The Rates of Income Tax in 1982–83 and 1983–84

Rate of tax (%)	*Slice of taxable income* (£) *1982–83*	*1983–84*
30	1 – 12,800	1 – 14,600
40	12,801 – 15,100	14,601 – 17,200
45	15,101 – 19,100	17,201 – 21,800
50	19,101 – 25,300	21,801 – 28,900
55	25,301 – 31,500	28,901 – 36,000
60	Over 31,500	Over 36,000

Notes: 1. There is also an investment income surcharge (see text).
2. The rates shown for 1983–84 were still being considered by Parliament while this book was in press.

applies to individuals over a very wide income range. For example, in 1983–84 an individual entitled only to the single person's allowance would pay the same marginal rate of tax whether he earned as little as £1,786 or as much as £14,600, a figure over eight times greater.

The effects that the long basic rate band have on work incentives are less clear cut. As we saw in Section 4.1, it depends on the reactions of taxpayers to the marginal and average rates of tax. It seems likely, however, that individuals who are just over the threshold are subject to considerable disincentives. At this level the marginal rate (discouraging work) is very high, while the average rate (encouraging work) is very low. Nevertheless, this is insufficient evidence for us to conclude that the overall effects of the tax structure are adverse to work effort.

So much for the taxation of earnings. We shall now look at the tax treatment of income from investment.

Investment Income Surcharge

As we saw above, in addition to income tax rates ranging from 30 to 60 per cent, there is a surcharge on investment income (or 'unearned income' as it is sometimes known). In 1983–84 investment income over £7,100 (1982–83:£6,250) was liable to the surcharge at a rate of 15 per cent.

Certain charges on income which are not related to earned income may be set off against investment income first. Examples include mortgage interest and any alimony or maintenance payments made under an enforceable arrangement. For instance, suppose that in 1983–84 a single individual has earned income of £7,785, investment income of £10,000 and mortgage interest of £1,000. His assessment will appear thus:

Total income	£	£
Earned		7,785
Unearned	10,000	
Mortgage relief	1,000	
		9,000
		16,785
Single allowance		1,785
Taxable income		15,000
Tax		
£0 – £14,600 at 30%	4,380	
£14,601 – £15,000 at 40%	160	
		4,540
Surcharge		
£0 – £7,100 at 0%	0	
£7,101 – £9,000 at 15%	285.00	285.00
Total tax		4,825.00

Several arguments have been used to justify tax discrimination against unearned rather than earned income. One of the main reasons is that it is possible that income from employment is generally less reliable than income from investment. It might be argued that earnings arise from a 'wasting asset' — a human being — and will cease when the individual retires or dies. Furhermore, it has been argued that the wage or salary may fluctuate more than, say, an investment in gilt-edged security. The fluctuations may arise either from the individual falling ill, becoming pregnant or whatever, or from the nature of the job itself. The argument is, of course, limited by the fact that a proportion of investment income arises from risky ventures, or assets with values related to the rate of interest.

A second justification for the favourable treatment of earned income is that there are expenses incurred in obtaining it which are greater than those incurred in obtaining investment income. As we shall see shortly, this argument is especially relevant when National Insurance contributions are considered. A further aspect is that expenses incurred in acquiring the education and skills needed to carry out a particular occupation are not taken into account in assessing tax liability.

A third argument for a surcharge on investment income is that the ownership of the capital from which it is derived confers benefits over and above the pecuniary return. These benefits, such as added security, independence and the ability to 'dis-save', are discussed at greater length in Sections 5.2 and 10.5 and will not be repeated here. The justification for the additional levy is that these extra benefits indicate a greater taxable capacity than that measured by the investment income alone.

A fourth argument, perhaps the strongest politically, is that earnings represent the return to current toil, whereas investment income represents the return to either past toil or inherited wealth.

There are also arguments against a heavier levy on investment income. The most important is that it may discourage saving. Such discrimination would be in addition to any 'double taxation of saving' feature of an income tax noted in Section 4.3.

However, the British income tax system has a number of built-in incentives for saving. These include the reliefs granted for expenditure on qualifying life assurance premiums and superannuation contributions. In addition, mortgage interest relief encourages saving in the form of home purchase.

Can we draw any conclusions from these points on the tax treatment of investment income? As we shall see in Chapter 10, the tax systems in many other countries have been based on the conclusion that there are benefits from capital over and above the income derived from it. The difference is that, in these countries, the extra benefits have been taxed by a wealth tax imposed directly on the capital, rather than a roundabout surcharge on the income it produces. It is argued in Chapter 10 that the same policy should be pursued in the United Kingdom.

Married Couples

The tax treatment of married couples is an aspect of the tax system which has received a great deal of attention in recent years. In 1980, the government published a Green Paper, *The Taxation of Husband and Wife*, which discussed a range of possible alternatives to the existing system.

Under the present system, when two people get married they lose their single person's allowances (£1,785 each in 1983–84) but gain the married allowance (£2,795). In addition, to encourage the participation of married women in the workforce, the wife is entitled to a further earned income allowance up to a maximum of £1,785). At modest levels of earnings, therefore, the tax treatment of married couples compares favourably with that of individuals. However, if the couples are taxed jointly, their threshold for higher rate tax (and investment income surcharge in the case of unearned income) on their combined incomes is clearly lower than if they were taxed as single people. One curious result of this arrangement is that if the wife is the only breadwinner, the couple receive both the married and the wife's earned income allowances (a total of £4,580 in 1983–84); but if the husband is the only earner, they can claim only the married allowance of £2,795. Where both are earning, they receive higher allowances than two single people.

The normal procedure is for husband and wife to be treated as a single unit for tax purposes, and the husband to be responsible for his wife's tax affairs. This basis was originally enacted in 1806. Now it appears in Section 37 of the Income and Corporation Taxes Act 1970:

> A woman's income chargeable to income tax shall ... (for any year) during which she is a married woman living with her husband be deemed for income tax purposes to be his income and not to be her income.

To overcome some of the tax disadvantages of this arrangement, there are two sets of provisions for the wife's income to be treated separately. These provisions, known as *separate assessment* and *separate taxation*, are quite distinct and should not be confused.

Separate *assessment* was introduced in 1914 and *does not* affect the total tax liability of the couple. The husband's and wife's incomes are assessed for tax in the normal way, except that the liability is then divided between them, usually in proportion to their own incomes. Both partners can then deal with their own tax affairs independently and can complete separate tax returns if they wish.

Separate *taxation*, also known as 'wife's earnings election', was introduced in its present form in 1971, though the original provisions date back to 1894. It is quite different from separate assessment and will usually result in a change in the couple's liability. The reason is that separate taxation involves both a gain and a loss and the final outcome depends on the couple's circumstances. The *loss* arises from the replacement of the married allowance and the wife's earned income allowance with two single person's allowances. In 1983–84 this would mean a loss of £1,010 worth of allowances in most cases (−£2,795, −£1,785 +£1,785 +£1,785). The *gain* may arise because, provided both the husband and wife have earned income, their threshold for higher rates of tax is higher than it would be if they were taxed jointly.

The result is that any advantage from separate taxation is confined to those couples earning sums which will push them well into the higher rate tax brackets. It should also be noted that separate taxation applies only to the wife's *earnings*; any investment income she receives would continue to be added to her husband's income for tax purposes. These calculations are technically complicated and may be of small interest to many readers. Therefore, they are not covered here, but in the *Workbook* published as a companion to this volume.

The tax treatment of married couples, as opposed to single people and those cohabiting, can be analysed in terms of the principles discussed in Chapters 3, 4 and 5. Clearly, within reasonable bounds, it is unlikely that the differential tax treatments have serious effects on efficiency, given the many other relevant considerations. As Frank McKinney Hubbard put it, 'nobody works so hard for his money as the man who marries it'. However, the effects of the UK income tax system would, if anything, encourage those on low and moderate incomes to marry and those on high incomes to cohabit or divorce. Regarding incentives, we have already seen that the wife's earned income allowance represents an attempt to improve work incentives. For instance, in 1942 it was increased to the level of the single person's allowance, specifically to encourage married women to remain in employment in the public interest.

Perhaps the area that has aroused most comment concerns equity. One approach might be that the tax system should not discriminate between taxpayers just because they are married. In other words, there should be no tax advantage or disadvantage to marriage. Another approach is that there should be no discrimination between married couples with the same income. These two approaches lead to two different possibilities — taxation on an individual basis and taxation on an aggregation basis.

On the individual basis everyone is taxed as if they were single. On the aggregation, or 'unit', basis the income of the family is added together and then subject to tax, after appropriate allowances, as if the family were one unit. This latter basis is essentially the UK system with certain exceptions, by far the most important of which is the option of separate taxation of wife's earnings.

The advantage of the individual basis of taxation is that it would be neutral with respect to marriage. Yet it can easily be argued that marriage alters taxable capacity. It could be asserted that, if the wife (or husband) does not have paid employment, the remaining breadwinner has a dependent and therefore a lower taxable capacity. On the other hand, there may be economic benefits, in as much as a married couple living together can live more cheaply than two single adults can (though not if the latter cohabit!). In addition marriage will normally generate non-pecuniary income. For example, when a bachelor employs housekeeping and similar services, the transaction goes through the market and so is subject to tax. In marriage, the implicit income from a housewife's services is not taxed. Therefore, so the argument runs, marriage confers a greater taxable capacity which, on equity grounds, should be taxed.

In principle one could extend the argument even further, though the practical implications are somewhat worrying. One of A.P. Herbert's famous cases (Herbert, 1966) comes to mind where marriage, as a popular commodity, might have the potential to raise considerable revenue if it were treated as a taxable luxury:

> Marriages, like intoxicating liquors, might be graded according to their strength; and the most passionate, happy, or fruitful couples could be made to pay more than the lukewarm or miserable!!

However far this is taken, it seems reasonable to conclude that marriage does change taxpayers' circumstances, and the case for the individual basis of taxation is limited by the extent that it does.

The problem is that immediately the tax system is altered to take account of marriage, it necessarily ceases to be neutral with respect to marriage. For example, take an extreme form of the aggregation principle where husband and wife are treated as a single person. This would mean a tax penalty on marriage. The penalty would be greater the more progressive the tax system, since the couple's aggregated income would be pushed into higher rate bands. For the same reason, the penalty would be greater the more equal the partners' income.

The aggregation basis can, of course, be modified to reduce this penalty, or to provide some tax advantage to marriage. One method is the quotient system under which one-half of the aggregated income of the couple is allocated to each spouse, who is then taxed as a single person. One example is the French *quotient familial* system under which the incomes of the married couple, dependent children and certain close relatives are all aggregated. This income is then divided by the number of people in the family — with children counting as a half for this purpose. The tax liability on a single part is then multiplied by the number of parts to give the total amount of tax due.

As an example of the effects of the quotient system, a couple with a combined income of £20,000 would be taxed as two individuals each receiving £10,000. If the two partners actually received the same income, such a system would be neutral with respect to marriage. However, if, as is more likely, they receive different amounts, there might be a tax advantage to marriage. This advantage would be greater the greater the difference in income and the more progressive the tax system.

This result hardly seems equitable. For instance, take two couples whose joint incomes are both £20,000. With couple A, the total is earned by the husband while the wife remains at home. With couple B, both spouses earn £10,000. Couple A gain the imputed income from the wife's work around the home and avoid the costs of earning income (such as travel to and from work) that would arise if the wife did take paid employment. Yet both couples would pay the same amount of tax under the quotient system. Furthermore, there is an impediment for the wife in couple A to take paid employment, since she would face the couple's highest marginal tax rate from the beginning.

Further problems arise in other areas. For example, under a system of independent taxation, investment income can be transferred between spouses to reduce tax liability. Other considerations include children, single parent families, other dependents and the treatment of the elderly. Nevertheless, even from this brief discussion, it can be seen that, whichever basis of taxation is employed, some anomalies will arise and the best arrangement depends on social preferences as to which anomalies are disliked the most.

National Insurance Contributions

It is appropriate to treat National Insurance contributions under the general heading of taxation because most types are compulsory and are not always related to entitlement to National Insurance benefits. For example, Class 4 contributions do not attract any benefit at all. Another example is the extra levy imposed on employers' wage bills by the National Insurance Surcharge Act 1976. Although this levy was imposed under the name of National Insurance, it is a tax in every other sense (in this case a 'payroll tax') and not a contribution to the National Insurance Fund.

There are four classes of contribution. Class 1 contributions are levied in respect of employees, Class 2 and Class 4 contributions are levied on the self-employed and Class 3 contributions are voluntary.

Since 1975, the Class 1 contribution has taken the form of an earnings-related payment, part of which is payable by the employee and part by his employer. From 1975 to 1978 the contribution was levied at a single rate. In 1977–78, for example, the employees' rate was 5.75 per cent of gross earnings up to an earnings ceiling of £105 per week. The employer also paid a contribution of 8.75 per cent.

However, in April 1978 a new state pension scheme was introduced which has affected contributions. From April 1978, employees are divided into those who are contracted fully into the state scheme and those who are 'contracted-out'. In 1983–84, for those individuals who were not contracted-out, the employees' contribution was 9.0 per cent of earnings up to a ceiling of £235 per week and the employers' contribution was 10.45 per cent up to the same ceiling. For individuals contracted-out of the state scheme, the same rates applied to the first £32.50 of earnings. But for weekly earnings between £32.50 and £235, the contracted-out contribution was 6.85 per cent for employees and 6.35 per cent for employers. In both cases where employees earn less than the 'lower earnings limit' of £32.50, contributions are not payable by either employee or employer. The $1\frac{1}{2}$ per cent National Insurance surcharge is payable in addition to the above employers' contributions.

Class 2 contributions are payable by the self-employed and are levied at a flat rate which, in 1983–4, was £4.40 per week. This contribution is payable if earnings from self-employment exceed £1,775 per year. The self-employed are also liable to Class 4 contributions which are related to their level of profits. For the year 1983–84 the rate was 6.3 per cent of profits between £3,800 and £12,000.

Class 3 contributions are voluntary, and payable either by the non-employed, who wish to preserve their entitlement to benefit; or by the employed or self-employed who wish to increase their entitlement to benefit. Class 3 contributions are payable at a flat rate (£4.30 per week in 1983–84).

There are a number of comments that can be made regarding National Insurance contributions. The first is that, as we saw in Chapter 5, the actual incidence of these contributions may be quite different from the intended incidence. For example, the 2 per cent (as it was then) National Insurance surcharge on employers introduced by Denis Healey, Labour's Chancellor in 1976, may have been partially passed on to employees through wages being lower, or unemployment higher (or both) than might otherwise have been the case.

A second equity problem arises with the relationship between the rates of income tax and National Insurance contributions. For, while the former is a progressive tax, the latter is regressive over a wide range of earnings. It should be noted that the income tax is progressive even over the long basic rate band. The reason is the tax-free personal allowances. They mean that the *average* rate of tax rises as income rises, even though the marginal rate of tax remains the same. The income tax is therefore progressive throughout the basic rate band, provided the taxpayer is entitled to some allowances.

The structure of National Insurance contributions is quite different. Although employees earning less than £32.50 per week do not suffer any levy, for individuals who are not contracted-out, as soon as earnings exceed £32.50 the *whole* amount is liable to a contribution of 9.0 per cent. For these individuals, therefore, the contribution is proportional to earnings between £32.50 and £235.

Beyond that point no further contribution is payable, so on higher incomes the average rate is lower and the contribution therefore becomes regressive. The situation is similar for the self-employed, because the Class 4 contribution is not levied on earnings over a ceiling (£12,000 in 1983–84). The flat rate Class 2 contributions also introduce a regressive element much further down the income scale.

It should also be pointed out that the effects of National Insurance contributions largely offset the discrimination against unearned income provided by investment income surcharge. As we saw above, the rate of the surcharge was 15 per cent in 1983–84. It is easy to show that earned income usually suffers a similar burden in the form of National Insurance contributions.

Consider £100 paid to an employee who is not contracted-out of the state pension scheme. An employee's contribution of £9 will usually be deducted from this figure and the employer will pay a contribution of £10.45 plus £1.50 'National Insurance Surcharge'. The gross payment by the employer is therefore £111.95 (100 + £10.45 + £1.50). The total National Insurance liability on this is £20.95: some 19 per cent of the gross figure.

There are several qualifications to this comparison, in particular it will be affected by the incidence of National Insurance contributions in different circumstances. Yet, in general, there is still some discrimination against investment income where a person receives sufficient to be liable to the surcharge. Income tax is not levied on the employer's share of the National Insurance contribution, whereas both income tax and investment income surcharge are levied on the full amount of the investment income. Nevertheless, we may conclude that discrimination against investment income is much smaller than it appears at first sight.

8.3 Capital Gains Tax

It is appropriate to deal with capital gains at this point because most forms of capital gains have much the same characteristics as income. Several types of capital gain are really income in disguise. For example, the value of National Savings Certificates is increased during their life as a method of paying interest. Similar forms of 'income' include the increase in value of bonds arising from the approach of the date of redemption, and the capital appreciation of all kinds of securities resulting from ploughing back profits. To consider other types of capital gain, we should examine carefully what we mean by 'income'.

The precise definition of income has been the subject of considerable debate. Haig (1921), for example, gave the following definition: 'income is the money-value of the net accretion to economic power between two points of time'. Another is the comprehensive definition of income of Henry Simons (1938): 'Personal income may be defined as the algebraic sum of (a) the market value of rights exercised in consumption and (b) the change in the value of the store of property rights between the beginning and end of the period in question'. Hicks' (1974) definition took income as the 'maximum amount of money which the individual can spend this week, and still be able to spend the same amount *in real terms* in each ensuing week'.

The definition that seems to be increasingly accepted is that of total accretion, that is the accrual of wealth. This includes as income an individual's spending in a given period, plus any changes in his net wealth. For example, if an individual spent £2,500 in one year, and the real value of his assets increased by £500, his income by this definition is £3,000 in that year.

Many more types of capital gain may be considered as income. This definition includes inheritances, gifts, winnings from gambling and any 'windfall' gains. In principle, all these items might be considered as income for tax purposes.

The case for taxing capital gains can now be summarised under the twin headings of equity and efficiency. On equity grounds, if capital gains are equivalent to income, they should equally be subject to tax (see Chapter 5). The equity argument is reinforced as capital gains accrue unevenly among the population. Gains can only accrue to owners of assets and, as we shall see in Section 10.1, wealth is unevenly distributed in the United Kingdom.

The efficiency argument has two main aspects. The first is that, as many types of income can be converted into capital gains, to exempt the latter from tax would encourage such conversion. This might involve economic costs for the individuals taking such action and economic costs for the Revenue in trying to prevent them. The second, and perhaps more important aspect, is that a tax on capital gains reduces the attraction of investment in 'non-productive' assets such as antiques, coins, paintings, precious stones and stamps, which are bought because of anticipated increases in their value, rather than any productive purpose.

So, in theory, there is a straightforward case for treating all capital gains as income. Needless to say, there are many practical difficulties.

Practical Problems

The first and most obvious difficulty concerns capital gains which arise only through increases in the price level. Such nominal gains do not, of course, increase an individual's real spending power and should not in principle be counted as income. However, there are other considerations which are discussed in Chapter 5, and there is also the practical problem of selecting an appropriate index number to take account of inflation.

A second problem is that, in principle, capital gains tax should be levied on an accruals basis. In practice this would involve the valuation of capital assets each year, so imposing a considerable administrative burden. It would also involve the risk that individuals might be forced to liquidate assets in order to pay the tax.

Capital gains tax in Britain avoids these problems because it is imposed on a realisation basis. But this in turn poses difficulties. First of all, asset-holders may be 'locked-in', in the sense that they have an incentive to postpone payment of the tax by not realising the asset. Second, because assets are realised in uneven lumps, it is difficult to make the tax progressive. To do so would require complex averaging provisions, as otherwise there would be an incentive to realise assets in an even flow, which may be economically inefficient. This difficulty is aggravated because an individual's capital gains, whether realised or not, occur irregularly.

Administration is another major problem. Even with the realisation basis, a valuation is sometimes required both when an asset is bought, and when it is sold. For some types of assets, such as shares quoted on the Stock Exchange, valuation is relatively simple. For other types of assets, such as unquoted shares, it can be very much harder.

Capital Gains Tax in the UK

Although there had been previous attempts to tax certain types of capital gains, especially from land, the systematic taxation of gains did not begin until 1962. In that year a tax on short-term gains was introduced. In 1965 a more comprehensive capital gains tax came into operation. The tax is levied on a wide range of assets, but there are several exemptions including owner-occupied houses, motor vehicles, and gambling winnings. The justification for exempting the last of these was that, as there is no capital asset, there cannot be a capital gain!

There is also a separate tax on the gains made by changing the use of land from, for example, agricultural to housing estate property. The tax, called Development Land Tax, was introduced in 1976. It is not dealt with in this book.

The rate of capital gains tax has been 30 per cent since 1965. However, several different schemes for exempting small gains have been used from year to year. These cut down the number of taxpayers and, hence, the administrative costs. In 1983–84, there is an exemption of £5,300 of gains. This is, in effect, a zero-rate band. The Finance Act 1982 provided for this exemption to be indexed by using the change in Retail Prices Index in the year up to the December preceding the tax year (and then rounding to the nearest £100).

Capital gains accruing to companies are also in effect charged at 30 per cent, though companies do not pay capital gains tax but corporation tax on (part of) their gains (see Section 13.2). The rules for the calculation of the size of a corporate chargeable gain are much the same as those for capital gains tax, which will now be discussed.

Although there have been several different ways of taxing a chargeable gain, the calculation of the gain itself has remained much the same. As one might expect, this is basically the sale proceeds less the purchase cost.

One way in which the gain may work out to be smaller than at first expected is due to the sensible treatment of expenses. Those paid at acquisition are added to the original costs; those paid at disposal are deducted from the proceeds. This is illustrated below.

	1984 disposal price		2000
	1984 cost of sale		200
	1984 net proceeds		1800
1970 purchase price		1500	
1970 costs of acquisition		150	
1970 total cost			1650
Taxable gain			150

A further aspect of the tax which reduces a chargeable gain relates to those assets being sold currently which were bought before 1965 when the tax was introduced. It would be inequitable (compared with those who realised gains just before the tax was introduced) to tax the gains accruing in the pre-tax period. For most such assets, taxpayers have a choice between using the actual gain since 6 April 1965, or a time-based apportionment of the total gain. For example, suppose that a painting was bought in September 1962 for £10,000 and sold in September 1983 for £22,000. Its value on 6 April 1965 was known to be £13,000, and expenses of purchase and sale were negligible. The two possible chargeable gains are:

(a) sale − 1965 value = £22,000 − £13,000 = £9,000

(b) $\text{total gain} \times \dfrac{\text{time after 1965}}{\text{total time}} = £12{,}000 \times \dfrac{18\frac{1}{2}}{21} = £10{,}571$

The taxpayer will choose the former in this case. The rules in the case of shares held before 6 April 1965 are more complicated and are not dealt with here. However, they are illustrated in the *Workbook*.

Yet another complication which reduces gains was introduced by the 1982 Finance Act. After years of criticism about the inequitable effects of inflation on capital gains tax (see Section 5.6), the government brought in a system of indexation based on the Retail Prices Index. The 'indexation allowance' (IA) relates to the gain since March 1982. It only applies to assets held for more than one year, and it cannot be used to create or augment a loss for tax purposes. These two aspects of the IA are administratively efficient and also reduce the revenue loss. However, there seems no equitable reason for either of them.

The allowance is worked out separately for each expense of a different date, like the initial purchase of an asset and a subsequent addition to it. The allowance is given by the formula:

$$IA = \text{expense} \times \frac{RPI_s - RPI_e}{RPI_e},$$

where RPI_e is the index at March 1982 or, if later, one year after the date of the expenditure; and RPI_s is the index at the date of sale.

For example, suppose that an asset was bought in 1978 for £10,000 (including expenses) and is sold in September 1984 for £25,000 (net). Let us suppose that the RPI in March 1982 was 200 and in September 1984 is 300. Then:

$$IA = £10{,}000 \times \frac{300 - 200}{200} = £5{,}000$$

$$\text{Chargeable gain} = £25{,}000 - £10{,}000 - £5{,}000 = £10{,}000$$

If the asset had been bought, for example, in June 1983, the relevant index for expenditure would be that for June 1984.

One might note that, for purchases before 1982, not only is the change in the index since the date of purchase to 1982 not taken into account (which seems reasonable for a system which commences in 1982), but also the allowance ratio only applies to the out-of-date cost (which seems less reasonable). For example, if the asset in the above example had been bought for £5,000 in 1970, the IA would only be £2,500, despite the fact that a larger amount of pre-allowance chargeable gain of £20,000 (i.e. £25,000 − £5,000) was a nominal or monetary gain.

The rules relating to chargeable gains on shares have always been complex. However, in an attempt to reduce the scope for manipulation of this new allowance, the rules have now become quite extraordinarily difficult to understand and implement.

Capital Gains Tax and Incentives

It is often asserted that enterprise and small businesses are discouraged by very high rates of income tax. Yet it should be pointed out that, where an entrepreneur can take his profits in the form of capital gains, such arguments are much less relevant. With a rate of capital gains tax of 30 per cent in 1983–84, it is still possible for an entrepreneur (but not an employee) to become rich by his own efforts.

8.4 Wages, Salaries and Pay-As-You-Earn

The United Kingdom's Pay-As-You-Earn (PAYE) mechanism for withholding tax from wages and salaries is quite unique, though a somewhat similar system was introduced in Ireland in 1960. The system is unique because it is capable of withholding tax extremely accurately. It is also unusual in that it requires very little co-operation on the part of taxpayers to work efficiently. This is because nearly all the work is done by employers and the Inland Revenue. However, before we examine the system in detail and discuss its advantages and disadvantages, we shall look at the reasons for its introduction.

PAYE was introduced in an attempt to overcome many of the difficulties of assessment and collection that arose during the Second World War. In the war the standard rate of income tax was raised to ten shillings in the pound (50 per cent) and the value of allowances reduced. The result was that large numbers of people were brought into the tax net who were unused to paying income tax — especially at high rates. In fact, the number of taxpayers rose from four million in 1938–39 to 12 million in 1943–44 (Inland Revenue 1976, p. 21).

Up to 1940, most employees who paid tax did so in two equal instalments each year. This soon proved highly unsatisfactory, especially for those paid weekly. Therefore, in 1940 a new system was introduced which spread the payments of tax over periods of six months. For example, the tax to be charged on wages earned between 6 April and 5 October was withheld from the wages of the six months commencing the following February.

The collection of tax in arrears caused many difficulties. There were many cases of hardship, especially in industries where earnings fluctuated seasonally. This meant that tax due on high wages earned in favourable periods was frequently withheld from lower wages received in other periods. Similar hardship often arose when an individual moved to a lower paid job.

As the war progressed there was increasing pressure for a system in which the amount of tax withheld in any pay period was based on the income received in that period. The Inland Revenue said that it could not be done (Barr *et al.*, 1977, pp. 23 and 24). However, pressure continued to increase, much encouraged by the fact that both Canada and the United States had introduced 'Pay-as-you-go' methods of withholding. Finally, the Inland Revenue relented, and in 1944 the Pay-As-You-Earn mechanism (widely known at the time as Pay-*All*-You-Earn!) was introduced.

The Operation of PAYE

The difference between the British system and those introduced in North America is that the former is operated on a cumulative basis, while the latter are run on a non-cumulative basis. Cumulation simply means that a taxpayer's pay and allowances are accumulated through the tax year so that the amount withheld in any one period is dependent on the income received throughout the tax year up to and including the current period. On the other hand, a non-cumulative system treats each pay period separately. Consequently, a cumulative system is capable of withholding the correct amount of tax throughout the year and can pay out a tax rebate when it falls due, rather than after the end of the tax year.

With a progressive income tax, a non-cumulative withholding system cannot achieve these results if taxpayers' incomes or allowances change or fluctuate during the tax year. The reason is that, since each pay period is treated in isolation, taxpayers are often pushed into higher tax brackets than would be appropriate if the position over the whole year were considered, and consequently too much tax is withheld.

The difference between the two systems is best illustrated by an example. Suppose that the basic rate of tax is 30 per cent. Suppose also that the individual in the example has total allowances of £2080 for the year in question, and that his income varies from week to week. We shall now examine the workings of first a pure cumulative withholding system, and then a non-cumulative system using these figures.

Cumulative System: The effect of cumulation is to divide the taxpayer's allowances by the number of pay periods (say 52) and then cumulate them as the year progresses. In this example, the allowances or 'free pay' accumulate at a rate of £40 per week (illustrated by column 4 in Table 8C). The cumulative free pay is then deducted from cumulative pay to date (column 3) to give cumulative taxable pay (column 5). Cumulative tax due is then calculated as 30 per cent of cumulative taxable pay, and the actual tax due is the difference between cumulative tax due, and the tax already withheld.

Thus in week 1 of the tax year, the individual earns £160 and has free pay of £40, leaving £120 of taxable pay. The tax due on £120 is £36. Similarly in week 2, when the individual's pay rises to £200 and cumulative free pay rises to £80, the cumulative tax due becomes £84. However, £36 has already been withheld in the previous week, so the final liability in week 2 is £48. Now suppose that in week 3 the individual's income falls to nothing. Free pay continues to accumulate and reaches £120 in week 3, which means that cumulative tax due falls to £72. However, £84 has already been paid in tax, so the individual should, in principle, receive a rebate for the difference that week. However, this feature has been restricted in the UK system. From 5 July 1982 a taxpayer who becomes unemployed will not normally receive any rebate due until after either he ceases to claim unemployment or supplementary benefit, or the end of the tax year. In addition, from 1982, rebates cannot usually be paid while a person is on strike.

Non-cumulative system: It can be seen that with a cumulative system the correct amount of tax should be withheld each period. This is not the case with a non-cumulative system. If the same example is followed through in Table 8D, the allowances are again divided between the number of pay periods, but are not accumulated. In the first two weeks the results are the same in both cases, but in week 3 the individual has not used up his full allowances.

There is no mechanism whereby the excess tax can be repaid during the tax year, and so by week 3 the non-cumulative system has withheld £12 too much. If, instead of using a single basic rate of tax in the example, a series of rates had been used, the withholding would have been even more excessive. The reason is that, in the high income weeks, the individual would be pushed into higher tax brackets than would be appropriate to his circumstances if the year

Table 8C An Example of Cumulation

(1) Week	*(2) Gross Pay*	*(3) Cumulative pay to date*	*(4) Cumulative free pay*	*(5) Cumulative taxable pay (col 3 – col 4)*	*(6) Cumulative tax due (30% of col 5)*	*(7) Actual tax due*
	£	£	£	£	£	£
1	160	160	40	120	36	36
2	200	360	80	280	84	48
3	0	360	120	240	72	–12

Table 8D An Example of Non-Cumulative Withholding

Week	*Gross pay*	*Free pay*	*Taxable pay*	*Tax due*
1	160	40	120	36
2	200	40	160	48
3	0	40	0	0

were taken as a whole. It is true that with a non-cumulative system the excess tax withheld would eventually be repaid, but this would have to be after the taxpayer's final liability had been calculated. This could not be done before the end of the tax year, and might be done well after that date.

The PAYE Code Number

Having described the principle of cumulation, it is now worth describing how the system is operated in practice. The first stage of the assessment process is that the taxpayer provides details of his personal circumstances to the Inland Revenue by completing a tax return. Most employees are not required to complete a return each year and, indeed, many go for several years without seeing one. As long as a taxpayer's circumstances do not change, the PAYE system makes an annual return unnecessary.

The allowances that the employee is entitled to claim are then translated into a code number. For example, a person entitled only to the single person's allowance (£1,785 in 1983–84) would be given the code 178L. A married man would be entitled to the married allowance (£2,795 in 1983–84) giving a code number of 279H. The suffixes L and H represent the (lower) single person's allowance and the (higher) married allowance respectively and their purpose is described below. Different letters apply to those entitled to age allowance and who have tax withheld through PAYE. In these cases, the suffix P refers to the single age allowance and V represents the married allowance. The numbers, 178 and 279, each represent a band of allowances £10 wide. The result is that PAYE does not withhold tax with perfect precision. However, any advantage is given to the taxpayer, so that PAYE tends to withhold marginally too little. However, amounts of tax outstanding as a result of this factor alone are not considered large enough to be worth assessing and collecting separately.

The next stage is to send a 'Notice of Coding' to the taxpayer. This shows the code number and how it was calculated so that the taxpayer can check the Revenue's figures. If he thinks they were wrong, he may appeal. The taxpayer is also warned to inform the tax office of any change in his personal circumstances which may subsequently affect his code, and not to wait until he receives a tax return.

The taxpayer's code number is then sent to his employer. Although the code is determined by the taxpayer's allowances, it does not disclose to the employer details of the employee's personal circumstances. The Inland Revenue also supplies the employer with the tax tables needed to calculate the correct amount of tax to withhold.

If, for some reason, the employer does not receive a code number for a particular employee, the emergency code (E) must be used. The emergency code is equal to the single person's allowance and must be operated on a non-cumulative basis. This is known as the 'week 1' or 'month 1' basis as the cumulative element is suppressed by treating each pay period as though it were the first in the tax year. This procedure means that anyone on an emergency code cannot receive a rebate from his employer.

At the end of the tax year (5 April) every employer is required to send to the tax office a list of his employees, together with details of their pay and tax withheld. The figures for each individual are then checked. Provided that the code number has been fixed correctly, and the PAYE system operated properly, no further adjustment should be necessary.

The Advantages of PAYE

The most important advantage of a cumulative PAYE system is that tax is withheld very accurately from employment income. This means that it is not necesssary to make an end-of-year adjustment (involving either a further tax demand or a rebate) to most employees' tax payments. It also means that the majority of employees do not have to complete a tax return every year.

PAYE also has a number of other advantages. When a taxpayer's entitlement to allowances increases during the tax year, his code can be increased so that he receives the benefit at once. (Note that an increase in the code number results in a *decrease* in the tax withheld.) If the taxpayer becomes entitled to a tax rebate, this also means that it can be paid during the current tax year, rather than after the end of the year.

However, it should be noted that, if the taxpayer's entitlement to allowances decreases, his code is not reduced in the same way. If it were, the extra tax (that should have been withheld week by week since the beginning of the tax year) would be withheld all in one go. This may mean hardship, and so the normal procedure is to reduce the code by the appropriate amount, but to operate it on the non-cumulative basis. This usually means that some tax liability is still outstanding at the end of the year, but less than would be the case if no action at all were taken.

Another advantage of PAYE is that it can be used to collect tax in respect of some forms of income not subject to withholding at source. A common example is bank interest. The method used, known as 'coding-out', is to reduce the taxpayer's code number sufficiently to allow the tax liability on these other sources of income to be withheld from his employment income. It is usually not necessary to make a separate assessment on the non-PAYE sources of income if it is 'coded out', but clearly this method is unlikely to be accurate where large amounts of non-PAYE income are received, or where the income is unpredictable or fluctuating.

There is also a technique which is sometimes known as 'coding-in'. This is used where a taxpayer has, for some reason, paid insufficient tax on his earnings at the end of the year. Instead of demanding immediate payment, the Inland Revenue may recover the oustanding tax slowly (and less painfully) over later years by reducing the taxpayer's code number by the appropriate amount.

The Disadvantages of PAYE

Given that the essential advantage of cumulative withholding is accuracy, the essential disadvantages arise from the need to maintain that accuracy in different circumstances. The disadvantages themselves fall into two categories. The first covers the difficulties in maintaining the cumulative process. The second is the need to design other aspects of the system to avoid large numbers of end-of-year adjustments.

The difficulty in maintaining cumulation occurs when an employee changes his job. There are two aspects to this: first, it is necessary to ensure that the new employer has the information to continue the cumulative process; second, the employee's file must be transferred to a new tax district. This is necessary because a key feature of PAYE is that the employee's tax papers are filed with reference to his current employer, and so a new employer usually means a new tax district.

The procedure for dealing with a change of employment is as follows. When an employee leaves his job, his employer issues a tripartite form (a P.45) which shows the employee's code number, gross pay, and tax paid to date. Part 1 of the P.45 is sent to the individual's original tax district, and parts 2 and 3 are given to the employee to pass on to his new employer. Part 2 of the form is retained by the new employer as an authorisation to withhold tax, and part 3 is sent on to the new tax district. The second tax district then contacts the first, and the employee's file is forwarded on.

The P.45 procedure has a number of drawbacks. The first is the amount of work involved. In tax districts dealing with PAYE (which are most of the 770 or so districts), at least 10 per cent of the districts' total staff resources can be employed on this work alone. A second drawback is that the complexity of the process means that parts of the P.45 are often lost or mislaid or issued well after the employee has left his original job. A third possible drawback (which may lead to employees suppressing their P.45s) is that the system may be considered to infringe on an individual's privacy, since the new employer can easily establish how much his new employee has earned in his previous job during the tax year.

In certain circumstances, it is not practicable to operate the cumulative element of PAYE accurately. This occurs, for example, with higher rate taxpayers who have more than one job. The problem is that if each job were treated separately, PAYE would tend to withhold too little tax. The reason is that too much income would be subject to tax at the basic rate, and too little at higher rates. The problem is dealt with by setting the taxpayers' allowances against one job (or possibly more than one) and allocating a D code prefix to any further jobs. There is one D code for each of the higher rates. Thus D0 represents the 40 per cent rate and so on. D codes are operated on a non-cumulative basis and, when a D code is issued, the employer must withhold tax at the appropriate rate on all payments to the employee.

Although the D code system improves the accuracy of PAYE in these circumstances, errors remain because of the non-cumulative element. For instance, if the taxpayer's income from his main job changes, the D codes in force on second and subsequent jobs may cease to be the appropriate ones and an end-of-year adjustment becomes necessary.

The D code system therefore provides an example of the difficulties involved in maintaining cumulation. It also shows why PAYE requires a long basic rate band to work efficiently. With such a band, straightforward withholding procedures can be used for many types of incomes; without it, withholding could not operate with the accuracy it does for most taxpayers, and many more end-of-year adjustments would be required.

We have seen that the cumulative element of PAYE avoids the need for most taxpayers to complete a return every year. This, however, has its disadvantages and can easily lead to the wrong amount of tax being paid. If an individual does not have to sign a statement of income each year, it is easy for him to 'forget' about casual earnings and occasional receipts. It is also possible that, without an annual return, taxpayers may not be aware of their entitlement to certain allowances and expenses, nor that it is up to them to claim. Some further discussion of PAYE is presented in the self-assessment section in the following chapter.

8.5 Schedule D and Other Incomes

Although the great majority of taxpayers are assessed under Schedule E, the other schedules should also be described. By far the most extensive of these is Schedule D.

Schedule D

Schedule D covers incomes from trades, professions, businesses and property. It is divided into six cases which may be listed as follows:

Case I	:	Trading profits
Case II	:	Income from professions and vocations
Case III	:	Interest not taxed at source
Case IV	:	Income from foreign securities
Case V	:	Income from foreign possessions
Case VI	:	Miscellaneous profits

Case I includes trading income from all sorts of ventures such as manufacturing, wholesaling and retailing. For the purposes of Case II, a profession is regarded as an occupation requiring certain intellectual and perhaps manual skills, for example, accountants, doctors of medicine and lawyers. A vocation describes the way a person spends his life; the main category is authors, but other examples are actors and singers.

Case III deals with interest not subject to withholding at source, unless it is assessed under Schedule C (see below). The main example here is bank interest. Incomes from foreign securities and possessions (Cases IV and V) are one of the most complicated areas of income tax, the details of which need not concern us here. Case VI, casual and miscellaneous profits, as the name suggests, is a sweeping-up section covering profits not dealt with under any of the other cases of Schedule D. Examples include income from furnished lettings and income from guaranteeing loans.

The operation of Schedule D provides several contrasts with the operation of Schedule E. Two of the most noticeable differences are the treatment of expenses (Cases I and II) and the use of the preceding year basis rather than a current year basis for Cases I to V.

For Schedule D, S130 of the 1970 Taxes Act provides that expenses are only deductible if they are incurred *wholly and exclusively* for the purposes of the trade, profession or vocation. In practice, the calculation of taxable income begins with the net profit for accounting purposes. Thus, the following would normally not have been deducted as expenses, nor should they be for tax purposes: capital items, taxation paid and appropriations of profit (like drawings or partnership profit sharings). As far as the calculation of taxable income under Schedule D Cases I and II of income tax is concerned, the statutory and case rules are much the same as for companies. These can be found in Section 13.2. Here we will examine some other cases relating particularly to individual taxpayers, though some of them have relevance for corporations.

Case law has clarified what a 'trade' is. For example, *C.I.R. v. Rutledge* (14 TC 490) concerned a businessman who bought one million rolls of toilet paper in Berlin, and sold them in one lot on his return to England. Despite the fact that this was an isolated transaction, it was held that it was an adventure by nature of trade. This was partly because Rutledge was a businessman and partly because the goods were not normally associated with investment! As another example, in *Pickford v. Quirke* (13 TC 251) it was held that making gains from buying companies and 'asset-stripping' did constitute a trade because the taxpayer had done it four times, whereas it would not have been if done once only.

In another case, *Norman v. Golder* (26 TC 293), it was held that a sick person could not claim that doctors' bills were 'wholly and exclusively for the purposes of the trade', because they were also 'for the advantage and benefit of the taxpayer as a living human being.'

Similarly, in *Bowden v. Russell and Russell* (42 TC 301) it was held that a solicitor travelling to America to attend a conference and to have a holiday could not charge his expenses against tax, because they were not exclusively for his profession. There was said to be 'duality' of purpose.

Travelling expenses *on* business, but not *to* business from one's home, are allowed. A number of cases have dealt with this (Pinson, 1982).

For Schedule E, S189 of the 1970 Taxes Act provides that expenses are only deductible if they are incurred *wholly, exclusively and necessarily in the performance* of the duties of the employment. This makes it even clearer than for Schedule D that, for example, travelling to and from work are not allowable because they are not *in the performance of* duties. These words and the word 'necessarily' make the rules for Schedule E much stricter than those for Schedule D.

Several expenses are not regarded by the Revenue as *necessarily* incurred. For example, in *Simpson v. Tate* (9 TC 314) it was held that a doctor could not claim subscriptions to medical societies, because keeping up to date was not necessary for the performance of duties, though it might be necessary for the fit performance of them. It is also clear that employees cannot in general claim expenses of tools, or clothing, unless these can be proved to be essential to the continuation of the employment.

However, the 1970 Taxes Act does allow deductions for certain subscriptions to professional bodies, which might be deemed to be necessary for some employees to join, e.g. architects or accountants. Furthermore, in practice, the Inland Revenue allows dons to claim for books purchased!

It is clearly useful for a taxpayer to try to establish that his income falls under Schedule D rather than Schedule E. The latter applies where there is a contract of service (whether written or verbal) and where the method of performance of duties is laid down by the employer. Even gifts which arise because of the employment are included; in *Cooper v. Blackiston* (5 TC 347) it was held that a vicar's receipts from an Easter offering were taxable because they arose from the vicar's job. On the other hand, it was held in *Hochstrasser v. Mayes* (38 TC 673) that compensation paid to an employee for loss on a house as a result of his being asked to move was not taxable, because it was not paid in respect of his services to the company.

Further, many benefits in kind received by employees are also taxable. For example, free or subsidised accommodation is regarded as an emolument under S33 of the 1977 Finance Act, unless the job requires the employee to live in the accommodation provided. Also, even clothing provided by an employer is an emolument; in *Wilkins v. Rogerson* (39 TC 344) it was held that the taxable benefit of a suit was its second-hand value.

As a final example, the benefit derived by an employee from the provision of a car by his employer is also taxable under a scale set out in the Finance Acts.

Having looked at the differences between Schedule E and Schedule D, it now seems appropriate to ask whether they are defensible. One strong argument for retaining the very strict rules of Schedule E, which disallow nearly all expenses, is that this is administratively efficient. Since there are so many Schedule E taxpayers, for the Inland Revenue to have to enter into a process of checking all their claims and arguing against some of them would be very expensive. At present, many Schedule E taxpayers do not even have to fill in returns; this is partly because they would not be allowed to claim expenses and partly because the PAYE system copes with personal allowances and other complications.

In addition to this, it might be expected that Schedule E

employees would normally be provided with the necessary special clothing, tools of the trade, etc. In contrast, it is clearly necessary to allow expenses of various sorts to the self-employed, who provide their own workplaces, capital equipment, etc. In order to charge tax on *profit*, which is the balance of revenues less expenses, it will always be necessary to have more complex returns for Schedule D taxpayers. Fortunately, there are relatively few of them compared to Schedule E payers. (For a detailed statistical analysis of the differences in incomes and conditions of the employed and the self-employed, see Diamond Commission, 1979.)

Nevertheless, the Royal Commission on the Taxation of Profits and Income (*Final Report*, 1955) found that the administration of the Schedule E rule 'is attended by rather widespread dissatisfaction' (para. 137). It recommended that the rule should be revised to the less restrictive 'all expenses reasonably incurred for the appropriate performance of the duties of the office or employment' (para. 140). This particular sentence was chosen in order to bring the Schedule E practice closer to the Schedule D provisions.

Despite this recommendation, the treatment of expenses under the two schedules has not yet been reformed. The economic implications of the more generous treatment under Schedule D are twofold. First, there is an artificial incentive for individuals to become self-employed even when it might be economically more efficient for them to work as employees. The Revenue, of course, also has problems in ensuring that taxpayers do not manipulate their employment status illegally. Second, in so far as employees see the differential treatment of expenses as unfair, it may lead to a loss of 'tax-morale' and a reduction in the willingness of taxpayers to comply with the requirements of the tax system.

The other major contrast between Schedules D and E is the basis of assessment. Schedule E is administered on a 'current year' basis, which simply means that the liability to tax in any one year is based on the income received in that year. Schedule D Cases I to V (but not Case VI), in contrast, are operated on a 'preceding year' basis. This means that the assessment to tax in any one year is based on the taxable income of the preceding year.

The preceding year basis may be illustrated by looking at the profits of firms and individuals assessed under Cases I and II. In these cases, liability to tax in any one year will normally be based on the profits shown in the person's accounts for his financial year ending in the tax year preceding the year of assessment. A tax year ends on 5 April. Now, suppose a shopkeeper makes his accounts up to 31 December each year. The shopkeeper will be assessed in the tax year 1984–85 on the profits he made during the year ending 31 December 1983. Payment of half the liability is then due on 1 January in the tax year and the rest on the following 1 July. In our example, half the liability would be due on 1 January 1985 and the rest on 1 July 1985.

The preceding year basis has some drawbacks. One of the main ones is that, in the first year of a business, there is no preceding year figure on which to base the assessment. The result is a fairly complicated procedure for firms which are just starting in business, and a further set of special rules for firms ceasing to trade.

The special rules applying to a new business are as follows. In the first year, the assessment is based on the profits accruing from the starting date to the following 5 April. In the second tax year, the assessment is usually based on the profits for the first 12 months of the business. In the third tax year, the assessment is normally on the preceding year basis. However, these special rules may bear unfairly on the taxpayer, so he has a right to elect to have the second and third year (but not just one of them) based on the actual profits of those years.

The rules for closing businesses are similar. For the tax year in which business ceased, the assessment is based on the actual profits from the previous 6 April up to the closing date. For the two years up to the final year, the assessment would have been on the preceding year basis. But the actual profits may have been higher than the profits assessed. The Inland Revenue therefore has the power to determine that the assessments are made on the basis of actual profits in each of these two years (but not just one) if such assessments increase the taxpayer's liability. These provisions are summarised in Table 8E.

The preceding year basis may have some advantages for taxpayers. The income of the preceding year is, in effect, being used as an estimate of the income received in the current year, and if incomes were constant the procedure would be accurate. However, if real or nominal incomes are rising as a result of growth or inflation, the tax liability on the increase may be deferred for a long period. In the example of our shopkeeper above, the tax on any

Table 8E *Schedule D Opening and Closing Provisions*

OPENING PROVISIONS

	Normal basis	*Election by taxpayer*
First year	Start date to 5 April	–
Second year	First 12 month's profits	Actual profits
Third year	Preceding year's profits	Actual profits
Subsequent years	Preceding year's profits	–

CLOSING PROVISIONS

	Normal basis	*Election by Revenue*
Pre-penultimate year	Preceding year's profits	Actual profits
Penultimate year	Preceding year's profits	Actual profits
Last year	6 April to cessation date	–

increases in his income may be deferred for an average period of 21 months. (As the accounts are made up to 31 December 1983 and, assuming that income accrues evenly over the year, the profits relate on average to 1 July 1983. However, the tax is not paid until 1 April 1985 on average.) If the accounting year of a particular business ended on 30 April, for example, the delay would be even longer.

The benefits of the delay may be interpreted either as an interest free loan which Schedule E taxpayers do not receive or (in inflationary times) the right to pay part of one's tax liability in depreciated pounds. The economic implications of this are again clear. There is an incentive, other things being equal, for people to become self-employed, even if they can be more productive as employees.

One other aspect that might be mentioned is the co-ordination and the administration of some other forms of income. We have seen that one of the main advantages of the PAYE system is that it avoids large numbers of end-of-year adjustments. The system has been carefully designed and modified to achieve this wherever possible. A similar need arises with other forms of income.

One of the major examples of this is building society interest. Most building societies have an arrangement with the Revenue that they pay a special average or composite rate of tax. Although this composite rate is below the basic rate, it means that the building societies can pay interest free of basic rate tax. However, investors not liable to tax cannot claim a rebate. This avoids the need for the Revenue to deal with a large number of end-of-year adjustments. A similar example is bank interest. Tax is not withheld on such interest because it would frequently have to be repaid.

Other aspects of the administration of incomes under Schedule D, such as capital allowances and stock relief, apply to incorporated businesses as well. These are described in Chapter 13.

Schedule A

Schedule A is concerned with income from land. In 1963, it was abolished and replaced with a new case under Schedule D — Case VIII. In 1969, Case VIII was renamed Schedule A and has continued as such since that time.

The new Schedule A deals with annual profits or gains to which an individual 'becomes entitled' from land (and buildings) in the United Kingdom. This means that most rents, feu duties and so on are dealt with under Schedule A. An exception is furnished lettings. In this case the fraction of the rent attributable to the furnishings is assessable under Schedule D Case VI. The rent itself may also be chargeable under Case VI. However, the taxpayer may elect to avoid this provision, in which case payment for the furniture will be dealt with under Case VI and the rest under Schedule A. This may be worthwhile if the expenses and losses are treated more favourably under Schedule A.

The Schedule A provision 'become entitled' means that tax is chargeable on the income an individual is entitled to receive in the tax year, regardless of whether it was actually received. There are two exceptions to this provision. The first occurs where reasonable steps were taken to enforce payment, but payment was not made by the tenant. The second exception is where payment was waived to avoid hardship, provided of course that no other form of benefit was received instead of the rent.

In contrast to Schedule D (apart from Case VI), Schedule A is administered on a current year basis, and tax is payable on 1 January in the tax year. Income dealt with under Schedule A is usually treated as investment income, and so is subject to investment income surcharge.

Schedule B

Schedule B once covered almost every type of occupation of land and buildings. Over the years, however, Schedule B has been steadily eroded until the only part of its former glory that remains is tax chargeable on the occupiers of commercial woodlands. Liability is calculated on the basis of the 'assessable value' of the woodlands.

The 'assessable value' is one-third of the woodlands' annual value, which is the annual rent that would be received if the woodlands were let in their natural and unimproved state. No expenditure may be deducted under Schedule D Case I on the actual profits from the woodlands. If the election is made, expenditure can be deducted, but the election cannot be reversed. However, this poses no problem to the tax planner. The most favourable strategy is to start with assessment under Schedule D when the trees are growing. Income is then low or zero, and losses may be deducted from other forms of income. When the trees mature and are ready to be felled, the woodlands are transferred to a company and switched back to Schedule B.

Schedule C

Schedule C is concerned with interest paid on government securities. Tax is withheld at source, unless the securities are held through the National Savings Stock Register or the Trustee Savings Bank Register. Schedule C is operated on a current year basis.

Schedule F

As we shall see in Section 12.3, the system of company taxation means that dividends are distributed together with a tax credit. This tax credit represents an imputation of the corporation tax on a company's profits, and is of sufficient value to offset any liability to income tax at the basic rate. The purpose of Schedule F is to cover any liability for tax at the higher rates or for investment income surcharge. Where there is further liability, it is calculated with reference to the 'grossed-up' value of the dividend; that is the dividend plus the tax credit.

8.6 Administration and Enforcement

The Inland Revenue

The administration of income tax is divided into two parts, assessment and collection. The assessment process is carried out by Inspectors of Taxes who are responsible for establishing each taxpayer's liability. The actual collection is then undertaken by Collectors of Taxes, who are quite separate from the Inspectors. The original reason for the separation was to prevent corruption. Indeed Johnston (1965, p. 135) reports that it was once thought 'essential to the maintenance of security that Inspectors were even forbidden to lodge in the same house as Collectors'! However, the separation has led to some confusion on the part of the public, and difficulties when the actions of a tax office and a collection office have been at variance. It has been suggested that the structure be reformed (Inland Revenue, 1975) but little progress has yet been made.

The Inland Revenue is a decentralised body, operating mainly through some 770 tax districts and about 250 collection offices spread throughout the country. Traditionally, taxpayers have been dealt with by their local offices, but increasingly taxpayers are being administered by a tax office located in a different part of the country. There are three main reasons for this. First, employees' tax files are kept by the office which deals with their *employers*, even if a company has establishments in different parts of the country. As there is a tendency to concentration in industry, it is increasingly the case that employees do not work in the same area as their employer's head office. Second, many taxpayers in London are dealt with by tax offices which are located outside the capital. Third, a single office (Centre 1) at East Kilbride deals with all employees in Scotland.

Enforcement

The Revenue has the power to inflict penalties for various offences, and some of these are shown in Table 8F. Nevertheless, the normal practice is to avoid the use of penalties if some other method of encouraging compliance can be used instead.

The most common example of this is dealing with taxpayers who do not complete a tax return when required to do so. In theory, the Revenue could impose a penalty of £50 for each missing return, plus £10 a day for a continuing offence. However, in practice, the normal procedure is simply to reduce the taxpayer's code number to the value of the single person's allowance (or perhaps even less), so that the PAYE system withholds too much tax. As soon as the taxpayer conforms, his code is calculated accurately and the tax he has overpaid will be returned. The Revenue does not generally need to rely on penalties as much as some foreign administrations because, as we have seen, the PAYE system can extract tax from most individuals without any co-operation from the taxpayer.

When the Inland Revenue has insufficient information to raise an accurate assessment, the Inspector may make an estimated

Table 8F Examples of Penalties

Offence	*Maximum penalty*
Failure to make a return when required	£50 plus £10 for each day the failure continues
Inaccurate returns	£50 plus the additional tax (or twice the additional tax in the case of fraud)
Assisting someone to prepare an inaccurate return	£500
Failure to give notice of liability to tax	£100
False statement by a sub-contractor made in order to obtain exemption from withholding	£5000

assessment which, if it is excessive, will force the taxpayer to appeal and so reveal his circumstances. Furthermore, unpaid tax is subject to an interest charge of twelve per cent per annum from the date the tax should have been paid. Official efforts to counter evasion are given in the annual reports of the Inland Revenue (e.g. 1982, pp. 16–19).

Appeals

If a taxpayer does not agree with an assessment to income tax, capital gains tax, or corporation tax, he may appeal. The appeal must be in writing and made within 30 days of the date of the assessment. Most appeals are settled between the taxpayer and the Inspector but, if no agreement can be reached, the appeal will be heard by the Commissioners of Income Tax.

There are two categories of Commissioners: the General Commissioners and the Special Commissioners. The General Commissioners are unpaid members of the public and perform a role similar to that of lay magistrates. There are no General Commissioners in Northern Ireland, their role being performed either by the County Court or by the Special Commissioners. The Special Commissioners are full-time civil servants and normally have extensive experience of tax law, having practised as barristers or solicitors either in the private sector or within the Inland Revenue.

In many cases, the taxpayer can choose whether the General or the Special Commissioners should hear the appeal. It is often suggested that the best policy for the taxpayer is to elect for the General Commissioners if the case is based on 'an appeal of the heart' and to the Special Commissions if there is a good legal case (Hepker, 1975, p. 37; Hambro, 1982, p. 166).

Hearings before the Commissioners are informal. The Inspector will normally conduct his own case, though the appellant may be represented by his accountant, solicitor or barrister. After the hearing, the Commissioners have the power to reduce, or confirm the original assessment.

On questions of fact, the Commissioners' findings are final. On a point of law, however, a further appeal may be made, and the appeal structure is described in Figure 8B. Thus, in England and

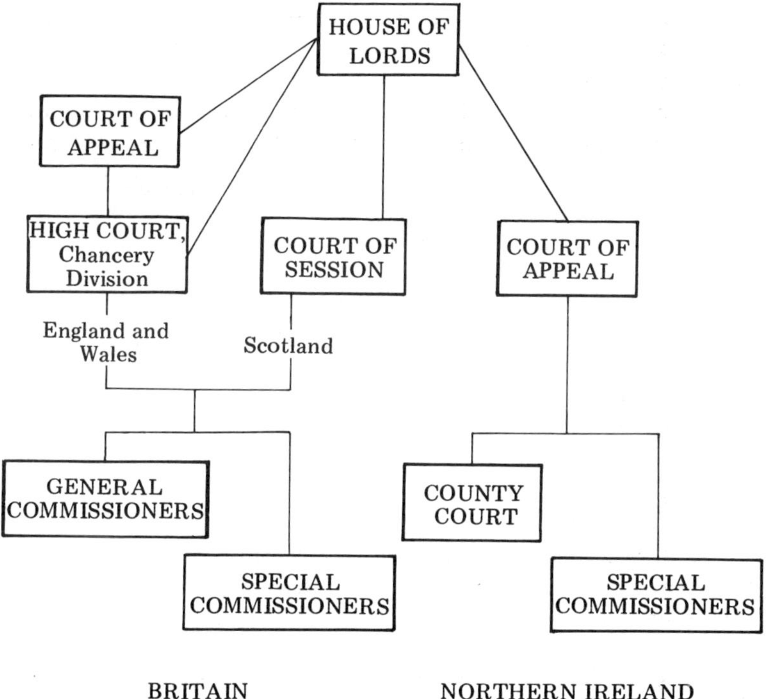

Figure 8B *Appeals in the United Kingdom*

Wales, the case would go first to the Chancery Division of the High Court, and then either to the Court of Appeal or directly to the House of Lords.

Further Reading

Details of the operation of the UK income tax are to be found in *The Hambro Tax Guide* (latest edition). Age allowance is considered in Morris (1981). Taxation and marriage are considered in Barr (1980), *The Taxation of Husband and Wife* (1980), Morris and Warren (1981) and Andic (1981). National Insurance contributions are discussed in Creedy (1981) and Williams (1978) and described in detail in Williams (1982). A history of the income tax is provided by Sabine (1965) and an account of the psychology of taxation is presented by Lewis (1982). Other useful information appears in the Inland Revenue's annual *Reports*.

References

Andic S. (1981), 'Does the personal income tax discriminate against women?' *Public Finance* No. 1, pp. 1–15.

Barr N.A. (1980), 'The taxation of married women's incomes', *British Tax Review*, I & II, pp. 398–412.

Barr N.A., James S.R. and Prest A.R. (1977), *Self-Assessment for Income Tax*, Heinemann.

Creedy J. (1981), 'Taxation and national insurance contributions in Britain', *Journal of Public Economics*, Vol. 15, pp. 379–88.

Diamond Commission (1979), *Report No. 8*, Cmnd. 7679, HMSO.

Farnsworth A. (1951), *Addington, Author of the Modern Income Tax*, Stevens.

Greenhalgh C. (1981), 'The taxation of husband and wife: equity, efficiency and female labour supply', *Fiscal Studies*, July, pp. 18–32.

Haig R.M. (1921), 'The concept of income', in R.M. Haig (ed.), *The Federal Income Tax*, Columbia University Press.

The Hambro Tax Guide (1982–83), Oyez Longman.

Hepker M.Z. (1975), *A Modern Approach to Tax Law*, 2nd edn., Heinemann.

Herbert A.P. (1966), *Wigs at Work*, Penguin Books, p. 100.

Hicks J.R. (1974), *Value and Capital*, 2nd edn, Oxford University Press.

Inland Revenue (1975), 'Proposals of the review committee for the structure of the Department', *Inland Revenue Management Review*, January.

Inland Revenue (1976), *118th Report* (for the year ended 31 March 1975), Cmnd. 6302, HMSO.

Inland Revenue (1978), *120th Report* (for the year ended 31 March 1977), Cmnd. 7092, HMSO.

Inland Revenue (1982), *124th Report* (for the year ended 31 March 1981), Cmnd. 8514, HMSO.

Johnston, Sir Alexander (1965), *The Inland Revenue*, Allen and Unwin.

Lewis, A. (1982), *The Psychology of Taxation*, Martin Robertson.

Morris, C.N. (1981), 'The age allowance', *Fiscal Studies*, November, pp. 29–36.

Morris, C.N. and Warren N.A. (1981), 'Taxation of the family', *Fiscal Studies*, March, pp. 26–46.

Pinson B. (1982), *Pinson on Revenue Law*, 15th edn, Sweet and Maxwell.

Royal Commission on the Taxation of Profits and Income (1955), *Final Report*, Cmnd. 9474, HMSO.

Sabine B.E.V. (1965), *A History of Income Tax*, Allen and Unwin.

Simons H.C. (1938), *Personal Income Taxation*, University of Chicago Press.

The Taxation of Husband and Wife (1980), Cmnd. 8093, HMSO.
Williams D.W. (1978), 'National Insurance contributions — a second income tax', *British Tax Review*, No. 2.
Williams D.W. (1982), *Social Security Taxation,* Sweet and Maxwell.

9

Further Aspects of Income Tax

Having examined the British system of income tax in Chapter 8, it is now appropriate to look at some possible reforms. As in Chapter 8, we are not concerned here with the overall level of income tax, but with the tax structure and methods of administration.

Given the extensive and complex nature of the present tax system, a general survey of potential reform would fill a much larger volume than this one. In order to keep our discussion within reasonable bounds, therefore, we shall confine ourselves to discussion of negative income tax, to the arguments concerning a possible personal expenditure tax, and to self-assessment.

9.1 Negative Income Tax

One reform which has attracted a great deal of interest is negative income tax. Many different schemes have been suggested under names such as income maintenance, reverse income tax, social dividend and tax credits, as well as negative income tax. Although the various schemes have many differences, the general aim is to provide an alternative method of taxing and redistributing income.

The main characteristic of these schemes is that they combine the income tax and important elements of social security into a single co-ordinated system. The basic idea, therefore, is that the income of each person or family unit would be assessed. If the income exceeded a certain amount, then tax would be payable in the usual way. However, if the income fell below the relevant amount, then it would be supplemented with a cash payment.

At present it is quite possible for individuals and families to be liable to income tax and National Insurance contributions at the same time as they are entitled to a wide range of cash and other benefits. Family Income Supplement (FIS) provides just one of many possible examples, although it is one of the most important. It also gives entitlement to certain other benefits. FIS was introduced in 1971 in an attempt to reduce the problem of low pay. It is payable to people bringing up children, where the head of the family is in full-time employment (or self-employment), but is earning an amount regarded as inadequate to meet the needs of the family.

Nevertheless, although officially recognised as having insufficient income, many recipients of FIS will still pay tax and National Insurance contributions. In 1983, families (including single parent families) could claim FIS if their earnings were less than the following:

Number of children	*Earnings per week (£)*
1	82.50
2	91.50
3	100.50
4	109.50
5	118.50

and so on, adding an extra £9 for each child. Yet in 1983–84, a married couple with children and the wife without paid employment could be liable to income tax if the husband's weekly earnings were as low as £54. A similar overlap occurs with a large number of other income-related (or 'means-tested') benefits.

The 'Poverty Trap'

The simultaneous taxation and subsidisation of low-income families is not the only feature of the present arrangements. Another very important one is that individuals can face very high 'implicit' marginal rates of tax. The reason is that many payments of benefit are, in fact, related to the recipients' income. When a claimant's earnings rise, therefore, he may not only incur more tax and contributions, but also lose part or all of any benefit payments he was receiving. The combined effects can lead to erratic and often very high implicit tax rates. This in turn can make it difficult for low-income families to improve their position through increases in gross pay: a situation commonly referred to as the 'poverty trap'.

For example, Family Income Supplement is reduced by 50p for every extra £1 earned, since the amount of the benefit is equal to half the difference between the qualifying levels of income shown above and the actual income received. There is an important offsetting factor in that FIS (and some other benefits) are usually awarded for periods of 12 months at a time. Permanent changes in income will not, therefore, affect the level of benefit until the end of the period. Temporary changes will not affect the level at all unless they happen at the wrong time, in which case they *might* result in a reduction in benefits for a whole year. Another offsetting factor is that many people do not claim their full entitlement, though this can hardly be considered an advantageous feature of the system in any other respect. Also, people may not be deterred from earning more in these circumstances if they do not understand the system, but that again does not seem to be a desirable state of affairs.

Nevertheless, the problem is not confined to FIS. In their evidence to the Select Committee on Tax Credit (1973), the Department of Health and Social Security and the Inland Revenue stated that there were 42 income-related benefits in the United Kingdom. Two more applied in Scotland. The main benefits include not only FIS, but also rent rebates and allowances, rate rebates, student grants and allowances, and free school meals and milk. Also included are such items as legal advice and assistance, legal aid, free National Health Service benefits, educational maintenance allowance, and school uniform and clothing grants.

The combined effects of these income-related benefits can raise implicit tax rates to very high levels indeed. The actual rates vary enormously between recipients depending on their circumstances and the benefits claimed. For illustration, take a married couple with the wife not earning and with two dependent children. To keep things reasonably simple, the only benefits we shall consider are FIS, rent rebate or allowance, and rate rebates. It might be added that the arrangements for rent and rate rebates are not uniform throughout the country because local authorities have the discretion to draw up their own schemes, though they can do so only within certain limits. Whatever the scheme, suppose that our family pays £12 a week in rent and £4 a week in rates. The couple would also receive child benefit but, as this is not related to income, it does not affect the following calculations. Let us further suppose that for income tax purposes, the couple are entitled to the married allowance only and that, for the purposes of National Insurance contributions, the husband has not contracted out of the state additional pension scheme. In these circumstances, using the rates of tax, contributions and benefits in force at the end of 1982, the implicit marginal rates of tax as calculated by the authors were as follows:

Earnings per week	*Marginal rate of tax*
£	%
40	59
50	89
60	110
70	120
80	119
90	112
100	62
110	62
120	62
130	39
150	39
200	39
250	30
300	40

Note that the marginal rates have been rounded to the nearest percentage point.

The implications for incentives are obviously serious. In the above example, if the husband were earning £80 a week, an increase of £1 could reduce his disposable income by 19 pence. If the husband was earning £60 a week, he would need an increase of nearly double that to make any significant difference to his spending power. Indeed, with an increase of anywhere between £1 and £40 he would probably make himself worse off financially.

Something may also be said about this on equity grounds. The very high rates of implicit tax faced by many families on low incomes provide a strong contrast with the explicit rates faced by those on higher incomes. For families such as that described above, the 39 per cent marginal rate applied to earnings ranging from just over £120 to £220. (Strictly, the 39 per cent consisted of the 30 per cent tax and the $8\frac{3}{4}$ per cent National Insurance contributions which applied in 1982–83.) On earnings in excess of £220, no further contributions were payable, so the marginal rate fell to 30 per cent. This continued until higher rates of tax were reached at £293. The maximum rate on earnings was 60 per cent, but our family would have had to have been earning £650 a week (or £34,000 a year) before they incurred such a rate again!

Naturally, some of the high implicit marginal rates in the above example would have been even higher if other benefits were included in the calculations. One in particular is where FIS is withdrawn, since FIS is also a passport to a number of other benefits. These were valued by the Department of Health and Social Security in their leaflet *FIS1/Nov82* as follows:

Free school means — up to £3 a week for each child at school.
Free milk and vitamins — about £1.40 per week for each child under five and for expectant mothers.
Free dental treatment — up to £90.
Free glasses — from around £10 up to £39.
Free prescriptions — £1.30 on each item needed.

Clearly, anyone in receipt of FIS might well be reluctant to pursue extra earnings which jeopardised his claim to the supplement. As William E. Simon, a former Secretary of the US Treasury, once said in an American context: 'the nation should have a tax system which looks like someone designed it on purpose' (US Treasury, 1977).

Unclaimed Benefits

A different problem with the present system is that many people do not claim the benefits to which they are entitled. For example, in

March 1973 it was thought that 'only about half the total numbers eligible were actually receiving payments under FIS' (Select Committee on Tax Credit 1973, Volume I, para. 30).

There are several reasons why individuals may not claim their full entitlement. In 1965 an enquiry was undertaken by the Ministry of Pensions and National Insurance (1966) into the financial and other circumstances of pensioners. The results suggested that there were two main reasons why many pensioners did not claim their entitlement to National Assistance. The first was that many were unaware of their entitlement. The second was the stigma attached to claiming assistance. Between a quarter and a third of pensioners who did not claim gave their reasons as disliking charity or the National Assistance Board, or that their pride prevented them from applying for assistance.

Benefit in Cash or in Kind

A separate aspect concerns the method of assisting poorer families. Many benefits take the form of either free goods and services (for example, free National Health Service prescriptions, and free dental treatment), or money related to particular forms of expenditure (for example, rent rebates).

It has often been argued that poorer families would be better off if the assistance they received were not tied to particular goods and services in this way. If poorer families had the cash, they could spend it on what they wanted most. In a recent proposal for a 'reverse income tax', for instance, it is argued that: 'Those who best understand the most urgent needs to which (social security) funds should be devoted are not the politicians and the bureaucrats, but the poor themselves' (Clark, 1977, p. 25).

There are, of course, limitations to this argument. Some individuals may be incapable of managing their own finances. Alternatively, the benefit of the payment may be intended for people other than the recipient. For example, the government may wish to ensure that children are adequately nourished.

Administration

A fourth aspect of the overlap between tax and benefits is

administration. Some integration between the two systems is likely to reduce the costs of administration. The Green Paper *Proposals for a Tax-Credit System* (1972) stated that its proposals 'would enable an eventual saving of some 10,000 to 15,000 civil servants to be made' (para. 47). A better integrated system would also be easier for the public to understand.

For a number of reasons, therefore, various schemes for reform have been proposed. There are substantial differences between many of the schemes, and we shall look first at the social dividend scheme and then at aspects of some others.

The Social Dividend

A social dividend scheme was first proposed by Lady Rhys Williams in 1942 and has been much discussed and developed since. The basic idea is that all social security benefits and the income tax would be replaced by a single scheme. Everyone would be paid a social dividend. The size of the payment would depend on family circumstances and the scheme would be financed by a proportional tax on all income.

A simple social dividend system is described in figure 9A. At the pre-tax level of income (I_1) the individual would pay as much in tax as he received as a social dividend. Below I_1, the dividend would

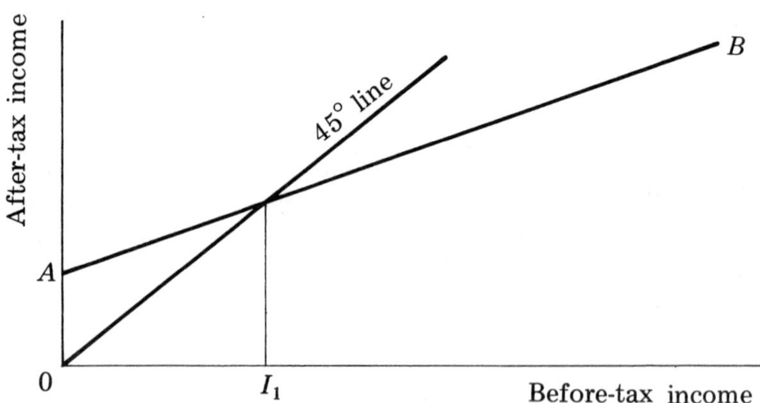

Figure 9A *A Simple Social Dividend Scheme*

exceed tax liability, and above I_1, the reverse would be true. The level of the social dividend is then represented by OA, and the income tax is shown by the line AB. The rate of income tax is shown by the slope of AB.

The advantages of such a scheme are clear. The social security and tax systems would be co-ordinated, with a constant marginal rate of tax. As everyone would receive a payment, the take-up problem would disappear. Individuals would be given the cash to spend on what they wished, and there would also be a potential administrative saving.

The main problem with the scheme is raising sufficient revenue. If the level of the social dividend was to be sufficiently high to enable a family to meet certain minimum needs, the level of income tax would have to be raised considerably. For example, suppose that on average (allowing for differences in family status) the value of the social dividend was set at £60 per week and the proportional income tax at 33.3 per cent. On these assumptions, the break-even point would be a weekly income of £180, leaving vast amounts of revenue to be raised from higher incomes. A more realistic tax rate would be 50 per cent; the break-even point would then be £120. However, such a rate would appear to be politically unacceptable. Even with progressive tax rates, such a scheme provides formidable problems of financing.

A second problem involves the calculation of the social dividend. In practice, the circumstances of low-income families can vary considerably. For example, different families face different housing costs, and many families have dependents with particular disabilities or special needs. It is difficult to see how the size of the social dividend payment in each case can be tailored to such individual circumstances without involving at least some of the administrative complexities and difficulties that are to be found under existing arrangements.

Other Schemes

The difficulties and the very high costs associated with a pure social dividend scheme have led to a number of less radical proposals. One involves higher rates of withdrawal of the subsidy. Another possibility is that much of the existing income tax and social security systems be retained. Many of the proposed schemes incorporate both of these modifications. Both would reduce the amount of revenue required to finance some form of negative income tax.

Schemes proposing higher rates of withdrawal include those by the Institute of Economic Affairs (1970), which proposed a withdrawal rate of 100 per cent, and Clark (1977) who proposed a rate of 70 per cent. Other suggestions have involved rates of $66\frac{2}{3}$ and 50 per cent. Among the schemes which have envisaged only a partial replacement of existing arrangements are the proposals of Tobin, Pechman and Mieszkowski (1967) and the *Proposals for a Tax-Credit System* (1972) put forward by a Conservative government. The main characteristic of the Conservative plans was that income tax allowances would have been replaced by a weekly tax credit. This would have assisted those who did not benefit fully from the personal allowances because they were below the tax threshold. It was intended that the scheme would come into effect by the end of the 1970s, but when the Labour Party was returned to office in 1974 it was shelved. It might be noted, however, that some progress has been made in this direction in as much as child tax allowances have been replaced by payments of child benefit.

One of the main reservations which has been voiced about a negative income tax, especially in the United States, has concerned the possible effects on incentives. Certainly in comparison with a system involving no redistribution of income, the introduction of a negative income tax would be very likely to involve both income and substitution effects which are adverse to work effort. Naturally, these effects would be less serious if the comparison was between a negative income tax and the present arrangements in the UK.

Nevertheless, several experiments have been undertaken in the USA to try to discover the extent of these effects. Summaries of these studies appear in Ferber and Hirsch (1978) and in Brown (1980). It should be pointed out that the findings of these experiments should be treated with some caution. First of all, there is the celebrated 'Hawthorne effect' in which the very act of participating in a social experiment may affect behaviour. Incidentally, this effect refers to a series of experiments in the 1920s when it was observed that productivity increased each time the workers' environmental conditions were changed — even when they were eventually restored to their original state. It appeared that the workers thrived more on attention than on any particular environment! A second problem is that experiments which involve a tiny proportion of the population for a limited time will almost certainly have different results from a nationwide scheme which was considered to be permanent. Even so, these studies have provided a valuable contribution to the issue.

The first study was commissioned in 1967 and took place in urban areas in New Jersey and Pennsylvania. The actual experiment ran for three years. The results are presented in Kershaw and Fair (1976) and Watts and Rees (1977a and 1977b) and further discussion appears in Pechman and Timpane (1975). The analysis by Hall (1975) suggested that the experiment reduced the work of white husbands significantly, and another analysis by Cogan (1978) found more substantial disincentive effects. For blacks, work actually increased (Watts and Rees, 1977a), though Hall suggested that the data for this group was unreliable on account of a high rate of attrition. It should also be pointed out that the experiment took place at the same time as the State of New Jersey improved its system of welfare payments. This must have affected behaviour. In addition there may well have been self-selection bias by the participants in what were anyway small sample sizes.

Another experiment was carried out in two rural areas — in North Carolina and Iowa. Another, in Indiana, concentrated on urban black families, many of whom contained only one adult. Experiments at Seattle and Denver tried to assess the effects of a system in which the rate of tax declined as income rose. Also, in order to capture long-term effects, part of the sample was enrolled for 20 years, the others for 5 or 3 years. The results of these later experiments were similar to many of those of the original New Jersey study. Negative income taxes appear to reduce work effort for most people and, in the case of married women, do so substantially — a result which is compatible with other evidence on taxation and the labour supply presented in Section 4.2.

9.2 An Expenditure Tax

The possibility of a tax based on consumption expenditure rather than on income has already been mentioned, and some of the arguments with respect to saving appear in Section 4.3, and with respect to equity in Section 5.2. However, the possibility of an expenditure tax merits further discussion in its own right, and it was one of the main proposals of the Meade Committee (1978).

The idea of an expenditure tax is not a novelty. Its history can be traced back to Thomas Hobbes and it has been discussed by people such as John Stuart Mill, Alfred Marshall, Irving Fisher and Lord Kaldor. In fact, Kaldor (1955) deals with the arguments for an expenditure tax more fully than does the Meade Report. The implications of an expenditure tax have also been discussed overseas. Professor Sven-Olof Lodin designed an expenditure tax for the Swedish Royal Commission on Taxation and *Blueprints for Basic Tax Reform* (US Treasury, 1977) discussed the tax in the context of the United States.

One of the reasons for introducing an expenditure tax is to have a tax system based on a set of clear principles. In the absence of such a basis, a whole range of anomalies of the sort already discussed will evolve over time. The Meade Committee considered the possibility of moving to a comprehensive income tax defined as a tax on the 'accretion of economic power'. However, the Committee were convinced that 'it would be extremely difficult, if not impossible, to introduce all the features of a comprehensive tax. In particular, we think that many of the measures which would theoretically be necessary to index the system for proper capital-income adjustments against inflation would not be practicable' (p.500). Therefore the Committee favoured a move towards an expenditure basis. They thought this would be feasible provided a system of self-assessment were first introduced for direct taxation.

A further argument concerns saving. The Committee argued that, 'a progressive expenditure tax is a tax which, by exempting savings and investment from tax, gives a maximum opportunity for economic growth and development in a mixed economy' (pp. 5 and 6). As they also pointed out: 'with a progressive income tax a wealthy man with a high marginal rate of income tax of 83 per cent (which was the maximum rate on earned income at the time) will be able to use only £17 out of £100 of profit for the development of his business, whereas with a progressive tax on expenditure he could use all his profit to develop his business' (p. 33). The argument assumes, of course, that more saving will mean more investment which in turn will mean a higher rate of economic growth.

Nevertheless, whether or not the overall level of saving would be affected by a change to an expenditure tax, it has been argued that such a change would radically improve the taxation of different types of saving and investment. The present system, as the Meade Committee showed, is highly arbitrary. The yield on different types of saving is affected by the interaction between income tax, capital gains tax and corporation tax. In addition, the yield is affected by such considerations as whether the investment is made through an incorporated or unincorporated business; the particular tax rules governing the depreciation of different assets; and whether the savings are channelled through loan or equity capital. The combined effects of all these factors mean that the treatment of saving ranges from the generous to the extremely severe. An expenditure tax, it is argued, would avoid such arbitrary effects.

Another major argument is that the proper basis of taxation is the amount an individual takes out of society's pool of resources (in other words the individual's consumption) rather than the amount he puts into it (as represented by his income). A particular aspect of this is consumption out of inherited capital. Such expenditure avoids income tax, but would be caught by an expenditure tax.

The Meade Committee's Proposals

The Committee presented four possible ways by which the principle of an expenditure tax could be operated in practice. The one which found most favour with the Committee would require a taxpayer's consumption expenditure to be calculated in each period as follows:

1. The taxpayer's total realised income would be established.
2. Any capital receipts, such as the proceeds from the sale of capital assets and sums borrowed, would be added on.
3. All expenditure for purposes other than consumption would be deducted. This would include expenditure on capital assets, and sums lent out or repaid.
4. The final figure would be the amount spent on consumption. The main advantage of this method over others is that, by providing a figure for each taxpayer's total consumption, it would permit an expenditure tax to be levied at a series of progressive rates.

The second method of taxing spending rather than saving would be a tax on value added. The third would be an income tax which exempted investment expenditure with a system of 100 per cent capital allowances, and the final method, again an income tax, would exempt investment income from tax.

After considering these various possibilities, the Committee came down firmly behind two particular forms of expenditure tax. The first was a 'universal expenditure tax' (UET) which would be based entirely on the first method described above. The second was a two-tier expenditure tax (TTET). The lower tier would consist of a single basic rate levied through a value added tax. The upper tier would be a restricted version of the UET and would allow tax to be levied at higher rates on taxpayers with higher levels of expenditure. It would work in a similar way to the pre-1973 income tax system, whereby most taxpayers were subject to tax at the standard rate, and more prosperous individuals to surtax as well. Indeed, it would also resemble the present income tax with its long basic rate band. A TTET could be introduced more gradually than a UET, and could also provide a transitional stage in a move to a fully-fledged UET.

The Limitations of the Arguments

There are several limitations to the arguments in favour of an expenditure tax. First, there does not appear to be a strong relationship between the level of saving and the return to saving. Therefore, although an expenditure tax would increase the return to saving, this would not necessarily increase the level of saving substantially.

Second, even if the relationship were a strong one, there is still no close link between an increase in saving and an increase in economic growth. An increase in the amount that people wish to save does not necessarily lead to an increase in the amount that people wish to invest. On the contrary, as Keynes demonstrated convincingly, it is quite possible that saving, if carried to excess, could lead to a lack of aggregate demand and to economic recession.

A third limitation is that an expenditure tax may have adverse effects on work incentives. It is likely that an expenditure tax would have to be levied at higher rates than an equivalent income tax, since savings would be treated more favourably for tax purposes. It is not certain whether higher rates of tax would increase or decrease the incentives to work. However, if people are mainly concerned with immediate consumption rather than saving, it is possible (but not certain) that an expenditure tax may discourage work effort. If it did, and incomes fell, then the absolute level of savings might also fall, even if the proportion of income saved rose.

A fourth factor is uncertainty. The rates of income tax on income currently received are fairly easy to establish. With an expenditure tax, things are more complicated. It is true that an expenditure tax allows a greater yield to savings. However, taxpayers cannot know what the rates of tax will be when the amounts saved come to be spent.

A fifth limitation is that an expenditure tax does not necessarily treat spending and saving equally. Wealth confers benefits on its owners over and above any pecuniary yield, these benefits taking the form of security, independence, influence and so on (see Section 10.5). Therefore a person who saves might be considered to have a greater taxable capacity than a similar person of equal income who does not save. An expenditure tax on its own would not cover such additional taxable capacity.

Sixth, if one takes a taxpayer's life cycle as a whole, the expenditure tax would be more likely to impose hardship than an income tax. The expenditure tax would weigh more heavily in those years when a family's financial commitments were high relative to its income. This is likely to be the case with young families and for those living off their savings in retirement.

Practical Considerations

One of the main arguments for an expenditure tax is that it is designed from basic principles. It may therefore be preferable to introduce such a new tax than to continue to patch up the existing tax system in an *ad hoc* manner. It is true that many of the existing defects and anomalies have been generated by departures from a well-defined set of underlying principles. Nevertheless, there must be some concern that a new tax, however well-designed, may not survive the transition from the fiscal drawing board into practice in a recognisable form. Many of the anomalies of the present system have arisen as a result of pressure from special interest groups. There is no guarantee that such pressure would not also mutilate any future expenditure tax. It might even eventually become as complex and unco-ordinated as the present system. Perhaps someone might then suggest another radical reform with the introduction of a simple income tax!

Some idea of the possible complexity of an expenditure tax in practice can be gained from looking at attempts to introduce such a tax in the past. Plans for a personal and progressive 'spendings' tax were submitted by the United States Treasury to the Senate Finance Committee in 1942. The proposed tax had the twin aims of controlling inflation by taxing private spending and providing funds for war finance. The tax was to have been administered within the existing arrangements for income tax, but nevertheless was rejected by Congress largely because of the novelty and complexity of the proposals. In what seems to have been a typical reaction at the time, Senator Harry Byrd described the proposed tax as, 'the most complicated and unworkable plan' the US Treasury had submitted in nine years (Paul, 1954).

In India, following a report to the Indian government by Kaldor (1956), an expenditure tax was introduced in 1958. Although the Indian government had accepted Kaldor's proposals in principle, the tax as enacted differed substantially from the original proposals. Certainly it could not be described as a simple tax, and its repeal in 1962 was apparently 'welcomed in all quarters' (Khanna, 1964). However, 'the joy was short-lived' when the tax was reintroduced in 1964. The revived expenditure tax also proved to be short-lived, and was repealed once more in 1966. Although the Finance Minister at the time felt that 'on purely economic grounds, it would be a very sound principle to replace the income tax increasingly with a tax on expenditure', he went on to say, 'given ... the administrative difficulties and inconvenience to assessees involved in the assessment of expenditure, it is, however, not possible to attempt this substitution on any significant scale at the present stage' (*Bulletin for International Fiscal Documentation,* 1966, p. 201).

In Ceylon (now Sri Lanka) an expenditure tax was introduced in 1959, also following proposals made by Kaldor to the government. The tax was repealed in 1963, though it was reintroduced on a limited basis in 1976 and then withdrawn once more. Taking these three experiences together, therefore, it can be seen that previous attempts to introduce an expenditure tax have not been showered with success.

The introduction of an expenditure tax in the United Kingdom would also raise many practical administrative problems. First of all, there would be the transitional problems associated with any major change of the tax system — especially in relation to the re-education of taxpayers, tax advisers and tax administrators. Moreover, with a switch from an income to an expenditure tax base, existing savings require special consideration. When savings have been accumulated under an income tax regime, it is hardly fair to penalise them when they come to be spent under an expenditure tax regime. Like many other similar problems, it could be overcome, but only at the cost of greater administrative complexity and expense. A similar problem arises with emigration. Unless there were special provisions, individuals would be able to save under a favourable expenditure tax in the United Kingdom, and then emigrate to a country with an income tax system to dis-save. One possible answer might be some sophisticated form of emigration tax, but it is hard to see any satisfactory solution to this problem.

Finally, there are other ways of achieving the effects associated with an expenditure tax, which are based on the existing income tax system. We have already pointed out that an income tax that exempts investment income gives a similar result — though such an exemption may be unacceptable politically. Another possibility suggested by the Meade Committee (1978, Chapter 8) is an income tax with 100 per cent capital allowances (explained in Section 13.2) against investment expenditure.

This list of limitations and difficulties suggests, therefore, that the case for an expenditure tax is not as strong as might appear at first sight. We now turn to the potential for a greater degree of self-assessment for direct taxation. Although this topic is highly relevant to any proposals for an expenditure tax, it will be discussed here in the context of income tax.

9.3 Self-Assessment

The basic principle underlying self-assessment is that the taxpayer rather than the tax authorities is primarily responsible for calculating tax liability and ensuring that payment is made promptly. The principle forms an essential part of many overseas tax systems, and elements of self-assessment can be found in the United Kingdom in the administration of value added tax and capital transfer tax (Barr *et al.*, 1977, pp. 52, 53). In addition, a large element of self-assessment was contained in the wealth tax proposals of a former Labour government (*Wealth Tax*, 1974). These generated a great deal of controversy, both before the Select Committee on a Wealth Tax (1975) and elsewhere, but the suggestion that the wealth tax should be self-assessed was not seriously disputed. There are, however, virtually no elements of self-assessment in the administration of the British income tax.

To bring out the contrast between British and overseas systems, it is useful to list the four stages in the calculation of tax liability. They are in turn:

1. The calculation of total income.
2. The calculation of total tax-free income, that is the sum of the allowances and expenses to which the taxpayer is entitled.
3. The calculation of total taxable income by subtracting 2 from 1.
4. The calculation of tax due.

In many foreign tax systems (but not in the UK), the first three stages are the responsibility of the taxpayer. The fourth stage can be performed by either the taxpayer or the revenue service. The role of the tax authorities is to ensure that tax is withheld from certain sources of income, to provide assistance to taxpayers where necessary, and to check the returns prepared by taxpayers.

Tax is normally withheld at source from wages and salaries, and there are usually special provisions relating to other sorts of income. For example, in many countries, provisional or estimated tax payments are required on non-employment income during the year in which the income is received. The number of such payments during the year varies from country to country. For instance, instalments are required six times a year in Sweden; four times a year in Australia, Canada and the United States; twice a year in Japan, New Zealand and South Africa.

These current payments of tax are usually based on the income received in the preceding year. However, if a person's income changes substantially during the current year, particularly if his income falls, the provisional payments of tax can be based on a revised estimate of liability made by the taxpayer himself.

The Operation of Self-Assessment

It may be helpful to present a stylised sketch showing how self-assessment operates in several countries overseas. Needless to say, the details of the operation vary considerably from one country to another.

Each year, every taxpayer had to complete a return by a specified date after the end of the tax year. For many taxpayers, particularly employees, the returns can be very simple. For example, the United States form 1040EZ (get it?) is much simpler in terms of layout, number of questions and instructions than its nearest British equivalent — the form P1.

Considerable efforts are made by the revenue services to assist taxpayers. Instructions and advice appear on television, the radio and in the press. This is helped by the fact that taxpayers are accustomed to completing a return every year (unlike most British taxpayers). In addition, because everyone has to complete their returns at the same time, the publicity can be concentrated in the appropriate period.

In the return, the taxpayer must calculate his final tax liability for the year. If his liability exceeds the amount of tax that has already been withheld or otherwise paid, he should enclose a cheque for the difference with his return. If, on the other hand, he is owed tax, a rebate is paid as soon as possible after the return is submitted.

When the returns are received by the tax authorities, they are subject to a check for arithmetical errors. A small proportion is selected for a more thorough audit. For example, in the United States and Canada, only between two and five per cent of returns are intensively investigated. To increase the chances of unearthing evasion, the returns are selected according to the potential for inaccuracy. For example, in Canada, a return from a taxpayer with a very low income which is all from employment has much less chance of being thoroughly audited than a return from a self-employed person with a high income.

The withholding of tax from wages and salaries is undertaken by employers on a non-cumulative basis. As we saw in Section 8.4, a non-cumulative system will tend to withhold too much tax if the employee's income or allowances change during the tax year. Nevertheless, withholding too much tax provides a substantial incentive for taxpayers to complete their returns promptly and accurately in order to speed up their rebates. In addition, surprising though it may seem, it appears that in those countries where it happens (such as the United States and Australia) over-withholding is widely popular. For example, many taxpayers in the United States take steps to ensure that too much tax is withheld (Barr *et al.*, 1977, p. 61). Presumably they find it a convenient method of saving.

It is therefore clear that there is a considerable contrast between a system of self-assessment and the British system. A more specific comparison between countries appears in Table 9A.

The Potential for Reform

There are several reasons why the reform of the British system should be considered seriously. None of these reasons is sufficient on its own to demonstrate that change is either necessary or

Table 9A Features of Self-Assessment in Different Countries

Feature	*Australia*		*New Zealand*		*Canada*		*Sweden*		*US*		*UK*	
	a	b	a	b	a	b	a	b	a	b	a	b
1	√	√	√	√	√	√	√	√	√	√	×	×
2	√	√	√	√	√	√	√	√	√	√	×	×
3	Optional		√	√	√	√	×	×	√	√	×	×
4	×	×	×	×	√	√	×	×	√	√	×	×
5	NA	√	NA	√	NA	√	NA	√	NA	√	NA	×
6	√	√	√	√	√	√	√	√	√	√	√	×
7	√	√	√	√	√	√	√	√	√	√	×	×

Key: a Income from employment
b Other income

Features: 1 Taxpayer works out his gross income.
2 Taxpayer calculates his tax-free income.
3 Taxpayer calculates the tax payable.
4 Taxpayer sends cheque for tax due, together with his return soon after the end of the tax year.
5 Taxpayer should change his current tax payments if his income changes significantly.
6 Tax is paid on a current basis (at least approximately).
7 Returns are subject to sample checking.

NA: Not Applicable √: Yes ×: No

Note: This table presents only a rough summary: there are many detailed differences between countries.

desirable, but together they suggest that there may well be considerable scope for reform.

The first reason concerns the costs of administering the present UK system; these are very high by both international and historical standards. Detailed comparisons between countries are difficult because of the different administrative arrangements in each country; nevertheless the Inland Revenue in a memorandum dated 17 May 1976 to the Expenditure Committee (Session 1975/76, HC 368—iv) gave the following estimates of overseas costs of collection as percentages of receipts:

	Per cent
USA	0.49
Canada	0.80
Australia	1.00
Sweden	1.00
Republic of Ireland	1.94

The figure for Inland Revenue duties in 1974–75 was 1.75 per cent, a figure considerably higher than all the above countries except Ireland.

The second reason for considering reform is that the British methods of administration are so different from the methods employed abroad. One of the main examples of this is that, apart from Ireland, the cumulative system is found only in the United Kingdom. This may partly explain why administrative costs are very similar in Britain and Ireland, but very much higher than in many other countries. There may also be other reasons why foreign countries have not adopted cumulative withholding, as mentioned below.

Third, the present system of cumulative withholding was introduced during the emergency conditions of the Second World War. While an old system is not necessarily an obsolete system, PAYE should perhaps be re-examined lest the major reason for its retention be inertia.

The Advantages of Self-Assessment

The case for self-assessment is based in the following three areas: savings in the costs of administration, greater flexibility in the tax structure, and greater taxpayer understanding of the tax system.

The potential scope for reducing the costs of public administration is illustrated by the contrast between revenue staffing in the United Kingdom and in other countries. Such contrasts should be qualified because different revenue services have different responsibilities. Nevertheless, it may be noted that approximately the same number of staff are employed by the Inland Revenue as are employed by the Internal Revenue Service in the United States, even though the latter deals with four times as many returns.

The main public sector economies that would arise from the introduction of self-assessment in the United Kingdom would be associated with changes to PAYE. Because each taxpayer would assess his own liability, the constraint of having to avoid many assessments and end-of-year adjustments would disappear. So too, therefore, would the main reason for cumulation.

The disadvantages of cumulation have already been discussed in Section 8.4. The main problems are that it is both an expensive and difficult system to operate accurately. The Inland Revenue itself has made a rather interesting comment on the situation. It suggested that 'it is not entirely light-hearted to compare the PAYE system to a vintage Rolls Royce which the Revenue laboriously if not lovingly maintains' (Inland Revenue, 1978, p. 280). It might, of course, be the case that society would prefer a more economical administrative vehicle. Some savings should be made as computerisation proceeds, but without self-assessment a great deal of work would remain with the Inland Revenue.

A further point which may be raised in this context concerns the future possibility of a local income tax. The Inland Revenue, in its evidence to the Layfield enquiry into *Local Government Finance* (1976), stated that the administration of a tax such as that outlined by the Layfield Committee would necessitate the employment of an additional 12,000 staff. This could well be true if a local income tax were to be grafted onto the existing system. However, it would be unlikely to be the case if self-assessment were introduced. As the taxes operating in Canada, Sweden and the United States show, provided the national income tax is self-assessed, the administration of a local income tax does not impose a large additional burden on either the authorities or the taxpayers.

The second area to benefit from self-assessment would be the flexibility of the tax structure. For example, the need to have a long basic rate band to avoid end-of-year adjustments would disappear. So too, would many of the current problems associated with the taxation of 'short-term' National Insurance benefits.

Finally, under self-assessment, the tax system would have to be designed and operated so that the average taxpayer could understand it. This in itself might lead to a number of economic benefits, such as a possible reduction in both administrative and compliance costs. Moreover, because taxpayers would be more involved with the assessment process, changes to the tax system might well attract greater public attention. This might result in taxpayers exercising greater influence over the ways in which they are taxed. It might also provide a constraint on the apparent propensity of the administration to complicate the system.

Arguments Against Self-Assessment

There are also several arguments which have been used or might be used against the introduction of self-assessment in the United Kingdom. The first is that self-assessment would impose costs of its own. There would be the cost of changing over to a new system. Some of the savings of public sector expenditure might be replaced by an increase in compliance costs. Also, the increase in the number of returns and end-of-year adjustments, plus the problems associated with a peak load of activity when the returns were completed, would also impose costs on the public sector. This argument is not altogether convincing. We have already seen how public sector costs tend to be lower in countries where taxpayers assess themselves. There is also some evidence to suppose that compliance costs may be higher in the United Kingdom than, for example, in the United States (Barr *et al.,* 1977, p. 151).

A second argument, or rather assertion, against self-assessment is that it would be associated with a higher level of evasion. There is no reliable evidence to support this. Indeed, because returns are not sent to every taxpayer each year at present, there must be a much greater temptation not to disclose casual and other receipts in the United Kingdom than in other countries.

The third argument is that self-assessment would lead to a system of 'rough justice'. In other words, it might be suggested that self-assessment could lead to a greater variance of tax actually paid by taxpayers in identical circumstances. There are a number of responses to this argument. One is that the lack of a universal annual return may mean not only that some forms of income remain hidden, but that some taxpayers remain unaware of allowances to which they are entitled. A second response is that it ignores the present costs incurred in reducing 'rough justice', even supposing that it can be reduced by operating an expensive and complicated tax system. It may be that a complex tax system, even if designed to be equitable, benefits only those who have the ability or the resources to take advantage of its complications.

Further Reading

For suggested reforms to the tax system, the best place to start is probably the Report of the Meade Committee (1978). The arguments for and against an expenditure tax are discussed in Pechman (1980) and the introduction of a system of self-assessment into the United Kingdom is examined in Barr, James and Prest (1977).

References

Barr N.A., James S.R. and Prest A.R. (1977), *Self-Assessment for Income Tax*, Heinemann Educational Books.

Brown C.V. (1980), *Taxation and the Incentive to Work*, Oxford University Press.

Clark C. (1977), *Poverty Before Politics*, Institute of Economic Affairs, Hobart Paper No. 73.

Cogan J. (1978), *Negative Income Taxation and Labour Supply: New Evidence from the New Jersey-Pennsylvania Experiment*, Santa Monica, Rand Corporation.

Ferber R. and Hirsch W.Z. (1978), 'Social experimentation and economic policy: a survey', *Journal of Economic Literature*, Vol. XVI, pp. 1379—1414.

Hall R.E. (1975), 'Effects of the experimental negative income tax on labour supply', in J.A. Pechman and P.M. Timpane (eds), *Work Incentives and Income Guarantees: The New Jersey Income Tax Experiment*, Brookings Institution.

Inland Revenue (1978), *120th Report* (for the year ended 31 March 1977), Cmnd. 7092, HMSO.

Institute of Economic Affairs (1970), *Policy for Poverty.*

Kaldor N. (1955), *An Expenditure Tax*, Allen and Unwin.

Kaldor N. (1956), *Indian Tax Reform*, Ministry of Finance, Government of India.

Kershaw D. and Fair J. (1976), *The New Jersey Income-Maintenance Experiment*, Volume 1, *Operations, Surveys and Administration*, Academic Press.

Khanna K.C. (1964), 'An expenditure tax in India', *Bulletin for International Fiscal Documentation*, p. 361.

Local Government Finance (1976), Report of the Committee of Enquiry, Chairman F. Layfield, Cmnd.6453, HMSO.

Meade Committee (1978), *The Structure and Reform of Direct Taxation*, Institute for Fiscal Studies.

Ministry of Pensions and National Insurance (1966), *Financial and Other Circumstances of Retirement Pensioners*, HMSO.

Paul R.E. (1954), *Taxation in the United States*, Little Brown, p. 312.

Pechman J.A. (1980), *What Should be Taxed: Income or Expenditure?*, Brookings Institution.

Pechman J.A. and Timpane P.M. (eds) (1975), *Work Incentives and Income Guarantees: The New Jersey Negative Income Tax Experiment*, Brookings Institution.

Proposals for a Tax-Credit System (1972), Cmnd. 5116, HMSO.

Select Committee on Tax-Credit (1973) *Volume I*, HC 341-I, HMSO.

Select Committee on a Wealth Tax (1975), *Volume I,* HC 696-I, HMSO.

Tobin J., Pechman J.A. and Mieszkowski P. (1967), 'Is a negative income tax practical?' *Yale Law Journal*, Vol. 77, No. 1, pp. 1—27.

US Treasury (1977), *Blueprints for Basic Tax Reform*, Washington DC.

Watts H.W. and Rees A. (eds) (1977a), *The New Jersey Income-Maintenance Experiment*, Volume II, *Labour Supply Responses,* Academic Press.

Watts, H.W. and Rees A. (1977b), *The New Jersey Income-Maintenance Experiment*, Volume III, *Expenditures, Health and Social Behaviour; and the Quality of the Evidence*, Academic Press.

Wealth Tax (1974), Cmnd 5704, HMSO.

10

The Taxation of Wealth

'Wealth is not without its advantages, and the case to the contrary, although it has often been made, has never proved widely persuasive' (Galbraith, 1962, p. 13). It is the taxation of these advantages with which we are concerned in this chapter. Initially we shall examine the definition of wealth and its distribution in the United Kingdom. Then we shall look at some historical attempts to tax items of wealth and at the operation of the modern capital transfer tax. We discuss the pros and cons of net wealth taxes and consider the wealth taxes currently in operation overseas. Finally, we shall examine some of the proposals for introducing a wealth tax in the United Kingdom.

10.1 The Definition and Distribution of Wealth

When considering the taxation of wealth, the first task clearly is to define what is meant by wealth, and then to attempt to discover how that wealth is spread throughout the community.

Definition of Wealth

Wealth, like income, represents the command a person has over economic resources. The difference between wealth and income is that wealth represents a *stock* of resources at any one point in time, whereas income is a *flow* of resources over time. For example, a person may own a government bond worth £100 which yields £10 per year. The £100 is clearly part of the person's wealth, while the £10 may be considered part of his income.

In practice, of course, deciding which assets to include in a person's wealth is a more complex problem. So too is deciding how much various assets are worth. Some assets, like the government bond mentioned above, have unambiguous market prices, but many other assets do not. As we are concerned here with personal wealth, perhaps the best way to examine these difficulties is to look at the wealth of a specimen household.

The most valuable asset that many people possess is their house. The value of a house is relatively easy to ascertain as reasonable estimates can be made on the basis of prices paid for similar houses in the same area. However, the total value of the house can be included as a net asset only if the person owns it outright. If the house is mortgaged to a building society, then clearly a liability is also involved. Only the net worth of the house, that is the value of the house less the mortgage, should be counted. For illustrative purposes, the list of the specimen household's assets in Table 10A includes a gross figure of £30,000 for a house, minus a liability of £18,000 which represents a debt to a building society.

Similarly, the contents of the home and any other personal belongings such as jewellery should be counted as wealth. If the family has a car, then it ought to be included as well. Any loans incurred to buy these items, whether from a hire purchase company, a bank, or an individual, should be deducted. Financial claims against other people or institutions, such as deposits in a bank or building society, must be treated as assets.

Presenting rather more difficulty are those items which are not immediately recognisable as wealth, such as life assurance policies and pension rights. Clearly, they represent command over economic resources as both life assurance policies and pensions are bought and sold for capital sums. As might be expected, there are considerable difficulties in valuing assets such as pension rights, and

Table 10A The Net Wealth of a Specimen Household

	£		
Assets			
House	30,000		
Furniture and other contents	4,000		
Car	2,400		
Pension rights	2,000		
Life assurance policy	1,000		
Building society deposit	500		
Cash	100		
		40,000	
Liabilities			
Mortgage	−18,000		
Bank overdraft	−800		
HP loan	−1,200		
		−20,000	
Net wealth			£20,000

some of these problems are discussed in Section 10.6. However, there is no reason in principle why these items should not be included as wealth, and illustrative figures have been included in Table 10A. In fact, the argument can be carried further to include National Insurance pension rights, and even rights to sickness and unemployment benefit.

The wealth tied up in human beings, 'human capital', might also be mentioned at this stage. It is possible to invest in human beings, for example, by teaching them new skills, just as it is possible to invest in industry. Industrial investment yields a return and so does investment in human capital, though in the latter case it may be a non-pecuniary return. The topic is discussed in more detail by Schultz (1961). Including human capital as wealth raises some fairly obvious difficulties. It is therefore excluded from this example, but will be discussed further in Section 10.5.

To complete the list of assets of the specimen household, any deposits in financial institutions such as building societies must be included, and any cash. Similarly, any further debts must be included with liabilities. The difference between the two is the net wealth of the household, and this is the figure that would be relevant for a wealth tax. Although the figures in Table 10A ignore the problems of valuation and are only for illustration, they do show that quite ordinary households have ‘wealth’ by the definition used here. We can now go on to see how wealth is distributed in the wider community.

The Distribution of Wealth in Britain

There are a number of ways by which the distribution of wealth in Britain may be measured. One method would be to derive estimates based on a sample survey of wealth holding. A second method would involve the use of figures collected by the Inland Revenue for investment income. Yet a third is to begin with the Revenue figures for the estates of deceased individuals. Each of these methods has its drawbacks. A sample survey, for example, would encounter difficulties in obtaining an accurate and unbiased response. Two particular problems are the valuation of non-marketable assets, and the estimation of the wealth of individuals who are not covered by the Inland Revenue’s statistics. These issues are dealt with in more detail by Atkinson (1975, Chapter 7).

The figures used in Table 10B are those provided by the Inland Revenue (1981) and are based on information about the estates of deceased persons. Column 1 covers marketable wealth only. Column 2 includes an estimate of the value of occupational pensions, and column 3 also adds in a value for state pension rights.

We can see at once from Table 10B that the figures of the distribution of wealth depend largely on what is included as wealth. If the definition of wealth is confined to marketable assets (column 1) 24 per cent of personal wealth was owned by the top one per cent of the adult population in 1979; 45 per cent was in the hands of the top five per cent of the population, and 59 per cent was owned by the top ten per cent.

If, however, the definition of wealth is widened to include certain non-marketable assets, the picture changes. The figures provided by the Inland Revenue are confined to the value of pension rights,

Table 10B The Distribution of Personal Wealth in the UK in 1979

	Column 1 *Marketable Wealth*	*Column 2* *Wealth including occupational pension rights*	*Column 3* *Wealth including occupational and state pension rights*
Top 1 per cent of adults	24	20	13
Top 2 per cent of adults	32	26	18
Top 5 per cent of adults	45	38	27
Top 10 per cent of adults	59	51	37
Top 25 per cent of adults	82	75–79	58–61
Top 50 per cent of adults	95	89–93	79–83

Source: *Inland Revenue Statistics* (1981), p. 60.

partly because pension rights are one of the most valuable non-marketable assets an individual possesses, and partly because of the difficulty involved in obtaining reliable values for other assets. The result of including figures for pensions is to make the distribution of wealth look more equitable. If occupational pension rights are included then, for example, the share of the top five per cent of the adult population of personal wealth falls from 45 per cent to 38 per cent. If the value of rights to state pensions is included as well, the share of the top five per cent falls to 27 per cent of wealth. Unless more reliable figures become available, we can only speculate on what the distribution of wealth would look like if estimates of the value of other non-marketable assets were to be included.

10.2 Historical Aspects of Capital Taxation

Taxes on items of wealth have a long history. The earliest forms consisted of the straightforward requisitioning of men and materials when needed. More formal arrangements were introduced in ancient Rome in the form of a tax known as the *tributum* which was levied when necessary. The assessment of this tax was undertaken by a local magistrate who kept a register known as the *census* which recorded the property of each citizen. The rates at which the tax was levied varied between 0.1 and 0.3 per cent of an individual's property, though the normal rate was 0.1 per cent (i.e. one-thousandth part). The *tributum* was abolished in 167 BC when the spoils of war made it no longer necessary to raise large sums from Roman citizens.

However, a five per cent inheritance tax was introduced in Rome in AD 6 on the estates of deceased persons and on legacies, but it was levied only on Roman citizens. The extension of Roman citizenship to all the inhabitants of the Empire by Caracalla (AD 198–217) may well have been influenced by an early desire to expand the inheritance tax base. The Emperor and the poor were exempt from the tax. So too were near relatives on the grounds that an inheritance tax is likely to be more of a burden for closer heirs than for more distant beneficiaries. In fact, this last exemption did not lead to as much avoidance as one might at first suppose, as a result of the Roman habit of leaving property to friends rather than to children. Deductions were allowed for the costs of the funeral and a single monument — provided it was not too expensive!

A problem that faced the old estate duty in the United Kingdom and still to some extent faces its successor, capital transfer tax, is the potential delay in tax collection as a result of a contested will. In Roman days the problem was overcome by Emperor Hadrian who directed that the heir be put in immediate possession of the property, provided the will appeared valid. So long as the tax was paid, any arguments over the remaining spoils could then continue.

Various other taxes on types of property have existed from time to time. In Britain in the thirteenth century, a tax system of fifteenths and tenths developed, which was imposed on moveable goods. An individual was taxed on moveables such as coin, plate, household goods and debts owed to him (less debts owed by him), though there were some exemptions for certain personal goods such as clothes and armour. The tax was not levied on a regular basis, but only in times of particular financial need.

In more recent times, taxes on capital have slowly become more systematic and widespread. In several European countries, for example, annual wealth taxes have been established for more than half a century. For instance, a wealth tax was introduced in the Netherlands in 1892, in Denmark in 1904, in Sweden in 1910 and in Norway in 1911. A wealth tax was also introduced in Germany in

1922, though this was based on an earlier Prussian tax of 1893. A wealth tax was introduced in Ireland in 1975, though it has since been abolished. More recently a net wealth tax on 'large properties' (*impôt sur les grandes fortunes*) came into force in France in 1982.

In the United Kingdom the two approaches to capital taxation in the twentieth century up to 1975 have been to tax wealth at death and to tax the income from wealth (that is investment income) at a higher rate than income from employment. It was proposed as early as 1803 to incorporate an element of tax relief for earned incomes of less than £150 per year, the main argument for such a relief being that incomes from employment are less reliable and, since they have to be earned by personal effort, involve more 'pain' than incomes from investment. In fact, such a relief was not introduced in the United Kingdom until 1907. It is interesting to note that this was during the same period that a number of European countries were introducing taxes on wealth itself, rather than discriminating against the income from wealth.

Although the evidence suggests that the first death duties were levied in Egypt in the second century BC, they do not appear to have been used in Britain until the introduction of Probate Duty in 1694. The modern estate duty was enacted in 1894. It was introduced partially to pay for an expanding navy, and partially to reform the taxation of the existing death duties which numbered five by 1894. The Chancellor at that time, Sir William Harcourt, particularly felt it to be correct that the state should have the first claim on the estate of a deceased person. However, estate duty was abolished entirely for deaths occurring on or after 13 March 1975, and replaced by capital transfer tax.

At first sight, a tax such as estate duty would appear to be difficult to avoid. It is hard to imagine avoidance along the lines described by Will Rogers (1962) that 'you won't catch those old boys dying so promiscuously like they did'! However, in practice, estate duty was thought to have a number of limitations. It is not clear that it contributed in any major way to the redistribution of wealth. More specifically, it appeared to be easy to avoid by the transfer of wealth at least seven years before death; by investment in assets which were subject to low rates of duty (agricultural land and private business assets); by the manipulation of legal trusts; or by emigration (e.g. see Atkinson, 1974, Chapter 7). Although the tax never formed a very large part of total revenue, its yield rose to a maximum of

£458.6 million or three per cent of total tax revenue in 1972–73 (Inland Revenue, 1977). Presumably some taxpayers were over-optimistic about the timing of their demise, or disliked or mistrusted their relatives even more than they disliked or mistrusted the government!

To reform the taxation of wealth, the government of the time, in a White Paper of August 1974, proposed the introduction of capital transfer tax to tax property passing in life as well as at death. In the same month, it produced a Green Paper containing plans for an annual tax on personal net worth. The wealth tax proposals have not been put into effect, but capital transfer tax was introduced by the Finance Act 1975.

10.3 Capital Transfer Tax

The main justification for the introduction of capital transfer tax was to reduce the avoidance associated with estate duty, and to tax *all* transfers of wealth and not just those occurring at, or shortly before, death. Originally, therefore, it was chargeable on the capital values of transfers of property made either during a person's lifetime or at death. The tax was levied on the cumulative total of all gifts made, with the final stage including property passing at death. However, in 1981, the period of cumulation was limited to 10 years. When a person makes a taxable transfer, it is added to all chargeable transfers made in the previous 10 years, but any made before that are not counted.

The rates of tax are progressive, and those applying to transfers made after 5 April 1983 are shown in Table 10C. The lower rate scale normally applies to transfers made during life, but if an individual dies within three years of making a taxable transfer, an additional charge is levied to bring liability up to the scale applicable on death. In the 1982 Finance Act, provision was made for both scales to be indexed to rises in the retail price level. For the purposes of capital transfer tax, assets are normally assessed at their open market value at the time of the transfer.

The tax may be paid by either the donor or the recipient. If the donor pays, the assessment is on the value of the transfer 'grossed up' to include the tax. If the recipient pays, the tax is not included in the assessment. For example, suppose a rich uncle faced a tax rate of

Table 10C The Rates of Capital Transfer Tax from 5 April 1983

Slice of chargeable transfers	*Lifetime tranfers*	*Transfers on death (or within 3 years before death)*
£'000s	%	%
0– 58	0	0
58– 80	15	30
80– 106	17½	35
106– 138	20	40
138– 174	22½	45
174– 211	25	50
211– 264	30	55
264– 686	35	60
686–1,318	40	65
1,318–2,636	45	70
Over 2,636	50	75

20 per cent and wished to give his lucky nephew something valued at £10,000. If the uncle paid the tax, the bill would be £2,500 (i.e. 20% of £10,000 plus 20% of £2,500). If the nephew paid the tax it would be £2,000 (i.e. 20% of £10,000). If the transfer were cash, the uncle could keep £2,000 to pay the tax and give his nephew the net £8,000. If the uncle wished his nephew to end up with £10,000 net, either of them could pay the £2,500 tax due, (i.e. if the uncle paid, the actual transfer would be £10,000, and if the nephew paid it would be £12,500). Whatever happens, the rate of tax is that of the donor and not the donee.

There are several exemptions for transfers made during life. In 1983–84 a person may transfer up to £3,000 per year and if any of this allowance is unused, the balance may be carried forward for one year only. Small outright gifts of up to £250 per year per person are exempt. So too are transfers which may be regarded as 'normal expenditure out of income'. For this to apply, there has to be a degree of regularity about the transfer, and the taxpayer has to be left with sufficient income to maintain his normal standard of living. Also allowed are gifts made in consideration of marriage — up to £5,000 from a parent, £2,500 from a grandparent or great grandparent, and £1,000 from anyone else.

In addition, there are exemptions which apply if the transfer is made either during life or at death. One of these is transfers between husband and wife. As an aside, it might be mentioned that this exemption has led to some speculation that wealth could pass between generations and avoid tax if the surviving spouse of the older generation married the future partner of an heir. This leads to further speculation on the numbers of elderly gentlemen (and presumably gentlewomen) either expiring with shock, or perking up, to live to ancient age at the prospect! Other exemptions include gifts to charities and political parties, though in both cases there are limits if the transfers are made within a year before death, or at death. Also allowed are gifts for national purposes made to organisations such as the National Trust, universities and certain museums and art galleries.

Furthermore, there are various reliefs for certain other transfers. One is the relief for business property. This is given at a rate of 50 per cent for transfers of the whole or part of a business. There is also relief for agricultural property and for woodlands. Finally, there is a quick succession relief which reduces any tax payable when a person dies within five years of receiving a transfer on which tax has already been paid. For individuals domiciled in the United Kingdom, capital transfer tax covers all their property whether situated at home or abroad. For other people, only property within the United Kingdom is included.

The tax on a transfer made during life is due at the end of the sixth month after the transfer or, if the transfer is made between 5 April and 1 October in any year, on 30 April in the following year. Normally the tax on transfers made at death becomes due at the end of the sixth month following death. Overdue tax, arising from transfers made either in life or at death, is subject to an interest charge. Some examples of the calculation of CTT are shown in the *Workbook*.

Despite various myths about the burden of 'death duties', capital transfer tax is not onerous. Although the *marginal* rates rise to 75 per cent, this is for estates valued in excess of £2.5 million and does not take account of the extensive exemptions and reliefs and the 10 year limit to cumulation. Sutherland (1981) pointed out that 'even without sophisticated tax avoidance, over 99 per cent of wealth owners will now be able to pay zero CTT when they hand on their assets. The burden to be borne by most of the remaining one per cent has also been greatly reduced.' He went on to conclude that 'CTT has become, as estate duty was, a voluntary tax'!

10.4 An Accessions Tax

Although capital transfer tax is a more comprehensive tax on gifts and inheritances than its predecessor, estate duty, it still has some disadvantages in terms of equity. The main reason for this is that capital transfer tax retains the old estate duty principle of basing tax liability on the amount given rather than the amount received. This apparently innocent feature conflicts with the principle of horizontal equity and provides no incentive for inherited wealth to be distributed more evenly.

The principle of horizontal equity is that people of a similar taxable capacity should be taxed similarly. This does not happen with a progressive donor-based capital transfer tax. Consider two individuals with the same financial circumstances who each receive an inheritance of the same gross amount but from different benefactors. On grounds of equity, each inheritance should be equally taxed. However, with the present capital transfer tax, liability in each case will depend on the cumulative amount each of the *donors* has transferred, rather than on the circumstances of the recipient.

For the same reason, capital transfer tax provides no incentive for a more even distribution of inherited wealth. Consider a rich person who is faced with a choice of leaving his money either to distant relation A, who has already inherited a large amount, or to distant relation B, who has so far inherited nothing. The amount of tax payable would be the same whether the money went to A or B, simply because the assessment is based on the amount given rather than the amount received.

Contrast these two situations with those occurring when there is a tax based on the amount *received*—an 'accessions tax'. With such a tax, liability would be based on the cumulative amount of gifts or inheritances an individual has received, regardless of the circumstances of the donor. In the first case, our two individuals in similar circumstances would now be taxed similarly. In the second case, less tax would be payable if the rich person left his money to individual B who had so far received nothing, than if he left his money to A. It might be argued, therefore, that inherited wealth might be spread more evenly under a donee-based tax than under the present capital transfer tax. It would depend on how far donors' choices are affected by tax considerations.

There is a qualification to this second case, where the donor is concerned not only with how much he leaves to his immediate beneficiaries, but also with how much they in turn leave. For example, suppose we have a rich uncle who is considering whether to leave his money to nephew A or to nephew B. Suppose, as before, that A has already received a substantial inheritance but that B has not. It is true that, under the donor-based capital transfer tax, the initial liability would be the same whether the money were left to A or B. But when the wealth came to be passed on again, liability would depend on the wealth of A and B. In these circumstances, therefore, even with the present tax, the rich uncle would minimise overall eventual liability by leaving his money to the poorer individual.

This qualification is unlikely to be very important in practice. Donors may not be very concerned with such long-term considerations. In addition, the future is uncertain and so benefactors cannot know which of the potential recipients will have the higher liability to capital transfer tax when the time comes for them to pass on their wealth.

A donee-based accessions tax is generally, therefore, superior to the donor-based capital transfer tax on grounds of both horizontal equity, and incentives towards a more equal distribution.

10.5 The Arguments in Favour of a Wealth Tax

The main arguments put forward in favour of an annual wealth tax usually centre around the concepts of equity and efficiency, and the extent to which a wealth tax could be used as a method of redistribution and administrative control.

Horizontal Equity

As discussed in Chapter 5, the principle of horizontal equity is that people of a similar taxable capacity should be taxed similarly. It will be shown below that the possession of wealth confers advantages over and above the pecuniary income derived from that wealth. It may be argued therefore that an income tax on its own is insufficient to achieve horizontal equity. A striking illustration is Kaldor's example (1956, p. 20) of a beggar and a rich man who keeps all his wealth in the form of gold and jewels. Neither individual has any income; yet the latter, despite his lack of money income, clearly has the greater taxable capacity.

Leaving aside any direct pecuniary income, the benefits of wealth include the ability to dis-save, the control of economic resources, non-pecuniary income and status.

The ability to dis-save has two important advantages. First of all it provides security. An individual with wealth is less dependent on earned income than someone without wealth. To some extent the need for economic security, narrowly defined, has diminished since 1945 with the growth of public welfare provisions. Nevertheless, the possession of capital makes it easier for an individual to maintain his standard of living if his earnings should fall. Even if his earnings do not fall, a wealthy individual is secure in the knowledge that unforeseen expenditure can be met from capital. Such economic security is particularly desirable in old age. People are notoriously nicer to rich old men and women than to poor ones!

Secondly, wealth allows its owner greater power to take advantage of any economic opportunities that may arise. Given imperfect capital markets it is not always possible for individuals without capital to undertake promising ventures, however profitable they may seem. For example, a particular course of full-time education or training may lead to increases in earnings that would more than cover its cost, including the earnings forgone during training. A person without capital may not be able to borrow the necessary money, whereas a person with wealth can always borrow from himself, as it were, and pay for the course out of his capital.

Wealth can also confer control over economic resources. Clearly, the amount of control can vary a great deal. The small saver has little more power than the ability to withdraw his savings from a particular institution, and sometimes, as in the case of National Insurance pension rights, even this power does not exist. In other circumstances, however, the situation may be quite different. For instance, after an examination of the subject, Atkinson concluded that:

> despite the separation of ownership and control in the modern corporation, the wealthy shareholder may well be in a position to exercise considerable influence over a company's policy, and in a substantial number of cases the owners retain full control.
>
> (Atkinson, 1974, p. 44)

In addition to these advantages, wealth usually yields benefits which we would classify as income under the definitions in Section 8.3, but which are not considered to be so for income tax purposes. The two most important are capital gains and the implicit income derived from wealth. A capital gain in *real* (as opposed to money) terms may be considered a form of income as it can be spent without reducing the owner's original wealth. Suppose, for example, a person owned £100 worth of gold and the price of gold suddenly doubled. Clearly the lucky owner could sell half his gold, spend the proceeds, and still own £100 worth of gold. Although there is a capital gains tax in the United Kingdom, it is levied at a rate of 30 per cent, which is less than the tax on many other incomes when investment income surcharge, National Insurance contributions and higher rates of income tax are taken into account. Further, the tax may be deferred until the value of the asset is realised. In addition, there are a number of important exemptions such as owner-occupied houses. It would seem, therefore, that even some of the explicit income from wealth is not taxed properly.

Perhaps more important in this context is the value of implicit income from wealth. What is meant by 'implicit income' here is the value of the services an owner receives from his property. For example, a person living in his own home enjoys the benefit of accommodation for which a tenant would have to pay rent. Similar benefits are received by owners of works of art and suchlike. Clearly, a comprehensive tax on income could in principle cover such non-pecuniary income, and indeed until 1963 the imputed benefit received by owner-occupiers was included in the United Kingdom income tax base.

A final advantage of wealth is the status it confers. Scientific evidence is somewhat light on this particular aspect, and it is tempting to retire behind anecdotal evidence concerning conspicuous consumption. Perhaps we can leave the description to Galbraith (1962, Chapter 7): 'Wealth has never been a sufficient source of honour in itself. It must be advertised, and the normal medium is obtrusively expensive goods'. Similarly with the other incidental benefits associated with wealth; perhaps these are best described by the immortal words of Zsa Zsa Gabor: 'No rich man is ugly'.

So, for all these reasons wealth provides benefits for the owner, over and above current pecuniary income. It may be argued, therefore, that on the grounds of horizontal equity an income tax alone is not sufficient to cover the full benefits derived from the ownership of wealth. The argument is the same as the 'ability-to-pay' approach discussed in Section 5.2.

Benefit Approach

A case for a wealth tax may also be made on the lines of the benefit approach to taxation (Section 5.2). In its most basic form it is derived from Locke's theory of the state as a protector of property. The argument suggests that those who require the state to protect their wealth should pay more in tax than those who do not require such protection. However, we have seen in Section 5.2 that there are limitations to the benefit approach. In addition, it seems reasonable to think that some types of property require more protection than others. Therefore, the benefit approach suggests a differential tax on particular items of property, rather than the more global net wealth tax with which we are concerned.

Efficiency Arguments

The main efficiency argument rests on a comparison between a wealth tax and an income tax of equal yield. The two areas normally considered are the effects on the supply of labour and enterprise, and the effects on the use of existing assets.

It may be argued that a wealth tax would have a less adverse effect on work incentives than an equi-yield income tax, on the grounds that the former would apply to past rather than present effort. In other words, people are less likely to be discouraged from working longer hours or applying for more productive and highly paid jobs if they are taxed on their *past* efforts (i.e. their wealth) rather than on their present efforts (i.e. their current income). However, this line of argument is limited by the extent to which income taxes encourage people to work harder or less hard (see Sections 4.1 and 4.2) and the extent to which the object of work is saving (i.e. future consumption) rather than current consumption.

The second point is that a tax on income from wealth rather than on wealth itself provides an incentive for people to invest in assets with low pecuniary yields, or in assets with non-pecuniary yields that cannot be captured by an income tax. At the extreme, an income tax could be avoided altogether by investing in an asset which has no pecuniary yield at all, such as a painting for a private collection. In contrast, a wealth tax would be levied on various assets at the same rate, and so would not discriminate against assets with a high yield. For example, suppose an investor had a choice between two assets. Asset A yields a pecuniary income of £20 a year, but has no non-pecuniary benefits, while asset B produces no money income, but yields other benefits which may be valued at £12 a year. To keep the example simple, suppose that the private benefits received by the owner are the same as the benefits to society, that is there are no effects external to the market. Secondly, suppose that the price of the two assets is the same (£100) and is not affected by different income or wealth taxes. Finally, suppose that the choice of tax is either a 50 per cent income tax or a 5 per cent wealth tax. We can then see that, without either a wealth tax or an income tax, the investor would be better off with asset A:

	Pecuniary income	*Non-pecuniary income*	*Total income*	*Net income with 50% income tax*	*Net income with 5% wealth tax*
	£	£	£	£	£
Asset A	20	0	20	10	15
Asset B	0	12	12	12	7

An income tax, however, captures the pecuniary income of A and so makes it more profitable to invest in B, even though the private and social benefits of owning B are less than A. In contrast, a wealth tax does not discriminate between assets of different pecuniary yields and so would restore the incentive for our investor to choose asset A. A similar result applies where an owner can control the yield of an asset. A farmer with a field, for example, may be said to have an incentive to use it productively under a wealth tax — even if for no other reason than to pay the tax. No such incentive exists with an income tax.

Redistribution

A wealth tax could be a powerful instrument for the redistribution of wealth. If the community has a preference for a more equal distribution of wealth than currently exists, it would be difficult to redistribute wealth if the only taxes that could be used were levied on the income from, or the movement of, wealth. Taxes on the income from wealth are limited by the pecuniary yield of that wealth. Capital transfer tax is limited by the degree of movement of capital. Death duties also have a number of problems, not least of which is that they are imposed on a near random basis, that is death. Only an annual wealth tax would cover wealth as it stands.

The incidence of a tax and its resultant expenditure is a complex matter (Chapter 5). If a wealth tax were to redistribute resources, it would have to be implemented with that specific purpose in mind. Otherwise, the equalising effect of the wealth tax might be offset either because the revenue was used for the benefit of the wealthy, or because the expenditure had the effect of increasing the return to factors of production owned more by the rich than the poor.

The state of near insolvency of one of the authors has suggested to us the novel solution of a negative wealth tax which would operate where an individual's net wealth was low or even negative!

Administrative Control

The argument here is that a wealth tax would generate information which could be used by the administration to tighten up the control of evasion and avoidance of income tax. Any apparent inconsistency between an individual's wealth and his income could be followed up by the revenue authorities. This was one of the reasons behind the introduction of the French wealth tax in 1982, and such cross-checking takes place, for example, in Sweden. A further incidental benefit would be the availability of more reliable data on the distribution of wealth, at least insofar as it is measured for tax purposes!

Wealth Tax and Human Capital

For administrative reasons that are discussed below, if for no other reason, it is highly unlikely that a wealth tax could be levied on the capital tied up in human beings. We include in this concept of human capital the investment in time and money spent to allow individuals to acquire education, training and skills. It might be asserted, therefore, that a wealth tax would discriminate between different forms of investment: that there would be a tendency to invest in human capital even in cases where it might be socially more productive to invest in non-human capital. Any redistributive aims of tax policy might also be frustrated. The rich might still be able to transmit their wealth to their offspring in the form of human capital and so avoid both wealth and capital transfer taxes, that is by making sure that their children are highly educated.

There are two things that may be said about this sort of argument. First, there is some reason to suppose that the market, if left to itself, will result in under-investment in education (e.g. see Blaug, 1970); and that education is something valuable and requires public encouragement. Second, for administrative reasons, the income tax system in the United Kingdom discriminates against investment in human capital. While any increase in income resulting from an increase in skill is subject to income tax, any costs involved in the acquisition of such skill, for example costs of tuition, are not deductible. It is not recognised in income tax law that human capital can depreciate in the same way as non-human capital. The reasons for this are perhaps understandable. As the 1955 Royal Commission in its *Final Report* pointed out, 'the practical difficulties of producing any system that would give verifiable figures for expenditure on the acquisition of personal capital are overwhelming'.

While some of the distortions against investment in education may be offset by state subsidy of education, a further offset would be provided by a wealth tax which discriminated in favour of such investment. It is not possible to say whether this is an advantage or a disadvantage of a wealth tax. Offsetting one distortion with another is almost certain to introduce a further set of anomalies. So we can only conclude that the fact that a wealth tax in practice normally discriminates in favour of investment in human capital is, on efficiency criteria, not necessarily a disadvantage, and could be an advantage.

10.6 The Arguments against a Wealth Tax

As we have seen, one of the main arguments in favour of a wealth tax is that a man with more wealth has a greater taxable capacity than a man with less wealth. However, it has been suggested that the validity of this argument is not as obvious as might appear at first sight (see Prest, 1976).

The suggestion is that taxable capacity can be covered adequately by a perfect income tax; that is a tax on all accretions, including capital gains as they accrue, gifts and bequests. Suppose that such an income tax existed. Suppose also there are two individuals who have the same wage income and, to begin with, have no wealth. One of the individuals then accumulates a capital sum through saving while the other does not, and the first individual as a result pays income tax on the interest from that saving. The argument then suggests, on equity grounds, that he should not be subject to an additional tax, as both individuals had the same opportunity to accumulate wealth.

There are difficulties with this line of argument because clearly we do not have a comprehensive income tax as described above. So we turn back to the more orthodox arguments which centre around the effects on saving and the practical difficulties associated with the operation of a wealth tax.

The Effects on Saving

Wealth is accumulated saving. Therefore it might be asserted that a tax on wealth would discourage saving. However, this is not necessarily true. As we have seen in Section 4.3, we cannot say, *a priori*, that an increase in taxation will lead to either an increase or a decrease in saving. Given that income taxes involve the 'double taxation of saving' (Section 4.3) it is possible that the replacement of a tax on investment income by a wealth tax would encourage saving.

Practical Difficulties

The main practical difficulty that emerged from the evidence presented to the Select Committee on a Wealth Tax (1975) concerned the valuation of assets. The valuation of pension rights and life assurance policies poses particular difficulties. A memorandum by the Government Actuary's Department demonstrated the very wide range of values that would result from relatively modest changes in the assumptions underlying the calculations. An example was based on a 30 year old man entitled at age 60 to a pension of £1000 a year plus a lump sum payment of £3000, both assumed to rise in line with the cost of living. Depending on a limited number of assumptions, the capital value of these pension rights varied from £580 to £60,190!

Other problems would be associated with the valuation of items such as stamps, books, coins, antiques and the like. One way round these difficulties, commonly used abroad, is simply to exempt these assets. More generally, many of the other practical considerations, such as the methods of administration and the treatment of the 'national heritage', have not caused the problems in overseas wealth taxes that the more fervent opponents of a wealth tax have suggested they might in the United Kingdom.

10.7 Wealth Taxes Overseas

Wealth taxes are now employed in about 20 countries. The tax is largely confined to Europe, the Indian sub-continent, and Central and South America and, as already seen, a number of these taxes are well-established. As we are concerned with the implications of existing taxes for the potential introduction of a wealth tax in the United Kingdom, we shall confine our attention here almost entirely to those of the above countries with a similar socio-economic background, that is European countries. It should be noted again that the details of foreign tax systems can change rapidly, and that the operation of wealth tax in different countries often takes place in different circumstances. The main areas of interest are the structure and the rates of the taxes, and how the practical problems of operating a wealth tax have (or have not) been overcome.

The Structure and Rates of Wealth Taxes

In Europe, wealth taxes are raised in the four Scandinavian

countries and in Austria, France, Germany, Iceland, Luxembourg, the Netherlands, Spain and Switzerland. They are imposed in addition to national (and often local) income taxes, but are levied in place of higher rates of tax on investment income. It is interesting to note that many of the continental taxes were introduced at about the time that the United Kingdom income tax was reformed to discriminate against investment income (see Section 8.2).

Except for the Swiss cantons, European wealth taxes are administered centrally, though Norway has both a national and a local wealth tax. In some countries the practice is to confine the tax to individual persons. This is in line with a general principle that the net wealth of corporations should be imputed to their owners. However, in Germany, Norway, Finland, Switzerland and Luxembourg wealth tax is levied on companies in their own right.

The tax unit normally includes the combined net wealth of husband and wife. Up to the age of majority, children's assets are also usually included with their parents'. This is the case in Germany, Norway and Sweden and was proposed for the United Kingdom in the 1974 Green Paper, *Wealth Tax*. It is not the case in the Netherlands and only so in Denmark if parents have transferred capital to the children.

The annual rates of wealth tax vary significantly. The tax is levied at a flat rate in some countries, such as Germany and Luxembourg (0.5 per cent), Austria (1 per cent) and the Netherlands (0.8 per cent). In other countries the rates are more progressive, for instance Denmark (0.9 rising to 1.1 per cent), France (0.5 to 1.5 per cent), Finland (0.8 to 1.7 per cent) and Sweden (1 to 2.5 per cent). Norway has gone a step further and has both a national wealth tax levied at rates of 0.4 to 1.6 per cent, and a flat rate local wealth tax. The flat rate varies from 0.4 to 1 per cent depending on the local authority, but like the local income tax in Norway, nearly all districts impose the tax at the maximum rate.

Wealth taxes are not normally deductible against income taxes. However, there may be a possibility that combined income, net wealth and other income-related taxes may consume a very large part of, or even exceed, an individual's income. Consequently, several countries have an upper limit to the percentage of a taxpayer's income that may be paid in tax. Thus in Finland, national and local income taxes, net wealth tax, church taxes and social insurance contributions may not exceed 90 per cent of income. In the Netherlands there is a ceiling of 80 per cent of taxable income which can be paid in income and wealth taxes. In Norway and Sweden there are graduated limits. In Norway, total liability may not exceed 80 per cent of the first Nk 150,000 plus 90 per cent of the remainder of income liable to national income tax. In Sweden, the figures are 80 per cent of the first Skr 200,000 and 85 per cent of the rest.

Practical Problems

On a number of occasions, particularly before the Select Committee (1975), it has been asserted that the introduction of a wealth tax in the United Kingdom would present a whole range of practical difficulties. These difficulties include decisions regarding the scope of the tax, that is which assets to tax and which (if any) to exempt; the problems of valuation; the treatment of agriculture and the national heritage; and which methods of administration to employ. Of the studies that have been made of foreign wealth taxes, especially the study by Sandford *et al.* (1975), it would appear that these potential problems do not cause a great deal of difficulty in practice, normally being dealt with by a judicious combination of principle and pragmatism.

Starting with the scope of the tax, in principle all types of assets should be included in a wealth tax. However, in practice this may be considered excessive, either because some assets are exceptionally difficult to value, or because society may regard certain possessions as 'necessities' and therefore not the proper subject for taxation. Thus, every wealth tax in operation seems to have some form of exemption for household and personal effects, though this may be limited as, for example, in Germany where 'luxury' items are taxed if their value exceeds a certain sum.

The valuation of the assets that are taxed should, in principle, be based on their open market value. Yet in practice this may lead to a number of difficulties. For example, if the market prices of some assets are relatively volatile, conscientious valuation may lead either to high administrative and compliance costs, or to a lack of certainty about current tax liability until a valuation is made. However, it would appear that the valuation of assets overseas is neither expensive nor the basis of much argument, perhaps because the methods are well-established and generally produce conservative values. For example, in Sweden land is valued every five years at the open market price, but that figure is then reduced by 25 per cent.

For various reasons, agriculture is a sector that receives a number of fiscal favours. Apart from the political power historically associated with land ownership, farmers have attracted sympathy for reasons such as the volatile price and output of agricultural products, the low rate of return to farming, and an apparent national desire towards self-sufficiency in food. Further factors are the unstable, and generally high price of land, and that the farm itself often forms the vast bulk of the wealth of its owner: about half of all agricultural land in the United Kingdom is owner-occupied.

These problems may be less serious on the continent, as the average size of farm is smaller than in the United Kingdom. However, while many countries such as Norway and Sweden do not give explicit relief for farming, agricultural land is still usually treated favourably in comparison with other assets. If the rate of return on agricultural land is very low, either in a particular year or in general, the ceiling in Denmark and the Netherlands, for example, limits the amount of wealth tax payable. In addition, the methods used to value land for the purposes of wealth tax normally produce a figure below the open market price. This benefits farming, sometimes deliberately as in Germany.

The 'national heritage', in the form of works of art, is completely exempt from wealth tax in countries such as Denmark and Sweden, not only to preserve the heritage, but also because of the difficulties of ensuring their disclosure and valuation. In other countries, works of art may be granted exemption if, as in Germany for example, they conform to certain requirements regarding artistic, historical or scientific interest. Historic buildings do not generally receive the generous concessions often afforded works of art, but may still be treated leniently in comparison with other assets.

The administration of wealth taxes abroad is usually at least partially integrated with the administration of income taxes. In Denmark, the Netherlands, Norway, Sweden and Germany, both taxes are dealt with in the same office, and in the first four of these countries, taxpayers make a combined annual return of income and wealth. In Germany, the wealth tax return is separate and is required once every three years. The combined returns can be relatively simple. In Sweden, a straightforward four-page return covers both national and local income taxes, as well as the wealth tax; and the space for the details of net wealth is only about half a page. Some form of joint administration can have a number of benefits, such as the cross-checking of wealth and income information. In addition, valuations made for a wealth tax can also be used for other taxes, such as gift or inheritance taxes. In those countries that have been studied in detail, it appears that the administrative and compliance costs are not remarkably high (Sandford *et al.*, 1975, pp. 250–253).

So, in considering these various potential problems of operating a wealth tax in the United Kingdom, our brief survey of taxes operating overseas seems to suggest that, once a wealth tax is established, the practical difficulties are unlikely to be as great as might at first be thought.

10.8 Proposals for a Wealth Tax in the United Kingdom

The preliminary proposals of a former Labour Government's Green Paper, *Wealth Tax* (1974) were based on two rate scales, one rising from 1 to 2½ per cent, the other from 1 to 5 per cent. In both cases the first £100,000 of net wealth was exempt and the maximum rate was applied to wealth in excess of £5 million. Investment income surcharge was to remain. The reason given for not proposing a lower wealth tax threshold combined with the abolition of investment income surcharge was the administrative difficulties that a lower threshold would imply for both taxpayers and the Inland Revenue. It was also proposed to operate the tax on the basis of self-assessment with sample checks by the Inland Revenue.

The Green Paper proposals were subsequently examined by the Select Committee on a Wealth Tax (1975). The Report of the Select Committee states, somewhat briefly, that the Committee was unable to agree on a report. There then follow five minority reports, and three volumes of evidence submitted to the Commitee. The five reports consist of a draft report proposed by the Chairman, a draft proposed by the Conservative group, the Chairman's report as amended by the Committee but not adopted, and two other minority reports.

There is insufficient space here to discuss each report in detail.

Suffice it to say that, perhaps as expected, the main areas of disagreement and concern were the threshold and rates of a wealth tax, and issues such as whether children's wealth should be aggregated with that of their parents, and how far owner-occupied homes, chattels, productive assets and 'the national heritage' (e.g. historic homes) should be subject to the tax. The reason for the rejection of the Chairman's amended report was essentially the absence abroad of two Labour MPs when the crucial vote was taken. Yet we might note the reasons put forward by the Committee for rejecting the Chairman's amended report were as follows. First, it was felt that the report failed to ensure that the proposed wealth tax would be substitutive rather than additive, in other words, to ensure that the proposed tax would be met from income, after allowing for a reasonable level of consumption, rather than by running down the taxpayer's assets. Second, the Committee would not accept the amended report because it failed to ensure a protective ceiling on tax payments. Third, the Committee was concerned about the problems of introducing a wealth tax during 'a time of high inflation and economic crisis'. With the possible exception of the third reason, we may conclude from the reasons given in the brief agreed report, that the members of the Committee who were present at the time of the critical vote were by no means in favour of a powerful wealth tax.

Further Reading

An accessions tax is discussed in detail in Sandford, Willis and Ironside (1973). The same authors also cover the pros and cons of wealth taxes and the operation of some wealth taxes overseas (Sandford *et al.*, 1975). A description of the new French wealth tax and a summary of the wealth taxes in certain European countries appears in *European Taxation* (1981). Other proposals for a wealth tax in the UK have been put forward by Flemming and Little (1974) and Meade *et al.* (1978). Finally, evidence on the relative importance of inherited as opposed to 'self-made' wealth is provided in Harbury and Hitchens (1979).

References

Atkinson A.B. (1974), *Unequal Shares*, Penguin Books.
Atkinson A.B. (1975), *The Economics of Inequality*, Clarendon Press.

Blaug M. (1970), *An Introduction to the Economics of Education*, Penguin Books.

Capital Transfer Tax (1974), Cmnd. 5705, HMSO.

European Taxation (1981), Vol. 21, No. 10, pp. 307–18.

Flemming J.S. and Little I.M.D. (1974), *Why we Need a Wealth Tax*, Methuen.

Galbraith J.K. (1962), *The Affluent Society*, Penguin Books.

Harbury C.D. and Hitchens D.M.W.N. (1979), *Inheritance and Wealth Inequality in Britain*, Allen and Unwin.

Inland Revenue (1977), *119th Report*, Cmnd. 6734, HMSO.

Inland Revenue Statistics (1981), HMSO.

Kaldor N. (1956), *Indian Tax Reform*, Ministry of Finance, Government of India.

Meade J.E. *et al.* (1978), *The Structure and Reform of Direct Taxation*, Institute for Fiscal Studies.

OECD (1979), *The Taxation of Net Wealth, Capital Transfers and Capital Gains of Individuals*, OECD.

Prest A.R. (1976), 'The select committee on a wealth tax', *The British Tax Review*, 1976, No. 1.

Rogers Will (1962), 'A Roger's Thesaurus', *Saturday Review*, 25 August.

Royal Commission on the Taxation of Profits and Income (1955), *Final Report*, Cmnd. 9474, HMSO.

Sandford C.T., Willis J.R.M. and Ironside D.J. (1973), *An Accessions Tax*, Institute for Fiscal Studies.

Sandford C.T., Willis J.R.M. and Ironside D.J. (1975), *An Annual Wealth Tax*, Heinemann Educational Books.

Schultz T.W. (1961), 'Investment in human capital', *American Economic Review*, Vol. 51, pp. 1–17, reprinted in M. Blaug (ed.), *Economics of Education I*, Penguin Books, 1968.

Select Committee on a Wealth Tax, Session 1974–75, (1975), Volume I, *Report and Proceedings of the Committee*, HC 696–I, HMSO.

Sutherland A. (1981), 'Capital transfer tax: an obituary', *Fiscal Studies*, Vol. 2, pp. 37–51.

Wealth Tax (1974), Cmnd. 5704, HMSO.

11

Indirect Taxes

It was pointed out in Chapter 2 that the word 'indirect' when applied to a tax may be somewhat misleading. In this chapter, the word will be used in its common loose sense.

There are many 'indirect' taxes in operation in the UK. This chapter opens with a brief background on the arguments which might justify the use of indirect taxes, the types there may be, and the past and present taxes in use in the UK. Consideration is given in turn to excise and customs duties, purchase tax and selective employment tax (which have both been discontinued), and value added tax. Finally, there are sections about the overall regressiveness of the present system and possible future developments.

11.1 Background

Arguments for Indirect Taxation

Before looking at particular taxes, some of the reasons for using indirect taxes should be briefly mentioned. We saw in Chapter 5 that indirect taxes may assist in the redistribution of income, though various unfortunate side-effects were examined in Chapter 3. Also, indirect taxes may be able to correct for market imperfections, such as the effects of monopoly on the supply of particular goods and the existence of externalities ignored by producers.

In addition, where people are thought to under-estimate the dangers or disadvantages of particular products, a paternalistic government may use indirect taxes to guide them. There may also be the advantage that some indirect taxes have only minor disincentive effects on the supply of effort (see Chapter 4).

From the point of view of governments, some indirect taxes, like VAT, are appealing because they are related to prices and, hence, are bouyant. The tax take increases without the need for action by a government because, as prices rise, the proportional tax on sales also rises. The tax is index-linked, given that sales volume does not decline. However, other indirect taxes are not so attractive, as will be explained.

Types of Indirect Tax

A large variety of indirect taxes is possible. There may be overall sales taxes, which can include capital goods in their coverage. These overall taxes could use different rates for different goods. Alternatively, a sales tax could be selective in coverage. In each case, the stage of imposition is open to choice. The tax can be levied on the manufacturer or the wholesaler or the retailer. Indeed, it may be levied on all of them, as for value added tax (VAT).

If the taxes are selective on particular goods, it is much simpler to tax at the manufacturing stage. This means that the number of taxpayers is smaller and that they are mostly large companies which are capable of efficient book-keeping. The UK purchase tax system was like this (see below). On the other hand, if a uniform *ad valorem* tax is required, it is necessary to tax at the retail level because the ratio of retail prices to manufacturers' prices differs by industry and by product within an industry.

Within multi-stage taxes there is yet another pair of possibilities. There may be either a system (like our VAT) under which the total tax bill is related to the final price, because at each stage there are credits for the previous tax borne, or a 'cascade' system (like that which once existed in some continental countries) under which the tax added at each level is based on the gross price up to that stage, including tax paid so far. The cascade system means that there will be a higher total rate of tax on products which involve a larger number of stages in their production. This encourages vertical integration of industries and is clearly economically inefficient. It has been replaced by a VAT in most countries.

Another possibility for any degree of comprehensiveness and any stage of imposition is to have a unit (or specific) tax rather than an *ad valorem* tax. However, although this has the merit of a certain simplicity, especially when one is not dealing with a large number of small items, it is clearly not suitable if a uniform rate of taxation is required. This is because taxation will represent a different proportion of the final value, depending on the value of the unit. A tax of £1 per bottle of wine will be a larger proportion of the price of a cheap wine than of an expensive wine.

Also, unit taxation may produce socially inefficient changes, like larger sizes of product or larger packets, merely in order to reduce the proportion of the gross price which is paid in tax. This is not possible, however, for unit taxes *per gallon* of petrol or *per pint* of whisky, for example. There will also be a reduction in buoyancy because the tax revenue will not automatically increase with prices. Consequently, unit taxes have become less popular. We will see later that there has been a move away from various unit-based excise taxes.

History and Present Yields

Certain types of expenditure taxation on important goods (like slaves) can be traced back as far as ancient Rome. Usually taxation has been associated with the need to raise funds for fighting wars. Recent British tax history begins with the introduction of expenditure taxes on alcoholic drinks, tea and coffee in the 1660s. At the time, efforts were made to exclude the expenditure of 'cottagers and paupers'. However, by the seventeenth century, one half of the burden of excise taxes fell on beer which was the drink of the labourers. During the nineteenth century, the real essentials of life, such as food, were generally free of tax. It was in 1940, in order to help pay for the war, that purchase tax was introduced. By 1947 the rates of tax were very high, including 100 per cent and 125 per cent rates. However, the tax base was fairly narrow, excluding food, fuel and services. By 1958 there were three different rates of purchase tax: 10 per cent, 15 per cent and a luxury rate of 25 per cent.

The importance of purchase tax gradually declined. One way of broadening the base of taxation was to tax employment in service industries which did not bear purchase tax. This was achieved with the introduction of selective employment tax (SET) in 1966. Both these taxes were replaced by VAT in 1973. VAT in the UK has seen a variety of changes since 1973, particularly to the number and level of its rates.

The importance of the various indirect taxes over the last few years can be seen from Table 11A.

11.2 Excise and Customs Duties

The first four columns of Table 11A show that excise duties have generally been rising with inflation. In the period covered by the table, there were increases in rates of duty for specific taxes, though these often did not keep up with inflation. In volume terms, demand was broadly stable. It peaked for beer and spirits in 1979, slowly fell throughout the period for tobacco and slowly rose for wine (CSO, 1982). These shifts seem to be more connected with the state of the economy and changes in tastes than with the level of duty.

Tables 7A and 11A show how important excise taxes are as a source of revenue. However, it is clear that they are unattractive in some ways. First, although the government relies heavily on excise revenue, it nevertheless indulges in advertising campaigns and introduces controls against smoking and drinking. These campaigns would have disastrous effects on the budget if they were more successful. Fortunately for the government, it may reasonably be said that both its control activities and its fiscal activities are designed to fight smoking and drinking. A more serious problem is that some excise taxes might be regressive (see Section 11.5). In these cases, households with smaller incomes would spend a larger proportion on goods subject to these taxes and thus suffer proportionally more from the taxation. A contributory factor would be the low elasticity of demand for some of these goods. However, in fact, if the percentages of disposable income taken by excise duties on drink and tobacco are added together as in Table 11B, we

Table 11A Important Indirect Taxes (£m)

	Beer	*Wine*	*Spirits*	*Tobacco*	*Hydro-Carbons*	*Road Licences*	*VAT*	*Customs Duties*
1976–77	808	227	867	1872	2065	816	3765	676
1977–78	893	243	873	2054	2458	1055	4230	681
1978–79	893	287	1103	2445	2467	1124	4832	735
1979–80	916	321	1151	2579	2928	1147	8179	937
1980–81	1048	343	1152	2816	3576	1358	10960	816

Source: *Financial Statistics*, HMSO, June 1982, Tables 3.3 and 3.4.

can see that a general charge of regressiveness would be unfounded. An overall view of regressiveness is taken in Section 11.5.

Similar selective imposts will now be briefly discussed. The taxes on hydrocarbon oils are imposed partly to reduce demand for these goods and are no doubt successful because of the availability of alternatives. Some uses for hydrocarbon oils are exempted, like fuel for fishing boats. The revenue raised by this taxation is also extremely useful. Road licences are a second example of duties applied to goods which are not in highly inelastic demand. There is some application of the benefit approach here, although the split of costs and benefits between private and commercial vehicles, and between stationary and moving vehicles is open to manipulation. There may also be an element of expenditure-directing towards the railways.

Customs duties are levied on imported goods and some goods manufactured from them. They may also be levied on some exported goods. As well as raising revenue, these duties have included some which are designed to give protection to certain industries, or preference to imports from certain countries. As a result of entry into the EEC and the resulting objective of removing customs barriers, protective duties are being absorbed into the other customs duties, which in turn are being adjusted to the EEC Common Customs Tariff or converted into internal excise duties.

11.3 Sales Taxes

As was mentioned in Section 11.1, purchase tax was introduced in 1940 and by the late 1950s was operated with three rates up to 25 per cent. Therefore, there was an element of progressiveness in the tax because the higher rates applied to the sort of goods which form a small proportion of the budgets of low-income families. As the ownership of televisions, record players, and so on became more widespread, the progressivity of purchase tax declined. Nevertheless, since food and fuel were untaxed, it never became regressive.

This tax on these relatively few types of goods was simple to collect from the manufacturers. There were between 60,000 and 80,000 collection points, and only about 1,500 civil servants involved in the collection. Nevertheless, purchase tax was a

Table 11B Drink and Tobacco Taxes as Percentages of Disposable Income, 1977

	Decile groups									
	1st	*2nd*	*3rd*	*4th*	*5th*	*6th*	*7th*	*8th*	*9th*	*10th*
Original Income £	20	390	1440	2700	3610	4410	5190	6100	7390	11080
Disposable Income £*	1380	1560	2270	2790	3320	3800	4380	5030	5970	8550
Percentage of Taxes	4.9	5.9	7.4	7.4	7.3	6.6	6.2	5.8	6.1	5.1

Note: * After tax and subsidies.

Source: *Economic Trends*, CSO, January 1979, Tables D and G, pp. 99 and 103.

considerable revenue earner (£1429m in 1971–72, about the same as hydrocarbons).

Partly because services were outside the scope of purchase tax, a further tax called selective employment tax (SET) was introduced in September 1966 as a tax on all payrolls which was then refunded to manufacturing industry, in some cases with a bonus. Its purpose was to encourage labour to move from service industries, which were allegedly 'unproductive', towards manufacturing industry (for analysis, see Reddaway, 1970).

It was always very unpopular with small traders, and its abolition became an aim of the Conservative Party in opposition. It was removed with purchase tax when VAT was introduced in 1973. However, those service industries which had complained about the effect of SET on their margins and administration costs were in for an unpleasant shock when they exchanged SET for VAT!

The UK System of VAT

VAT was introduced in the UK in 1973, partly in order to satisfy the requirements of the EEC. Harmonisation of indirect tax systems is called for by Article 99 of the Treaty of Rome; it should eventually extend to excise taxes, and it includes rates of tax as well as the tax base and the system.

In the UK, VAT began with a single rate of 10 per cent covering about 55 per cent of expenditures. Other goods were either exempt or (more favourably, as explained below) zero-rated. Later a 'luxury' rate was temporarily introduced. In 1977–78–79 the rates were 8 per cent and $12\frac{1}{2}$ per cent. There were some problems in defining luxuries, of course. For example: ironing boards and films were taxed at the lower rate, whereas irons and cameras were taxed as luxuries.

The Conservative Party was returned to office in 1979 pledged to shift the balance of taxation from income tax to indirect tax. The argument concerned incentives, as discussed in Chapter 4, where it was pointed out that both theory and empirical evidence are inconclusive about the effects of lowering income tax (both marginal and average rates). Further, as the compensation for lower income tax is higher VAT, it should not take the average taxpayer/consumer too long to work out that extra disposable income has become less attractive because the average price of goods has risen.

Nevertheless, almost immediately after taking office, the Conservative government unveiled a Budget in which income tax rates were significantly lowered and VAT was raised to 15 per cent. This had a considerable effect on the inflation rate and brought cries of outrage from the Labour benches. However, one tangential advantage was a considerable step towards the harmonisation of rates of VAT in the EEC (Dosser, 1981). For an analysis of the switch from direct to indirect taxes, see Atkinson (1981) and Kay and Morris (1979).

VAT is a multi-stage tax which involves credits at each stage. Suppose that there is a manufacturer (M), a wholesaler (W) and a retailer (R) involved in supplying a good to a customer. Let us further suppose that there is a 10 per cent VAT rate and that the manufacturer extracts his own raw materials and pays no VAT for any purposes.

Table 11C shows that, assuming the net prices are not adjusted as a result of the effect of VAT on demand, the traders do not directly bear any of the VAT. The customer bears the full 0.90, which is 10 per cent of the retail price and which is fully received by the Customs and Excise. It should be pointed out, however, that the *effective* incidence of VAT may rest partly on the suppliers because demand for their goods may fall.

The goods which are *exempt* from VAT include postage and services like education, health, finance and insurance. No VAT is to be charged on these goods, but no VAT can be reclaimed on inputs. On the other hand, there are *zero-rated* goods like food, fuel, exports, construction, books, newspapers and medical

Table 11C VAT Example

	VAT paid on inputs	*Net price*	*VAT charged*	*Gross price*	*VAT to Customs and Excise*
Goods leaving M	0.00	4.00	0.40	4.40	0.40
Goods leaving W	0.40	6.00	0.60	6.60	0.20
Goods leaving R	0.60	9.00	0.90	9.90	0.30
					0.90

prescriptions. For these, no VAT is charged on outputs and VAT suffered on inputs is reclaimable. So zero-rated goods escape entirely from VAT, whereas exempt goods do not suffer any tax on the value added at the final stage.

A further detail of administration which is of great importance to many businesses is that there is a lower turnover limit below which traders need not register for VAT purposes. For many small traders this saves much administration and means that VAT need not be charged and paid over on their outputs. However, it also means that any VAT borne on inputs cannot be reclaimed. This lower limit changes fairly often. For 1983–84 it was £18,000.

Arguments For and Against VAT

The Green Paper proposing VAT (NEDO, 1971) said that indirect taxation should become a 'more broadly based structure which, by discriminating less between different types of goods and services, would reduce the distortion of consumer choice'. Since there was a Conservative pledge to remove SET, and since it was difficult to extend purchase tax to include services, VAT was proposed. It was argued that this would reduce the misallocation of resources of selective taxes (see Chapter 3). VAT is neutral between all goods (and services) if it is levied at a single rate on everything; it is neutral between vertically integrated companies and others (unlike the cascade system mentioned earlier); it is also neutral between companies with different ratios of labour costs to profit (unlike SET) (Johnstone, 1975).

However, although VAT is theoretically an overall tax with some exceptions, its actual coverage (according to Field *et al.*, 1977, p. 102) is only 55 per cent of expenditures. In addition, there are still excise taxes at higher rates and VAT itself involves two percentage rates (0 and 15). Therefore, although the neutrality argument was reasonably used for the introduction of a wide-based single-rate VAT system, it would be misleading to use it in defence of our present VAT.

There is some effect on the encouragement of exports. This is because exports are zero-rated for VAT which can, therefore, be completely recovered. Previously, purchase tax and SET were charged on some inputs to exports, like stationery and office equipment. However, adjustments could have been made to the former taxes to achieve the same effect. It is additionally argued that it is easier to exempt capital formation under VAT.

VAT was also said to be more difficult to evade because, if a trader does not issue an invoice, then another trader is not receiving one. Therefore, the net effect should be less evasion. However, invoices to final customers can be omitted. In addition, since there are now around two million collection points rather than about 70,000, there are more opportunities for evasion and overdue payment. It has been estimated that 5 per cent of the due revenue may be lost in this way, although the rates in other countries are even higher: they are estimated at over 20 per cent in France and as much as 50 per cent in Italy (Field *et al.* 1977, p. 106).

A disadvantage that also follows from the increased number of collection points is the high cost of administration (Sandford, 1981). This does not include the great amount of extra work created for industry and commerce in recording and processing VAT information. The present system of VAT assessment based on invoices could be greatly simplified if an alternative system based on accounts were used. Here there might be approximate self-assessment by companies each quarter using their sales and purchases figures. These could be checked more thoroughly and agreed by chief accountants, auditors and excise officials once every year.

11.4 Local Authority Rates

'Rates' are levied by local authorities at amounts based on the 'rateable value' of 'rateable property', which includes land, houses and buildings. The rateable value of a property is its net annual value. This value is taken to be the notional annual market rent of the property, less the cost of its upkeep. The ratepayer's liability on his rateable value is calculated with reference to the 'rate poundage', which is fixed by each rating authority. The rate poundage is the percentage of tax due on each pound's worth of rateable value. The annual bill for rates is therefore calculated by multiplying the rateable value of the property by the rate poundage.

The rate poundage varies considerably from one area to another. It also varies between commercial and industrial ratepayers on the one hand and domestic ratepayers on the other. In this way, the burden on domestic ratepayers is reduced. There is also a system of rate rebates. The amount of the rebate is calculated by reference to a ratepayer's income, family commitments and the rates due.

Charities occupying property for charitable purposes pay half rates. Local authorities also have the power to reduce or remit the rates for a range of non-profit-making bodies. Agricultural property, except for dwellings, is exempt from rates. Churches are also exempt.

There have been many criticisms of rates as a tax. It is said that rates do not take an individual's ability to pay into account and that they are regressive (see Section 11.5). Conscious of these criticisms, successive governments have tried to shift the burden away from domestic ratepayers and to alleviate hardship by rebates. Other criticisms come from the Local Authorities, who complain that rates are not a buoyant source of income and that they are too unpopular to raise the increasing revenues needed. Such criticisms are recorded in the reports of successive government enquiries into local government finance (e.g. Layfield, 1976, pp. 12, 155–65).

The Layfield Report suggests that a change to a capital value basis is necessary for greater comprehensibility and fairness. Also, other sources of local revenue should be developed. The most appropriate is seen to be a local income tax (Layfield, 1976, pp. 168–172, 196–208). The administrative difficulties of these alternative local taxes, and the aversion of the Chancellor to losing control of taxes on income or expenditure, are serious obstacles. However, there have been two government Green Papers on this subject, the former based on the 1976 Layfield Report (Department of the Environment, 1977 and 1981). For further discussion, see Prest (1982) and Crawford and Dawson (1982).

11.5 Regression

The definition of a 'regressive' tax was considered in Section 2.2. It has been used in this chapter in its normal context, that is in relation to income or disposable income. At its simplest, the reason why indirect taxes may be regressive is because there is no equivalent of the zero-rate band in income tax. A tax on beer is paid by poor consumers and rich consumers alike. To the extent that poor

Table 11D Indirect Taxes as Percentages of Disposable Income, 1977

	Decile groups										*Average over all decile groups*
	1st	*2nd*	*3rd*	*4th*	*5th*	*6th*	*7th*	*8th*	*9th*	*10th*	
Rates	6.6	5.2	4.4	3.8	3.4	3.1	3.0	2.7	2.5	2.1	3.1
Beer	0.9	1.0	1.5	1.7	1.7	1.7	1.6	1.5	1.5	1.4	1.5
Wines & spirits	0.8	1.0	1.3	1.3	1.3	1.5	1.4	1.4	1.7	1.6	1.5
Tobacco	3.2	3.9	4.6	4.4	4.3	3.4	3.2	2.9	2.9	2.1	3.2
Value added tax	2.5	2.4	2.9	3.1	3.1	3.4	3.4	3.4	3.3	3.1	3.2
Oil	0.7	0.9	1.6	1.8	1.8	2.1	1.9	2.0	1.8	1.6	1.7
Import duty	0.5	0.4	0.5	0.5	0.5	0.5	0.4	0.4	0.4	0.4	0.4
Intermediate taxes	6.0	5.5	5.8	5.7	5.4	5.6	5.4	5.2	5.1	4.8	5.3
Other	1.3	1.3	1.6	1.6	1.5	1.5	1.3	1.3	1.2	0.9	1.3
Total indirect taxes	22.4	21.7	24.0	23.8	22.9	22.7	21.7	20.8	20.5	18.0	21.1

Source: *Economic Trends*, HMSO, January 1979, p. 103, Table G.

consumers spend a greater proportion of their incomes on beer, the tax on beer will be regressive. To the extent that the poor consume a greater proportion of their incomes (on goods that are taxed), the whole indirect tax system may be regressive.

In total, the system does in fact seem to be slightly regressive, as Table 11D shows. However, it is not seriously so; for example, the 2nd and 7th decile income groups spend the same proportion of disposable income on indirect taxes. Within this, the VAT system is also broadly neutral.

The most regressive form of taxation can be seen to be local rates. This regressiveness remains despite a tempering due to charging much higher poundages on commercial and industrial property than on domestic property, and by allowing rate rebates for low-income sections of society.

A note of caution must be sounded about the remarks in this section, however. It has been pointed out that the redistributive effects of indirect taxes are usually measured using nominal income rather than real purchasing power. In times of high inflation this can be misleading (Levitt, 1976).

Further Reading

Value added tax is discussed in detail in Prest (1980) and Chown (1973) relating to the UK, and in Aaron (1981) for other European countries. More general coverage of indirect taxation may be found in Kay and King (1980), Musgrave and Musgrave (1980), Prest and Barr (1979) and in a special edition of *Fiscal Studies* (Symposium, 1982).

References

Aaron H.J. (ed) (1981), *The Value-Added Tax: Lessons from Europe*, Brookings Institution.

Atkinson A.B. (1981), 'On the switch to indirect taxation', *Fiscal Studies*, July.

Central Statistical Office (CSO) (1982), *Monthly Digest of Statistics*, Tables 6.13, 6.14, HMSO.

Chown J. (1973), *VAT Explained*, 2nd edn., Kogan Page.

Crawford M. and Dawson D. (1982), 'Are rates the right tax for local government?', *Lloyds Bank Review*, July.

Department of the Environment (1977), *Local Government Finance*, Cmnd. 6813, HMSO.

Department of the Environment (1981), *Alternatives to Domestic Rates*, Cmnd. 8449, HMSO.

Dosser, D. (1981), 'The value added tax in the UK and the EEC', in A. Peacock and F. Forte (eds), *The Political Economy of Taxation*, Basil Blackwell.

Field F., Meacher M. and Pond C. (1977), *To Him Who Hath*, Penguin Books.

Johnstone D. (1975), *A Tax Shall be Charged*, HMSO.

Kay J.A. and King M.A. (1980), *The British Tax System*, Oxford University Press, Chs 9 and 10.

Kay J.A. and Morris C.N. (1979), 'Direct and indirect taxes: some effects of the 1979 budget', *Fiscal Studies*, November.

Layfield F. (1976), *Local Government Finance*, Cmnd. 6453, HMSO.

Levitt M.S. (1976), 'The redistributive effects of taxation', *Economic Journal*, September, p. 582.

Musgrave R.A. and Musgrave P.B. (1980), *Public Finance in Theory and Practice*, 3rd edn., McGraw-Hill, Ch. 20.

NEDO (National Economic Development Office) (1971), *Value Added Tax*, HMSO, para. 5.56.

Prest A.R. (1980), *Value Added Tax: The Experiences of the United Kingdom*, American Enterprise Institution.

Prest, A.R. (1982), 'On Charging for Local Government Services', *The Three Banks Review*, March 1982.

Prest A.R. and Barr N.A. (1979), *Public Finance*, 6th edn., Weidenfeld and Nicolson, Ch. 19.

Reddaway W.B. (1970), *Effects of the Selective Employment Tax*, First Report, HMSO; Final Report, Cambridge University Press, 1973.

Sandford C. *et al.* (1981), *Costs and Benefits of VAT*, Heinemann.

'Symposium on Local Government Finance' (1982), *Fiscal Studies*, March.

12

Company Tax Systems

This chapter looks at the background to the UK corporation tax by discussing the general purpose of such a tax, and by examining some of the different types of corporate taxation that there have been or might be. The following chapter is concerned with a more detailed examination of the calculation of corporate tax liabilities in the UK.

12.1 Special Taxation for Companies

It was only during the First World War that companies in the UK began to be treated differently from individuals for the purposes of taxation. Special taxes on companies were in force from 1915 to 1924, and then from 1937 onwards. However, the question whether a business is a separate entity from its owner or owners has a long history in the thought and practice of disciplines like accounting, company law and economics. Italian accountants had decided by the thirteenth century that they wished to separate the business from its owners, so that the latter could see more clearly how the former was doing. Consequently, balance sheets of businesses show amounts called 'capital' that represent amounts contributed by the owners. During the nineteenth century, various laws were enacted in the UK to the effect that all companies have perpetual succession independently from their owners, that these companies may sue and be sued in their own names and that the owners are not liable for the debts of a company beyond their capital contributions. Economists have extended the separation of the owner from his business. When calculating the profit of the business to a sole trader, for example, the costs of the business would include the opportunity costs of the amounts the owner could have earned with his time, his property and his money if they had not been invested in his business.

It was not until this century that revenue law caught up with this separation and that companies began to be taxed in a different way from individuals. As is frequently the case with taxation, the change was associated with the need to finance warfare. In particular, the rearmament before the Second World War imposed a heavy burden on the Exchequer, which was partly supported by the revenue from a new profits tax on companies. This was an additional tax to the existing income tax paid on the income of companies, partnerships, sole traders and other individuals. This profits tax was already providing 3 per cent of the total tax yield by 1938–39. By 1950–51 it provided 7 per cent, but by 1960–61 only 5 per cent, due to the substantial rises in the yields of income tax and indirect taxes.

This important step involving the taxation of companies at different rates from individuals and unincorporated businesses was followed during the Second World War by the introduction of a system of capital allowances for all businesses. This system has, from time to time, involved a number of different tax allowances and reliefs aimed at encouraging investment by deferring or permanently reducing tax for those businesses which purchase capital equipment. In addition to this economic role of shifting the allocation of resources towards investment, the capital allowances system has been used to try to allocate resources to designated 'development areas' by making allowances more generous for companies operating in those areas.

We will look at capital allowances in more detail in Chapter 13. What should be noted here is that, for the purposes of capital allowances, partnerships and sole traders' businesses are included with companies. This seems reasonable, as the investment of unincorporated businesses probably needs even more encouragement than that of companies, because the former generally find it more difficult to raise finance for investment.

The next important change occurred in 1965 when the Finance

Act of the Labour Chancellor, James Callaghan, introduced corporation tax to replace both income tax and profits tax on companies. The dividing line between businesses which pay corporation tax and those which do not remains the same as for profits tax. That is, partnerships and sole traders do not pay corporation tax. Their profits are split up amongst the owners, who add this to their other income and pay income tax on it. The dividing line is drawn in this way as part of the means of separating those businesses whose owners control and manage on their own account from those, typically larger, businesses whose owners are clearly separate from their businesses and who appoint directors to manage them. (However, the separation is not as simple as this; see Section 13.5 on close companies.) So, the corporation tax was brought in partly to effect a greater separation of the taxation of incorporated businesses from that of individuals. This allows more flexibility for the Exchequer in fiscal policy. For example, the government might wish to reduce the taxation paid by companies, in order to encourage more investment. It would not be necessary to reduce personal taxation as well, now that the corporation tax rate is not tied to the income tax rate. The yield of corporation tax was discussed in Section 7.1.

Other arguments for the separate or additional taxation of companies include the benefit principle. It could be said that the tax that a company pays is the price for its legal privileges. However, the company also pays by having to disclose financial information. Anyway, it is not easy to measure the cost or benefit of the privileges, or to establish a relationship which justifies a tax proportional to profit; a licence would be more appropriate. This argument and others, which are all acknowledged to be weak, are mentioned by other writers (e.g. Prest and Barr, 1979). Kay and King (1980, pp. 172–3) point out that limited liability is a voluntary agreement entered into by both sides, who can adjust the terms on which they are prepared to accept or contribute capital. Also, they note that, as companies are owned by individuals, there is no *separate* taxable capacity in a company. A corporation tax affects the owners, workers, or customers of a company.

There is an argument that, since corporation tax exists, it should not be removed because this would be 'capitalised' as unexpected windfall gains for the existing shareholders, who have adapted to the existence of the tax (see Section 5.4 and Meade, 1978, p.227).

The need for a separate levy in order to tax the retained profits of companies is discussed in Section 12.3, after corporation tax systems have been outlined.

A brief note on the incidence of corporation tax seems appropriate at this point. There is no theoretical conclusion about whether company entrepreneurs, company owners or consumers bear a corporation tax in the last analysis. The initial incidence of the tax can be seen to depend upon exactly which system is adopted (Kay and King, 1980, Chapter 12). Much, also, depends on the degree of imperfection in the markets for products, labour and capital. Econometric studies are, unfortunately, equally indecisive about the incidence of corporation taxes (Musgrave and Musgrave, 1980).

12.2 Differences in Taxes

Corporation taxes differ from country to country and from time to time. The two fundamental areas of difference might be called tax bases and tax systems. The differences between tax bases (or definitions of taxable income) may be very great. In some countries, like France and West Germany, taxable income is very closely linked to accounting profit, and therefore varies with the particular countries' rules in this area. In other countries, like the UK, the Netherlands and the USA, there are substantial differences between accounting and taxable incomes; and the nature of these differences varies by country. Even when concentrating on one country, like the UK, the tax base changes from year to year. This is examined in greater detail in the following chapter. Further information on corporate taxation in the countries mentioned above may be found in Nobes and Parker (1981).

The second basic type of difference lies in tax *systems*, to which most of this chapter is devoted. Once taxable income has been determined, its interaction with a tax system can vary, in particular with respect to the treatment of dividends. Corporations, unlike partnerships whose business income in most countries is taxed as though it were all distributed at the end of each tax year, may have both retained and distributed income for tax purposes. If business income is taxed only at the corporate level and only when it is earned, then different shareholders will not pay different rates of personal income tax. If income is taxed only on distribution, taxation may be postponed indefinitely. On the other hand, if income is taxed both when it is earned and when it is distributed, this creates 'economic double taxation' which could be said to be inequitable and inefficient (see below).

Another way in which taxes may vary is by the level of the tax rate. Table 12A shows the systems and rates of corporation tax for some countries. As will be mentioned, these differences in tax bases, rates and systems could lead to several important economic effects: for example, on dividend policies, investment plans and capital raising methods.

12.3 Systems of Corporation Tax

Systems of corporation tax are often divided into three types: classical, imputation and split-rate (van den Tempel, 1974; OECD, 1974). The UK system in 1965–73 was a classical system. Under such systems, company profits are taxed without a deduction for dividends paid; then the dividends are fully taxed as investment income in the hands of the shareholders. The United States, the Netherlands, Luxembourg and Australia are examples of countries which still have classical systems.

There are two main criticisms of classical systems; both rest upon what has been called the 'economic double taxation of dividends', whereby distributed income is taxed both to corporation tax and then to personal income tax. First, this double taxation is said to be inequitable when compared to the treatment of the distributed income of *unincorporated* businesses (e.g. partnerships). Income of such businesses, whether physically distributed or not, bears no corporation tax but bears current income tax in the hands of the owners of the businesses. Such single taxation would not be so easy to arrange for corporations. This is because retained profit does exist, both in reality and for tax purposes, and so, if there were no separate corporation tax, taxation could be indefinitely postponed if companies delayed distribution. As has been mentioned, the alternative of taxing income only at the corporate level would mean that all individual recipients would have borne the same rate of tax. This would be unacceptable as part of an otherwise progressive income tax system. Thus, double taxation of the distributed income

Table 12A EEC Corporation Tax Systems in 1980

(1) Country	(2) *Imputation Introduced*	*(3)* *National Corporation Tax Rate %*[a]	*(4)* *Tax Credit as proportion of dividend*	*(5)* *Tax Credit as % of underlying CT*
Belgium	1963	48	57.5	62.29
France	1965	50	50	50
UK	1973	52	42.9 (i.e. 30/70)	39.56
Ireland	1976	45	42.9 (i.e. 30/70)	52.38
W. Germany	1977	56 & 36	56.25	100
Denmark	1977	40	15	22.50
Italy	1977	25[b]	33.33	100
Netherlands	(Classical)	48	–	–
Luxembourg	(Classical)	40	–	–

Source for columns 3 and 4: Section E of *The Taxation of Private Investment Income,* International Bureau of Fiscal Documentation.

Notes: [a] Withholding taxes have been ignored throughout.
[b] There is also a deductible local income tax of 15% making a total of 36.25%.

of corporations results from a desire by governments to ensure proper taxation of retained income.

The second case against economic double taxation is that it introduces a bias against the distribution of dividends. Since both total income and then distributed income are fully taxed, the larger the distribution, the larger is the total tax borne by a company and its shareholders. It might be thought that such an encouragement to retain profits would promote investment. However, more subtle economic thinking might suggest that profitable and efficient investment would be more likely to occur if companies distributed their profits and then shareholders allocated these funds through the new issue market to the most profitable companies. Unfortunately it is not proven that companies with a good earnings record will remain the most profitable (Whittington, 1971).

It should also be noted about this second argument that, even if there were no effective corporation tax on distributed income (i.e. no double taxation), there would still be a bias against distribution if there were an income tax which had to be paid only when dividends were distributed.

The two cases against the economic double taxation of dividends have given rise to other systems of taxation which are designed to mitigate these effects of classical systems. Because of these arguments, the UK moved in 1973 to an imputation system. Such systems approach the mitigation of double taxation by imputing to the shareholders some or all of the tax paid by companies. For example, taxpayers in the UK are deemed to have paid tax at the basic rate of income tax on their dividends grossed up at the basic rate. Split-rate systems tax distributed profits at a lower rate than retained profits.

Imputation Systems

A frequently used way of mitigating the effects of economic double taxation is to impute to the recipients of dividends some of the tax paid by a corporation on the income out of which the dividends are paid. Imputation systems are used in EEC countries, apart from the Netherlands, Greece and Luxembourg, and also in Canada. Tables 12B and 12C illustrate the contrast between the UK's pre-1973 classical system and its imputation system in 1982–83.

In the UK there is a 'basic rate' of income tax, which is the marginal rate for a majority of taxpayers; it has been assumed that this is 30 per cent, that the classical corporate tax rate is 40 per cent, and that the imputation rate is 52 per cent. The rate of classical corporation tax in the UK between 1965 and 1973 was between 40 and 45 per cent. Such rates raise about the same revenue as a 52 per cent imputation rate. This is because, under the latter system, some of the corporation tax is imputed to the recipients of dividends as an income tax credit. In the UK, the tax credit is linked to the basic rate of income tax for administrative reasons, as will be explained later. From 1979–80 to 1982–83, when the basic rate was 30 per cent, the tax credit was 30/70 or 3/7. Under the pre-1973 system, there was a withholding of standard rate income tax at source.

Let us look at the figures in Tables 12B and 12C in more detail. They assume that the taxable and accounting incomes are the same, and £10,000 in each case. Under the classical system shown on the left, corporation tax at 40 per cent is borne, and then income tax at 30 per cent is deducted at source. Thus, for basic rate taxpayers, there is no further income tax to pay. As the first column of Table 12B shows, the tax liability is £600 (i.e. 30 per cent of the gross dividend of £2,000). The tax already deducted by the company and paid to the Inland Revenue is also £600. Thus, there is no net liability.

The imputation system illustrated on the right in Table 12B is based on the UK system in 1982. Corporation tax of 52 per cent is borne, and a tax credit of 3/7 the size of the dividend is given to shareholders. No further tax is deducted, so the dividend received by shareholders cannot sensibly be called 'net'. The tax liability is worked out on the cash dividend which is grossed up to include the tax credit. In this case, the example has been chosen to keep the 'grossed up' (and post-tax) dividends the same for the two systems. Thus, the tax liability on the 'grossed up' dividend of £2,000 is £600, but this may be settled with the tax credit of £600, leaving no net liability.

It should now be clear how useful it is administratively to set the tax credit (and the former tax deduction at source) at a rate related to the basic rate of income tax. It means that many taxpayers have no net liability to tax on dividends. In most other countries, where there is an absence of a long basic-rate band, such an advantage cannot be gained because there is no particular marginal rate which is predominant.

Table 12B Classical and Imputation Systems (low payout)

		Classical £		Imputation £
Company				
income (say)		10,000		10,000
corporation tax	(40%)	4,000	(52%)[a]	5,200
distributable income		6,000		4,800
distribution (say) gross		2,000		
less income tax deducted at source (30%)	600			
net	1,400		cash	1,400
retained income		4,000		3,400
Shareholders (basic rate)				
dividend: cash received		1,400		1,400
income tax deducted at source		600		0
tax credit received ($\frac{3}{7}$)		0		600
gross dividend		2,000	'grossed up' dividend	2,000
income tax liability (30%)		600		600
less tax already deducted		600		0
less tax credit		0		600
tax due		0		0
Total Tax	(4,000 + 600)	4,600		5,200

Note: [a] Ignoring the 'small companies' rate, see p. 299.

Table 12C Classical and Imputation Systems (high payout)

			Classical £		*Imputation* £
Company					
income (say)			10,000		10,000
corporation tax		(40%)	4,000	(52%)	5,200
distributable income			6,000		4,800
distribution (say) gross			5,000		
less income tax deduction (30%)		1,500			
	net	3,500		cash	3,500
retained income			1,000		1,300
Shareholders (basic rate)					
dividend: cash received			3,500		3,500
income tax deducted at source			1,500		0
tax credit received ($\frac{3}{7}$)			0		1,500
gross dividend			5,000	'grossed up' dividend	5,000
income tax liability (30%)			1,500		1,500
less tax already deducted			1,500		0
less tax credit			0		1,500
tax due			0		0
Total Tax		(4,000+1,500)	5,500		5,200

Table 12C shows a similar example, but one where the company pays out a high proportion of its post-tax profits. A comparison of Tables 12B and 12C shows that, for shareholders who pay only basic rate tax, the UK imputation system fully removes the double taxation of dividends. The total tax of £5,200 under the imputation system does not alter as the level of dividends rises; under the classical system, the total tax rises.

However, the case is different when there are shareholders who pay a higher rate of personal income tax. Then there is still a double taxation under the imputation system, and the bias against distribution remains. Table 12D illustrates this by showing that total taxation is higher for higher rate taxpayers when there is a larger payout, not only under the classical system but also under the imputation system. Examination of the top right-hand quarter of Table 12D shows that, where a taxpayer has a marginal rate of 50 per cent, the £600 tax credit is insufficient to cover the liability on the £2,000 'grossed up' dividend.

The present UK system, like most existing imputation systems, involves *partial* imputation. That is, only part of the corporation tax paid by companies is imputed to shareholders. In 1982–83, the part imputed is 39.56%, as Table 12E shows.

The partial imputation systems of France, Belgium, Denmark and Ireland are broadly similar to that in the UK. A summary of rates is shown in Table 12A. It can be seen, for example, that France has a corporation tax rate of 50 per cent and a (partial) imputation of 50 per cent of the amount of corporation tax underlying any dividend. Apart from the size of the tax credit, French imputation works in the same way as that in Table 12B.

Unlike these systems, Table 12A shows that the West German and Italian systems involve *full* imputation. This removes the economic double taxation of dividends. It means that the eventual effect of the whole federal taxation system for distributed income is as though there were no separate corporation tax. However, this is much too simple a picture to give an accurate impression of overall taxation, which needs to include other federal and local taxes. Note also in Table 12A that the German system has a higher rate for retained than for distributed profits.

Returning to the UK system, one might notice that it is possible to work out the effective rate of tax on cash dividends under the UK imputation system. The 'effective rate' is given by $(m - b)/(1 - b)$,

Table 12D Classical and Imputation Systems (higher rate taxpayers)

low payout		*Classical* £		*Imputation* £
Company (as table 12B)				
Shareholders (50% marginal rate)				
dividend: cash received		1,400		1,400
income tax deducted at source		600		0
tax credit received ($\frac{3}{7}$)		0		600
gross dividend		2,000	'grossed up' dividend	2,000
income tax liability (50%)		1,000		1,000
less tax already deducted		600		0
less tax credit		0		600
tax due		400		400
Total Tax	(4,000+600+400)	5,000	(5,200+400)	5,600

high payout				
Company (as table 12C)				
Shareholders (50% marginal rate)				
dividend: cash received		3,500		3,500
income tax deducted at source		1,500		0
tax credit received ($\frac{3}{7}$)		0		1,500
gross dividend		5,000	'grossed up' dividend	5,000
income tax liability (50%)		2,500		2,500
less tax already deducted		1,500		0
less tax credit		0		1,500
tax due		1,000		1,000
Total Tax	(4,000+1,500+1,000)	6,500	(5,200+1,000)	6,200

Table 12E UK Partial Imputation 1982–83

	£
Company	
income	1,000
corporation tax	520
	480
dividend	480
	0
Shareholders	
cash receipt	480
tax credit ($\frac{3}{7}$)	205.7
'grossed up' dividend	685.7

partial imputation = $\frac{205.7}{520} = 39.56\%$

where *m* is the taxpayer's marginal rate and *b* is the basic rate. Table 12F shows a list of such rates. For those who pay no income tax, the tax credit is reclaimable. Thus, on the arrival of a dividend, they are better off by 43 per cent more than the apparent face value of it. Their 'effective rate' is *negative*. The rates in Table 12F may be useful as a ready means of calculating the post-tax value of a cash dividend received by a shareholder. Also, the average 'effective rate' of its shareholders is that which a company's management may wish to bear in mind as the extra tax to be borne by the company-plus-shareholders on payment of a dividend.

It should be noted, in summary, that even a partial imputation system *can* totally remove double taxation and the bias against distribution in circumstances where the tax credit cancels the personal liability. Alternatively, the double taxation can be removed by fully imputing the corporation tax to shareholders. However, in this case, even if there is no double taxation because there is no effective liability to corporation tax, there could still be some bias against distribution if personal income tax is larger than the underlying corporation tax and if it operates only when dividends are paid.

Table 12F 'Effective Rates' on Cash Dividends (1982)

Individual's Marginal Tax Rate (m) %	*Effective Rate on Cash Dividend (b) %*
0	−43
30	0
40	14
50	29
60	43
75	64

Advance Corporation Tax

A further complication was introduced with the imputation system, partly in order to maintain the government's cash flow. Under the classical system 1965–73, the income tax deducted at source from dividends was payable to the Revenue soon after the distribution. Since there is now no basic rate tax deducted from dividends, there would have been no tax payment until the corporation tax was paid (9 to 21 months after the company's year-end, as explained in the following chapter). In order to obtain some revenue before this, *Advance Corporation Tax* (ACT) was invented as part of the imputation system. ACT equal to 30/70 of any distribution (when the basic rate of income tax is 30 per cent) is to be paid on a quarterly basis soon after the distribution (see *Workbook* for details). It is not a separate tax, but only an advance payment of corporation tax. This 'staggering' of the receipts of tax from corporations was not only useful in the transitional period of 1973, but is an advantage that has continued. Because most companies have March 31 or December 31 year-ends, the tax receipts would be very 'lumpy' without an ACT.

The net amount of corporation tax which is paid later is known as *Mainstream Corporation Tax* (MCT). It is the remaining *Corporation Tax Liability* (CTL) after ACT has been paid:

$$\text{MCT} = \text{CTL} - \text{ACT}$$

Some more detail on the calculation of ACT may be useful at this point. Dividends received by companies from other UK resident companies are treated as *Franked Investment Income* (FII). The income is called 'franked' because it has been paid out of a pool of profits which have already borne corporation tax. Recipient *companies* cannot benefit from the tax credits associated with the FII in the way that individuals can, because companies do not pay income tax. However, recipient companies can use their FII to reduce their payments of ACT on distributions of dividends. Under normal circumstances, this does not alter the total corporation tax liability, but it does reduce the amount that needs to be paid in advance.

For example, let us take a company with taxable profit of £300,000 for the year ended 31 March 1983. During the year the following transactions occur:

(i) Dividends received, £14,000 : associated credit received (14,000 × $\frac{3}{7}$) =	£6,000
(ii) Dividends paid, £21,000 : associated ACT (21,000 × $\frac{3}{7}$) =	£9,000
Thus, ACT to pay =	£3,000

The company's Corporation Tax Liability (CTL) will be £156,000 (i.e. 52 per cent × £300,000). The advance of £3,000 on this corporation tax has been paid during the year. The rest of the tax, the Mainstream Corporation Tax (MCT), is due on 1 January 1984. In this case, MCT is £153,000 (i.e. £156,000 less £3,000).

In the financial accounts of the company, the above dividend *received* would be shown 'gross' as £20,000, with a corresponding increase of £6,000 in the tax figure disclosed. In fact, the FII does not bear corporation tax in the receiving company (see Section 13.2). The above fiction is recommended by Statement of Standard Accounting Practice No. 8 of the Accountancy Bodies. The dividends *paid* are shown as the cash amount of £21,000.

It will probably have been noticed that the size of the ACT relating to a particular dividend is the same as the size of the tax credit. This should not be taken to mean that the two are the same thing, or that ACT is an essential feature of an imputation system. As explained above, the tax credit is an imputation based on the fact that *corporation tax* has to be paid; the ACT is mainly a device to collect some corporation tax early. The imputation system introduced in Ireland in 1976 illustrates this point: there was no

ACT in Ireland until 1983, but there is a similar system of imputation credits to that in the UK. Other EEC imputation systems also have no general ACT.

However, under certain circumstances, ACT does fulfil another function which is connected with the funding of tax credits. The problem occurs when there is insufficient *taxable* income to cover the tax credits associated with dividends. This is possible in those countries, like the UK, where taxable income may be considerably lower than accounting profit, due to generous capital allowances, stock relief and other deductions made in the calculation of taxable income (see following chapter).

For example, suppose that accounting net profit is £500,000:

		£	£
	Accounting net profit	500,000	500,000
Less	Adjustments to calculate taxable income (e.g.)	300,000	
	Taxable income	200,000	
	Corporation tax (52%)		104,000
	Distributable profit		396,000

Suppose that the company wishes to pay out £350,000 in dividends. The tax credits received by shareholders with this will be £150,000 (i.e. £350,000 × $\frac{3}{7}$). Thus, the tax credits exceed the CTL of which they are supposed to be a partial imputation. This problem, which is solved by ACT, has affected about $\frac{2}{3}$ of UK companies for at least one year in the late 1970s or 1980s (Treasury, 1982, p. 9).

This illustrates the second reason for ACT. That is, ACT ensures that imputation credits are not granted to recipients of dividends when there has been no underlying payment of corporation tax to impute. ACT is paid on dividends irrespective of a company's taxable profits and can normally only be relieved against CTL. Consequently, the shareholders' tax credits will always have been paid for. In order to make this operate more exactly, the ACT set-off in any year is limited to the amount of ACT that would relate to a dividend that, when 'grossed up' for the ACT, would absorb all the taxable income. To reduce the harshness of this, unrelieved ACT can be carried back for a number of years (two years for 1982–83 and progressively up to 6 years by accounting years ending after 31 March 1987[1]), or forward indefinitely against other years' CTL.

Most other countries with imputation systems do not have large differences between accounting and taxable incomes. Thus, the above problem does not arise, and they do not need an ACT. However, many such countries do have a special tax which comes into force when tax credits could exceed corporate tax revenues, for example when dividends are paid out of some foreign incomes. The French compensatory tax of this sort is called a *précompte*.

Split-Rate Systems

A second way to reduce the effects of double taxation is to charge a lower rate of tax on distributed income than on retained income. The West German system up until the end of 1976 was a split-rate system with a 51 per cent rate for retained income and a 15 per cent rate for distributed income. The Austrian split-rate system continues.

It is possible to re-organise a partial imputation system into a split-rate system with identical tax liabilities and therefore, unless they are perceived differently, identical economic effects (Nobes, 1980). Therefore it could be said that, for the purposes of classification, split-rate systems and partial imputation systems are in the same category.

Other Ways to Mitigate Double Taxation

There are many other ways to reduce double taxation. In the USA for example, the classical system is modified in that the first $200 of dividends (plus interest) received by an individual each year are exempted from personal income tax. Alternatively, the 'primary dividend' system allows companies to deduct some proportion of dividends in the calculation of their taxable incomes. Such a system has operated in Sweden and Iceland.

---

[1] Proposals in the 1983 Finance Bill.

12.4 Interest

At this stage it is probably sensible to discuss the other important payment to providers of long-term finance, that is, interest. Whereas dividends are not treated as expenses for the purposes of calculating taxable profit under most tax systems, interest payments nearly always are. This is because dividends are a share of post-tax profit paid to the owners of the company, whereas interest is a fixed payment which *must* be paid to outside lenders of money. Consequently, under most types of system, paying out £2,000 in interest is about half as expensive for the company in post-tax terms as paying £2,000 cash dividends, because the former payment reduces tax by £1,040 (assuming a corporation tax rate of 52 per cent). On the other hand, as shown below, £2,000 of cash dividends is worth more to an individual than £2,000 of gross interest. This is because, although they are both investment income, the dividends are treated as though basic rate tax had already been paid. The following example assumes a basic rate of income tax of 30 per cent, and a corporation tax rate of 52 per cent.

	Dividend payment £	*Interest payment* £
Net profit before interest and tax	10,000	10,000
less Interest (£1400 net, £600 income tax deducted at source)	–	2,000
Net profit before tax	10,000	8,000
less Tax at 52%	5,200	4,160
Net profit after tax	4,800	3,840
Dividend (equivalent to £2000)	1,400	–
Retained profit	3,400	3,840

The recipient of dividends, in this example, gets £1400 which is the equivalent of £2000 gross dividend with £600 tax paid. This is exactly what the recipient of interest gets, because the company deducts £600 basic rate tax at source and pays it to the Revenue. The net effect is still that the interest payment is cheaper, leaving a greater retained profit. The company will consider this and many other relevant factors when choosing between alternative ways of raising external long-term finance. One of the criticisms of the UK and other tax systems is that they are not 'neutral' in this respect, as they introduce a bias in favour of debt finance.

For the treatment of interest *received*, see Section 13.2.

12.5 Harmonisation

The existing differences between effective taxation burdens in different countries give rise to great difficulties for the Revenue Authorities who tax multi-national companies. These companies themselves put considerable effort into reducing overall taxation by moving capital and profits around the world. However, these are matters of international business finance and management accounting, rather than the province of this chapter. The existence of these differences has not yet given rise to the same plethora of proposals and committees for international harmonisation as have the differences between accounting systems. However, within the EEC, harmonisation of taxation is in progress. Many Directives on the harmonisation of VAT and other forms of indirect taxation have been passed. Direct corporate taxation, with which we are concerned here, has also been the subject of proposals for harmonisation. Progress in this area has been slow because of the reluctance of governments to lose any control over direct taxation, which is such an important source of revenue and regulator of the economy.

The Treaty of Rome calls for the elimination of customs duties between member states, the introduction of common tariffs with third countries, and the removal of barriers to the free movement of persons, capital, goods and services. The interest in taxation shown by the EEC Commission, which is the guardian of the Treaty of Rome, stems from this desire to promote free movement. The free movement of goods and services implies particularly the harmonisation of indirect taxes. Similarly, the free movement of people and capital implies the harmonisation of direct taxes. If there were no harmonisation of taxes and if barriers to movement were eliminated, there might then be encouragement or obstruction of flows of people, capital and so on to particular countries within the

EEC for purely fiscal reasons.

It is the aim of harmonisation (Dosser, 1973; Burke, 1979) that the conditions of competition and the returns to capital and effort should not be significantly affected by differences in effective tax burdens. So far, the EEC Commission's proposals have covered only tax systems rather than tax bases. The Commission's activity in this area will now be outlined.

In 1962, the Neumark Committee (1963) recommended to the Commission that a split-rate system should be adopted. Later, the van den Tempel Report (1974) described the three types of corporation tax systems, and recommended the classical system. However, the Commission's draft Directive (EEC Commission, 1975; Nobes, 1979) on the harmonisation of corporate taxation proposes the imputation system. This must be partly due to the fact that a majority of EEC countries were already using such a system or had plans to introduce one. In 1975, Belgium, France and the UK were using an imputation system. Since then, Germany, Denmark, Ireland and Italy have introduced one (see Table 12A, column 2).

Some of the reasons for choosing an imputation system have been mentioned. They include the fact that the tax credit reduces the bias against distribution and favours small investors (lower rate taxpayers). Also, the system should reduce the incentive for evasion by lowering the effective marginal rate of tax on dividends. In addition, since the corporation tax rate tends to be higher under an imputation system, there is a fairer comparison between the rates of tax borne on company retained profits and partnership profits (European Taxation, 1976; OECD, 1974).

Article 3 of the draft Directive proposes that there shall be imputation systems in operation with a single rate of tax between 45 and 55 per cent. Also, Article 8 proposes that imputation credits shall be between 45 and 55 per cent of the corporation tax that would have to be paid on a sum equal to the taxable income out of which the dividend could be paid (i.e. on the dividend increased by the corporation tax; see Table 12A). The rates in force in the EEC in 1980 are shown in Table 12A, which reveals that little notice has been taken of these proposals even in recently introduced imputation systems. Other proposals are that there should be a compensatory tax like an ACT or a *précompte* (Article 9); that there should be a withholding tax of 25 per cent unless shares are registered, as in the UK (Articles 14–17); and that tax credits should be available to shareholders irrespective of their member state (Article 4). This last requirement is clearly designed to promote the free movement of investors' capital. These various requirements would not necessitate important adjustments to the UK corporation tax system. The tax systems of some other EEC countries would need greater adjustments, as Table 12A suggests.

The draft Directive has been criticised on many grounds. The omission of a proposed treatment for capital gains is important. Unless their taxation is also harmonised, there will be much wasteful manoeuvring in order to create capital gains in favourable member states, rather than *income* in any state or capital gains in unfavourable states. Another criticism is that other corporate taxes, like net worth, turnover and local taxes, ought to be included in the harmonisation. More generally,the different rules relating to the calculation of taxable income need attention if total effective tax burdens are to be harmonised. A further criticism is that some countries in the EEC are intrinsically less attractive to companies for economic, geographical and political reasons; and that these countries need advantageous corporate tax regimes if they are to encourage investment and employment. Therefore, to harmonise taxation without altering these other factors might give rise to undesirable regional side-effects.

The 'opinion' of the European Parliament (Official Journal, 1979) on the draft Directive has stressed the need to include the problem of different tax bases as well as tax systems. Partly as a result of this and partly because member states are not enthusiastic about changing their tax systems or losing flexibility, the 1975 draft Directive — and that concerning the taxation of financial institutions (EEC Commission, 1978) — have been delayed and may need considerable amendment. However, the proposals may give an indication of the direction of future changes in corporation tax in the EEC.

12.6 Reform

There have been many suggestions for the reform of corporation tax (e.g. Meade, 1978; Kay and King, 1980; Alworth, 1980; Mayer, 1982). Despite, or perhaps because of, many tinkerings with the system to take some criticisms into account, it still seems to be the case that 'the system is in total disarray' (Kay and King, 1980, p. 171). Some suggestions for reform will be considered below. However, it should be remembered that a strong argument against structural change is that companies have already had to cope with two major changes of system in the last two decades. Further, since the corporation tax is still a major source of revenue in the UK (see Table 7A) the government has expressed an unwillingness to consider abolishing it or substantially reducing its total tax take (Treasury, 1982, p. 5).

The Meade Committee (Meade, 1978) devoted some attention to the major problem in corporate taxation which imputation is designed to solve, that is, the different taxation of retained and distributed profits. On the one hand, it might be argued that any double taxation of income (on the company and on the shareholder) is inequitable when comparisons are made with unincorporated businesses. This argument is used to justify imputation of corporation tax to the shareholders. On the other hand, it is argued that it is inequitable, again compared with unincorporated businesses, to allow companies to accumulate retained profits which have not borne tax at the shareholders' marginal rates. This argument may justify a separate corporation tax at a higher rate than basic rate income tax, if shareholders are assumed to pay higher rates of tax.

One approach to solving these problems is that of the split-rate systems, which have a lower rate of corporation tax for distributed income than for retained income. Other approaches seen above are to tax corporate profits at fairly high rates and then to impute all or part of this tax to shareholders with their distributions. Also, a shift to expenditure tax rather than income tax was discussed by the Meade Committee.

The Committee reasonably proposed that one theoretically sound solution is for retained profit to be apportioned to shareholders just as if they were partners ploughing profit back. This apportionment would be taxed with the dividends at the shareholders' marginal tax rates. There would be a full imputation of corporation tax via a tax credit on both distributed and apportioned profit. In this way, the company would effectively bear no tax, and corporation tax would be a sort of withholding tax. This would solve the problems of double taxation and retained profits. Incidentally, it would be necessary to adjust capital gains tax in order to avoid a double taxation of the gains arising from retained profits.

Clearly, there would be some administrative problems with this system and some unfortunate implications for the cash flow of shareholders of companies which retain a high proportion of profits. However, the idea is very attractive theoretically.

The government published a Green Paper called *Corporation Tax* in 1982 (Treasury, 1982). This provides a mass of fascinating statistics about corporation tax, and discusses various possible reforms. It looks at different tax bases (e.g. using cash flows or current cost accounting profit for taxation), different tax systems (e.g. split-rate), and less drastic changes (like changing loss reliefs or tax depreciation allowances). The Green Paper constitutes a useful, wide-ranging discussion of possible reforms. However, it does not come to firm conclusions, and in many places seems to be merely a marshalling of all the available arguments against a particular proposed reform. For a review of this Green Paper, see Edwards (1982).

Further Reading

For a general treatment of corporate taxation, see Musgrave and Musgrave (1980) and Prest and Barr (1979). For more lengthy consideration of alternative systems, see OECD (1974). For more details on overseas systems, see Nobes (1981). For corporation tax reforms, see Meade (1978), Treasury (1982) and Edwards (1982).

References

Alworth J. (1980), 'Are there feasible reforms for corporation taxes?', *Fiscal Studies,* July.

Burke R. (1979), 'Harmonization of corporation tax', *Intertax,* June–July.

Dosser D. (1973), *British Taxation and the Common Market*, Charles Knight, Chapters 1, 4 and 6.

Edwards, J. (1982), 'The Green Paper on corporation tax: a review article', *Fiscal Studies*, July.

EEC Commission (1975), *Proposal for a Directive Concerning the Harmonization of Systems of Company Taxation and of Withholding Taxes on Dividends*, COM(75) 392 final, Brussels.

EEC Commission (1978), *Proposal for a Directive on the Application to*

Collective Investment Institutions (of the 1975 draft Directive), COM(78) 340 final, Brussels.
European Taxation (1976), International Bureau of Fiscal Documentation, Amsterdam, Vol. 16, Nos 2, 3 and 4, pp. 41–51.
European Taxation (1978), *Guides Volume II,* International Bureau of Fiscal Documentation, Amsterdam.
Kay J.A. and King M.A. (1980), *The British Tax System*, 2nd edn, Oxford University Press.
Mayer C. (1982), 'The structure of corporation tax in the UK', *Fiscal Studies*, July.
Meade J.E. (1978), *The Structure and Reform of Direct Taxation*, IFS/ Allen and Unwin.
Musgrave R.A. and Musgrave P.B. (1980), *Public Finance in Theory and Practice*, McGraw-Hill, Chapters 18 and 19.
Neumark Committee (1963), *EEC Reports on Tax Harmonization*, International Bureau of Fiscal Documentation, Amsterdam.
Nobes C.W. (1979), 'Fiscal harmonization and European integration: a comment', *European Law Review*, August.
Nobes C.W. (1980), 'Imputation systems of corporation tax in the EEC', *Accounting and Business Research,* Spring, Appendix.
Nobes C.W. (1981), in C.W. Nobes and R.H. Parker (eds), *Comparative International Accounting*, Philip Allan, Chapter 13.
OECD (1974), *Theoretical and Empirical Aspects of Corporate Taxation*, Paris.
Official Journal of the EEC (1979), C140; see also report in *Intertax*, October.
Prest A.R. and Barr N.A. (1979), *Public Finance*, Weidenfeld and Nicolson, Chapter 17.
Treasury (1982), *Corporation Tax*, Cmnd. 8456, HMSO.
van den Tempel A.J. (1974), *Corporation Tax and Individual Income Tax in the EEC,* Brussels.
Whittington G. (1971), *The Prediction of Profitability*, Cambridge University Press, Chapters 4 and 5.

13

The UK Corporation Tax

In Chapter 12, a number of introductory matters concerning corporation tax were discussed. Also, the UK's imputation system was examined at some length. With that background, this chapter looks in more detail at the workings of the UK corporation tax. The most important matter concerns the tax base, that is the definition of taxable income. Also, this chapter discusses loss reliefs, the 'small companies' rate, close companies and partnerships, and the effects of inflation. Before examining these areas, the general scope and administration of corporation tax will be briefly looked at.

13.1 Scope and Administration

Corporate taxation in the UK is controlled, as with most other taxes, by statute, case law and the practice of the Inland Revenue. The 1970 Income and Corporation Taxes Act contains many of the relevant provisions. This is supplemented by yearly Finance Acts, which are preceded by the related 'Budget' statements and Finance Bills. In addition, a number of cases are relevant to the definition of income and to many other matters. Many of these statutory rules and cases apply to unincorporated businesses as well as to companies. This chapter includes some references to statute and case law. Those studying taxation specifically as an aspect of law would need to refer to many more.

Corporation tax is chargeable on resident UK companies and unincorporated associations (e.g. sports clubs or trade unions). It is not charged on partnerships, sole traders, charities, or local authorities. Building societies and insurance companies are subject to special rules. As with income tax, there are different schedules and cases; for example, Schedule D Cases I and II are for trading profit. The tax is chargeable on a current year basis for a 'chargeable accounting period', which is normally the company's accounting year. The rate of tax relating to the fiscal year (1 April to 31 March for companies) is fixed in the Finance Act following the year. For example, the 1983 Finance Act sets the rate for the corporation tax year 1982: that from 1 April 1982 to 31 March 1983. If the accounting period straddles two fiscal years and if the corporation tax rate changes, an apportionment must be carried out.

The due date for payment of corporation tax depends on the date of incorporation of a company. For those companies formed before 1 April 1965 (when corporation tax started), the due date remains as it would have been under the income tax rules, except that all payments must be made on January 1 (not split between January 1 and July 1). Thus, older companies pay their MCT between 9 and 21 months after their accounting year-ends. Companies formed on or after 1 April 1965 pay MCT 9 months after their year-ends. As the previous chapter mentioned, ACT is paid on a quarterly system (see *Workbook* for details).

13.2 Taxable Income

The determination of taxable income is broadly similar for companies and unincorporated businesses. It begins with net profit (that is, revenues less expenses) as calculated according to accounting conventions. One important convention used by accountants is the *realisation convention* which is that revenues will be recognised, for the purposes of calculating profit, not at the point of completion of a product ready for sale, nor necessarily at the point of collection of cash, but at the usually intermediate point when the sale is made, by the buyer and seller setting up legally enforceable obligations to each other. Consequently, a business will include sales on credit as part of its revenues, even though no cash has been received. The business has debtors instead of cash. Taxation is based on the profit calculated by using this realisation convention.

Another connected convention used by accountants is the *accruals convention* which is that the revenues of a year are only those receipts (of any year) which *relate* to that year. Similarly, the expenses of a year are the payments (of any year) which *relate* to that year. For example, rent received in advance for next year, or receipts of cash from debtors gained last year, are not revenues of this year. Insurance payments for next year's premium or payments to suppliers for last year's bills are not expenses of this year. A very significant example of the effect of this convention is the fact that purchases of fixed assets are not treated as expenses of the year of purchase, because the assets will be used up over several years. Part of the cost (in proportion to the amount of the asset that is used up) is charged against revenues each year as an expense called depreciation.

However, there are several ways in which accounting profit, calculated using the above and other conventions, is different from taxable profit. These include capital allowances, unallowable expenses, untaxed incomes, and special reliefs. Also, taxable income does not use the accruals convention as fully as accounting profit does. These matters are discussed below. A numerical example which includes these points may be found in an Appendix.

It should be remembered that it was mentioned in Chapter 12 that, as for accounting net profit, dividends are not deductible but interest payments are deductible in the calculation of taxable income.

Depreciation

As we have seen, one of the expenses that a business charges against its revenues is depreciation. Each year in which the asset is used, part of its cost is charged in the profit calculation. Under traditional accounting, it is historic cost that is allocated; for companies using current cost accounting it is the replacement cost (Kirkman, 1978, Chapter 5).

Depreciation is one of the expenses which is not allowed in the calculation of taxable profit. Instead, there is a scheme of accelerated depreciation called the *capital allowances* system. One of the reasons for this is that the estimation of depreciation is a fairly subjective matter. Many companies and many accountants come to many different answers to the questions of what rates and what methods of depreciation should be used. Consequently, it might be found that high depreciation charges were being used to calculate profit merely in order to reduce taxation. This occurs in many other European countries. Fortunately, it is not the case in the UK, so accountants can charge what they consider to be fair amounts of depreciation without affecting the tax bill.

The main reason for capital allowances, as we have seen, is that they are a means of encouraging certain types of investment by postponing amounts of taxation paid by a company in proportion to the investment it carries out. Postponement of any payment is clearly useful to a company because the money can be used for other purposes in the interim period. Postponement is particularly useful in times of inflation when the real value of the eventual payment falls. From time to time, the government has given cash grants in addition to or instead of tax allowances. Since 1970 the system has been reasonably simple. Plant and machinery have attracted substantial first-year allowances and subsequent writing down allowances; industrial buildings (but not commercial buildings like shops and offices) have attracted initial allowances and writing down allowances that start in the first year. This is illustrated in Table 13A.

When an asset is sold, it may be found that the capital allowances have exceeded or fallen short of the actual loss in value. This gives rise to 'balancing charges' or 'balancing allowances' to correct the difference. In the case of buildings, for example, it may also be that an asset is sold for more than its purchase cost; in which case there is a capital gain as well as a balancing charge. These problems are discussed in the *Workbook*.

In order to illustrate the advantage given by capital allowances, suppose that a company spends £1m on machinery, as follows:

	Non-spending company £'000s	*Spending company £'000s*
Taxable profit before allowances	5000	5000
Capital allowance	–	1000
Taxable profit after allowances	5000	4000
Taxation (52%)	2600	2080
Profit after tax	2400	1920

Table 13A Capital Allowances

(i) *Plant and Machinery bought:*
27.10.70–19.7.71: 60% first year allowances
20. 7.71–21.3.72: 80% first year allowances
22. 3.70–present: 100% first year allowances

Any amount not allowed against profit in the first year attract writing down allowances of 25% each year on the reducing amount.

(ii) *Industrial Buildings bought:*
5. 4.70–21. 3.72: 30% initial allowance
22. 3.72–12.11.74: 40% initial allowance
13.11.74– 9. 3.81: 50% initial allowancs
10. 3.81– present: 75% initial allowance

In addition, 4% of the *cost* is allowed as a writing down allowance each year (including the first) until all the cost has been used up by these two sorts of allowance.

(iii) *Patents created or bought:*
based on life of patent up to 17 years.

(iv) *Industrial or Scientific 'know how':*
based on 6 years.

(v) *Business Cars:*
writing down allowances of 25% per year on the written down (reducing balance) value. Lorries are considered to be plant. Expensive cars (over £8,000 in 1983) receive yearly allowances restricted to £2,000.

The expenditure of £1m leads to a tax reduction of £520,000. Similarly, if a company spends £100,000 on a factory it achieves a £41,080 tax reduction (allowances of 75 per cent and 4 per cent).

The reason for saying that capital allowances 'postpone' tax rather than permanently reducing it rests on a comparison between this scheme of accelerated depreciation allowances and the smaller depreciation charges used by accountants, which could be taken to be the alternative to capital allowances. Assuming that, under either system, the maximum eventual allowances against profit sum to the asset's cost, the system of capital allowances allows a higher charge against taxable profit in the first year, but lowers the charge in later years:

	Accounting treatment	*Tax treatment*
Purchase of asset (expected to last 5 years)	1000	1000
Depreciation or capital allowance, year 1	200	1000
	800	0
Depreciation charge, year 2	200	–
	600	
Depreciation charge, year 3	200	–
	400	
Depreciation charge, year 4	200	–
	200	
Depreciation charge, year 5	200	–
	0	

During the mid-1970s, it was usual to find large amounts in a company's balance sheet called 'deferred taxation' which represented amounts that accountants had charged against profit in order to recognise the tax postponed due to capital allowances and other reliefs. In 1977 this practice was discontinued in many cases on the grounds that, for a company with a continuing capital expenditure programme, the deferred tax is postponed indefinitely and therefore does not represent a reasonable liability for a going concern (ASC, 1975 and 1978).

The estimated reduction in corporation tax receipts due to capital allowances was £6700m in 1980–81. The tax receipts after this and other reliefs were £4650m (Treasury, 1982, pp. 134, 136).

Suggestions for the reform of capital allowances include extending them to commercial buildings, like offices and shops, and basing them on current cost accounting depreciation. The government regards the former as expensive and a reduction in the bias towards investment in manufacturing industry (Treasury, 1982, Chapter 15). The latter is seen as approximately accomplished already (see Section 13.6 below).

Unallowable Expenses

In addition to the disallowance of depreciation because of the alternative granting of capital allowances, all other forms of capital expenditure are also disallowed because they are not used up to earn the year's profit. Also, some other payments are disallowed because they are deemed to be unconnected with trading. These include taxes paid, fines and legal costs involved in breaking the law, the costs of tax appeals (a wry piece of humour), and political donations that cannot be clearly shown to be spent in order to preserve or enhance the trading of the business.

These disallowances follow from S.130 of the 1970 Taxes Act which disallows expenses which are not 'wholly and exclusively laid out for the purposes of the trade'. This matter was considered in Chapter 8 with respect to the words 'wholly and exclusively'. It might be noted here that case law has further defined 'the purposes of the trade'. In *Strong and Co Ltd v. Woodifield* (5 TC 215) it was held that 'It is not enough that the disbursement is made in the course of, or arises out of, or is connected with the trade ... it must be made for the purpose of earning the profits'. In this case the cost of damages paid to a customer who was hurt by a chimney falling from the taxpayer's premises was disallowed. As another example, in the case of *Smith Potato Estates Ltd v. Bolland* (30 TC 267) it was held that tax appeal expenses were not allowable.

In practice, the Revenue allows apportionment of expenses like rates or car running expenses when they do not exclusively relate to a business. However, it is clear that any private benefit gained from the business's assets or current expenditure should lead to a reduction in the amounts allowable against profit of the business. This provides the ground for many a skirmish between the Revenue and the taxpayer; for example, the case of *Sharkey v. Wernher* (36 TC 275). Lady Wernher transferred horses from her (taxable) stud farm to her (untaxed) racing stables. It was held that the stud farm should be deemed to profit from the market value of the horses, not their cost. This also applies to the private use of business stocks; for example, the use by a grocer of his business's lettuces for his own lunch.

The cost of entertaining customers who are UK residents, the cost of any gifts (unless they are under £2 each and constitute advertising) and part of the costs of hiring expensive cars (i.e. over £8,000 in 1983) are unallowable for tax purposes, presumably on the grounds that the government does not wish to subsidise extravagance or provide easy ways in which tax can be avoided. Entertainment of overseas customers is still an allowable expense in order to encourage exports. It has been suggested that now no party of UK customers is complete without an overseas member; one supposes that Rent-a-Sheikh is doing brisk business! Various legal charges which should properly be added to capital expenditure (like legal fees for negotiating long leases or buying a factory) are not allowable as charges against current profit. However, since they increase capital expenditure, they will increase capital allowances.

Another area in which some expenses are not allowed for tax purposes concerns the bad debts which a business may suffer after having included the related credit sales in revenues. Any debt which is *certain* to be uncollectable is charged against accounting profit and is allowable for tax purposes. Any identified debts which are considered *likely* to be uncollectable are dealt with by creating a *specific* provision for doubtful debts. The creation or increase of such a provision is also charged against accounting profit and is allowable for tax purposes. This implies that any 'bad' debts which are later recovered and any specific provision which turns out to have been unnecessary will cause an *increase* in taxable profit. In addition, accountants often charge an additional amount against profit as a *general* provision for possible bad debts. This will be based on past experience; it might be five per cent of debtors at the end of the accounting year. This is not allowed as a charge for the calculation of taxable profit, because it is subjective and therefore too easy to manipulate, rather like depreciation expenses.

A further point which may need clarification is that the splitting up of profit between shareholders (dividends) and internal uses (transfers to reserves) are not expenses but *appropriations* of profit. Consequently, the payment of dividends or the transfer of amounts to reserves are not deductible in the calculation of taxable profit.

Without going into further detail (of which there is a great deal) this section has outlined several principles which cause payments to be disallowed. For example, non-trading expenses or expenses for private benefit cannot be allowed against the trading revenues of the business: distributions of profit cannot be treated as expenses; any form of capital expenditure must be allowed under the capital allowances system or not at all; and expenditure which is too subjective is disallowed to avoid manipulation. These adjustments cause permanent changes in tax, unlike capital allowances which might be said to cause a postponement.

Financial Income

Some revenues of the company are not taxable for corporation tax purposes. First, incoming dividends from UK companies are not taxed, because they will have been paid out of profit which has already borne corporation tax in the paying company. For this reason such income is called 'franked' investment income. (Income which has not borne corporation tax in the paying company, like interest receipts, is called 'unfranked' investment income.) Second, a large part of any sale of fixed assets will not be taxable profit; and even that part which *is* will usually not be included in taxable profit, but will cause an immediate or eventual adjustment to capital allowances. There are more details in the *Workbook*.

In addition, companies are not subject to personal income tax. Therefore, any receipt (like interest or patent income) that has suffered an income tax deduction at source will give rise to a reclaim by the company. Similarly, companies deduct income tax at source, on behalf of the Inland Revenue, when they pay interest, patent royalties or annuities. This tax then becomes due to the Revenue, but may be set off against the reclaims mentioned above.

For example, suppose that a company receives debenture interest (unfranked investment income) of £7,000 and pays interest of £2,000. When it receives the interest it can make a claim to the Inland Revenue for £3,000, which will have been deducted at source as income tax by the paying company. When it pays out its own interest, it must similarly deduct income tax at the basic rate (i.e. for 1983–84, 30% × £2,000 = £600). Thus, on balance, it reclaims £3,000 – £600 = £2,400. In practice this paying or reclaiming is done using a quarterly system, as illustrated in the *Workbook*. For both corporation tax and financial accounting purposes, the interest receipts and payments are treated *gross* of income tax.

Stock Relief

There are some special reliefs for businesses, which reduce the taxation paid. The most important of these is stock appreciation relief which aims to alleviate the taxation of 'profit' caused by unrealised gains on stocks. Consider this case in a simple retail organisation:

		£	£
	Sales		80,000
	Opening stock	10,000	
plus	Purchases	50,000	
		60,000	
less	Closing stock	11,000	
equals	Cost of goods sold		49,000
	Gross profit		31,000

If the increase in stock of £1,000 does not represent a physical increase but has been caused by inflation, it is an unrealised nominal gain which is locked into the company. If it gave rise to a tax liability, the business might have to reduce its scale in order to pay the tax, and there would often be liquidity problems. From 1973 there has been relief in this area. In 1980–81, for example, the total corporation tax yield was £4,650 million, with the stock appreciation relief having been £2,050 million (Treasury, 1982, p. 136).

The system for granting stock relief has changed frequently since its introduction. It applies to companies, partnerships and sole traders, so such stocks as professional work-in-progress may be included. Under the 1975–80 system, stock relief was an amount equal to the excess of any increase in stocks over 15 per cent of adjusted profit less capital allowances. This stock relief was then deducted during the calculation of taxable profit.

The 1981 Finance Act introduced a new system whereby an 'all-stocks index', published by the government, is applied to a company's opening stock (less £2,000). This system moves closer to the accountant's idea of a 'cost of sales adjustment' (Kirkman, 1978, Chapter 6). It also removes the effect under the previous system whereby stock relief was gained due to increasing volume as well as increasing value.

In the above numerical example, the index change would be applied to the opening stock less £2,000, i.e. £8,000 in this case. Suppose that the all-stocks index for the year-end is 200, and the index for the previous year-end had been 180, then the stock relief will be:

$$\text{£}8{,}000 \times \frac{200 - 180}{180} = \text{£}889$$

This is a further deduction in the calculation of taxable income.

Unused relief is to be written off after six years. Also, within this period, it is possible for previous relief to be clawed back, but only if the trade ceases or virtually ceases.

Capital Gains

Capital gains of companies as well as those of individuals and unincorporated businesses are taxed. In all cases, there is no tax to be assessed until the gain is realised. The rules relating to the calculation of the gain are the same for all taxpayers. However, for businesses of all sorts, capital gains tax can be postponed indefinitely because of 'roll-over' relief. When a business replaces an asset, it may deduct any gain on the old asset from the cost of the new asset. This increases the eventual gain on the new asset, but then this cumulative gain may once more be rolled over into the next replacement. Assuming that assets are always going to be replaced, capital gains tax will never be paid, particularly in times of inflation when replacement costs are rising. Let us look at a simple example where there have been no capital allowances because the asset is a commercial building:

		£	
Asset A sold in 1984 for		10,000	
less costs of sale		600	
		9,400	
Purchase of A in 1974	5,000		
plus costs	500		
		5,500	
Realised gain on A		3,900	untaxed (see below)
Purchase of replacement B in 1984		15,000	
Costs		1,500	
		16,500	
less realised gain on A		3,900	rolled over
Purchase price used for eventual calculation of gain on B		12,600	

Companies do not pay capital gains tax as such. They pay corporation tax on their chargeable gains. However, the rate of tax on capital gains for companies is, in effect, still 30 per cent. In practice, for the purposes of corporation tax calculations a *proportion* of the capital gain is added to other income and the total is taxed at the corporation tax rate. For example, if the rate is 52 per cent, then 15/26 of any capital gain is included ($(15/26)G \times 52\% = G \times 30\%$). There is an example of a corporate capital gains calculation in the *Workbook*.

The indexation of capital gains applies for companies as for other taxpayers. This was discussed in Chapter 8. However, the zero-rate band (£5,300 in 1983–84) which applies to capital gains of individuals is not available for corporate capital gains.

13.3 Loss Reliefs

There are many ways in which the losses of a company may be used to reduce taxation by absorbing taxable income of various sorts. Unfortunately, the rules relating to different types of losses are different, and there are some special reliefs for companies which are ceasing to trade and for companies which are part of a group. This section will briefly outline these reliefs, leaving more detailed consideration and examples to the *Workbook* for readers who require it.

Trading Losses

Trading losses of a fiscal year may be set against any other income of the same year, or carried back against income of the previous year. If the loss was caused by claiming first year allowances, it may be carried back against the income of up to two further years. Income includes the reduced portions of capital gains. If there are still unrelieved trading losses, these can be carried forward against *trading profits only* of future years. Rules for this are in Section 177 of the Income and Corporation Taxes Act, 1970.

Charges on income, like interest or patents, can create or increase a loss that can be carried forward against future trading profits.

Non-Trading Losses

Examples of non-trading losses are capital losses or losses on property rental. These may be relieved against present or future profits or gains *of the same type* but may not be carried back.

Other Reliefs

If a company ceases trading and cannot relieve its losses in other ways, it may be able to take advantage of 'terminal loss relief'. Any unrelieved losses of the last 12 months may be carried back against the *trading profits* of the previous 36 months (S178).

Members of a group of companies can set off trade losses, charges and capital allowances against profits of another member (S258). If a company has unrelieved losses and a surplus of franked investment income (FII) over its franked payments, it may opt to treat this as subject to corporation tax. This has two effects, which can be reversed in later years. First, the surplus FII is absorbed by the losses. Second, the tax credit attached to the FII can be claimed (S254).

The *Workbook* has details of these various loss reliefs.

Unincorporated Businesses

Loss reliefs for partnerships and sole traders bear similarities to the above reliefs for companies. The rules are to be found in SS 168–176 of the 1970 Taxes Act. S168 gives relief of losses against other income of the same or preceding year. S171 allows losses not relieved under S168 to be carried forward against profits from the same trade. S174 allows a terminal loss relief.

13.4 'Small Companies' Relief

In 1973, with the imputation system, a reduced rate of corporation tax was brought in, designed for small companies. Because it is difficult to define a small company, it actually applies for those companies with small taxable incomes. The reason for the lower rate is that small companies are particularly dependent on retained profits as a source of finance, since, for example, they are not able to afford an issue of shares or debentures to the public. Also, these companies are the most like partnerships, and a lower rate may reduce the taxation effects which would accompany the transition from one form of business to the other.

The definition of small profits changes from year to year. For 1982–83, as proposed in the 1983 Budget, the lower rate of 38 per cent applies to 'profits' below £100,000. (The profits are specially defined to be net taxable income after trading losses and annual charges, but including chargeable gains and grossed up FII. See *Workbook* for a numerical example.) The 52 per cent rate applies fully to profits above £500,000. In between these two levels, there is a tapering relief which gradually raises the average rate from 38 to

52 per cent. This tapering relief is necessary in order to avoid the very high marginal rates that there would otherwise be if the average rate suddenly rose from 38 to 52 per cent as soon as profits exceeded £100,000.

Thus, the lower rate does not apply to a band of income for all taxpayers, as occurs in income tax. The relief is specifically designed to benefit small profits only. To give such small profits a similar advantage using a true lower-rate band would involve the loss of much more tax revenue, because all corporation taxpayers would benefit.

In 1980–81 it was estimated that a remarkable 95 per cent of all companies either take advantage of the small companies relief or pay no tax at all (Treasury, 1982, p. 119). The cost of the relief was about £150m a year.

Returning to the tapering relief, it should be clear that the maximum benefit of 14 per cent occurs at £100,000. This reduces to nil by £500,000. Thus the tapering proportion (as proposed in the 1983 Budget) may be shown for 1982–83 to be:

$$\frac{14\% \times 100{,}000}{500{,}000 - 100{,}000} = \frac{7}{200},$$

or 3.5 per cent of each pound that the profit is below £500,000.

The details of the application of this to a specific example are shown in the *Workbook*.

Despite this tapering, the *marginal* rate of tax is obviously still above 52 per cent for profits between the two threshold levels. Since so many companies are within the scope of the relief, the existence of high and varying marginal rates may act as a serious disincentive (Mayer and Morris, 1982).

13.5 Companies and Partnerships

There are many factors, relating to taxation and other matters, which a business should take into account when deciding whether to operate as a company or as a partnership. Before discussing these, we should briefly examine a few distinctions between types of company.

Companies must have two or more shareholders, and must obey a large number of rules to be found in the Companies Acts 1948, 1967, 1976, 1980 and 1981. These include compulsory disclosure of substantial amounts of financial and other information in companies' annual reports and accounts (Lee, 1981). These accounts must be audited by independent qualified accountants. Other rules about disclosure and behaviour are made by the accountancy bodies and, if the company is listed, by the Stock Exchange.

Private companies are those which may not offer their securities for sale to the public. Some requirements, particularly those relating to disclosure, are less onerous for private than for public companies. No distinction is made for tax purposes between public and private companies. However, a distinction is made between companies controlled by their directors or by five or fewer persons or families, and those less closely controlled. The former are called 'close' companies and can include public companies, but not if 35 per cent or more of the shares are publicly held. 'Controlled' means that either the majority of the capital or of the voting rights or of profit rights are held by the five or fewer associates or by the directors. Close companies constitute, for the purposes of taxation, the border area between individuals operating in business and corporations with a separate identity from their owners. On one side of the border, individuals operating as sole traders or partners pay personal income tax on the whole taxable profit of the business. On the other side, corporations pay tax on taxable profits, without reference to the owners' tax situations. Any of the profits of the corporation which are distributed may cause a recipient's tax bill to be adjusted. Consequently, for corporations whose owners pay higher rates of tax, there is a saving of immediate tax if profit is retained.

Since close companies are similar to partnerships in their ownership and control, it would seem unfair to tax the whole of partnership profits as though they had been distributed, yet not to tax the profits of close companies in a similar way. So, from the introduction of corporation tax, close company shareholders have had to pay personal income tax as though some proportion of the profits had been distributed. Up until the Finance Act 1980, this was a serious problem for many close companies. However, that Finance Act did away with 'apportionment' of *trading* profits to shareholders. It now only applies to part of estate and investment incomes.

Close Companies versus Partnerships

The question whether to run a small business as a partnership or a close company may well be decided by tax matters. The decision will depend upon the detailed circumstances of each case and, in real situations, professional advice should be sought. We can look at some main points here (using 1982–83 rates).

Partnerships: All profit is treated as distributed for tax purposes. Therefore the partners pay up to 60 per cent income tax on marginal trading income and 30 per cent on capital gains.

Companies: All profit is taxed at average rates of between 38 per cent and 52 per cent, depending on the size of profit (the 'between' is due to tapering relief). Any distributed profit is treated as though basic rate tax had been paid, but must be grossed up for possible taxation at higher rates as investment income (see Section 12.3). The company pays 30 per cent tax on its capital gains. A way of extracting more money at lower tax rates would be to sell shares and pay capital gains tax on them. A way to reduce corporation taxation is to arrange for the company to pay directors' salaries and fees. This reduces the company's taxable income and gives the owners earned income. This is clearly better than receiving dividends after corporation tax and then paying higher rates of tax on them as unearned income. However, the earned income is obviously subject to income tax.

Although the tax rates on retained profit may be lower for companies once profit reaches a certain level, the owners of the business must consider the additional eventual tax rates to be paid when the benefit is taken from the business, that is, they must remember the possibility of 'double taxation'. The combined corporate and eventual personal taxation on income or capital gains may be higher for companies than for partnerships. Note that, in either case, interest paid to outsiders is deductible from profit for tax purposes, and capital allowances are claimable. Also, the personal tax allowances of the owners can be used against their partnership or company income.

One particular advantage for companies which has become more prominent in recent years is their ability to fund large pension schemes for their employees (e.g. directors). Payments into tax-exempt pension schemes for present and past years are tax deductible for corporation tax purposes. This is greatly more advantageous than the limited contributions ($17\frac{1}{2}$ per cent of relevant income for many taxpayers) which partners can use as deductions for income tax purposes.

Another tax consideration that may be important is that, by careful planning, a *partnership* can arrange to delay payment of any year's tax until up to 21 and 27 months after the related accounting year end. The partnership must pay some tax for each year of business, but the rules relating to the opening years of a trade can be used to advantage (see Chapter 8). However, a *company* formed now would have to pay MCT nine months after its accounting year end, and ACT soon after any distribution. On the other hand, a company may have rather more advantageous ways of using up losses against the past, present and future profits; and it is able to smooth out fluctuations in the personal income of its owners which will be of advantage under a progressive tax system.

There are also several important factors unconnected with tax which must be considered. First, many professional bodies do not allow their members to form limited companies. Consequently, solicitors, accountants, architects and other professionals operate as partnerships or sole practitioners. Solicitors and accountants may become directors of companies not engaged in professional practice, but architects may not even do this. The reason for this ban is that the professional bodies wish to preserve reputations for high standards of practice and conduct, which might be damaged by some of their members if they had limited liability for the results of their firms' actions. The law allows such professional partnerships to exceed the normal limit of 20 partners.

Second, disclosure requirements do not apply to partnerships. This may be important to a business in a competitive or sensitive area. Other legal requirements are also less onerous for partnerships. On the other hand, as we have noted, a company's owners have limited liability for the debts of the company, whereas partners are jointly and severally liable for all debts of the business. Flowing from this is the important consequence that some owners of companies need not be managers, because they are reassured by limited liability. Therefore, even if a business needs to turn only to family and friends for share finance, it will be a great advantage to both sides if becoming an owner does not have to imply becoming a manager in order to safeguard one's personal assets. This becomes particularly important for public companies, of course, whose size is only feasible because their many owners are prepared to delegate management to directors. Another factor which may weigh in favour of the formation of a company is that it is easier to fragment a company, because the ownership shares are precisely defined and easier to transfer. For retirement or estate problems, this may be a considerable advantage.

13.6 Inflation

Since the early 1970s, inflation has been running at such high rates that traditional accounting has become increasingly unrealistic, because it is based on historic cost figures. Profit figures have been seriously overstated for two main reasons. First, depreciation charges (the recognition of the using up of assets to produce profit) are based on the historic costs of assets not on their current values to the business. Second, holding gains on stocks are included in profit. Many methods of adjusting accounts for the effects of inflation have been proposed and experimented with (Kirkman, 1978). In 1980 the accountancy bodies published an accounting standard (SSAP 16) requiring listed and large companies to publish supplementary current cost accounting (CCA) statements. CCA takes into account the current cost of using up fixed assets and stocks. However, taxable income calculations still begin with historic cost net profit.

The 'overstatement' of profit under historic cost accounting is important because it gives a false view of the operating success of the business, affecting different companies and industries by different amounts. Also it may lead to excessive distributions of profit to the shareholders, excessive claims against profit by employees and excessive demands by the Revenue. However, there are two important counteracting features in the tax system, which we have already met. Stock appreciation relief approximately adjusts historic cost profits for the stockholding gains. Capital allowances, since they allow 100 per cent first year depreciation on many assets for tax purposes, cause a full tax reduction at a time when an asset's historic cost *is* approximately its current value. Consequently, the corporation tax system from the mid-1970s has been approximately index-linked (see the figures quoted in Section 13.2).

Because of these two main allowances the effective rate of corporation tax on companies (excluding financial companies) for the period 1976–80 averaged only 25 per cent (or 15 per cent excluding ACT) of historical cost profit (Treasury, 1982, p. 138). If the corporation tax had been levied on CCA profits for the same period, the yield would have represented a 65 per cent tax (or 40 per cent excluding ACT). For more discussion of these points, see Gibbs (1979), Richardson (1980) and Meade (1980).

As has been mentioned, since the 52 per cent rate is a flat rate of tax, indexation of bands is not necessary in the way that it is for income tax. However, the thresholds for the small companies relief are raised regularly.

13.7 Petroleum Revenue Tax

Petroleum Revenue Tax (PRT) is a system of taxation, set up by such regulations as the Oil Taxation Act 1975, which taxes profits arising from the extraction of oil and gas in British territory (land and sea). The tax is chargeable on each field separately, and the liability is apportioned among the participants. The tax has been amended several times by Finance Acts. The position after the 1983 Finance Act is as follows.

The tax is charged at a rate of 75 per cent on the net income from a field. The net income is the gross revenue less royalties, operating costs and some other taxes. The royalties include those to the government, which are really a separate tax. The operating costs exclude interest payments. The tax is assessed on a half-yearly basis but paid monthly. There is also an advance PRT based on 15 per cent of gross revenues (for 1983 and 1984, to be abolished by 1987).

There are allowances in the PRT system. First, for most purchases of fixed assets there is a 'capital allowance' of 135 per cent, which may be spread over several years. The 35 per cent uplift ceases when cumulative income has exceeded cumulative outgoings. Nevertheless, this does mean that PRT need not be paid until net income (as defined above) considerably exceeds capital expenditure on exploration and development.

Secondly, there is an 'oil allowance' of one half a million metric tonnes per chargeable period, up to a maximum of ten million tonnes. Unused allowances cannot be carried backwards or forwards.

There are a few implications for corporation tax. First, PRT and royalties are deductible in the calculation of profit for corporation tax purposes. Second, in order to stop manoeuvres that would reduce corporation tax, a company is prevented from setting losses and capital allowances from other activities against its net income from oil and gas extraction.

For a more detailed analysis of the system after the important changes in the 1979 Finance Act, see Johnson (1979) and Kemp and Cohen (1980).

Appendix An Example of a Corporation Tax Calculation

The accountants of Ganymede Ltd have calculated the company's profit in this way for the year ended 31 March 1984:

			£000s
	Sales		10,000
	Cost of goods sold		7,600
	Gross profit		2,400
	Dividends received		400
	Bank interest		200
			3,000
Expenses:	Salaries	500	
	Rent	170	
	Rates and insurance	165	
	Depreciation	400	
	Office expenses	140	
	Travelling	190	
	Directors' fees	120	
	Auditors' fees	30	
	Legal fees (note 1)	30	
	Miscellaneous (note 2)	15	

Bad debts (note 3)	10	
		1,770
Net profit		1,230

Note 1

	£000s
Legal fees: Defending the company in a tax case	10
Work connected with new factory	12
Debt collecting work	8
	30

Note 2

Miscellaneous: Donation to Liberal Party	10
Subscription to local Chamber of Commerce	5
	15

Note 3

Bad debts: Specific debts written off	3
Specific provisions for bad debts	3
General provision for 4% of debtors	4
	10

Note 4

Capital expenditure for the year (£000s):

	Costs	*Capital allowances*
Machinery	250	250 (100% first year allowances–FYA)
Factory	200	158 (75% FYA, 4% writing down allowance — WDA)
Shop	39	– (no allowance for commercial buildings)
Cars (5 at £4,000)	20	5 (25% WDA)
		413

The adjustment of net profit to get to taxable profit proceeds like this:

Net profit as in the accounts	1230

Untaxable income:		
Franked dividends		400
		830
Unallowable expenses:		
Depreciation	400	
Legal expenses	22	
Miscellaneous	10	
Bad debts	4	
		436
		1266
Less Capital allowances	413	
Stock relief (e.g.)	180	
		593
		673 × 52% = 350

The corporation tax liability for the year 1983–84 is £350,000, which should be paid on 1 January 1985, less any ACT paid during the year 1983–84.

Further Reading

The technical details of the UK tax system are discussed in Carmichael, Harvey and Young, and Pritchard (latest editions in each case). More general coverage may be found in Brown and Jackson (1982), Kay and King (1980), Prest and Barr (1979) and White (1981).

References

Accounting Standards Committee (ASC) (1975), *Deferred Taxation — SSAP 11*, Professional Accountancy Bodies.

Accounting Standards Committee (ASC) (1978), *Deferred Taxation — SSAP15*, Professional Accountancy Bodies.

Brown C.V. and Jackson P.M. (1982) *Public Sector Economics,* 2nd edn, Martin Robertson, Chapter 18.

Carmichael K.S., *Corporation Tax*, HFL, latest edition.

Gibbs M. (1979), 'Inflation accounting and company taxation', *Fiscal Studies,* November.

Harvey E.L. and Young D.G., *Tolley's Corporation Tax*, latest edition.

Johnson C. (1979), 'The improvement of the North Sea tax system,' *Fiscal Studies*, November.
Kay J.A. and King M.A. (1980), *The British Tax System*, Oxford University Press.
Kemp A.G. and Cohen D. (1980), 'The New System of Petroleum Revenue Tax', *Fiscal Studies*, March.
Kirkman P.R.A. (1978), *Accounting Under Inflationary Conditions*, 2nd edn, Allen and Unwin.
Lee G.A. (1981), *Modern Financial Accounting*, Nelson, Chapter 16.
Mayer C. and Morris N. (1982), 'Marginal rates of corporation tax: a disaggregated analysis', *Fiscal Studies*, July.
Meade J.E. (1980), 'Companies, Inflation and Taxation — Comment', *Fiscal Studies*, March.
Prest A.R. and Barr N.A. (1979), *Public Finance*, 6th edn, Weidenfeld and Nicolson, Chapters 16 and 17.
Pritchard W.E., *Corporation Tax*, Polytech Publishers, latest edition.
Richardon G. (1980), 'Companies, inflation and taxation', *Fiscal Studies*, March.
Treasury (1982), *Corporation Tax*, Cmnd. 8456, HMSO.
White, R. (1981), 'The changing face of taxation — corporation tax', *British Tax Review*, No. 6.

Index

W indicates that the subject is covered in the *Workbook*

George Myerson is Lecturer in English at King's College, London

The argumentative imagination

'A sufficient and at the same time general criterion of truth cannot possibly be given.'

Kant, *Critique of Pure Reason*,
translated by N. Kemp Smith

The argumentative imagination

Wordsworth, Dryden, religious dialogues

George Myerson

Manchester University Press
MANCHESTER AND NEW YORK

distributed exclusively in the USA and Canada by St. Martin's Press

Published by Manchester University Press
Oxford Road, Manchester M13 9PL, UK
and Room 400, 175 Fifth Avenue, New York, NY 10010, USA

Distributed exclusively in the USA and Canada
by St. Martin's Press, Inc., 175 Fifth Avenue, New York,
NY 10010, USA

British Library Cataloguing-in-Publication Data
A catalogue record for this book is available from the British Library

Library of Congress Cataloging-in-Publication Data
Myerson, George, 1957–
The argumentative imagination : Wordsworth, Dryden, religious dialogues / George Myerson.
p. cm.
Includes bibliographical references and index.
ISBN 0-7190-3676-3
1. Wordsworth, William, 1770–1850. Excursion. 2. Dryden, John, 1631–1700. Hind and the panther. 3. Bible, O.T. Job—Criticism, interpretation, etc. 4. Bhagavadgītā. 5. Religious literature––History and criticism. 6. Persuasion (Rhetoric). 7. Imagination. 8. Dialogue. I. Title.
PR5858.M9 1992
808′.93382—dc20 91-44097

ISBN 0 7190 3676 3 *hardback*

Photoset in Linotron Galliard
by Northern Phototypesetting Co. Ltd, Bolton

Printed in Great Britain
by Biddles Ltd, Guildford and King's Lynn

Contents

Preface and acknowledgements

The main structure of this book consists of four readings: Wordsworth's *The Excursion* (two chapters), Dryden's *The Hind and the Panther*, the Book of Job in a translation by Robert Gordis, and the *Bhagavad Gita* in a translation by Juan Mascaro. The first and last chapters extend theoretical contexts. There are two sets of footnotes. At the end of each chapter, there are publication details and references for texts cited, together with other interpretations of the four central works. At the foot of the text in the readings, there are notes referring to specific comparisons with relevant theories.

I am grateful for the following permissions:

The University of Chicago Press and Professor Robert Gordis for permission to quote passages from *The Book of God and Man: A Study of Job* © Robert Gordis 1965. Professor Gordis's translation belongs to this volume.

Penguin Books for permission to quote passages from the Penguin Classics volume, *The Bhagavad Gita*, translated with an introduction by Juan Mascaro © Juan Mascaro 1962.

Lorna Ziegler has produced the typescript with her exemplary professionalism and good humour, as ever. I am grateful to my friends in the Department of English at Bristol University, for their help and support throughout my five years there, and for a finely strategic sabbatical term. I am also grateful to Anita Roy at Manchester University Press, for her enthusiasm and care.

Many dialogues have accompanied this work. John Lyon and Paul Kenny have been essential other voices of true exchange. Cliff Myerson has been the source of creative encouragement at all stages, and the book's own close reader. Syb Myerson has shown me personal research entering the public domain. Yvonne Rydin, in our life together, has really made it all conceivable. Simon has come along with us in his own true style.

George Myerson

Introduction: argument, dialogue, story

Arguments as stories

Four stories make up this book, four stories which depend completely upon the representation of arguments. This book is about the specific power of such stories, the power of inescapable processes which raise necessary questions. How much hope can we place in the exchange of differing views? How is good argument to be conceived? When do we recognise that we are in the presence of good arguing? And how much hope springs from that presence? What can arguments do about strong beliefs? The stories make the questions resonate, the questions drive the stories: in that circle, reading arguments becomes a great experience of imagination.

The stories belong to diverse works of poetic vision. The cumulative outcome – and, I hope the unified outcome – is a book of readings engaging with argument in imagination, where it may become many things: a hope of curing ills, a prospect for the victory of truth, a glimpse of reciprocity between people, an endless and even menacing vista of reversals, a comic series of twists and turns in language, a tragic ideal, a skill, a passion, a duty, a vocation . . . . There is no simple relation between what can be imagined and what can happen – but imagination's scope is an essential part of all situations.

A poem by Wordsworth – *The Excursion* – and one by Dryden – *The Hind and the Panther*; translations of The Book of Job and the *Bhagavad Gita*: the chosen texts are from different places. But each is a vision which has a central dialogue of differing voices. Any text will include different voices. These poetic visions rely upon their power to create differing voices: without these voices, there would be no development. These are also whole, poetic worlds which would not exist except through the representation of argument. Such worlds are arguable worlds, even when one of their voices has more authority than any other, even when one voice speaks much of that world's truth.

Each chapter pursues a story by giving a close reading – each takes the form of a continuous act of recall. Though continuous in a narrative sense, these recalls are still selective; such texts respond to other questions, naturally. Without claiming to settle such texts, the book does lay claim to a repertoire of necessary stories. These stories are diverse and yet also comparable. The repertoire constitutes – so I argue throughout – a distinctive understanding of argument, a literary understanding of a human problem and potentiality.

* * *

Any interpretation implies a point of view. The readings represent a consistent view of argument, a view which then comes to life in relation to the particular texts. There are two stages in the making of this view of argument. First, argument is understood primarily as the dialogue between differing voices; and, second, that dialogue is conceived as a story, an interaction between characters with motives and goals that combine to dictate a dynamic shape. It is more common to think of argument as primarily a monologue, the presentation of a single case. A persuasive monologue is clearly not a form of narrative, even if it includes elements of story-telling. The narrative requires an interaction between different agents, with their own ends in view. Therefore, the shift to argument as dialogue is essential to the idea that we can conceive of arguments in narrative terms. The argumentative dialogue may be taken over by one of the agents within the interaction – and a single case then comes to the fore. Nevertheless, that case would have emerged in the context of the interaction. The process begins with exchange: without that starting-point, there is no momentum for the individual cases.

What makes for a good story? And how do arguments have the makings of good stories? It is possible to think of arguments as suppressing narratives – *if* 'argument' only refers to a single case composed of linked propositions. Of course that is one sense of 'argument', but in the other sense it is the whole exchange of voices. Without that exchange, these readings insist, there can be no argumentative significance to any sequence of propositions. The exchange makes the cases truly argumentative; without the other side, we can hear only flat statements. Fundamentally, argument is a living relationship, a relationship between differing voices.

When this relationship between voices lives imaginatively, there are the makings of a good story in it. Not all differing voices make for good stories, of course: but, then, not all sequences where a good man falls from grace and favour with the gods make for successful tragedies. What are the other factors, the reasons why some arguments hold the imagination? That is another way of defining the interest of the readings.

The answer is the process of reading and experience. We need to follow the whole process, for only then can we recognise an inescapable quality. *Argument* has the makings of good stories when there is an inescapable rhythm. We hear the alternations of justification and challenge, assertion and criticism, insistence and rejection – and in rare cases, we also feel that the process is all of a piece, like the best stories. The pattern of exchange keeps us following: we want to discover what can be said on the other side, after what has just been said against it, and we also need to know how the underlying motives will dictate the outcome. Argument is truly inescapable if the competing cases are coherent and yet we can also feel the driving force of human motives.

To cure; to cheer; to console; to convert; to unsettle; to establish an identity; to unmake an identity; to rearrange history; to serve a cause; to justify a life; to make an action possible; to change the world; to preserve the world: there is no limit to the human motives which can provide the driving force to the rhythms of competing cases. And all the time, those cases must make their own sense too, otherwise the arguing is not real, but only a cover for other acts. Such stories evolve where strong beliefs are in question – for it is these beliefs which link the serious cases to the passionate motives. The works represented here are both poetic and religious: the quality of the beliefs dictates the poetic heightening of language and of world; the same beliefs create a religious intensity. These arguments are stories of strong beliefs – of the characters and relationships which belong with strong beliefs.

These are stories about belief in argument. People are inclined to think of belief as something to be held, something which is not subject to argument. The stronger the belief, the less argument is relevant. But experience shows that we cannot help but argue about our beliefs – and equally, the stronger the belief, the more compelling the motive of argument, whether to convince or defend. These four works take us into the centre of such tensions – which are tensions that compose the texture of experience, rather than flaws to be set straight by logic.

'The argumentative imagination' is the power of creating and re-creating the process of exchange between differing voices. This power is an under-recognised part of creativity. It is a power to tell stories which embody essential questions, questions of hope. The role of the argumentative imagination is not to answer these questions, but to make them real, to realise them fully. The stories are that realisation of the profound questions implicit in human arguing. What are the sources and resources with which to approach these stories?

Arguments and dialogues: Bakhtin and some Aristotles

> The word is born in a dialogue as a living rejoinder within it . . . .
>
> The world of poetry, no matter how many contradictions and insoluble conflicts the poet develops within it, is always illumined by one unitary and indisputable discourse.[1]

These poetic stories of arguments are about a type of *dialogue*. Any contemporary study of dialogue necessarily enters the domain of Bakhtin. To me, the brief transition between these two passages of Bakhtin is one of the most significant and disappointing moments in modern literary thought – and a generative moment for this book. His idea of dialogue is strong and open-ended; his idea of poetry is nebulous (yet doctrinaire). In between, Bakhtin begins by projecting a profound image of human speech. He maintains that:

> The word in living conversation is directly, blatantly, oriented towards a future answer-word: it provokes an answer, anticipates it and structures itself in the answer's direction . . . Such is the situation in any living dialogue. (p. 280)

So far, so rich; then the approach alters. Although such 'dialogism' is 'present to a greater or lesser extent in all realms of the life of the word' (p. 284), there are near-exceptions to the rule. Poetry is the greatest exception:

> In genres that are poetic in the narrow sense, the natural dialogization of the word is not put to artistic use. (p. 285)

The way is prepared for the crucial contrast in this great essay on 'Discourse in the Novel', the contrast between the novel and poetry.

The novel enhances the 'dialogic essence' (p. 300) of language; poetry does not recognise dialogue as the linguistic imperative.

Bakhtin does not intend a value-judgement *for* the novel and *against* poetry. Yet those 'genres that are poetic in the narrow sense' do sound narrow indeed, when we look beyond them at the other 'realms of the life of the word' outside. To the novel goes that 'dialogic imagination' which realises Bakhtin's vision of language itself in artistic form: the novel fully recognises that words are always replying to the words of another, whether or not anyone else is actually there to speak them. These ideas are influential – because the central concept of language as dialogue is enabling. But we should not let the appeal of that one idea validate Bakhtin's whole theory. This book implicitly endorses his notions of 'rejoinder' and 'living conversation', but I also wish to argue with Bakhtin. Why (to adopt his terms for argument's sake) should 'poetic' be the contrary of 'dialogic'? Why is poetry the great exception?

Bakhtin is difficult to argue with: he has ways of circumventing examples that conflict with his theory:

> It goes without saying that we continually advance as typical the extreme to which poetic genres aspire; in concrete examples of poetic works it is possible to find features fundamental to prose, and numerous hybrids of various generic types exist. (p. 287)

The poems of Auden, for instance, might include such 'hybrids', and many 'features fundamental to prose'; or the poems of Browning; or Pope's *Moral Epistles* . . . . In fact, the list is so long that Bakhtin might be underrating the extent of his concession! In the end, Bakhtin's definition is circular: if a work is a true dialogue, then it is not poetic; if a work is poetic, then (to that extent) it cannot be a dialogue of different voices (either directly or implicitly). But I am not interested in these logical objections to Bakhtin's theory, since this book partly endorses something in Bakhtin's views.

It seems to me that Bakhtin was over-ambitious. He defined genres so that *every* work can be classified, even if that meant allowing for 'hybrids' and hybrid-hybrids. He also based a system on one central concept or truth – language having a 'dialogic essence'. The problem with the genre scheme is that the labels help to begin discussion, not to resolve it. (No single genre scheme could unite the works in this study; yet they need discussing together.) And any master concept will always betray its inventor. Where does dialogue end and monologue begin? Can we always be sure which is which? How can we be certain whether 'the internal dialogization of the word' is or is not being 'put to artistic use'?

Bakhtin is trying to short-circuit the critical process. He treats the distinction between 'dialogization' and 'unitary discourse' as objective, as if that difference were not a matter of interpretation. His genre theory then supports that objectivity, by adding a historical dimension to the claim that dialogue and monologue are distinct. My counter-claim is through works which might be taken for a 'single unitary discourse', but which represent the most profound dialogue imaginable. That they are imaginable is important: imagination is the crux.

The idea of a 'dialogic imagination' conflicts with Bakhtin's watertight theory. Imagination is not an objective phenomenon. *It takes imagination to understand imagination* – and indeed Bakhtin demonstrates his own imagination in a ghostly blueprint for a hypothetical conversation and by passages on Dickens in the same essay. It is in imagination that interpreters make their choices: how to imagine the world of the text? We could interpret *The Excursion* as if it were a monologue. But much more is revealed about the poem's world by re-imagining the whole dialogue as argumentative exchange, placing the more self-contained utterances in that context. We can set the whole of the *Gita* inside a monologue of truth, *but then we would lose the experience of re-imagining the whole dialogue*. That whole dialogue is the living context within which the voice of truth is heard, a context with a benign yet argumentative dynamic. Bakhtin encourages the narrow choice in these cases; I think we should choose the more generous way.

Bakhtin is not alone when he excludes poetry from the realm of authentic dialogue. In his *Discourse on the Art of the Dialogue*, Tasso asserted:

> Furthermore, as others have said, dialogues should not be written in verse; they should be in prose, which is the form of speech that suits both the speculative man and the civil man who reasons about duties and virtues.[2]

And yet the argumentative imagination finds outstanding representations in poetic texts, as I shall attempt to show. I shall connect these poetic arguments and other prose dialogues. These connections make explicit some historical implications of the readings, and confirm the connection between these heightened visions and other representations.

* * *

Bakhtin provides an essential approach to *language* as dialogue, although he almost excludes poetry. Rhetoric offers a specific approach to *argument* as dialogue. Rhetoric analyses figurative language, and, by extension, may deconstruct texts into contrary figures. However, Aristotle begins his *'Art' of Rhetoric*:

> Rhetoric is a counterpart of Dialectic; for both have to do with matters that are in a manner within the cognizance of all men and not confined to any special science. Hence all men in a manner have a share of both; for all, up to a certain point, endeavour to criticise or uphold an argument, to defend themselves or to accuse.[3]

The terms are paired: 'to criticise or uphold . . . to defend . . . or to accuse'. Aristotle conceives the art of rhetoric as a study of opposing viewpoints and their interaction. We cannot understand the act of defending an argument except in terms of the dialogue with a critical viewpoint. This idea is also explicit in Aristotle's works on logic. We might expect logic to pursue argument in the individual case; but Aristotle sees logic as argumentative *dialogues*:

> A proposition is one part of a contradiction or the other part. A contradiction is an opposition which of its very nature excludes any middle. That part of a contradiction which affirms something of something else is an affirmation; that which denies something of something else is a negation.[4]

Propositions do not exist separately. We can understand propositions only as parts of a contradiction. These contradictions require different voices to represent their different dimensions, dimensions of 'affirmation' and 'negation'. When Aristotle analyses the mechanisms of logic, he discerns the interaction between different viewpoints: 'If a syllogistic question is the same as a proposition stating one half of a contradiction . . .'.[5] Syllogistic questions advance a particular view, but they make sense only by interacting with the opposing viewpoint.

Bakhtin perceives opposing positions in dialogue:

> Thus, all real and integral understanding is actively responsive, and constitutes nothing other than the initial preparatory stage of a response.[6]

But he considers explicit oppositions constitute only one form of dialogue and distinguishes his model of dialogue from what he terms:

> The narrow understanding of dialogism as argument, polemics, or parody. These are the externally most obvious, but crude, forms of dialogism.[7]

He also denies that his theory deals with actual interactions or imagined interactions between particular speakers:

> But dialogic relations, of course, do not in any way coincide with relations among rejoinders of real dialogue – they are much broader, more diverse, and more complex. (p. 124)

This book deals very much with the 'rejoinders of real dialogue'. Aristotle's model of argumentative interaction is followed and is more sympathetic to the understanding of texts as they are interpreted. These texts are stories of direct exchanges between differing views. Rhetoric explores the nature of these exchanges. Bakhtin is a stimulus, but introduces problems by narrowing the field of vision. Rhetoric is an open-ended historical resource.

* * *

Rhetoric has no single history. But Aristotle's ideas of argument recur and are reinterpreted by others in rhetorical contexts. Juan Luis Vives appears in this book with his concept of 'pseudodialectic'. In 1520 he wrote against the authorities whom he termed 'the Pseudo-dialecticians'. He accused them of dealing in 'strange and unusual meanings', 'wondrous suppositions', 'wondrous ampliations, restrictions, appellations'.[8] By pursuing arcane methods based on dialectic, these 'pseudodialecticians' had made rhetoric into an overcomplex system of arguing and analysing arguments. Vives connects the analysis of argument with real experience and practice. Aristotle began by recognising that 'all men in a manner have a share' of rhetoric and logic. Vives returns rhetoric to ordinary disputes and debates: 'Aristotle does not entangle and detain his pupil in these stupid and dreary suppositions, ampliations, restrictions, and verbal quibbles.' (p. 79)

Vives re-establishes rhetoric around argument between familiar human beings, as they seemed to him at the time. He was aware that there was an objection to doing so:

> And at this point the dialecticians always say, with sidelong nods and

> haughty air, 'Words take their meaning by convention'. Perfectly true, but still we must understand from whose will and convention they take their meaning. (p. 67)

Rhetoric should realise that large contexts shape argumentative interaction. But nothing is gained by a system which claims to be independent of experience.

Tasso foreshadowed the Bakhtinian preference for prose as the medium of dialogue. However, he also has an Aristotelian understanding of *argument* as dialogue. He recognises that many people are 'skilled in logical demonstrations'.[9] They seem to have mastered argument as a technique for presenting one case. Tasso accepts that mastery. But he warns that 'if the man who is skilled in logical demonstrations is not also skilled in asking questions, he ought not to write dialogues.' In other words, the gulf is wide between mastering the art of putting a viewpoint, and mastering the larger art of argument. Tasso attributes to Aristotle the view that 'every kind of knowledge must admit questions', and for him, therefore, Aristotle is the authority who presides over argumentative dialogues. The role of questions in the argumentative dialogue also arises in this book.

The philosopher Thomas Hobbes recreated Aristotle's contribution to rhetoric as an English work which he called *The Art of Rhetoric*. He brilliantly summarised each section of Aristotle's text:

> The Definition of Rhetorick.
> Rhetorick, is that Faculty, by which we understand what will serve our turn, concerning any subject to win belief in the hearer.[10]

Rhetoric concerns the relationship between argument and *belief*: 'belief is not gotten only by proofs, but also from manners' (Chapter 8, p. 20). Rhetoric depicts the point at which language engages with belief. Belief gives argument meaning, and, presumably, the more intense the beliefs, the more compelling the process of argument. The connection between argument and belief is explored throughout this book – *The Hind and the Panther* being closest in approach, as in time, to Hobbes. Hobbes also underlines the idea that argument is dialogue:

> Of the wayes to answer the Arguments of the Adversary.
> An Argument is answered by an opposite Syllogisme, or by an Objection. The Places of opposite Syllogismes are the same with the Places of Syllogismes . . . .

> The Places of Objections are four.
> First, from the same, as, To the Adversary that proves Love to be good by an Enthymeme, may be objected, that no want is good, and yet Love is want . . .
> The second from Contraries: as, if the Adversary say, A good Man does good to his friends, an Objection might be made, that then an evil Man will do also evil to his friends. (Chapter 27, p. 96)

Hobbes produces an Aristotle for whom arguments are dialogues in which belief is at stake. He also finds epigrammatic insights in rhetoric: 'Proofs are to be applyed to something Controverted' (Book 3, Chapter 16, p. 128),

In tones which we recall in Francis Bacon's famous essays on wisdom, Hobbes also transforms Aristotle into the most practical of English guides:

> Of Interrogations, Answers, and Jests.
> The times wherein 'tis fit to ask ones Adversary a *question* are chiefly four.
> 1. The first is, when of two Propositions that conclude an Absurdity, he has already uttered one; and we would by Interrogation draw him to confess the other.
>
> . . .
>
> 3. The third, when a Man would make appear that his Adversary does contradict himself. (Book 3, Chapter 17, p. 132)

> To equivocal questions a man ought to answer fully, and not to be too brief. (Chapter 17, p. 132)

Those epigrams pick from Aristotle insights into practical dialogue.

Rhetoric has continued to diversify since Aristotle. But there recurs an antithesis between 'basics' and systems developed from them. One supporter of the 'basic' Aristotle is Thomas De Quincey. De Quincey remembers learning systematic rhetoric in the style of the pseudo-dialecticians that Vives mocked. De Quincey too recreates rhetoric more cogently:

> Many years ago, when studying the Aristotelian Rhetoric at Oxford, it struck us that, by whatever name Aristotle might describe the main purpose of Rhetoric, practically, at least, in his own treatment of it, he threw the whole stress upon finding such arguments for any given thesis as, without positively proving or disproving it, should give it a colourable support.[11]

Much 'colourable support' finds its way into the rhetoric explored among the texts in this book. De Quincey also grounded rhetoric in everyday experience:

> Certainly we knew, what all the world knows, that an enthymeme was understood to be a syllogism of which one proposition is suppressed – major, minor, or conclusion. But what possible relation had *that* to rhetoric? (p. 87)

> The province of rhetoric, whether meant for an influence upon the actions, or simply upon the belief lies among that vast field of cases where there is a *pro* and a *con* . . . (p. 91)

Kenneth Burke, in his book *A Rhetoric of Motives*, connects modern thought about language with the basic idea of Aristotle's rhetoric:

> Rhetoric is the art of persuasion, or a study of the means of persuasion available for any given situation. We have thus, deviously, come to the point at which Aristotle begins his treatise on rhetoric.

Burke's concern was with antitheses, which seemed to him fundamentally the matter of classical rhetoric:

> for nothing is more rhetorical in nature than a deliberation as to what is too much or too little, too early or too late; in such controversies, rhetoricians are forever 'proving opposites'. [12]

In *A Grammar of Motives*, Burke converted rhetoric into 'dramatism', an approach which 'treats of human motives in the terms of verbal action'.[13] Dramatism consisted of five core terms: act, agent, scene, agency and purpose. With these five terms, Burke proposed to analyse the motives of human action, always beginning from language. He shows how rhetoric can construct the whole story, the story around any text or utterance. One agent implies others, one act implies others, one purpose implies other purposes . . . . In the pieces I have chosen for this book, dramatistic rhetoric has been foreshadowed by the telling of equivalent *stories* about dialogue.

In *The Theory of Communicative Action*, Habermas makes argument into the critical criterion of social analysis. A society is represented by the state of its arguments. The ideal argument is an 'unconstrained' interaction between equal representatives of differing viewpoints. Constraint and its effect on argument is a theme that recurs among my chosen texts, where authority is sometimes dominating. The 'unconstrained' reason moves freely towards the good argument and 'the better argument', also central themes of my analyses, and, where it does so, Aristotle's rhetoric and logic reappear:

> the theoretical perspectives from which the familiar disciplines of the Aristotelian canon can be delimited: Rhetoric is concerned with argumentation as a *process*, dialectic with the pragmatic *procedures* of argumentation, and logic with its *products*.[14]

Habermas relates each perspective to his sketch of an ideal argument:

> As a matter of fact, from each of these perspectives a different structure of argumentation stands out: the structures of an ideal speech situation immunized against repression and inequality in a special way; then the structures of a ritualized competition for the better arguments; finally the structures that determine the construction of individual arguments . . .

If we think about argument as a process, we will need to imagine 'an ideal speech situation', to advance the process. 'Pragmatic procedures' include the conduct of discussion between participants and the need to organise 'competition for the better argument' – what other procedure could be superior? 'Structures that determine the construction of individual arguments' are reached only *after* the other dimensions are cared for. Habermas makes the construction of individual arguments less important than the *whole* process of argument and the interaction between participants. The rhetorical process has been given an idealised twist in the location of good and better arguments.

Stanley Fish is another who sharpens Aristotle for later uses: Fish is attracted to the 'defences' of rhetoric which 'are offered by Aristotle in the *Rhetoric*'.[15] He returns to rhetoric as the study of interactions between viewpoints competing for persuasion, extracting from Aristotle the defence that: 'in short, properly used, rhetoric is a heuristic, helping us not to distort the facts, but to discover them' (p. 479).

Fish also finds in Aristotle support for his emphasis upon 'contexts or situations' (p. 344). Fish connects arguments with particular situations – just such situations as appear in my selected texts. Fish's rhetorician negotiates with the world. So must the figures in these stories. The possibilities are diverse. At the heart of this diversity is an idea: speakers for differing viewpoints must be engaged in exchanges. There may be an audience, or the object of the speakers may be to persuade each other; the consequences may be immediate, or they may be general. The rhetorical idea adapts itself to many uses, but the central point remains those differing voices.

Other modern writers have made contributions to thought that depend on rhetorical principles, and interpretations in the texts draw upon their contributions. Though they differ in approach and outlook, their common reference-point, almost a heritage, is in Aristotle, which links them, and links their practice to that adopted in this book. Barbara Johnson is questioning the received sense of texts in a project of literary criticism. She redefines deconstruction in terms that link with rhetoric generally, and that refocus and transform Aristotle's antithetical agents: 'deconstruction focuses on the functioning of claim-making and claim-subverting structures within texts'.[16]

Such structural tensions shape, undermine and reshape much of the writing analysed in this book. Douglas Walton, investigating informal logic, examines the logic of disputes, another matter which arises in this book. His study begins, just as Aristotle's does: 'One common and important type of goal is to convince or persuade another arguer with whom the first arguer is engaged in reasoned dialogue.'[17]

Hans-Georg Gadamer, considering hermeneutics, defends tradition, a theme that reappears in this book, where tradition is sometimes considered to uphold an argument. Gadamer attacks Habermas for supposing that tradition may suppress reason. But Gadamer, too, recycles rhetoric's central antithesis: 'Knowledge always means, precisely, looking at opposites.'[18] He goes so far as to make 'the art of finding arguments' a central ideal of his 'rhetorical and humanist culture' (pp. 21–3).

Rhetoric has a long history, with some common derivation and its own internal dissensions that have developed over the years. The texts examined here interact with that history, and hopefully this examination continues and extends that history. Though they are themselves texts from different historical periods, they elide in this sense: an examination of their arguments reveals an intact theme, consistent with ideas that have developed in the history of rhetoric. There is something in common in the nature of their arguments, and in arguing generally, which connects the different situations which are represented. Their common humanity – and their diversity – is expressed in the ways they seek and find differences between people and the ways they deal with those differences. Similar differences appeared to other writers of their time in the cases of Wordsworth and Dryden, and the arguments to which they led were set down by those writers in prose dialogues which are reproduced here. In the case of the translations, there are analogies with other traditions of translation. Those additional dialogues throw a tangential light upon the four main texts, and further illuminate the nature of argument itself, and the way it is rooted in dialogue with rhetorical implications.

The arguments dealt with in this book are conceived in imaginary and visionary terms. Between argument and imaginative handling is a delicate link, a symbiosis of feeling and thought which has called into being distinct rhetoric *and shaped great literature*. This link between imagination and argument, between literature and rhetoric, provides a fundamental motivation for this book. The book juxtaposes the work of two great poets with responses to two sacred texts: though the poems themselves deal with religious controversy and sacred matters, the overlying connection between all four is in the handling of the arguments they raise, and the rhetorical considerations that apply to all four texts, which overlap sacred and secular differences, just as they overlap differences in time and place. Since the sacred texts are in translation, the fidelity of translation might arise, but my concern is with the ways in which works conceived as translations contribute to the imagining of arguments. The way in which great writers and translators have handled differences of opinion can be analysed in terms that are rhetorical, terms ingrained in rhetoric's ongoing history, terms that now afford some understanding of differences which have been formulated over many centuries in many places, which reproduce and transform the main lines of rhetorical thinking and its history.

Argumentative dialogue

This book considers four works mainly, and extracts from others, on the basis that they are argumentative dialogues or contain them. There is also an examination of what is meant by the term 'dialogue' in the writings of Bakhtin. Very broadly, dialogue is taken to indicate some exchange of words, particularly where meaning is illuminated, or created, in the process of their interaction. The criteria for an *argumentative* dialogue extend this definition, and the way that the term is used in this book may be more readily grasped by considering some passages from John Stuart Mill's work *On Liberty*:

> The greatest orator, save one, of antiquity, has left it on record that he always studied his adversary's case with as great, if not still greater,

> intensity than even his own. What Cicero practised as the means of forensic success requires to be imitated by all who study any subject in order to arrive at the truth. He who knows only his own side of the case knows little of that.[19]

This passage alone may already suggest, to some extent, what is meant by an argumentative dialogue, *particularly as it applies in literature*, where both sides of the case implicitly are needed to make up the form. But Mill is more specific:

> So essential is this discipline to a real understanding of moral and human subjects that, if opponents of all-important truths do not exist, it is indispensable to imagine them and supply them with the strongest arguments which the most skilful devil's advocate can conjure up. (p. 99)

Embedded here is a profound rhetorical concept: that every argument is formed, or takes its content, from an opposition to some other opinion, or at least from a cognisance of some other opinion. It is this recognition of the mutuality of difference that underlies the meaning of argumentative dialogue. Moreover, there is no explicit requirement that the viewpoints be continuously exchanged, or be part of an exchange which is occurring all the time. To that extent, an argument can *occur* in what seems to have become a monologue, which states a case, or details the logic of a case. However, the implications are the same, in Mill's terms: such a would-be monologue refers *to*, or takes its form *from* consideration of another viewpoint which it has encountered, or which it may yet encounter. It may even be that arguments are partly offered to God, as they are in The Book of Job, without any expectation of answer: nevertheless they are adapted to God's point of view, as it is conceived in Job's mind, against which the form of his own words is shaped. And ultimately, in a divine way, God answers.

Another outcome of this whole arguing process by which one argument is shaped to another, shaped by another, is that an opposing viewpoint may be thoroughly tested and investigated, with results that are unforeseen. So it appears in the argumentative dialogues in this book. The effect of an unforeseen answer may be simple – to vitalise the argument, or change its course. But it may have more profound consequences. For the text, from whom a certain outcome may be expected according to all that is already given, may be profoundly troubled and unsettled by the opinions thrown up in an argumentative dialogue. The resulting illumination may be traumatic, straining all the work's resources and greatly heightening its effect as literature. Such are the problematic consequences of the Wanderer's intervention against darkness, against disillusionment, against the intellectual outcomes of a revolution in *The Excursion*, in which the ascendancy of any one point of view remains in doubt to the end, and there is certainly no finality that might have conveyed Wordsworth's own point of view, but its enhancement as literature by these precarious means is great.

Argument, dialogue, story: references

1 M. M. Bakhtin, *The Dialogic Imagination*, ed. Michael Holquist, translated by Caryl Emerson and Michael Holquist (Austin: University of Texas Press 1981), 'Discourse in the Novel' p. 279 and p. 286. Succeeding references given in text.

2 T. Tasso, *Dialogues with the Discourse on the Art of the Dialogue*, translated with intro. and notes by Carnes Lord and Dain A. Trafton (Berkeley and London: University of California Press 1982), pp. 23–5.

3 Aristotle, *The 'Art' Of Rhetoric*, with an English translation by J.H. Freese (London: William Heinemann 1926), Book I i (p. 3).

4 Aristotle, *Posterior Analytics And Topics*, with English translations by Hugh Tredennick and E. S. Forster (Cambridge, Mass: Harvard University Press and London: William Heinemann 1960), *Posterior Analytics* Book I ii (p. 33).

5 *Posterior Analytics*, Book I xii (p. 77).

6 M. M. Bakhtin, *Speech Genres And Other Late Essays*, translated by Vern W. McGee and edited by Caryl Emerson and Michael Holquist (Austin: University of Texas Press 1986), 'The Problem of Speech Genres' p. 69. Succeeding references given in text.

7 M. M. Bakhtin, *Speech Genres*, 'The Problem of the Text' p. 121. Succeeding references given in text.

8 Juan Luis Vives, *Against The Pseudodialecticians*, translated and introduced by Rita Guerlac (Dordrecht: D. Reidel 1979), p. 57. Succeeding references given in text.

9 Tasso, *Dialogues with the Discourse*, p. 27.

10 Thomas Hobbes, *The Art Of Rhetoric With A Discourse On The Laws Of England* (London: 1681), p. 3 (Chapter 2). Succeeding references given in text.

11 Thomas De Quincey, *Selected Essays On Rhetoric*, edited by Frederick Burwick (Carbondale and Edwardsville: Southern Illinois University Press 1967), pp. 85–6. Succeeding references given in text.

12 Kenneth Burke, *A Rhetoric Of Motives* (New York: Prentice Hall 1950), p. 46 and p. 45.

13 Kenneth Burke, *A Grammar Of Motives* (New York: Prentice Hall 1945), p. 33.

14 Jurgen Habermas, *The Theory Of Communicative Action* I, translated by Thomas McCarthy (London: Heinemann 1984), p. 26.

15 Stanley Fish, *Doing What Comes Naturally* (Oxford: Oxford University Press 1985), p. 478. Succeeding references given in text.

16 Barbara Johnson, *A World Of Difference* (Baltimore and London: The Johns Hopkins University Press 1987), p. 17.

17 Douglas N. Walton, *Informal Logic* (Cambridge: Cambridge University Press 1989), p. 1.

18 Hans-Georg Gadamer, *Truth And Method*, English Translation (London: Sheed and Ward 2nd ed. 1979), p. 328. Succeeding references given in text.

19 John Stuart Mill, *On Liberty* (Harmondsworth: Penguin 1974), p. 98. Succeeding references given in text.

The Excursion (I): arguing with hope

> . . . the noblest conversation poem I ever read. A day in heaven.
> Charles Lamb in a letter to Wordsworth (August 9, 1814), after reading the newly published poem, *The Excursion*.[1]

What is the status of hope, and what of despair, in this world? How far may we proceed through illumination; how much remains in darkness? These urgent questions were taken up in *The Excursion*. There is a literary background to Wordsworth's dilemma, going back at least as far as Cicero's dialogue, *The Nature of the Gods*:

> There are many questions in philosophy to which no satisfactory answer has yet been given. But the question of the nature of the gods is the darkest and most difficult of all.[2]

In that work, Velleius advances the Epicurian view that the gods are indifferent to human affairs:

> We have rightly said that a divine being is a happy being, but you involve him in all manner of vexation . . . . If on the other hand God dwells in the universe as its ruler and governor, . . . then he must be involved in all kinds of troublesome and laborious affairs. But we define the happy life as peace of mind and freedom from care. (Book I, pp. 90–1)

Among several replies, that of Balbus is the most forceful:

> we should be not only stupid but also impious if we deny the existence of the gods. It does not make much difference either, whether we deny it or merely deprive the gods of all activity and purpose. For it seems to me that anything which is entirely inactive might as well not exist. (Book 2, p. 140)

From the early days of recorded literature, hope and despair are in the balance, and the darkness is contested by human voices in argument.

Cicero's dispute on *The Nature of the Gods* was reconsidered by David Hume in *Dialogues Concerning Natural Religion*, published posthumously in 1779. Can we know about God from our own experience, he asks? His character, Philo, thinks we cannot, and that there are no grounds for supposing the deity to be specifically benign:

> And is it possible, Cleanthes, said Philo, that . . . you can still persevere in your anthropomorphism, and assert the moral attributes of the Deity, his

> justice, benevolence, mercy, and rectitude, to be of the same nature with these virtues in human creatures?[3]

In Cicero, on balance, the outcome suggests that we *can* know about the gods. Hume alters that balance. Philo makes a strong case against man's ability to conceive God, or derive general truths from the flux of experience:

> I have still asserted that we have no *data* to establish a system of cosmogony. Our experience, so imperfect in itself and so limited both in extent and duration, can afford us no probable conjecture concerning the whole of things. (Part VII, p. 48)

In reply, Cleanthes identifies a benign God, from a Christian standpoint:

> The only method of supporting Divine benevolence – and it is what I willingly embrace – is to deny absolutely the misery and wickedness of men . . . (Part X, p. 68)

Philo, however, cannot see the hand of a benign God at work in a world where accidents occur – a fundamental theme in *The Excursion*, too. According to Philo:

> A being, therefore, who knows the secret springs of the universe might easily, by particular volitions, turn all these accidents to the good of mankind . . . (Part XI, p. 74)

Philo has reached what might be for another type the verge of suicide at the scheme of things:

> Patience is exhausted, courage languishes, melancholy seizes us, and nothing terminates our misery but the removal of its cause or another event which is the sole cure of all evil, but which, from our natural folly, we regard with still greater horror and consternation. (Part X, p. 68)

But in the end he comes to accept 'a certain degree of analogy' between God and man and some hope from the comparison which favours Christianity. However challenges to that viewpoint remain ineradicably written into the dialogue.

Wordsworth's poem *The Excursion* appeared in 1814. Other controversies raged at the time in a post-revolutionary atmosphere which had unsettled received values in England as well as France and had also provoked a vigorous reaction to radical change. Politics overlapped with religious issues. *The Excursion* shared the preoccupations of the time and participated in current themes: besides the hopes and limits of religious belief, controversy centred on the need for revolutionary change and the need for rational and scientific solutions. Other writers, too, created argumentative dialogues out of the issues of the time. It is no simple coincidence that in 1814 Shelley published *A Refutation of Deism*, in part a reworking of Hume's dialogues in which religious matters connect with political issues. His first character, Eusebes, speaks for Christianity, but immediately raises political questions:

> . . . I have beheld the progress of your audacious scepticism trample on the most venerable institutions of our forefathers,until it has rejected the salvation which the only begotten son of God deigned to proffer in person to a guilty and unbelieving world.[4]

As with Hume, the argument between religious faith and scepticism turns upon suffering. Eusebes is offering a Christianity which makes life easier in his terms through: 'A patient acquiesence in injuries and violence; a passive submission to the will of sovereigns' (p. 120).

This provokes a response from Theosophus which rejects both the religious and the political values:

> The doctrine of acquiescing in the most insolent despotism, of praying for and loving our enemies, of faith and humility appears to fix the perfection of the human character in that abjectness and credulity which priests and tyrants of all ages have found sufficiently convenient for their purposes. (p. 125)

Theosophus is, nevertheless, a deist: he believes in a God; his objections are to the traditional God of Christianity. Since Theosophus has already rejected revelation and tradition, and Eusebes goes on to reject reason, the case ends by undermining both their avenues to religious belief.

In 1793, Hannah More produced a dialogue *Village Politics*, which takes a straight look at the revolutionary position, but steers cautiously for the conservative side, though amid the currents of dialogue its progress in that direction is far from straight and sure. Jack is a blacksmith, Tom a mason:

> **Tom**: Pooh! I want freedom and happiness, the same as they have got in France.
> **Jack**: What, Tom, we imitate them! . . .
> **Tom**: What do you mean by that? ar'n't the French free?

Jack: Free, Tom! ay, free with a witness. They are all so free, that there's nobody safe. They make free to rob whom they will, and kill whom they will.

Jack concedes that French justice always was very uncertain:

> . . . for they could clap an innocent man into prison, and keep him there too, as long as they would, and never say, with your leave, or by your leave, gentlemen of the jury. But what's all that to us?

The reply is sharp and leaves Jack somewhat lost:

Tom: To us! Why, don't our governors put many of our poor folks in prison against their will? What are all the jails for? . . .
Jack: Harkee, Tom, a few rogues in prison keep the rest in order.[5]

Tom is a voice much disturbed by new ideas being spread through the country, as the beginning makes clear, whatever the comic slant:

Jack: . . . Why dost look so like a hang-dog?
Tom: *(Looking on his book)*. Cause enough. Why, I find here that I am very unhappy, and very miserable; which I should never have known, if I had not had the good luck to meet with this book. (p. 221)

Tom *has* been given a vision of new possibilities:

Jack: What is it you are crying out for, Tom?
Tom: Why, for a perfect government.
Jack: You might as well cry for the moon. (pp. 225–6)

High hopes fostered by the revolution were to leave a disillusionment in their wake that comprised a significant part of the disenchantment recorded in *The Excursion*.

The movement towards and away from rational hopes pervades another dialogue of 1793, by Anna Barbauld – 'Between Madame Cosmogunia and a Philosophical Enquirer of the Eighteenth Century'. Mme. Cosmogunia half-opts for rationality in one prevailing trend of the times; but the philosopher finds her wanting, and her rational predilection shallow:

Enquirer: You must doubtless have made great advances in the art of reasoning, from the various lights and experiments of modern times: pray what was the last philosophical study that engaged your attention?
Madame Cosmogunia: One of the last was a system of quackery, called Animal Magnetism.

. . .

Enquirer: And pray what are you doing at this moment?

Madame Cosmogunia: I am going to turn over a new leaf. I am singing *Ca Ira*.

Enquirer: I do not know whether you are going to turn over a new leaf or no; but I am sure, from this account, it is high time you should.[6]

These argumentative dialogues explore the limits of reason, rather than being confidently rational. The exchanges are not smooth; the rules are not necessarily agreed or predictable. Conversations break down, change course, are interrupted or left unresolved. They do not advance deliberately towards a predetermined end; indeed, viewpoints opposed to the writer's own apparent inclinations sometimes surface with devastating effect and acquire great authority. The encounters are unstable, as human encounters are. Such was the dialogue form in use when Wordsworth was writing *The Excursion*: in many respect its responses were subtle and spontaneous and offer inherent opportunities to match the thrust of rhetorical theory.

In *The Excursion*, the recalcitrant figure of the Solitary is encountered. He has a profound disagreement about the value of life with a wise and generous friend, the Wanderer, which is recorded by a third character in the poem, the Poet. Ultimately all three turn for clarification to the Pastor, a figure of authority. The Solitary has lost all sense of the worthwhileness of life – his own life and life in general. The arguments between these characters concerning the value of life *are* religious, but the process of the argument – I shall suggest – represents an understanding of human exchange itself, an understanding which goes beyond the terms of the particular dispute and the doctrines that occur in it. At the heart of the poem – when we see it as a process – are no answers, but questions: how is it possible to sustain a constructive exchange with a rebel, a misanthrope, an individualist, an eccentric with a radically recalcitrant voice? Other questions follow: *why* should an articulate person – and the Solitary is articulate – turn against human exchange itself? How can others simultaneously create an interplay with his views *and* advance particular views of their own? What is the relation between having beliefs and being able to persuade others? What would happen to *our* beliefs in a world where *they* refused to argue?

Without the argument, *The Excursion* has no principle of development. To tell the story of the poem – or to interpret it – means telling an argument. But are arguments 'tellable' in that sense? If we naturally contrast narrative and argument, does that not mean reserving 'tellability' to the former and keeping logical analysis for the latter? Wordsworth challenges such assumptions, when he offers argument to the responsive imagination. The challenge is radical. Imagination must stretch to recognise how great is the potential in this enterprise, how it transforms our categories and opens new horizons.

A centre of dialogues

Soon after *The Excursion* begins, the Poet meets his friend, the Wanderer. One of the first things that we learn about the Wanderer is that from his early life 'on the lonely mountain tops' (l. 219):

> he acquired
> Wisdom, which works through patience; thence he learned
> In oft-recurring hours of sober thought
> To look on Nature with a humble heart,
> *Self-questioned* where it did not understand,
> And with a superstitious eye of love. (I ll. 238–43) (emphasis added)

Faith is never prior to questioning: the dialogue that leads to wisdom contains questions from the outset. Together, Poet and Wanderer gaze upon the ruins of a 'lonely cottage' which the Wanderer knew in his youth (Book I l. 568). The old man sees before him the evidence of mortality and transitoriness:

> I see around me here
> Things which you cannot see: we die, my Friend,
> Nor we alone, but that which each man loved
> And prized in his peculiar nook of earth
> Dies with him, or is changed . . . (I l. 469–73)

He does not have an easy, accepting view of death, as he envisages it in the ruined cottage. It recalls painful memories:

> . . . Oh, Sir! the good die first,
> And they whose hearts are dry as summer dust
> Burn to the socket . . . (I ll. 500–2)

'The good die first.' One would think these are the words of the Solitary, the notorious pessimist who subsequently confronts the Wanderer. In fact, these are the words of the Wanderer to the Poet.

But in this poem the Wanderer speaks *for* faith – so how can he begin the poem from such a low point? The fact is that the Wanderer's optimism is not facile. His faith acknowledges tribulation. He feels deeply the pain of life, and he expresses his pain in the story of Margaret, the young woman who once lived in the cottage. Years before, she lost her husband and children, one after another. From time to time, when he returned to the place he saw this good, virtuous woman's downfall in a series of terrible glimpses. He makes her sufferings resonate in moments that are *almost* ordinary, and all the more sinister for being commonplace, as when he heard from outside how

> Her solitary infant cried aloud;
> Then, like a blast that dies away self-stilled,
> The voice was silent. . . . (I ll. 736–8)

Disasters converge on Margaret: 'poverty and grief /Were now come nearer to her' (I. ll. 833–4). Surely, as a moralist, the Wanderer will extract a simple consolation from her situation? On the contrary, the sequel shows how difficult it is to find the consoling answer to grief. He surveys her life at its end, and he does reach for consolation in the idea that *she*

> learned, with soul
> Fixed on the Cross, that consolation springs,
> From sources deeper far than deepest pain, (I l. 936–8)

But the perspective is easy to reverse: the very soul is 'fixed' to anguish (in contemplation but also in imitation of Christ's agony); and 'consolation' seems to be as much extreme pain as antidote. The voice of consolation is contested; always on the verge of reversing into an opposing voice. Therefore, what the Wanderer offers, in the end, is a question:

> . . . Why then should we read
> The forms of things with an unworthy eye? (I ll. 939–40)

And the question is a real one, insomuch as the Wanderer himself has seen a world in which 'the good die first'. His, the affirming voice, finds there is already an argument to be had with a differing voice: each of us *is* drawn towards the unconsoling, the discouraging, the reading of things which strips them of value – but 'Why then should we read . . . things' in this way? Each of us must find a more constructive response. We must take that '*why then*' in the strongest possible way, as a full rejection of unworthiness. That is what the speaker advises, but he cannot enforce his advice on us or on anyone else as we shall soon see.

The Wanderer, at this point, is speaking with the Poet; the Solitary, their would-be antagonist, has not yet appeared in the poem. This is crucial to the dynamic of the work. Even before the Solitary appears with his entrenched pessimisms, the Wanderer has a case to answer, a case for taking the universe negatively. The poem is establishing that the dispute which follows is a real one, with general significance and not simply due to the awkward personality of the Solitary. Even without the intervention of that obstinate resister, the Wanderer lives in an arguable world: he lives by faith, but a faith that recognises the need to encounter other views. In other words, the poem is showing that the argument to come is intrinsic to the issues involved; it is an argument rooted in the human predicament and no mere by-product of personal defects.[7]

Can we find redeeming sense in the world? In fact, this is a profound aspect of the Wanderer's understanding of *argument* which appears at this moment. The universe itself is being recognised as a topic in the rhetorical sense, a focus of inevitable oppositions, a 'place' where contrary cases are necessarily found.[a] That recognition of opposed possibilities belongs to the voice which also speaks for faith. This radical way of faith – the Wanderer's way – links *faith* with a universe that is itself a topic of dispute, for that way there can never be any exemption from the contest to come, and from contest after contest. The effect, therefore, is to explain why the poem takes the form of a dialogue and a dispute, since that form will simultaneously express both the knowledge of life's value and the question: how can it be found? *We cannot choose between a world of contests and a world of beliefs: the two worlds are one, one arguable world.*

We can see this Wanderer who is going to take on the Solitary as a figure who stands for good arguing. People become wise only by making interpretations, but to interpret – a text or a life – is to

[a]Aristotle's *Rhetoric* (Cambridge, Mass: Harvard University Press 1926, translation and edition by J. H. Freese) declares that 'dialectical and rhetorical syllogisms . . . are concerned with what we call "topics," . . .' (Iii). That is, valid and plausible arguments derive from certain issues which require to be discussed in such terms.

recognise that other interpretations must exist. Every interpretation is part of an implied argument (not that all views are equal). Wisdom arises only *within* the arguable world of interpretations. The Wanderer has asked why we should 'read' the world without hope: *his* reading presupposes a contrary reading; wisdom comes from interpreting an arguable text, adducing an arguable world.

Viewing such a world, the Wanderer indeed adopts one perspective. 'The good die first,' but he proposes reading that knowledge with a worthy eye, though that implies the possibility of what to *him* is an unworthy eye which will read differently . When we opt for trust we acknowledge the other possibility; the shadow of lamentation falls across it. For the Wanderer, this is the universal argument, or argument at its most explicitly universal. Argument begins on the very edge of the unarguable, with the problem of suffering mortality. Almost reduced to silence or to exclamatory despair, ('Oh, Sir!') we have to make a positive effort. That effort may lead to resolution, even to stable faith, but we must never forget that it has been achieved on the very edge of another possibility. This need not make the chosen perspective less firm; on the contrary, we will realise why that perspective is so necessary to us – because it is threatened by a grim alternative.[b]

A question of exchange

On their way to the Solitary, the Wanderer and the Poet encounter a funeral which they fear may be the funeral of their friend. Clearly, in their minds he exists on the very verge of the living world. The Wanderer recounts the Solitary's story – and this establishes some of the terms for the arguing process which is to follow. He presents the Solitary as a chaplain who lost his faith with the death of his wife and children. He transferred his hopes to the French Revolution, only to be still further disillusioned by the outcome:

[b]The modern rhetoric of Kenneth Burke begins with a comparable choice between two perspectives on a single world: 'Acceptance and Rejection . . . then start from the problem of evil. In the face of anguish . . . one adopts policies . . .' (Burke, *Attitudes Toward History*, Boston: New Beacon 1961, p. 3).

this gone, he forfeited
All joy in human nature; was consumed,
And vexed, and chafed, by levity and scorn, (II ll. 296-7)

This Solitary seems to embody disbelief and cynicism. But to the Wanderer he represents more than that disbelief. The words 'levity and scorn' suggest also the idea of *a man who cannot be argued with*. Either he is not serious, or he is contemptuous. 'Levity' and 'scorn' precisely would undermine all exchanges. The Wanderer declares that the Solitary is possessed by:

a self-indulging spleen, that wants not
Its own voluptuousness; – on this resolved,
With this content, that he will live and die
Forgotten, – at safe distance from 'a world
Not moving to his mind' (II ll. 311–15)

The Solitary is 'resolved', beyond arguing. His horizons are closed, his attitudes are fixed and prevent him entering into the process of disagreement constructively. Either he will not take the issues seriously ('levity'), or he dismisses them ('scorn'), or he is already decided ('resolved'). We have seen that for the Wanderer issues are intrinsically arguable. For him the universe is a topic of opposing issues; beliefs are subject to reversibility. When he defines the Solitary as someone who refuses to argue, *a fundamental tension* is anticipated – between the drive towards the exchange of different positions, which leads to wisdom, and the refusal to engage in exchange, between a will to argue and its antithesis.

After the Wanderer has described the Solitary to the Poet, they meet the man in person. He is comforting a boy at the funeral, so he is not malevolent, whatever else he may be. However, when the Wanderer tries to discuss the funeral with him, he resists. The Wanderer proposes some notions that are comforting at a funeral:

Oh! Blest are they who live and die like these,
Loved with such love, and with such sorrow mourned! (II l. 591–2)

The reply is swiftly dismissive – and perhaps the comfort was a little too bland:

'That poor Man taken hence today,' replied
The Solitary, with a faint sarcastic smile
Which did not please me, 'must be deemed, I fear,
Of the unblest; . . .['] (II l. 593–6)

The Wanderer has already revealed that he lives in and with such challenges to hope and faith. His easy consolation – if it was easy – was offered out of kindness, not insensitivity. But the Solitary is already showing those qualities which the Wanderer anticipated: 'levity' and 'scorn', and, in a subtle way, he shows that he is already 'resolved' not to trade his position. That 'faint sarcastic smile' tells it all: the smile ought to make contact easier, but its faintly sarcastic character is a barrier. It is a parody of the goodwill which supports true exchanges between differing voices. The smile is dismissive, and dismissive both towards himself and towards the other. The Solitary is fixed in an attitude that can hardly be approached in argument through the ordinary use of words. For the Solitary, there is nothing to discuss. Though he does engage in a kind of differing, he does so in a way which seeks immediately to bring the process to a stop.[8]

The Solitary tells the story of the man being buried. Old and poor, he was – says the Solitary – exploited, unrecognised as a human being. After a storm he did not return from working on the hills. The Solitary went out to find him and, while looking for him, he had a vision – as in a dream, he seemed to see the perfect city:

> The appearance, instantaneously disclosed,
> Was of a mighty city – boldly say
> A wilderness of building, sinking far
> And self-withdrawn into a boundless depth,
> Far sinking into splendour – without end!
> Fabric it seemed of diamond and of gold, (II ll. 834–9)

This vision which the Solitary has had out in the hills seems to be connected with experiences of the old man himself on the same hills. The Solitary, however, is not concerned with such mysterious connections, and, on the contrary, gives a far more limited interpretation of his own story. Like the Wanderer's tale of Margaret, the Solitary's tale moves towards a question which he asked himself after his vision:

> 'And now I live! Oh! Wherefore *do* I live?'
> And with that pang I prayed to be no more! – (II ll. 876–7)

But the Solitary's question ('Oh! Wherefore *do* I live?') does not allow any space for different answers. The questioning construction has really become a kind of exclamation. It is enough to ask 'Wherefore do I live?' to pre-empt any reply of any kind. Further discussion is useless.

And now, looking back to that grand vision of the 'fabric' in the wilderness, we feel that the Solitary has deprived us of its positive possibilities, turning them to mere illusion. He has seen something of value in the world, something meaningful and splendid – and it was baseless. The Solitary's question: 'Wherefore do I live?' contrasts with the Wanderer's question 'Why then should we read/The forms of things with an unworthy eye?', and the contrast is central to the exchange that develops between them. The Wanderer reaches for conviction through confronting alternatives. There are many reasons why one might 'read' the forms of things in discouraging ways; he faces those ways; he wants to overcome the reasons for disparagement. He recognises the challenge of discouragement as a real one. He puts a poignant question, seeks an answer. For the Solitary, the 'wherefore' of 'wherefore do I live' is a dismissal of reasons for living, and it is final.[c] A man for whom questions have no interrogative force is unlikely to develop, to grow wiser or even survive in an arguable world. He is stuck with his preconceptions, confined within his limitations. Yet this awkward figure has his bearing upon arguing. The Solitary's presence points to a problem. He will not play: there is no strength, nor even relevance in anyone else's point of view for him. But we can already feel that this Solitary is a far from negligible opponent: any ideal of truth and knowledge which had no time for his voice would be gravely restricted.

The Solitary winds up the first encounter:

[c]The modern discipline of Informal Logic also studies argument – and makes some analogous judgements. Douglas N. Walton in his *Informal Logic* (Cambridge: Cambridge University Press 1989) addresses: 'The problems and errors of question asking' (p. 58, Chapter 2 *passim*). He notes the difference between productive and limiting questions and recognises that 'in evaluating dialogues, we should begin by examining the questions that were asked' (p. 40). Another analogy links the poem's story of argument with the thought of Hans-Georg Gadamer in the field of hermeneutics. In *Truth and Method* (English translation, London: Sheed & Ward 1979, 2nd ed. p. 328) Gadamer asserts that: 'Only a person who has questions can have knowledge, but questions include the antithesis of yes and no, of being like this and being like that.' We can see the affinity with the Wanderer and the contrast with the Solitary, whose apparent questions actually *suppress* alternatives.

> 'So ends my dolorous tale, and glad I am
> That it is ended.' At these words he turned –
> And, with blithe air of open fellowship,
> Brought from the cupboard wine and stouter cheer,
> Like one who would be merry. . . . (II ll. 896–900)

Partly, he is being hospitable; partly, he is evading further discussion, using what the Poet ironically calls 'stouter cheer' to avoid an exchange. The double emphasis 'so ends . . . it is ended' is symptomatic: as far as the Solitary is concerned, nothing remains to be said. The label 'dolorous' wraps up the whole story, although we might wonder whether he does not remember that 'fabric . . . of diamond and of gold' and whether it still indicates other possibilities. And was the life of the old man so unblessed? After all, others have mourned him sincerely. Some alternative interpretations to the Solitary's discourse linger as an after-effect in the poem, though his voice remains distinct and his recalcitrance problematic. The gesture of invitation signals that, for the Solitary, discussion is now closed, and the conclusion that there is no point in living remains in force – but the Wanderer still responds:

> Nay, nay,
> You have regaled us as a hermit ought;
> Now let us forth into the sun! . . . (II ll. 901–3)

'Nay, nay' the Wanderer says. He is refusing the invitation to wine, but also denying the Solitary's interpretation of his own story. So far as the Wanderer is concerned that tale was not 'merely dolorous' and he will not share the view: 'glad I am . . . that it is ended'. So 'regaled us' affirms the value of the tale, while implying that no further refreshment is required. The appeal 'let us forth into the sun' counteracts any negation left over from 'Nay, nay'. More deeply, the Wanderer is forecasting an answer to the Solitary's doom-laden question 'Wherefore do I live?'. No direct answer was possible. The answer comes obliquely in the invitation to go outside into the sun. We live to *move* 'into the sun', out of the darkness. Both sun and gloom are real. We can *choose* the one while recognising the other.

The Wanderer is at once challenging ('Nay, nay') and enticing ('Now let us forth'), and in microcosm, this is the essential dynamic of the way he will deal with the Solitary's obduracy. The Solitary needs to be persuaded, not merely challenged. And to be persuaded, he has to be enticed, drawn into argument and not merely subjected to opinions, while remaining outside argument. The will to argue *must* be goodwill – goodwill must be sought. How far can good arguing create goodwill – in an argumentative sense – where none is forthcoming? If *good* arguing is reciprocal, then it requires participants to share an equal commitment to the exchange. But the Solitary is hard to dismiss from an exchange, as hard to dismiss as he is to engage. He is a man of vision: his vision of the lost city is enticing, imaginative, full of affirmative possibilities though he treats it otherwise.

* * *

When the Wanderer offers to renew the exchange, the Solitary resists argument. He still tries to be negative without arguing. In other words, he is not merely adopting a negative position; he is negating all positions. Speaking of the child at the funeral, he says:

> 'Far happiest,' answered the desponding Man,
> 'If, such as now he is, he might remain!
> Ah! What avails imagination high
> Or question deep? . . .['] (III ll. 207–10)

The Solitary's renewed use of a question is even more deceptive. In reality, he is dismissing this particular question, and all other questions as well. It is crucial that he uses an interrogative form to do this. *His words take possession of the resources which might open up a discussion, and use them to close off the process.* There *are* great potentialities in linking 'imagination high' with 'question deep', great potentialities for probing and learning. But, at this point, the Solitary is exercising his scorn to the detriment of all argument. There is a very distinctive quality to the way he puts his ideas. His negation proceeds from a vivid imagination, with great power:

> what profits all that earth,
> Or heaven's blue vault, is suffered to put forth
> Of impulse or allurement, for the Soul
> To quit the beaten track of life, and soar
> Far as she finds a yielding element
> In past or future; far as she can go
> Through time or space – . . .

But the power of his imagination and address goes to close off the encounter again. What profits it indeed . . .

> if neither in the one,
> Nor in the other region, nor in aught
> That Fancy, dreaming o'er the map of things,
> Hath placed beyond these penetrable bounds,
> Words of assurance can be heard; . . . (III ll. 210–20)

Again, he appears to be asking something; in fact, he is dismissing the inquiry. He seems to glimpse a region of vast scope and promise, which dissolves like the visionary city. And he achieves this closure by using tactics which *could* have been accessible to debate. The key word is 'if': 'if neither in the one,/ Nor in the other . . ./ Words of assurance can be heard'. The 'if' seems to introduce premises for discussion – but this 'if' actually introduces definitive judgements. The repeated negative, '*neither* in the one,/ *Nor* in the other region, *nor* in aught', gives the force of absolute judgement, and it is a comprehensively absolute view – covering earth, heaven and even everything that Fancy can conceive. Everything open, everything hypothetical, everything arguable is drawn into an absolutely closed position. There really is no question about what 'Profits all?' – the answer: nothing. The Solitary's mode of address is far more challenging than obstinate belief. He represents the anti-arguer in people, in us all. Consider how he proceeds:

> if nowhere
> A habitation, for consummate good,
> Or for progressive virtue, by the search
> Can be attained, – a better sanctuary
> From doubt and sorrow, than the senseless grave?' (III ll. 220–4)

He moves by mock-syllogism: 'if neither in the one,/Nor in the other region' . . . 'if nowhere/A habitation'. The force of 'senseless' in 'the senseless grave' transforms those possibilities into absolutes – of course, we could not possibly find such 'a habitation'. The word 'senseless' combines the idea of death as the closing of awareness, with the idea that the grave deprives the world of meaning. He exploits the shock of 'the senseless grave' to close exploratory propositions. We can see how intensely this mind has been ingrained in arguing by the continued use of the most argumentative techniques – question and syllogism. This Solitary is a contrary function of arguing itself. He possesses total competence in argument; he has the arguer's full repertoire. Yet in his *life*, that argumentative competence is now a burden. He has suffered too painfully by entrusting his hopes to a world in which one perspective succeeds another, endlessly, without a final solution in the life of one person, or the continuity of history. No simple response is possible to his predicament and yet the Wanderer seems right not to exclude the Solitary because he is unco-operative. Argument is partly responsible for the Solitary – and must be responsible *to* him.

Acutely, the Wanderer responds to this enigma with a real problem:

> 'Is this,' the grey-haired Wanderer mildly said,
> 'The voice, which we so lately overheard, ['] (III ll. 225–6)

He refers to their meeting, when they found the Solitary comforting a boy at a funeral. Despite the slightly patronising tone, the question is a real one: is the voice in which the Solitary speaks now the same voice that spoke to the boy? In a way, it *is* (belonging to the Solitary); and in a way it is not (since it voices despair rather than consolation). The Wanderer is, in effect, trying to redeem the arguing process from the Solitary's closures and denials, by pointing to matter for new discussion. Of course, the Wanderer prefers the Solitary's consoling voice, but initially he fastens on the Solitary's possession of two voices. It is a sign that the Solitary is a complex figure when the strategy works: 'The Other, not displeased,/ Promptly replied' (III ll. 232–3). He is only half-responsive, but the half-response is still quick, quick with his suppressed life.[d]

The rhythm begins to move. The Solitary recalls all his *other* voices:

> in more genial times, when I was free
> To explore the destiny of human kind
> (Not as an intellectual game pursued
> With curious subtlety, from wish to cheat
> Irksome sensations; but by love of truth
> Urged on, . . . (III ll. 283–8)

He recalls an *exploratory* time, a time when he thought existence was open to possible interpretations. Furthermore, he actively distinguishes a genuinely exploratory *voice* from voices of 'curious subtlety'. The motive for exploring must be 'love of truth', all the stronger when

[d]The Wanderer is drawing his 'Other' into what Gadamer calls 'the to-and-fro motion of play' (*Truth and Method*, p. 94).

truth is a goal and not a starting-point. But then instead of offering these ideas about his former pursuit of truth for discussion, he turns against them pre-emptively: 'But why this tedious record?' (III l. 325)

One such 'question' dismisses further questions, such as the bearing of these memories on current issues. The Poet joins in[9] – first he encourages the Solitary: 'I said, "My thoughts, agreeing, Sir, with yours"' (III l. 332). He proposes a catalogue of problems about idealism and disillusion which include the thought that one cause for disillusion is starting with excessive idealism. One kind of false idealism which he criticizes is the Epicurean one of 'voluptuous unconcern' (III l. 351), and then he approaches nearer the Solitary's position by considering a possible defect in Stoicism:

> '. . . Or is she,'
> I cried, 'more worthy of regard, the Power,
> Who, for the sake of sterner quiet, closed
> The Stoic's heart against the vain approach
> Of admiration, and all sense of joy?' (III ll. 352–6)

He opens out two possibilities, those offered by the Epicurean and those of the Stoic – and then uses them to frame a question. In his view, neither school is adequate, but his use of questions is far from pre-emptive. The Solitary *is* freed to choose betweem these alternatives, and succumbs to the temptation to do so:

> Ah! gentle Sir,
> Slight, if you will, the *means*; but spare to slight
> The *end* of those [Stoics] . . . (III ll. 359–61)

The Poet did allow that the Stoics had *reasons* to be stoical – 'for the sake of sterner quiet' – and therefore the Solitary can rise to the question in their defence. One real question leads to others, and the recalcitrant Solitary is almost over-intense in his responsiveness.

But the problem of this figure is hard to *solve*, however promising the move. The more he does argue, the more sharply he re-turns against all exchanges:

> what good is given to men,
> More solid than the gilded clouds of heaven?
> What joy more lasting than a vernal flower? –
> None! . . . (III ll. 437–40)

He cannot bear to leave the question which has arisen open for discussion. Challenging voices are treacherous; they must be excluded.

This Solitary puts the arguable world in a problematic light. Does *any* assertion have sufficient weight to be worth testing in serious discussion? He anticipates every statement failing – even his own view that happiness dissolves fails the test of hypothetical time:

> Yet, ere that final resting-place be gained,
> Sharp contradictions may arise, . . . (III ll. 446–7)

Even contradiction has two sides to it. On the one hand the contradictions inside himself, which reappear in his attitudes, entice him into the play of voices which is argument; on the other hand the possibility of finding – in time – contradiction for what might have been worthwhile makes discussion treacherous. Since 'sharp contradictions' are always likely, we would do well to spare ourselves the demands of exchanging views at all.[e] The Wanderer – and the Poet – sense questions within all assertions: they face up to contradiction; the Solitary has been hurt, he stalls at contradiction. The Solitary understands *why* he will not argue seriously: no position is trustworthy enough to start an argument from. Only a potential arguer could present such a challenge to the idea of exchanging differences. The Solitary recounts his terrible story – a family lost, a political hope betrayed. He tells the tale with deep feeling – while urging through it, and through the pain it caused, a case against the merits of discussion. The beginning is the loss of two children, a loss which remains at the story's heart. These children's loss defies faith and hope:

> . . . Our blooming girl,
> Caught in the gripe of death, with such brief time
> To struggle in as scarcely would allow
> Her cheek to change its colour, was conveyed
> From us to inaccessible worlds, . . . (III ll. 638–42)

Loss succeeds on loss.[10] The pain of his wife's death is beyond *any* words, let alone the words of persuasive reasoning:

[e]Here Kant offers an alternative diagnosis of the Solitary: 'The proposition that no predicate contradictory of a thing can belong to it, is entitled the principle of contradiction, and is a universal, though merely negative, criterion of all truth. For this reason it belongs only to logic' (*Critique of Pure Reason*, translated by N. Kemp Smith, London: Macmillan 1933), p. 190. The Solitary is mistakenly applying the rigid rules of logic to experience more generally.

> What followed cannot be reviewed in thought;
> Much less, retraced in words. . . . (III ll. 680–1)

Speaking of the Revolution in France and its hopes, he pre-empts further argument, too, dismissing from the argument the very terms tried by the Poet and the Wanderer: 'Thus was I reconverted to the world' (III l. 734). It is no use *their* trying to reconvert him to the conditions of life; he has already experienced a reconversion 'to the world': all the reversals are done. Some experiences may be too severe for language; some histories may pre-empt all the questions on which our exchanges must turn:

> Yet, mark the contradictions of which Man
> Is still the sport! . . . (III ll. 806–7)

The Solitary is now generalising his perspective against argument by extending the negative aspects of contradiction. If there are always contradictions in the end, why should we ever embark on any arguments? Are justification and exchange not in bad faith if you know that contradictions ultimately wait for them in this world?

The Solitary has finished with humanity after his experience of the French Revolution:

> But that pure archetype of human greatness,
> I found him not. There, in his stead, appeared
> A creature, squalid, vengeful, and impure; (III ll. 951–3)

If we have dismissed humanity, then we have no grounds left for pursuing human exchanges:

> Enough is told! Here am I – ye have heard
> What evidence I seek, and vainly seek; (III ll. 956–7)

We glimpse a question opening – 'what . . . I seek' – and see the matter close – 'and vainly *seek*'. He has had enough! If people are worthless, then communicative exchange is pointless. The Solitary demands absolute assurance in the value of relations and discussion and their continuity before he will begin to discuss anything. We can see the anguish which caused him to exile himself from humanity as a recluse, the same anguish which keeps the arguer self-exiled from all argument.

Wordsworth's poem presents a crux in the portrayal of argument: one of the participants, the Wanderer, has a sense of the possibility of truth: he enters seriously into an exchange. But the other main participant, the Solitary, cannot any longer recognise truth as conceivable; therefore, he cannot enter seriously into an exchange. This is why the Solitary does not merely ignore argumentative techniques, but inverts them. But we can now see *how* the Solitary arrived where he has – and we cannot merely dismiss such annihilating interpretations, for to do so, would itself be to refuse argument.

Believing in argument

No one will influence this Solitary unless they justify argument. He will be inaccessible to particular cases unless arguing itself makes sense to him. (Yet his position – however awkward – is not to be dismissed: we now understand how much lies behind the 'levity and scorn': how much suffering has turned the arguer from exchange.) The Wanderer makes the attempt:

> One adequate support
> For the calamities of mortal life
> Exists – one only; an assured belief
> That the procession of our fate, howe'er
> Sad or disturbed, is ordered by a Being
> Of infinite benevolence and power; (IV ll. 10–5)

The key word here is 'support', which has a vital double sense. On the one hand, there is the emotional element in the meaning of 'adequate support': there is a presence which prevents the mind sinking, and the feelings withering. On the other hand, there is also the sense of intellectual support – 'support' in an argument, grounds for belief and reasoned back-up to conviction. In both senses an 'adequate support' enables us to make more sense of the 'calamities of mortal life', and sustains us in our sadness.

Yet there is something essentially provisional, or at least challengeable about a 'support' – it is very different even from a foundation, or a basis. So the 'belief' may be 'assured', but the result is still far from final. We can feel the scope for argument by the way in which 'howe'er sad or disturbed' breaks in upon the sentence before we arrive at 'is ordered by . . .'; and again when 'a Being' is slightly separated from that 'infinite benevolence and power'. The Wanderer's attitude here is precise and also subtle. It is not that the *belief* is at all provisional: on the contrary, he believes assuredly. But the consequences of that assured belief still leave us in the realm of the provisional assertion, in the arguable world. We will still need to make the assured belief apply to each new problem in 'the procession of our fate'. *The world remains one of process, at least as far as our experience goes.* Therefore, the Wanderer's response implies, the Solitary has expected too much from belief, from those 'words of assurance' which he has found lacking. Nothing about this 'belief', however 'assured', will prevent 'the procession' from throwing up some 'sharp contradictions', or will prevent the grave from making the world sometimes seem 'senseless'.

The exchange is asymmetrical, crucially so. The Solitary has been too disturbed to make acceptance a possibility, but the accepting position recognises the possibilities of rejection; it is essentially reversible – though not evenly reversible. So the Wanderer provides a striking version of the spirit of the universe, not the version ordinarily associated with an omnipotent power:

> Whose everlasting purposes embrace
> All accidents, converting them to good. (IV ll. 16–7)

Accidents occur – within the sphere of a purposeful order. The tension is real: there are 'everlasting purposes' being worked out but that does not rule out 'accidents'. We do experience these 'accidents' – and suffer from them, at least for a while, until they are converted to good by a benevolent authority. The Solitary has overlooked the alleviation possible in those 'everlasting purposes' – he sees all as necessarily accidental – that is part of his case against 'everlasting purposes'; nevertheless the Wanderer's defence of those 'purposes' recognises that we *will* often experience the accidental and may see life in terms of the accidental, even the apparently malign. The transformative word is 'converting', ('everlasting purposes embrace/All accidents *converting* them to good') and it is played off very directly against the Solitary's bleak memory of having been 'reconverted to the world' (III l. 734).

The point is not in the mere contrast. The Wanderer is creating a dialogue between his views and the Solitary's, despite the Solitary's resistance to exchange. The Wanderer's moves must be towards a dialogue of differing. It would not be helpful, or kind, or humane to leave 'hope' on this man's doorstep in the expectation that it would reach him. The Wanderer provides a hope that relates to the other view:

> Inspire me with ability to seek
> Repose and hope among eternal things – (IV ll. 62–3)

He asks only the '*ability* to seek', and nowhere talks simply of finding. Such a voice is adapted to dialogues, and indeed the words are responsive to particular terms from the other:

> Enough is told! Here am I – ye have heard
> What evidence I seek, and vainly seek; (III ll. 956–7)

The Wanderer has picked up the Solitary's closed word 'seek', and made it open. The search takes place in a different world from that of finding. True seeking is part of a world where *the reality is the process*. His reuse of 'seek' also stresses that the Wanderer lives consciously in an arguable condition, which the Solitary is unable to do. Contrast and dialogue: the double function is fragile indeed! Only a certain *voice* could live with the challenge. The Wanderer's is a voice which implies a surrounding dialogue, precisely where a monologue seems natural. His own voice is already full of exchange:

> 'And what are things eternal? – powers depart,'
> The grey-haired Wanderer stedfastly replied,
> Answering the question which himself had asked, (IV ll. 66–8)

The Wanderer is steadfast within the shifting process of challenge and response. Therefore he *needs* the questions which are real not self-closing. His 'answer' hardly ends the confrontation: 'powers depart'. For this Wanderer, some questions are real.

Term by term, the Wanderer goes on to weave dialogue around the Solitary's rejections:

> so senseless who could be
> As long and perseveringly to mourn
> For any object of his love, removed
> From this unstable world, if he could fix
> A satisfying view upon that state
> Of pure, imperishable, blessedness,
> Which reason promises, and holy writ
> Ensures to all believers? – . . . (IV ll. 154–61)

Now the key term provided by the Solitary – 'senseless' – reappears, and as in the Solitary's case, the context is death. The Wanderer turns his opponent's closures into starting-points, rather than rebutting everything. For the Solitary, the grave made all 'senseless'; for the Wanderer, despair would be 'senseless', if we could envisage salvation. But he is aware that no one can consistently adopt such a viewpoint.

Whereas the Solitary excludes other views than his own, the Wanderer's argument is inclusive. This inclusiveness involves far more than co-opting the word 'senseless'. The construction itself is taken from the way in which the Solitary expressed *his* sense of the world: 'so senseless . . . if he could . . . to all believers?' This corresponds very closely to the way in which the Solitary moved in his darkest moments:

> . . . What profits all that earth,
> Or heaven's blue vault, is suffered to put forth . . .
>
> if neither in the one,
> Nor in the other region, nor . . .
>
> if nowhere
> A habitation, for consummate good
> Or for progressive virtue, by the search
> Can be attained, – a better sanctuary
> From doubt and sorrow, than the senseless grave?

Their voices share a rhythm. That rhythm proceeds from a question through a hypothetical proposition back to the question. The Solitary uses this rhythm to close issues: his 'if' merely serves to introduce more negations which confirm the negative stance, and so turn what could be a real question into a merely ostensible one. By contrast, the Wanderer's hypothetical proposition – 'if he could fix . . . a satisfying view' really *is* hypothetical. In fact, he recognises, no one *can* assuredly achieve that 'satisfying view' in the face of death. Therefore, the question – 'So senseless who could be to mourn . . .?' – has a real force, since we all must 'mourn', here in this world.

All kinds of possibilities are opened up by the Wanderer's exposition. Ought we to mourn at all; or, since we *must*, ought we, at least, to try and overcome our sorrow? And, then, what is the relation between reason and holy writ and the 'satisfying view' they both offer – between the promise of reason and the assurance of holy writ?

Everywhere, at every stage, he expresses what he believes so as to acknowledge other positions, even to encourage a play of other positions. His belief is strong, yet recognises its own contexts, the dialogues without which no belief is possible. Could we have a 'satisfying *view*' of a state which was 'pure' and 'imperishable'? In one way, he is refuting what the Solitary has said – the grave need not be 'senseless' at all. In another way, he is also including – even intensifying – the darkened state of mind in which the Solitary has persisted. It is this double movement which constitutes the strange, rational magic of the Wanderer, and his claim to having a better argument than the Solitary.

The Wanderer demonstrates in practice that to argue with others is an essential part of his own belief – for the exchange follows directly from the self-arguing by which alone 'an assured belief' can be sustained. The Wanderer argues concertedly with himself, in every line, which makes his a voice always ready to argue with the Solitary, ready both in the sense of being willing and of being prepared. After all, he is the one to whom has occurred the most penetrating thought from the realm of the 'senseless' – 'the good die first'. Listening to the Wanderer, we recognise why those who cannot argue, will not retain their beliefs. Faith claims the status of *a good argument*, without surrendering other claims.[f]

This is a particular encounter between the Wanderer and the Solitary; it is also all encounters between those who trust and those who don't – who *humanly* cannot – including encounters between those who trust arguing itself, and those who must refuse the exchange. To possess knowledge – as the Wanderer feels he does – is not to stand above arguing. Truth may lose arguments on any occasion, even on most occasions. The Wanderer is well aware that he *may* lose any argument between the faith which is truth in the poem's arguable world and something darker, which speaks from the parts of experience that are outside hope's sphere:

[f]Kenneth Burke's terms 'acceptance' and 'rejection' are indeed suggestive. Each of us must return to the perspective from which things *do* seem 'senseless' – in the face of anguish, no support will ever be finally adequate. *But, because 'acceptance' is a larger position than 'rejection', people will always try to find another, a better, way of accepting their own lives.*

– And, if there be whose tender frames have drooped
Even to the dust; apparently, through weight
Of anguish unrelieved, and lack of power
An agonizing sorrow to transmute;
Deem not that *proof* is here of hope withheld
When wanted most; . . . (IV ll. 165–71) (emphasis added)

The word 'proof' extends the range of the dialogue which is needed to involve the Solitary. The intervention effectively counterposes the word 'proof' against the Solitary's use of the word 'evidence': that was what the Solitary was seeking, and what he could not find. The Wanderer acknowledges that the argument cannot be certainly ended with 'proof': in the face of such suffering, no way of putting the case can be relied upon to convince. The Wanderer then proceeds to a true arguer's insight: the fact that an encounter is lost does not mean that all cases of the same kind are necessarily lost and must be abandoned. In the phrase 'proof is here of hope withheld': what precisely is being 'withheld'? One possibility is that it is '*proof* . . . of hope' that is wrongly thought to be withheld. In other words, when hope is lost in an encounter, do not assume that there is no chance of showing on some other occasion that there are grounds for hope, even sure grounds. There *may* be a 'proof' which will make 'hope' convincing, even though we have not yet found it. The Wanderer's case is that 'proof' may still appear, may *always* be forthcoming, even though it is still to come. The argument for hope *may* be won, even though we have not won it on this occasion. But there is another interpretation possible: what we might assume to be 'withheld' is '*hope*' itself. This version is darker. The Wanderer would be warning that a lost case does not prove that '*hope*' is forever 'withheld . . . when wanted most'. It would be wrong to assume that the argument has been won finally and utterly by the other side, that the case against 'hope' is conclusive. That interpretation is much harder than the first, in which he is warning us only against assuming that the positive case can never be established.

In many instances , our minds cannot overcome 'agonising sorrow'; but the Wanderer simultaneously warns against drawing two possible conclusions from being unable to cope with sorrow. First, we should not conclude that we can never establish the case for hope because we cannot establish it in this instance, intellectually *and* emotionally. He implies that the case for 'hope' may be deferred, *may* be proven on another occasion. But the other view of hope is a darker one: the Wanderer is also warning us not to believe, in the face of catastrophe, that the negative view *has* been proven, that it has been established that there are no grounds for hope.[g]

Above all, there are the things which the Wanderer does not say: he issues no guarantee that, in any particular case, we can be sure of 'proof . . . of hope' being given to us. His point is that we do not need such a guarantee. The trust is in ongoing argument. It must be sufficient that the positive case may be successful on another occasion if not on this, if not for us then for others. That possibility is enough to make this exchange worthwhile and other exchanges worthwhile. Many arguments may end with untoward conclusions, intellectually and emotionally, from the point of view of participants. But it would be wrong to renounce the process of arguing – for in renouncing the process we give up our beliefs. We must argue: it is only a matter of time before our beliefs require defending against 'the senseless' or against 'sharp contradictions' or against lack of 'evidence'. It is the relation between our experience and our beliefs which renders believing inseparable from arguing. The world is dynamic – experience changes, and in doing so throws up problems and challenges. Even to keep our beliefs constant we will have to argue for them. Ceasing to argue means ceasing to believe.

But the Wanderer is also aware that he takes risks by creating dialogues. Arguing vitalises belief; but because exchange is open-ended, we cannot be sure of the outcome or that the outcome of exchange will be reassuring. The arguer needs courage:

> Here then we rest; not fearing for our creed
> The worst that human reasoning can achieve,
> To unsettle or perplex it: . . . (IV ll. 197–9)

The Wanderer half dismisses the threat of reason to his creed, but he also acknowledges it at the same moment. There *is* – he suggests – a higher perspective from which human reasoning is no threat; but none of us is guaranteed such a vantage-point. We must exert our will to find it, or at least, to pursue it. Only by accepting that defeat for a

[g]Aristotle is particularly concerned with different kinds of 'proof' in the *Rhetoric*, when defining the arguable world of the rhetorician. He sees a very narrow domain in which proof may be absolute, and self-contained. But outside that area, proofs will be either much more provisional, or even unattainable, and that area includes most of human experience.

credo is possible, does the need to justify it intensify. If there is no guarantee of success, you must try your hardest to win: win in the fullest sense, by true persuasion not by trickery.

The Wanderer's approach to the exchange has an imaginative and ethical pull which surpasses *doctrine*. What counts imaginatively is not what he believes, but the *way* he continues the discussion, after assessing the role of 'proof' in seeking 'hope'. What remains, after acknowledging that the 'proof' may be deferred?

> . . . What then remains? – To seek
> Those helps for his occasions ever near
> Who lacks not will to use them; . . . (IV ll. 214–16)

He continues to enrich the dialogue, to act *responsively*. His key word is still 'seek' – re-answering the Solitary's complaint that we 'vainly seek'. For the Wanderer, seeking is a worthwhile process, and not simply an indication that we lack what we need. Or, rather, it is both, a worthwhile activity and a sign of lack. We live amidst 'occasions', new experiences, new findings and renewed problems. In such a context, what is belief? Not a solution to problems that is provided in advance. To believe means to make the effort, to work away from the shadows of the 'senseless' and from the 'sharp contradictions' towards what is positive. In this struggle, there are 'helps for his occasions', which takes us back to that adequate *support* – those 'helps' are starting-points and not endings.

For the Wanderer, for one who has come to terms with the arguable world, it is enough to have recognised that there will always be some basis for the positive case – he does not want guarantees to make the process worthwhile. The Solitary has given up because he never found 'words of assurance' (l. 220). He has linked that doubt to his personal agonies and to his loss of ideals in a wider historical context. The Wanderer moves to recreate the dialogue at the historic level:

> For that other loss,
> The loss of confidence in social man,
> By the unexpected transports of our age
> Carried so high, . . . (IV ll. 260–3)

He re-presents the inflated ideal and its loss as two barriers separating some from the arguable world:

as, no cause
Could e'er for such exalted confidence
Exist; so, none is now for fixed despair: (ll. 265–7)

We must trust *without* 'proof . . . of hope' – our beliefs must be modest, on the human scale, sufficient to survive the uncertainty of living, otherwise they are not truly beliefs that engage with us and our world. Such trust ends in arguing – internally and with others.

As he advances the dialogue, the Wanderer creates a double case – for argument and for belief; which together define our un-assured condition. Yet the Wanderer's open-endedness lies in his *strength*. How could anyone sustain such a sense of opposition without strong beliefs? He moves towards a still more assertive view, claiming the voice of Providence:

. . . 'But Wisdom of her sons
Shall not the less, though late, be justified.' (IV ll. 293–4)

We inhabit the interval, the period for which this justification is deferred. For us, therefore, that final justification is itself a question of belief, and of argument. As yet we are still waiting; but the pause is now a time of dialogue.

What are the main implications of interpreting the story of the Wanderer and the Solitary in the perspectives of argument? The overwhelming sense is that the world of exchanges cannot do without the Solitary. His voice is necessary – he testifies to the hurt of loss, the bitterness of history. Furthermore, he has made himself an outsider by breaking with argument; competence is no guarantee of a will to argue. This Solitary casts an ironic light on all other arguers, taking their starting-points as dead ends. What remedy? Another irony suggests itself: to persuade such a Solitary, the Wanderer must first reintroduce him to questions, *real* questions which imply differing responses. There is no way towards belief without these questions. The problem is to recreate the need to argue – and questions are the source of that need.

The *Wanderer* finds ways of drawing questions to new life in the Solitary's own terms. He makes a possible dialogue out of the Solitary's refusal of dialogue. A new game is improvised out of the rejection of all games. We all feel the need to believe our lives are worthwhile. We feel, accordingly, the need for a dialogue with the Solitary, to extricate him from the predicament in which pain has left him.

The play of argument

The Wanderer needs the exchange not only as an end in itself, but also in order to persuade the Solitary. His *refutations* of the Solitary's position become stronger. Yet the words which refute the other voice are more vibrantly coloured by that contrary presence. The Solitary has been exploiting hypothesis and question to protect himself in his anguish from the challenges of exchange. The Wanderer has echoed constructions such as 'what avails imagination . . . if neither . . .'; now his echoes amount to imitation, as they recur and become more obvious:

> Ah! If the heart, too confidently raised,
> Perchance too lightly occupied, or lulled
> Too easily, despise or overlook
> The vassalage that binds her to the earth,
> Her sad dependence upon time, and all
> The trepidations of mortality,
> What place so destitute and void – but there
> The little flower her vanity shall check;
> The trailing worm reprove her thoughtless pride? (IV ll. 418–26)

The Wanderer gives the same force as the Solitary to mortality, and considers the tokens of mortality, tokens which show that some idealism is empty; as in 'vassalage that binds', the heart to the earth. He suggests that only a heart led astray by that kind of idealism would have ignored mortality in the first place – 'a heart too confidently raised' and 'lulled . . . too easily'. There should be no great shock in discovering you are mortal. The Wanderer is pointing out that the stunning insights offered by the Solitary are less striking in a fuller perspective; death then is an ordinary part of life. The shock impact of 'the senseless grave' has been defused into a generalised 'sad dependence upon time'. The Wanderer is pointing out that the most ordinary argument, the argument from commonplaces, would dispose of this kind of idealism. The Solitary need not have focused his own experience of loss into this intense argument.

But a great difference is made according to whether the argument is based upon the common experience of all, or on the unique and private experience of the individual. 'Commonplaces', in this sense, are the stored responses of a culture. And other commonplaces intro--

duce different ideas.[h]

A 'place destitute and void' is commonplace enough. And what *is* to be found in such places? Why, of course, other commonplaces: the 'little flower' and the 'trailing worm'. What *does* that 'flower' represent? Does it check the over-exalted view because, though humble and ordinary, it is beautiful and worthwhile? Is the point also that in a destitute void this flower represents the 'vassalage' which 'binds' the human being to 'the earth'? Presumably, the worm stands for the mortality which idealism ignores; but the worm is also a symbol of the idealist himself, necessarily earth-bound!

There is an advantage in arguing from the commonplace rather than from private experience. One commonplace leads easily to an awareness of other commonplaces. One person's experience does not readily lead to the awareness that there are other kinds of experience. So, whereas the experience of the Solitary is limited and confining, the Wanderer's view of the commonplace continues to widen:

> These craggy regions, these chaotic wilds,
> Does that benignity pervade, that warms
> The mole contented with her darksome walk
> In the cold ground; . . . (IV ll. 427–30)

That 'mole contented' represents the fittedness of things to their contexts. But that fittedness, like the sense made by the world, is complex: the wilds may fit some of their inhabitants but from another point of view they are 'chaotic'. And, the mole's 'walk' is 'in the cold ground', with its suggestion of the senseless grave. The consolations which the Wanderer finds in the commonplace are far from simple.

For the Wanderer, the wiser voice will be more open to the whole culture, less confined by a single perspective, the perspective from one man's experience. He seems to be advancing to a climax:

> We live by Admiration, Hope, and Love;
> And, even as these are well and wisely fixed,
> In dignity of being we ascend. (IV ll. 763–5)

[h]Aristotle points towards 'commonplaces' when he establishes that: 'Rhetoric . . . may be defined as the faculty of discovering the possible means of persuasion in reference to any subject whatever.' (*Rhetoric* Iii) Roman rhetoricians mapped the assumptions and expressions of their times in pursuit of the resources of argument (e.g. Cicero *De Inventione*; *Rhetorica ad Herennium*). Gadamer (*Truth and Method* p. 21) claims to defend the respect for 'the old topica' as the central resource in 'the art of finding arguments'.

But then the crossing-over of voices occurs in another way. The Solitary's style of stabbing questions returns in the Wanderer's tone: 'But what is error?' (IV l. 766). But there is a substantial point in the question. May we not be misled by the inherited voice of 'Admiration, Hope and Love'? We need these things, but they need to be 'wisely fixed'. If they are not, how can we ever distinguish the times when Hope, say, is fulfilled from the many occasions when hope is disappointed? 'Admiration, Hope and Love' are great criteria but can such criteria fail to be helpful sometimes?

The Solitary responds in a strange tone, a strained tone:

> 'Answer he who can!'
> The Sceptic somewhat haughtily exclaimed:
> 'Love, Hope, and Admiration – are they not
> Mad Fancy's favourite vassals? Does not life
> Use them, full oft, as pioneers to ruin,
> Guides to destruction? . . .['] (IV ll. 766–73)

The questions tumble out with eager pain. But where the Wanderer left 'error' an open question, the Solitary makes sure there can only be one answer. It is as if he were showing his mimic how it is *really* done, this negative turn of phrase! He brings the matter down to basics:

> . . . Who shall regulate,
> With truth, the scale of intellectual rank? (IV ll. 777–8)

Who can decide how the truth is determined? That is the question; the only answer is clear: no one possesses such authority. The Wanderer trumps that trick in turn:

> 'Methinks,' persuasively the Sage replied,
> 'That for this arduous office you possess
> Some rare advantages. . . .['] (IV ll. 779–81)

The Wanderer turns the Solitary's case on its head by offering him the role of judge. The very insight which remarks the complexity of the problem could find the solution! Every move of the Wanderer destabilises the Solitary's chosen role, the negating role, offering other roles in exchange. Whether by mimicry or by generous misunderstanding, the Wanderer suggests that his case already includes the position of the Solitary.

But a still more profound exchange of roles is possible. The narrative has just reidentified the Solitary as a 'Sceptic'. The Wanderer is about to risk casting himself in such a role. He turns to consider those people – such as the Ancient Greeks of pastoral times – whose lives were lived by faiths alien to his own faith:

> a Man so bred
> (Take from him what you will upon the score
> Of ignorance or illusion) lives and breathes
> For noble purposes of mind: . . . (IV ll. 828–31)

The Wanderer is affirming even the faith of pagans, which is preferable to the complete absence of all faith.[11] The dialogue quickens. The Solitary counter-proposes other examples of error exposed, examples which are closer to home and so more threatening, concerning Catholicism and the Scottish Church. Surely the reformers of the Scottish Church did mean to expose errors in earlier systems of belief:

> How, think you, would they tolerate this scheme
> Of fine propensities, that tends, if urged
> Far as it might be urged, to sow afresh
> The weeds of Romish phantasy, . . . (IV ll. 905–8)

The Solitary wittily recasts the Wanderer as a relativist. How can the Wanderer accept the wisdom in old traditions, pagan or 'Romish', without impairing his judgement? The exchange becomes inverted for a moment, the Sceptic claiming that the believer is too open-minded:

> This answer followed. – 'You have turned my thoughts
> Upon our brave Progenitors, . . .['] (IV ll. 919–20)

Far from being angry, the Wanderer delights in the enhanced dialogue. He broadens the issue. Error is not, he argues, simply the opposite of truth. Humanity has a power of creativity, a power which:

> feeds
> A calm, a beautiful, and silent fire,
> From the encumbrances of mortal life,
> From error, disappointment – nay, from guilt;
> And sometimes, so relenting justice wills,
> From palpable oppressions of despair. (IV ll. 1072–7)

'Error' may lead to a deeper truth; 'guilt' may lead to a more profound acceptance of one's own life. The Wanderer's sense of truth becomes a way of engaging *with* other voices, since he may discover in them other sources of the 'calm . . . beautiful . . . silent fire'.

The Solitary is half caught in the role of anti-relativist:

> The Solitary by these words was touched
> With manifest emotion, and exclaimed;
> 'But how begin? And whence? – . . .['] (IV ll. 1078–80)

The moment is enhanced by the fact that the Solitary's 'manifest emotion' leads to *questions*.[12] If the poem were less committed to exchange, perhaps the Solitary would have found the answers he seeks here. One could say that the poem is showing now how difficult it is to make someone accept answers. But, more profoundly, it shows how difficult it is to make another person accept questions, accept them as genuinely necessary. Here is another profound twist: it is the sceptic who has trouble accepting questions, and the believer for whom they are necessary. The Wanderer's achievement is to enable the Solitary to ask questions, not to make him decide what is truth. The Wanderer's central point is that there are diverse ways of creating truth, and none of them preclude 'error', or 'guilt'. Therefore, we *can* judge errors, and yet find truth in the same context. No wonder the Solitary is puzzled into responding! Can the balance between error and truth really be sustained? The Wanderer tempts fate by his reply, which proposes a good life as one where: 'he looks round /And seeks for good; and finds the good he seeks' (IV ll. 1222–3). The potential challenge is all too clear: *what we find is only what we look for*. Evidently, there could be a negative way of looking at the idea of discovering what you already believe: that you find only what you already believe. But we can make this idea creative. We need to believe in the most generous possible way, so that the search for truth in our lives is humane and humanising.

We live our lives, in practice, between the question and the answer. The Wanderer returns to his idea of 'support' – but this time the support is from 'science', or enlightenment, which has previously been problematic. Science is dangerous if it treats truth as an absolute and has no possible use for 'error'. But if we avoid such narrow criteria and rigid distinctions, then – in some better time – the scientific spirit will enhance creative hope:

> . . . Science then
> Shall be a precious visitant; and then,

And only then, be worthy of her name:
For then her heart shall kindle; her dull eye,
Dull and inanimate, no more shall hang
Chained to its object in brute slavery;
But taught with patient interest to watch
The processes of things, and serve the cause
Of order and distinctness, not for this
Shall it forget that its most noble use,
Its most illustrious province, must be found
In furnishing clear guidance, a support
Not treacherous, to the mind's *excursive* power. (IV ll. 1251–63)

His criterion is creativity, 'the mind's excursive power' – which the poem reclaims in its own name. We must ask whether ideas and observations enhance that 'power' to create, rather than settling merely for naive accuracy: accuracy which is 'chained to its object'. 'Things' belong to 'processes', and these exterior processes correspond to the 'excursive' life of the human mind.

This last interplay of voices interweaves the Wanderer's with his own utterances from an earlier stage. Previously 'support' was identified with religion; now the 'support' is science, or could be. The Wanderer has exchanged his own role, as he previously exchanged roles with the Solitary. The moves are almost bewilderingly intricate, quick with the play of a living process. At different moments, the Wanderer mimics the Solitary; the Solitary reclaims his tones; the Wanderer enables his adversary to cast aspersions of relativism on him; the Wanderer turns round his own terms, truth and error. Yet all the time, the Wanderer is advancing his case – first by negation and now with passionate affirmation. The poem gives us a character who is quickened by the play of exchange, whose fervent beliefs belong to this communicative process:

Here closed the Sage that eloquent harangue,
Poured forth with fervour in continuous stream, (IV ll. 1276–7)

And this word 'eloquent' focuses the issue of the preceding episodes: what does it mean to be 'eloquent', to have a persuasive voice?

The Wanderer's practice embodies a distinct theory of persuasive eloquence, capable of engaging with other theories. The first part of this theory concerns his power of sustaining dialogue. Unlike most theories, this approach can accept the Solitary's unco-operativeness. He can *create* exchange, without agreed rules. The second part of the implicit theory concerns the way of *developing* the exchange. The Wanderer relishes the play of voices; he allows roles to interweave and even to become reversed. His constant case – for faith in value – is all the more emphatic since it emerges from difference and reversal. Commonplaces become a necessary – and complex – resource; *questions* are urged on the Solitary; wittily, error ceases to be truth's antithesis. The case includes a play of ideas, as well as addressing the other side with playful energies. The Wanderer's persuasiveness is full of contraries and of contrariness, and yet he also has a voice to speak 'with fervour'.

But when the Wanderer has 'closed', for all his eloquence, the Solitary has not conceded. Is the discourse then persuasive in effect, as well as intention? There is no simple answer. The dialogue continues, and indeed the Solitary will abjure all influence from this encounter with the Wanderer. That is why the poem – and the exchange – now turns to the Pastor. Yet in another sense, the Wanderer's eloquence *has* succeeded. The Solitary is now part of a communicative process; moreover, he *has* been 'touched' by the Wanderer's words and felt again 'manifest emotion'. The Wanderer also represents a humane persuasiveness in his patience, which is more than tolerance. His patience testifies to a deep sense of the Solitary's being, his independent being as another centre of consciousness. Nothing can annihilate that centre, no imperial statement can invade it from outside. The Wanderer plays with this other consciousness – plays in a way which recognises the active being of the Solitary. We should not be distracted by the Wanderer's specific doctrine of faith from recognising his more general significance. He embodies a more general hope than the Christian 'Hope' for which he also speaks with such fine passion. He embodies the hope of engagement and exchange. The Wanderer shows us that it is possible to play with deep conviction – to play to win. The power of this hope is proportionate to the tensions in its path: indeed, hope is a reflex of the tension. In Wordsworth's argumentative imagination, the strained argumentative dialogues of his period become a scene for the discovery of hope.

The Excursion (I): further commentary and references

Text of *The Excursion* used is William Wordsworth, *Poems* Volume II, ed. John O. Haydon (Harmondsworth: Penguin 1977), with minor differences resulting from the identification of direct speech in my accompanying discussion.

1 Letter of Charles and Mary Lamb II, ed. E. V. Lucas (London: Dent and Methuen, 1935), p. 126.

2 Cicero, *The Nature of the Gods*, trans. by Horace C. P. McGregor with intro. by J. M. Ross (Harmondsworth: Penguin 1972), p. 69. Succeeding references given in text.

3 David Hume, *Dialogues Concerning Natural Religion*, edited by Henry D. Aiken (New York: Hafner Press 1948), Part X p. 66. Succeeding references given in text.

4 P. B. Shelley, *A Refutation of Deism*, collected in Shelley's Prose, edited by David Lee Clark with a preface by Harold Bloom (London: Fourth Estate 1988), pp. 118–37, p. 119. Succeeding references given in text.

5 Hannah More, *Village Politics*, collected in *The Works of Hannah More* II (London 1833), pp. 221–36, pp. 222–3. Succeeding references given in text.

6 Anna Laetitia Barbauld, 'Dialogue', collected in *The Works of Anna Laetitia Barbauld* II (London 1825), pp. 277–87, p. 287).

7 The heart of Book I of the poem began much earlier than the other books – the poem 'The Ruined Cottage' was first completed in 1797, whereas the whole poem belongs to the years from 1809–14. The story of 'The Ruined Cottage' and its evolutions is told in Jonathan Wordsworth, *The Music of Humanity* (London: Nelson 1969). The short poem has a high status. Jonathan Wordsworth invaluably prints the 'most coherent surviving version' (p. 31) of the original poem, composed 'up to and including March 1798' (p. 23). Several comparisons stand out, when *The Excursion* is considered. The terrifying metaphor of the crucified soul is absent. The Pedlar – the Wanderer's predecessor – advises the Poet: 'Be wise and cheerful, and no longer read/The forms of things with an unworthy eye.' (ll. 510–11) *The Excursion* has, therefore, created the question, however weighted, where the original has a plain statement. Bernard Groom in his study of *The Unity of Wordsworth's Poetry* (London: Macmillan 1966, p. 105) clarifies a common assumption when he claims that 'The Ruined Cottage' is too great a work to be considered as part of *The Excursion*'. The main objection is to the Wanderer's consolations, which are more elaborate than the speeches given to his predecessor, the Pedlar. But the detail can also support the rival view, that the Wanderer is more complex, rather than more dogmatic. An interesting contrast to my account is provided by Susan J. Wolfson, who finds in Book I 'Wordsworth's questioning presence' and sees the Wanderer not as the focus of questioning, but as a figure representing 'detachment from questioning pressure'. (Susan J. Wolfson, *The Questioning Presence*: 'Wordsworth, Keats, and the Interrogative Mode in Romantic Poetry' (Ithaca: Cornell University Press 1986, p. 99 and p. 105).)

8 The Solitary can be interpreted in many ways, like other great characters of the imagination. Kenneth Johnston has a profound account of the poem in his *Wordsworth and the Recluse* (New Haven: Yale University Press 1984). His Solitary is a symbol of a historical moment, a symbol of 'almost every personal, social, religious and philosophic catastrophe that could possibly befall a character born . . . in the last quarter of the eighteenth century' (p. 265). Other interpretations take the historical view more literally, drawing on remarks made later by Wordsworth himself. Carl Woodring in his *Wordsworth* (Cambridge, Mass: Harvard University Press 1968, p. 183) identifies specific models: 'The Solitary is founded on rationalistic liberals, particularly the dissenting preacher Joseph Fawcett, whom Wordsworth knew in London . . . John Thelwall and Gilbert Wakefield, among others, as well as the poet himself, must have contributed traits to the portrait.' On the other hand, Geoffrey Hartman gives a resonant interpretation in *Wordsworth's Poetry 1787–1814* (New Haven: Yale University Press 1964, p. 307) where he asks pertinently: 'Who is the Solitary, if not the Hamletian man in black, and a dangerous part of the poet's mind?'. Rightly, the dialogue is as rich and endless as its source!

9 William Howard has suggested ('Narrative Irony in The Excursion' in *Studies in Romanticism* 24 (1985) pp. 511–30, p. 512) that we should avoid a 'persistent confusion of Wordsworth with his narrator'. He regards the comments given to the Poet as contrivedly inadequate, and suggests that the reader should even be ironically inclined towards such labels as 'the Sage' for the Wanderer and 'the Sceptic' for the Solitary. The interpretation certainly encourages us to treat the whole exchange as an integral process, rather than abstracting one of the speakers from it.

10 Johnston (*op.cit.* p. 271) adds that the Solitary is here allowed to express particular catastrophic experiences of Wordsworth: 'Wordsworth goes out of his way to invest himself in the Solitary's character, most bravely by the late addition of mention of the death of two children, following the stunning double blow of the deaths of Catherine and Thomas Wordsworth in 1812, . . .'.

11 Alan G. Hill gives a tempting perspective on this passage in his 'New Light on The Excursion', in *Ariel* 5 (1974) pp. 37–47. He sketches an intriguing resemblance between the debate in the poem and a dialogue written in Latin by Minucius Felix in the second or third century A.D.. Wordsworth indeed possessed this work, called the *Octavius*, which was also admired by Coleridge: 'The author, as impartial arbiter, presides over the debate between Caecilius, the sceptical pagan traditionalist, and Octavius, champion of Christianity' (pp. 40–1). Hill is helpful in focusing on the point that the poem is truly a work of dialogue, and he also brings out by his comparison Wordsworth's 'feeling for the pre-Christian religions' (p. 46), though, of course, that feeling must have richer sources beyond any specific analogue.

12 Johnston (*op.cit.* p. 280) hears the questions in a different way, and interprets them not as part of a renewal but as signs of 'a debilitating self-consciousness' which he connects with the 'peculiar form of personal and religious doubt, notably commented on by Carlyle and Mill, Newman and Kierkegaard, . . .'. But Hartman (*op.cit.* p. 312) gives a psychological twist to this episode by commenting that: 'The despondency the Wanderer seeks to correct is less the opposite of hope than its strongest derivative,' which would allow the Solitary's questions to oscillate between the two states. The line is a fine example of the argument's arguability, without which it would hardly seem authentic.

The Excursion (II): an arguable progress

From refusal to critique

But the Solitary *is* unbeaten, or only persuaded into entering the process of exchange. Can *he* turn the play to his advantage? Can he play to bolster his negative position? What is the most profound challenge he can produce? These questions will turn the poem round: after them, there will be a new interplay, with the Pastor as a central voice. But the poem first marks the conclusion of the Wanderer's central role. Together with the Poet, the arguers set out towards the next stage of the excursion, literally and symbolically: the Pastor and his church.[1]

Walking through the Pastor's churchyard, the three visitors try to decipher the inscriptions on the stones:

> 'These dim lines,
> What would they tell?' said I, – but, from the task
> Of puzzling out that faded narrative,
> With whisper soft my venerable Friend
> Called me; . . . (V ll. 205–9)

The word 'narrative' prefigures the next phase in which the Pastor tells stories, mostly read off from the inscriptions on these stones. But for the moment, the Poet looks up from 'puzzling out that faded narrative' and says:

> looking down the darksome aisle,
> I saw the Tenant of the lonely vale
> Standing apart; . . . (V ll. 209–11)

Strangely, the Pastor resembles the Solitary, a man of a lonely region whom we see 'apart' from everyone else – nor is this resemblance the last.

The visitors continue their walk through the churchyard, where the Solitary utters his first challenge to the conclusion of the last exchange. He recalls being impressed with that exchange, only to dispel the impression:

'Much,' he continued, with dejected look,
'Much, yesterday, was said in glowing phrase
Of our sublime dependencies, and hopes
For future states of being; and the wings
Of speculation, joyfully outspread,
Hovered above our destiny on earth:
But stoop, and place the prospect of the soul
In sober contrast with reality,
And man's substantial life. . . .['] (V ll. 242–50)

The 'soul' has a 'prospect', but that perspective contrasts with our actual experience. There is a hopeful *perspective*, but it vanishes when we relate it to our familiar view of things. The move is much more subtle – argumentatively – than the Solitary's earlier tactics. He now allows that the other side has a perspective and he reduces its relevance to life; instead of denying it altogether. 'Dejected' he may be, but the Solitary can now make that dejection play an argumentative role. His voice has absorbed some of the Wanderer's flexibility, the use of qualification rather than blunt negation – albeit the winning for which he plays will also be to his own loss, as he perseveres in showing (his) life is not worthwhile.

The initiative passes to the Solitary. The Poet defends a greater trust in Providence, which provokes the animated desponder to further counter-claims:

Far better not to move at all than move
By impulse sent from such illusive power, –
That finds and cannot fasten down; that grasps
And is rejoiced and loses while it grasps;
That tempts, emboldens – for a time sustains,
And then betrays; accuses and inflicts
Remorseless punishment; and so retreads
The inevitable circle: . . . (V ll. 321–8)

For the Solitary, to have a point of view is to be deceived, perhaps not immediately, but nevertheless inevitably deceived. He argues that we only seem to advance until the next error emerges to dissolve the vision. His speech culminates in the image of the inevitable circle. For the Solitary, we see the beliefs we project, but neither the wish to believe nor the mind's projection can be stable. The mind's power is 'illusive' not 'excursive' because we people the world with phantoms, rather than creating a new sphere of vision.

The Solitary has found himself able to define the idea of 'illusive power' because the Wanderer had proposed 'excursive power'. He is doing far more than denying someone else's view – he is recreating that view in his own terms. The Solitary agrees that the issue is human subjectivity – and he even accepts for this subjectivity the term 'power'. But, whereas the Wanderer's 'power' acts on behalf of humanity, for the Solitary, our minds have 'power' *over* us. The central twist is that the Wanderer's emphasis on creative subjectivity now serves the Solitary's purposes as well. If our minds are creative, can they not create illusions? In that case, might not the Wanderer's own persuasiveness be itself a servant of illusion, indeed a *sign* of illusion? The more creative the mind, the more deceptive its ideas; so the Solitary's responsive logic runs.

Then the Pastor joins the group. Surely, he will right the balance which has tipped in favour of the Solitary? The Solitary does lose his greatest advantage, perhaps – for the moment. Meanwhile the Wanderer explains to the clergyman that they – the three who have arrived in the churchyard – have been arguing. Significantly, he outlines the argument in terms of questions:

'. . . Is Man
A child of hope? . . .
. . . Are we a creature in whom good
Preponderates, or evil? Doth the will
Acknowledge reason's law? . . .
These are the points,' the Wanderer said, 'On which
Our inquest turns. . . .['] (V ll. 465–81)

The argument may have progressed, but for the Wanderer questions still determine the nature of the discourse. Book V is the middle of the poem; the Wanderer outlines the argument near the centre of Book V: the poem is almost balancing itself upon these points. The word 'inquest' comes to life suggestively. They have been inquiring – and 'inquest' represents the quasi-legal rhythm of the enquiring. But we may also feel that the poem is a 'quest' – or journey or excursion – a quest which moves inwards. We may even sense that the journey moves inwards towards questions. We can hear the now matched voices of the Solitary and the Wanderer poised to contest these questions.

The Wanderer asks the Pastor to exercise his 'persuasive wisdom'

(Book V,l. 483), perhaps hoping for support in that contest. The Pastor immediately casts himself as the recipient of the poem's central problem, by now the question of point of view:

> and we
> Are that which we would contemplate from far.
> Knowledge, for us, is difficult to gain –
> Is difficult to gain, and hard to keep –
> As virtue's self; like virtue is beset
> With snares; tried, tempted, subject to decay. (V ll. 490–5)

But whose voice is audible within the first sentences of the Pastor? Whose voice but the Solitary's when he was defining the illusive power? The Pastor has not heard the Solitary's speech, but, given the Wanderer's explanation of the questions, the new voice binds itself into the play of exchange. The Solitary talked of a 'power' which 'tempts' and which 'loses while it grasps': the Pastor suggests that 'knowledge' is 'tempted, subject to decay'. Again, the two figures are joined. We have reached the centre of *The Excursion*, and there the Solitary's voice resonates, even penetrating the Pastor's first utterance. The Pastor – like the Solitary – insists upon linking point of view with its most difficult aspect, subjective emotion: 'Love, admiration, fear, desire, and hate, /Blind were we without these:' (V ll. 495–6). Different feelings make the world appear different: yet no emotion at all leaves us 'blind' rather than objective.

But the Pastor does begin to translate the problem – point of view – into new forms:

> if from the sullen north
> Your walk conduct you hither, ere the sun
> Hath gained his noontide height, this churchyard, filled
> With mounds transversely lying side by side
> From east to west, before you will appear
> An unillumined, blank and dreary plain,
> With more than wintry cheerlessness and gloom
> Saddening the heart. . . . (V ll. 532–9)

We may see the churchyard as 'mounds transversely lying', mounds which can even seem to fill the world 'from east to west'; death is everywhere. There is nothing perfunctory about this perspective from death: the Pastor conceives that the world may become for us 'an unillumined, blank and dreary plain'. Even that 'dreary plain' does not end the vision. When we reach 'wintry cheerlessness and gloom' we feel sure that the end of the portrayal has come. Yet that 'gloom' turns active: 'saddening the heart'. These lines convey the Pastor's intensity of *perspective*, since we seem to see beyond each final resting point, in a vista of never-ending dejection back to the Solitary's claims, as if his claims were in the very shape of this churchyard. But he goes on to suggest that light shines from a certain '*quarter*' and upon 'the southern side' of each grave (ll. 541–3). Humanity must see the world from points of view which differ, differ radically – hence the world is implicitly arguable. We want some perspectives to appear *stronger* or *larger* than others – without escaping perspective altogether, we can resort to 'the southern side' of every grave, if we choose, and choose we must.

The Pastor elaborates his terms and then, abruptly, inverts the argument:

> – This contrast, not unsuitable to life,
> Is to that other state more apposite,
> Death and its two-fold aspect! wintry – one,
> Cold, sullen, blank, from hope and joy shut out;
> The other, which the ray divine hath touched,
> Replete with vivid promise, bright as spring. (V ll. 552–7)

The argument about perspectives on life reverses to account for death. And what makes the case appropriate either to life or to death is precisely that the view is itself 'two-fold', bright and dark. There are always alternatives: other ways of seeing, other ways of saying, and other ways of judging. But the Pastor emphasises arguability in order to make his audience *choose*.

We feel the Pastor moving towards the centre of the argument – but he has not yet arrived. The Wanderer agrees with what he has said about perspectives on life and death; then he moves back to his questioning mode, and raises a question about an aspect of argument itself:

> . . . With joy sincere
> I re-salute these sentiments confirmed
> By your authority. But how acquire
> The inward principle that gives effect
> To outward argument; . . . (V ll. 569–73)

These terms link the concept of 'authority' with the process of 'argument'. Our assent to 'authority' is only strong when we have made 'argument' strong – with the more radical authority of an 'inward principle'. Here at the poem's centre, the word 'argument' stands for life itself, for life as we *enact* it. If we acquired the 'principle that gives effect/To outward argument', if the good argument entered our *lives*, then our lives would match our best hopes. In an arguable world, the way we live is itself an argument, and one which we must endow with all the authority we can discover. The Poet echoes the Wanderer's view of life as argument, and in doing so he praises the uncomplicated perspective of people who live by 'daily toil' (l. 600). But these words reveal a gap in the fairness of the arguable world in which people live and the Solitary exploits it to challenge the process of arguing itself. We can *hear* the animation entering his voice: ' "Yes," buoyantly exclaimed /The pale Recluse – "praise to the sturdy plough," ' (V ll. 601–2). The Solitary reaches his finest moment – the moment when his position impacts upon the argument from within, impacts ineradicably. Before the new centre of the Pastor's voice is strong, we encounter an alternative to his voice, strong with the argumentative power of response and anticipation.

Since agreement is the key note now, the Solitary avoids direct confrontation. Instead, he achieves his near-breakthrough by mimicking enthusiasm for:

– Inglorious implements of craft and toil,
Both ye that shape and build, and ye that force,
By slow solicitation, earth to yield
Her annual bounty, sparingly dealt forth
With wise reluctance; you would I extol;
Not for gross good alone which ye produce,
But for the impertinent and ceaseless strife
Of proofs and reasons ye preclude – in those
Who to your dull society are born,
And with their humble birthright rest content.
– Would I had ne'er renounced it! (V ll. 611–21; emphasis added)

For a second, the Wanderer – and the poem with him – is discomposed:

A slight flush
Of moral anger previously had tinged
The old Man's cheek; . . . (V ll. 621–3)

'Slight' and 'moral' qualify the 'anger' – but the Solitary has forced the great interlocutor away from his high ground of argumentative goodwill. The poem recognises the impact, though the recognition of the Wanderer's anger is half repressed into the past as we learn the awkward truth ('previously had tinged'). Indeed the Solitary has spoilt the charm of his achievement only by self-reproach. The Pastor has settled nothing as yet, which is the risk of his entering the argument. The Solitary has sensed that risk. If a positive perspective is wanted, then why argue? Does not the interminability of arguing reach beyond any hopeful perspective? Is not the double commitment – to arguing and to hope – an impossible commitment?

We have had contrary allusions to arguing itself: the Wanderer refers to 'outward argument', giving the best life to the best case; the Solitary counters, effectively, with the 'ceaseless strife' of argument. Now the Wanderer refocuses on argument's central dynamic of exchange:

> Said he,
> 'That which we feel we utter; as we think
> So have we argued; reaping for our pains
> No visible recompense. . . .[′] (V ll. 624–7)

The Wanderer too has his finest moment: his use of 'we' is the height of argumentative goodwill. He includes the Solitary in the very nature of the arguments. Here is goodwill to set against 'ceaseless strife' and the critique of exchange. As 'feel' is to 'utter' so 'think' is to 'argued'. For the Wanderer, the feeling and the thinking, the uttering and the arguing are inseparable.

We have come a long way from the Solitary's ironic smile, the block to participation, and the enticing questions with which the Wanderer lured him into discussion. It is the Solitary who has taken hold of the central issue – point of view itself. He refuses to see perspective in constructive terms, arguing first that the perspective of hope is remote, then that all perspective involves illusion, and finally that argument itself is a circulation of views, without prospect of resolution. Mimicry, turn-about, qualified echoes: all these techniques are inherited by the Solitary from the Wanderer. Through play, the Solitary converts his 'scorn' into a critique – the key difference being that 'scorn' cut him off, whereas 'critique' is responsive, and engages him with others.[a]

The hope of method

In the exchange, critique is born from despair. But the birth is difficult. The centre of the poem testifies to the nurturing powers of arguing, but a dilemma remains. The Wanderer has been playing to win his own argument, and not only to revive the discourse of the Solitary! How can the exchange respond to the Solitary's critique which has arisen in its heart? Another exchange of roles will be necessary – so the poem suggests. We have already heard the Pastor speaking, as an arguer; but now he must exchange that arguing voice for a different mode of address. There seems to be no other resource, and when the Wanderer asks the Pastor to join in again, he himself is turning away from further argumentative exchange:

> Give us, for our abstractions, solid facts;
> For our disputes, plain pictures. . . . (V ll. 637–8)

The Wanderer first defended arguments and promoted them; but now he *does* seem to waver, requesting 'facts' and 'pictures'. He wants these pictures and facts 'for our disputes' – *instead of* the arguing, though they are also part of the exchange.

What follows can be a disappointment, if we consider the play of exchange thus far. For the Pastor no longer plays that game. He tells long stories, and these stories seem to *contain* their own resolutions – instead of addressing themselves to other voices in debate.[2] But in another sense, the change of address means that the poem has taken

[a] *Kant*'s 'critique' is indeed aligned with the argument *against* scepticism. Nevertheless, his thought is no more a straightforward defence of orthodoxy for its own sake than is Wordsworth's poem: 'Our age is, in especial degree, the age of criticism, and to criticism everything must submit. Religion through its sanctity, and law-giving through its majesty, may seek to exempt themselves from it. But they then awaken just suspicion, and cannot claim the sincere respect which reason accords only to that which has been able to sustain the test of free and open examination' (*Critique of Pure Reason*, p. 9).

To bestow the honour of 'critique' – the most self-aware criticism – on the Solitary may seem paradoxical given his other roles in the poem. But the poem may even suggest questions about Kant's ideal of separating 'critique', which is legitimate criticism, from extremes of 'scepticism'.

seriously the Solitary's critique. The poem's insight is ironic – the Wanderer acknowledges that the Solitary has made a serious point by turning away from the play of arguing. The Wanderer is not abandoning his good faith in exchange. The other view must always be taken into account – even when that view requires the whole exchange to transform itself. The impasse is wittily constructed, with a wit that is structural. The Pastor's authority is a response to an insoluble crisis: it is a requirement that emerges from the preceding exchange, it relates to that exchange and the Solitary's critique, and is not simply grafted onto the poem. Indeed authority emerges as the other side of critique.

The clergyman begins by looking out from the churchyard and seeing 'High on the breast of yon dark mountain, dark /With stony barrenness, a shining speck' (V ll. 671–2). He focuses first on the human background to the scene in gloomy terms:

> those who occupy and till the ground,
> High on that mountain where they long have dwelt
> A wedded pair in childless solitude. (V ll. 690–2)

Despair almost fills the landscape and the lives of its inhabitants. The world succumbs to a hostile wind: 'the strong South-west /In anger blowing from the distant sea. . . .' (V ll. 702–3) Here is hardship: it will become the first pole of opposites in a synthesising process. It is the negative pole. The Pastor then recalls walking on that mountain in a dark night where he:

> saw the light – now fixed – and shifting now –
> Not like a dancing meteor, but in line
> Of never-varying motion, to and fro.
> It is no night-fire of the naked hills,
> Thought I – some friendly covert must be near. (V ll. 745–9)

The light is a counter-proposition to 'anger' and the 'distant sea'. Against the negation of hardship it proposes 'some friendly covert', the couple's home. The husband appears, and the Pastor enters the house with the couple:

> . . . From a fount
> Lost, thought I, in the obscurities of time,
> But honoured once, those features and that mien
> May have descended, though I see them here. (V ll. 786–9)

The Pastor has discovered a humane potentiality among the alien mountains. But his story has more complex associations. Locally, he has responded to the problems of perspective in the potentialities of the mountain. Structurally, he introduces a new rhythm, where opposition can lead to synthesis. The good woman speaks to him about that once-terrifying wind:

> And if the blustering wind that drives the clouds
> Care not for me, he lingers round my door,
> And makes me pastime when our tempers suit; –
> But, above all, my thoughts are my support,
> My comfort: – . . . (V ll. 820–4)

This goes beyond the dark landscape and the human welcome that awaits others there as a counter-affirmation to its alien harshness. In a new synthesis, her 'thoughts' raise a higher ideal. Oppositions are surpassed. Hostile wind and human welcome join together at another level of resolution, where the wind accompanies her thoughts, and her thoughts are her support.

No longer does the Solitary 'buoyantly' cry out his 'yes', animated by a hope of contradiction. Now his 'yes' is a cry of assent:

> 'Yes!' said the Solitary with a smile
> That seemed to break from an expanding heart, (V ll. 838–9)

The Solitary still criticises the Pastor's contribution – he looks across the graveyard and wonders what other stories could be told instead of that one. But the poem makes the Solitary assent fully, before dissenting marginally. We have not passed from an arguable world to an unarguable world. But the margin of difference between what is arguable and what is not has narrowed. This narrowing accompanies the assertion of the Pastor's authority, which claims a large space in the centre of the exchange. When the Pastor tells more stories, we begin to realise that his authority is grounded in a consistent *method*.[b]

[b]The story of the Pastor and argument has connections – as told here – with Plato. On the one hand, there is Socrates' commitment to exchange and dialogue. But there is also his ideal of method – the development of an approach which can systematically produce the truth:

> Well, Phaedrus, I am a great lover of these methods of division and collection as instruments which enable me to speak and to think, and when I believe that I have found in anyone else the ability to discuss unity and plurality as they exist in the nature of things, I follow in his footsteps 'like the footsteps of god'.
> (Plato, *Phaedrus*, translation by W. Hamilton, Harmondsworth: Penguin 1973, p. 82)

The strengths of the Pastor's method correspond to its limitations. A young man is dissolute:

> but all hopes,
> Cherished for him, he suffered to depart,
> Like blighted buds; . . . (VI ll. 313–15)

This negation is followed by a counter-proposition, an affirming movement: 'But soon revived /In strength, in power refitted, he renewed' (VI ll. 331–2). Negation returns; he goes to ruin again. But this time the opposition raises him to a higher stage. His last fall leads to his being saved:

> Till his deliverance, when Mercy made him
> One with himself, and one with them that sleep. (VI ll. 374–5)

The approach *is* dynamic, but the dynamism is self-contained. It is still threatened occasionally by attacks from the Solitary. But these are marginalised, and only point up the fact that the Pastor's authority is autonomous. Although the Solitary keeps agreeing ('True,' said the Solitary, VI l. 589), his critique also finds occasional space:

> but if the thing we seek
> Be genuine knowledge, bear we then in mind
> How, from his lofty throne, the sun can fling
> Colours as bright on exhalations bred
> By weedy pool or pestilential swamp,
> As by the rivulet sparkling where it runs,
> Or the pellucid lake. (VI ll. 593–9)

When we are confronted by synthetic wisdom, how can we distinguish the true point of view from another which resembles it closely, asks the critic. However the rules of the exchange have altered:

Socrates calls this 'method' a 'dialectical method' (p. 87) – and he seems to put great faith in it, as an ideal at least. Yet all the time, the exchange continues. What is the relation of dialogue to method? Where Socrates sees method in terms of dialectic – of synthesis from opposition, a later thinker will see method in terms of scientific method, and may then indeed regard Socratic dialectic as having more in common with dialogue. This is so in the way Gadamer has taken over and transformed the Platonic concepts (in his *Dialogue and Dialectic* as well as in *Truth and Method*).

'Small risk,' said I,
'Of such illusion do we here incur;[c]
Temptation here is none to exceed the truth; ['] (VI ll. 599–601)

A synthesising performance, such as the Pastor's, needs to proceed in peace, without interventions, subtle though the process may be. The poem avoids the *full* perplexity of the transition to method by imbuing the Solitary with sudden agreeableness. On the one side, the synthesising Pastor *can* make oppositions seem constructive; on the other side, to do so he needs to be protected against radically differing voices.

An essential feature of method – in whatever form – is that it is *repeatable*. The Pastor tells diverse stories, and he resolves each one in the same way. A woman has been unfortunate:

– Her wedded days had opened with mishap,
Whence dire dependence. . . . (VI ll. 716–17)

She becomes greedy and isolated, which is the negation in the process. The Pastor was passing her cottage one night, when he heard her voice:

it said, 'That glorious star
In its untroubled element will shine
As now it shines, when we are laid in earth
And safe from all our sorrows.' . . . (VI ll. 763–6)

The woman's own voice proposes the affirming proposition to counter the negation, and, finally, the narrative synthesises the contraries of suffering and hope to create acceptance:

. . . She, who had rebelled,
Was into meekness softened and subdued;
Did, after trials not in vain prolonged,
With resignation sink into the grave; (VI ll. 771–4)

We are able to anticipate the outcome: that is a sign of methodical skill, and also a problem.

The Wanderer becomes the Pastor's supporting voice:

[c]Kant expresses analogous resistance when he defines 'what the sceptic most desires' as the establishing of the view that 'all our insight, resting on the supposed objective validity of our judgments, is nothing but sheer illusion' (*Critique of Pure Reason*, p. 175). Like the Pastor, Kant needs to find a way of acknowledging 'our subjective constitution' (p. 84) without reducing all our perspectives to illusions.

> This tale gives proof that Heaven most gently deals
> With such, in their affliction. . . . (VI ll. 1072–3)

Yet we can also contrast the two characters, Pastor and Wanderer, and their two discourses. We may ask whether the Pastor could have drawn the Solitary into the discussion, as did the Wanderer? We may reflect that the Pastor's stories reduce the role for other speakers. We may compare the fabric of the language which the two use when speaking for faith. The Pastor qualifies ideas ('God, who takes away, yet takes not half . . . or gives it back' (VI ll. 1134–5)), but his qualifications are awkward to apply. He finds qualifications troublesome, they get in the way, because he is using every idea as a means to an end, which is synthesis. By contrast, for the Wanderer qualifications *are* necessary ideas. The good argument enhances qualifications, while the resolving method tolerates them.

Since the poem is argumentative, we can also argue *with* it. Has *The Excursion* fully recognised the cost of exchanging the Wanderer for the Pastor, the loss to the poem as it moves from dialogue to synthesising method? Another way to put the question – more acutely – is in terms of the Solitary's critique, his reworking of point of view and the possibilities of exchange. That critique enforces the move from Wanderer to Pastor. Has the Solitary thereby won more of a victory than the poem can acknowledge? Is articulate anguish as manifested in the Solitary too cogent for the whole design of the poem to bear? A further question would be: has the poem underestimated the *motives* of critique? Is it *only* the Solitary's agony which motivates his rejection of argument? There is a quality in the Solitary's voice which makes the question relevant. Is there not also an animated side of critique, a positive side? Could it not even be said that without the Solitary, the Wanderer would have no way of displaying his art of dialogue, nor the Pastor his dialectical method? Are there not more *energies* implicit in the Solitary than the poem can openly admit? But to argue thus is also to acknowledge the possibilities which *The Excursion* has created. Above all, the poem makes the arguments about arguing matter – emotionally and philosophically.

Ideals at the end of exchange

The Pastor persists with the method, which ultimately becomes systematic because, being methodical, it eventually produces a predictable result. The system is the sum of these predictable results. The stories are patterned to represent an understanding which has become systematic. We begin Book VII with a story of a clergyman, 'a simple Clerk' (VII l. 129); we end with a story about a 'courteous Knight' (VII l. 1008). Polar oppositions are multiplied in the application of synthesis. In between the poles of church and clerical state, of meditation and action, we have the deaf and the blind, the old and the young, the ignorant and the learned.[3] We apprehend the system because the examples are so diverse. Yet without repeatability, there is no method, and it is method which generates a sense of system. It is this system which embodies the highest claim to have reconciled diversity with a single approach – an *ideal* claim in its comprehensiveness. Yet the poem does not find systematic method sufficient for an ending.

The problem is that method and dialogue are not easy to reconcile with one another. Each is a process, and both processes originate in differences of opinion and perspective. But, where method resolves the differences internally, dialogue makes of them an interplay. Method would have provided an easier ending – but the poem returns *towards* a fuller dialogue. Once again, there is an exchange of roles. First, the Solitary – always the transforming influence – renews his more critical effect. He starts from a subsidiary point in the Pastor's last tale, the Tale of the Knight. He compares the Knight to the Wanderer, praising both types:

> Their tardy steps give leisure to observe,
> While solitude permits the mind to feel;
> Instructs, and prompts her to supply defects
> By the division of her inward self
> For grateful converse: . . . (VIII ll. 54–8)

The Solitary is endorsing the Pastor and the Wanderer. Yet his endorsement is slippery, because he is also defending 'solitude', which takes us back to his own point of view. Now the Solitary who accepted exchange gives a new defence of solitude: he suggests that the lone figure can still argue, argue *within his own mind*! The Solitary is also further eroding the Wanderer's position: if the Wanderer is like the Knight, then is he not a man of the past? And, if so, how pertinent are the Pastor's tales to the contemporary world? Endorsing both the Wanderer and the Pastor, the Solitary also asks questions about both men. He also questions the distinction between social exchange and isolated thinking: but that question could strike at the heart of the poem, at least in its earlier stages. The Solitary has recovered the power to criticise arguing from within the process, which is his version of good arguing. The Wanderer treats the words as simple praise:

> 'Happy,' rejoined the Wanderer, 'they who gain
> A panegyric from your generous tongue!['] (VIII ll. 82–3)

But after taking the praise, the Wanderer must respond to the challenge. Since the Solitary has identified him with older times against modernity, the Wanderer's reply is that:

> – An Inventive Age
> Has wrought, if not with speed of magic, yet
> To most strange issues. . . . (VIII ll. 87–9)

The Wanderer is going to argue that the new age is dangerous, and often impoverishing:

> . . . That birthright now is lost.
> Economists will tell you that the State
> Thrives by the forfeiture – . . . (VIII ll. 282–4)

He still thinks by qualifying, and so he complicates his own reply to the Solitary's view that he may be out-of-date:

> yet do I exult,
> Casting reserve away, exult to see
> An intellectual mastery exercised
> O'er the blind elements; a purpose given,
> A perseverance fed; almost a soul
> Imparted – . . . (VIII ll. 199–204)

In tune with *his* form of good arguing, the Wanderer includes the other view as a counter-force: 'yet . . .'. Such inclusion is distinct from the synthesis achieved by the Pastor. The Wanderer can never resolve the opposition, only recognise the differences while he advances his own case. He reintroduces his key note, hope; after the complex admission that the modern has new powers:

For with the sense of admiration blends
The animating hope that time may come
When, strengthened, yet not dazzled, by the might
Of this dominion over nature gained,
Men of all lands shall exercise the same
In due proportion to their country's need; (VIII ll. 208–13)

The Wanderer's voice can still quicken an exchange. The dialogue moves back and forth. What of the dispossessed whom the Wanderer himself identified? Have such any 'animating' prospects? The Solitary erupts:

'Hope is none for him!'
The pale Recluse indignantly exclaimed,
'And tens of thousands suffer wrong as deep.['] (VIII ll. 334–6)

The elements of a counter-case exist within the Wanderer's arguing – the Solitary has only to alter the emphasis to take it up. If the Wanderer acknowledges such anguish, where is the space of hope?

Once the Wanderer takes over the central role from the Pastor in extending the case for faith, the Solitary too recovers a voice, a *critical* voice. Yet the exchange between them has changed. The Wanderer and the Solitary are exchanging different ideas, in a way which is only possible because of their earlier interplay, but emotional tensions between them are now unusual or absent. After method has spoken, the exchange is purified or simplified. The dialogue inherits a certain ease from the preceding dialectic, an ease which was notably lacking in the early confrontation.[d] The poem reaches an impasse, when the focus returns from the Solitary to the Wanderer:

This ardent sally pleased the mild good Man,
To whom the appeal couched in its closing words
Was pointedly addressed; and to the thoughts
That, in assent or opposition, rose
Within his mind, he seemed prepared to give
Prompt utterance; . . . (VIII ll. 434–9)

[d]Gadamer (*Truth and Method*, p. 331) even transfers the term 'dialectic' to refer also to this type of uncontentious argument: 'Dialectic consists not in trying to discover the weakness of what is said, but in bringing out its real strength.'

In such an idealised exchange of views it becomes difficult to distinguish between 'assent or opposition' – difficult for those taking part in the exchange, and difficult for us, the readers.

Significantly, the Pastor intervenes while the poem is hesitating, but only with an invitation to the parsonage. When the exchange continues later, the Wanderer assures the Solitary of: 'A wide compassion which with you I share' (IX l. 155). Agreement can be taken for granted, where goodwill is so complete. The idealised dialogue that results risks becoming predictable in the same way as dialectical method is ultimately predictable. After acknowledging the Solitary's compassion the Wanderer laments the fate of the modern labouring child: 'The senseless member of a vast machine, /Serving as doth a spindle or a wheel;' (IX ll. 159–60). He connects the victim of industry with rural children:

> Think not, that, pitying him, I could forget
> The rustic Boy, who walks the fields, untaught;
> The slave of ignorance, and oft of want, (IX ll. 161–3)

The two perspectives are narrowly distinct, the Wanderer's emphasis falling on the total horror of modernity with greater intensity than on the effects of poverty on children in the traditional countryside. But the Wanderer and the Solitary have only a difference of emphasis between them – and as the differences shrink, the dialogue consumes its own pre-conditions. So idealised are their relations, that they turn from differing to echoing each other, until the exchange subsides. From the idealised exchanges emerges – in the Wanderer's words – an ideal which they might share concerning education and that State which

> shall admit
> An obligation, on her part, to *teach*
> Them who are born to serve her and obey; (IX ll. 296–8)[4]

The poem's story of an argument ends with this ideal dialogue. But that ending also contains three separate conclusions – corresponding to the Wanderer's, the Pastor's and the Solitary's.[5] The Wanderer's personal conclusion has been that we must hold to hope:

> we see by the glad light
> And breathe the sweet air of futurity;
> And so we live, or else we have no life. (IX ll. 24–6)

But how close the argument still comes to its opposite, the negative inversion: for he is just one step away from admitting that it is *only* hope which makes life worthwhile. So close here is the balance between hope and its opposite that it may be left to the reader to decide on which side to come down and what has been the effect on the Wanderer of his Excursion with the Solitary. The Pastor, too, remains aware of darkness: 'This dire perverseness . . . Shall it endure?' (IX ll. 660–1) The Pastor's concluding vision springs up with the force of prediction out of the whole experience:

> Almighty Lord, Thy further grace impart!
> And with that help the wonder shall be seen
> Fulfilled, the hope accomplished; . . . (IX ll. 675–7)

The Solitary's departure is left for the last words. Returning from an evening walk we see the Solitary as we knew him at the start of *The Excursion*, and sense his previous alienation:

> but ere the Vicar's door
> Was reached, the Solitary checked his steps;
> Then, intermingling thanks, on each bestowed
> A farewell salutation; . . . (IX ll. 769–72)

He appears friendlier, but he still insists on being separate and prematurely going his own way. But, it develops, he has moved on from this entrenched position:

> 'Another sun,'
> Said he, 'shall shine upon us, ere we part;
> Another sun, and peradventure more;
> If time, with free consent, be yours to give,
> And season favours.' (IX ll. 779–83)

He no longer considers himself to be entirely separate. The Solitary can envisage contact, further communication, further developments – and, significantly, the sun shall shine on these. The narrative of the poem ends by considering the position that the Solitary is now in – and the extent to which he may, or may not, have shifted since *The Excursion* began. The Poet, who recorded these exchanges, and participated in them has the last words:

To enfeebled Power,
From this communion with uninjured Minds,
What renovation had been brought; and what
Degree of healing to a wounded spirit, (IX ll. 783–7)

What renovation? *What* degree of healing? The repeated 'what' seems to point towards possible change and improvement in the Solitary's condition. But the question – 'what renovation'? – cannot be answered, not yet. We still inhabit the space *between* the questions and their hoped-for answers:

How far those erring notions were reformed;
And whether aught, of tendency as good
And pure, from further intercourse ensued;
This – if delightful hopes, as heretofore,
Inspire the serious song, and gentle Hearts
Cherish, and lofty Minds approve the past –
My future labours may not leave untold. (IX ll. 790–6, the end)

The prospect remains open, stretching towards a horizon of resolutions.[6]

Argument at its limits

In *The Excursion*, argument reaches the limits of its usefulness: the problems inherent in arguing to any purpose are everywhere apparent. The Solitary refuses to enter into dialogue; later he is so critical that he undermines the point of further discussion. The Pastor places other limits to the value of argument. He embodies a split between argument as dialogue and argument as monologue, as his themes take their independent way. Further, he introduces method into argument – which reduces effective exchange while appearing to be part of a dialogue. Finally the poem reaches another limit to effective exchange: agreement is so desirable that the outcome is predetermined and differences are voiced in the most muted way possible. The poem becomes a story of argument coming up against these limits. The central meaning of the poem is in encountering these problems of argument: the obstacles to effective exchange, the strains on it, and its boundaries and limits.

In Wordsworth's poem, the hopes to be found in argument include this story of strains and limits. Other dialogues in the later eighteenth and early nineteenth century show the same sense of strain in the process of resolving disputes. Wordsworth's story overlaps with Hume's *Dialogues* in a number of places. Hume is very aware of the problems of arguing reasonably towards an effective solution. Cleanthes argues with Demea and Philo who hold that the Deity is unknowable; he argues, but he cannot restrain his impatience with their views:

> It seems strange to me, said Cleanthes, that you, Demea, who are so sincere in the cause of religion, should still maintain the mysterious, incomprehensible nature of the Deity, and should insist so strenuously that he has no manner of likeness or resemblance to human creatures . . . Is the name, without the meaning, of such importance? Or how do you mystics, who maintain the absolute incomprehensibility of the Deity, differ from sceptics or atheists, who assert that the first cause of all is unknown and unintelligible . . .
>
> (*Dialogues* Part IV, p. 31)

Hume is writing a philosophical dialogue: the emphasis is on the logic of opposing cases. But even here, human tensions creep in; Hume imagines such proceedings as being intensely strained, and Demea points out the strains:

> Who could imagine, replied Demea, that Cleanthes, the calm philosophical Cleanthes, would attempt to refute his antagonists by affixing a nickname to them, and, like the common bigots and inquisitors of the age, have recourse to invective and declamation instead of reasoning? (IV, p. 31)

To Hume, as to Wordsworth in his different way, argument is a *difficult* process. No story of argument will be plausible where these difficulties are suppressed. In Wordsworth's story, the difficulties are more subtle and pervasive than in Hume's, and amount to much more than unpropitious invective. But it is highly significant when such tensions creep into a 'philosophical' argument from the eighteenth century. The perspective unfolds in two directions. On the one hand, argument seems a testing engagement; on the other hand, the commitment to argument is all the more vivid for this acknowledgement of problems.

Shelley's *A Refutation of Deism* shows another kind of stress placed on the reasonable progress of an argument. Here are the terms in which Eusebes invites Theosophus to an exchange of views:

> Permit me to exhibit in their genuine deformity the errors which are seducing you to destruction. State to me with candour the train of sophisms by which the evil spirit has deluded your understanding. Confess the secret motives of your disbelief; suffer me to administer a remedy to your intellectual disease. I fear not the contagion of such revolting sentiments; I fear only lest patience should desert me before you have finished the detail of your presumptuous credulity.
>
> (*A Refutation, Shelley's Prose*, p. 121)

A charming approach, but it falls within the bounds of argument! Theosophus, of course, replies in kind:

> I am not only prepared to confess but to vindicate my sentiments. I cannot refrain, however, from premising, that in this controversy I labour under a disadvantage from which you are exempt. You believe that incredulity is immoral, and regard him as an object of suspicion and distrust whose creed is incongruous with your own.

The Wanderer invites the Solitary to argue in the hope of curing his despair. Eusebes parodies the hope of such a useful exchange, and consistent with such beginnings goes on to demolish his opponent's hope for a rational faith. *The Excursion* and *A Refutation of Deism* share the knowledge that argument involves mixed motives. Wordsworth tells how the Wanderer balances these mixed motives, keeping the good argument always in sight. In Shelley's work, ambiguous motives for discussion give a surprising twist to his argument: both works depend on an underlying perception that the motives for starting an argument are complex.

Anna Barbauld presents a different strain in argument, arising out of the choice of alternatives presented to an opponent in an exchange. The Philosophical Enquirer offers Madame Cosmogunia two alternative views of herself:

> I have often heard it asserted, that as you increase in years, you grow wiser and better; and that you are at this moment . . . more amiable in every respect, than ever you were in the whole course of your life; and others, – you will excuse me, madam, – pretend that you are almost in your dotage; that you grow more intolerable every year you live; . . .
>
> **M. Cosmogunia:** As to that, I am, perhaps, too nearly concerned to answer you properly. I will, therefore, only observe, that I do not

> remember the time when I have not heard the same contradictory assertions. ('Dialogue', *Works* II, p. 278–9)

Madame Cosmogunia is being offered the opportunity to confirm her shortcomings – a not very nice argumentative tactic which, at least, will leave behind a reference to her shortcomings, but she is not easily overcome by argumentative tactics, for Madame Cosmogunia is 'too nearly concerned' to give a proper answer. A point, indeed, but what kind of exchange would it be in which the parties were not concerned! Wordsworth's poem takes up both these difficulties. Assertions *may* be contained, but, once made, they will never entirely lose their effect. The Wanderer acknowledges the absence of 'visible recompense' for the whole process of exchange after the Solitary's assertion of 'impertinent and ceaseless strife' in the realm of debate. There are affinities, too, between the poem and Madame Cosmogunia's idea that she is too *close* to the issues to know the truth about them: the Pastor believes in subjective *truth*, but the Solitary sees in subjectivity only the dangers of illusion. Arguments matter because they engage with people's perspectives; but those perspectives also limit the range of an argumentative process. Anna Barbauld is mocking an exchange: *The Excursion* comes close to doing so in places.

It is possible to carry mockery of the uses of argument much further than Anna Barbauld, and end by undermining them entirely, as Blake does in *An Island In The Moon*:

> 'Pray,' said Aradobo, 'is Chatterton a Mathematician?'
> 'No,' said Obtuse Angle. 'How can you be so foolish as to think he was?'
> 'Oh, I did not think he was – I only ask'd,' said Aradobo.
> 'How could you think he was not, and ask if he was?' said Obtuse Angle.
> 'Oh no, Sir. I did think he was, before you told me, but afterwards I thought he was not.'
> Obtuse Angle said, 'In the first place you thought he was, and then afterwards when I said he was not, you thought he was not.'[7]

Walter Savage Landor pits the useful qualities of arguments against the drawbacks, satire against acceptance, in his *Imaginary Conversations*, which first appeared shortly after *The Excursion* in 1824. He projects the post-revolutionary arguments back into history. Walter Noble takes on Oliver Cromwell:

> **Noble:** I hope, General Cromwell, to persuade you that the death of Charles will be considered by all Europe as a most atrocious action.

> **Cromwell:** Though hast already persuaded me: what then?[8]

Cromwell accepts the arguments of his adversary, but does not alter his actions. In fact, he ends with an emphatic statement of the revolutionary position: 'Where there is a crown there must be an axe:' (p. 108). On the one hand, this voice has great power; on the other hand, it participates only superficially in the argument. To Landor, argument is essential – and yet of dubious value. As in Wordsworth's poem, there is no escaping the need to argue, but the effect of argument is vitiated.

'Dialogue' may suggest a composed medium: voices in balance or even harmony. Yet a dialogue can also – as we have seen – register strains and tensions in its very procedures. Or a dialogue can be poised between division and resolution. Another such poised work is Robert Southey's strange book, *Sir Thomas More or Colloquies on the Progress and Prospects of Society*. In a ghostly echo of *The Excursion*, Southey (renamed 'Montesinos') takes the shade of More on some walks in the Lake District. Their most interesting subject is hope, the issue which pervades *The Excursion*. More criticises a third party who hopes for progress:

> He believes the world to be in a rapid state of sure improvement; and in the ferment which exists everywhere he beholds only a purifying process; not considering that there is an acetous as well as a vinous fermentation.[9]

The reply is almost querulous, before harmony returns:

> **Montesinos:** Surely you would not rob us of our hopes for the human race.

The pair then consider history, a consideration which leads to 'the manufacturing system'. As at the end of *The Excursion*, a debate on this issue is muted by a desire for harmony. Yet the issue still breaks through as a sense of crisis:

> **More:** Society has its critical periods, and its climacterics . . . This is one of its grand climacterics. A new principle, . . . a *novum organum* has been introduced, . . . the most powerful that has ever yet been wielded by man. If it was first *Mitrum* that governed the world, and then *Nitrum*, both have had their day, . . . gunpowder as well as the triple crown.

> Steam will govern the world next, . . . and shake it too before its empire is established. (pp. 198–9)

Even this wise ghost cannot settle the question!

The Excursion belongs to a period in which argumentative dialogues test the process of arguing from different viewpoints. Perhaps this questioning is connected with wider issues concerning reason, general problems which are heightened by particular contexts. Argumentative exchanges are not purely rational, nor are they possible without reason. These dialogue works, therefore, tell stories which test reason's status, a status possibly in doubt through wider events and crises leading to and from the French Revolution. From Wordsworth's story, too, emerges an exchange which tests contrary reasons, and expresses different feelings. There is a profound sense of strains on the process of argument and limits to its achievements. The poem concentrates the whole exploration of argument, reveals how necessary it is, shows its requirements and its limits. The comprehensiveness of this story of argument is far more significant than the weighting given to any belief. The poem's viewpoint is finally not identified with any particular character. Perhaps Wordsworth partly intended the Pastor to solve the Solitary's problems. If so, his commitment to the whole narrative obscured that solution in the end. Rhetorical versions of argument help to understand this situation. These rhetorical analyses are themselves part of another history, a rhetorical history outlined in the introduction. In particular, Burke and Gadamer look at the problems of argument through the traditions of rhetoric and seek some hope in argument. Burke and Gadamer both believe, with Wordsworth, that arguments *continue*. To Gadamer, argument continues through inexhaustible *questions*; Burke sees that accepting an argument must be followed by endless *criticism* and *renewal* of the argument: both draw on a sense that oppositions are inherent in issues. Wordsworth is also intensely relevant to this history at the present moment. In our time, there threatens to be a split between the recognition of argument's limitations and argument's fulfilment. Argument is either forbidden: or its outcomes are final and binding. Wordsworth's story makes the hopes engendered by argument inseparable from the strains that it imposes and the limitations that it has. Such a story belongs with the rhetorical efforts of Burke and Gadamer: encouraging argument, it does not conceal the extreme difficulties, and the ongoing, shifting balance in its outcomes.

The Excursion (II): further commentary and references

1 What are the places of the poem's excursion? The Ruined Cottage episode originally belonged to a walk over Salisbury Plain. Book II describes the arrival of the Poet and his friend at the Solitary's valley and then at his cottage. The scene has moved to the Lake District, with the cottage itself 'situated on the high ridge between the Great and Little Langdales' (Groom, *The Unity of Wordsworth's Poetry*, pp. 104–5). The Pastor has his church at Grasmere.

2 The tales which the Pastor is going to tell have troubled sympathetic interpreters of the poem – and necessarily so. In his larger perspective on Wordsworth, Johnston sees the Pastor as advancing *The Excursion* at the expense of the whole design of which this poem was meant to be a part – the magnificent idea of the Recluse: 'Wordsworth turned in the last five books to a sacramental priestly style of natural interpretation which enabled him to complete *The Excursion* – but it finished *The Recluse*' (*Wordsworth and The Recluse*, p. 284). Yet he, like the others of us who wish to interpret the poem in its best possible light, finds a redeeming motive: 'These stories complete one of the deepest intentions of *The Recluse*, the decentralization of imagination from its traditional location in privileged classes in capital cities.' (p. 286) Johnston's interpretation is inspiring in its humanity and shows a way for generous interpreters: 'The ideal of democratized imagination to which Wordsworth here sacrificed his egotistical genius gradually became, in the decades after 1815, the goal of enlightened social thought, the spirit of reform' (p. 290).

3 The grouping of the tales supports diverse interpretations. Johnston (*op.cit.* p. 299) remarks 'a set of binary oppositions that would please a structural anthropologist'! While some readings find comfort in the scheme, others are troubled. Laura Dabundo discovers a consoling unity in her 'The Extrospective Vision: The Excursion as Transitional in Wordsworth's Poetry and Age' (*The Wordsworth Circle* 19(1988) pp. 8–14, p. 11): 'Beneath the sense of community in Books Five, Six and Seven of *The Excursion*, can be found a sense of cross-grave community . . . '. But Hartman (*Wordsworth's Poetry 1787–1814*, p. 299) has an almost visionary discomfort at the same vista: 'Yet, as the poem proceeds, and more ghosts are raised, nature takes on the aspect of a large graveyard.'

4 The Wanderer proposes a system whose detail recalls the ideas of Dr Andrew Bell, whose 'Madras System' of teaching the poet admired. The system, first attempted in India, relied on older pupils to teach the younger classes – that was how the hope of universal schooling seemed practicable in an immediate way. Critical reactions differ. Characteristically and enrichingly, Johnston is expansive (*op.cit.* p. 320): 'Wordsworth's vision of a national or imperial education system is not a tacked-on digression . . . but an integral culmination of his wish to generalize and decentralize imagination. Pupils teaching each other are not very far removed from poets speaking as men to men.' Carl Woodring is more sceptical. In his study of *Politics in English Romantic Poetry* (Cambridge Mass: Harvard University Press 1970), Woodring refers to such education as 'this steam-intellect system' (p. 136) and views it as a symptom of just how deep were the causes of that very 'mechanization of the human spirit' which the scheme was designed to alleviate. Woodring adds more generously, and in line with Johnston: 'The significance of all this, for Wordsworth's politics generally, lay in his insistence that the state, responsible for the welfare of all whose allegiance it claimed, had a moral obligation to make life humane for the poor and the unfortunate.' (p. 138) These readings share an identification of the views with Wordsworth, no doubt justified by other sources – yet it is also valid to persist with the story of the whole exchange and consider the Wanderer at this moment in that story, and the overall unfolding of the various modes of debate.

5 It is a characteristic of *The Excursion* that different interpreters can – indeed must – give the work different endings. The reason is that almost every passage in Book IX serves as an ending in one way or another. Johnston concentrates on two emblems which greet the characters as they walk onto the hills around the parsonage and overlooking the lake of Grasmere in the evening light. One is a 'snow-white ram' reflected in the water (Book IX ll. 447–51) and the other is a sunset which prefigures 'unity sublime' (l. 608). Division becomes unity in these fine passages. But Hartman has a story which must end without being resolved: 'At the dramatic center of the poem stands the Solitary: can this mind be restored to health? Wordsworth is honest enough not to resolve the question.' (*op.cit.* p. 300) A story of argument must necessarily end *The Excursion* with the characters in their arguable world, of which indeed the diversity of interpretations becomes an extension!

6 The reputation of *The Excursion* is another story in itself, a story told most fully by Judson S. Lyon in his *The Excursion: A Study* (New Haven: Yale University Press 1950). The most notorious episode of that story would have to be the review by Francis Jeffrey (*Edinburgh Review* 24 (1814) pp. 1–30) with its memorable opening of dismissal, 'This will never do.' Although it is a symptom of the poem's ill-fortune that Jeffrey's review as a whole is more complex than this famous exclamation. Even the next sentence suggests a tension which is more representative of Jeffrey's troubled reaction: 'It bears no doubt the stamp of the author's heart and fancy; but unfortunately not half so visibly as that of his peculiar system.' Jeffrey seems – like others subsequently – uneasy about his recognition of the poem's powers:

> The conversation (of Book III) is exceedingly dull and mystical; and the Solitary's confessions insufferably diffuse. Yet there is considerable force of writing and tenderness of sentiment in this part of the work (p. 8).

Other poems by Wordsworth have had richer inheritances of interpretation and affirmation – *The Prelude* being the closest rival, if rivalry is the relation. *The Excursion* has had profound interventions, particularly in the voices of Kenneth Johnston and Geoffrey Hartman. Yet these voices have had to resonate against a background of dismissal, which can be expressed with contempt rather than with interpretive reason: 'the philosopical arguments of *The Excursion*, especially of The Wanderer, are simply childish', declares John Hodgson in his study of *Wordsworth's Philosophical Poetry* (Lincoln, Neb: University of Nebraska Press 1980, p. 168). How a poem of such delicate touch and essential development has not registered more richly would be subject for another study . . . the answer has probably more to do with the different virtue of Wordsworth's other poems than with anything in *The Excursion* itself. Perhaps some assumptions about Romanticism have also directed attention away from a poem whose attention is on the interplay of people rather than on the inner life – though the day of such assumptions is surely passed.

It is nonetheless reassuring that Keats recognised *The Excursion*, and recognised it richly: 'In a note to Haydon about a week ago . . . I said if there were three things superior in the modern world, they were 'The Excursion', 'Haydon's pictures' and 'Hazlitt's depth of Taste'. So I do believe – Not thus speaking with any poor vanity that works of genius were the first things in this world.' (letter to George and Thomas Keats, 13 January 1818, *Letters of Keats*, edited by Robert Gittings (Oxford: Oxford University Press 1970), p. 49).

7 *An Island In The Moon* in *William Blake: Poetry and Prose*, edited by Geoffrey Keynes (London: The Nonesuch Press 1948), Chapter 5 p. 676.

8 'Oliver Cromwell and Walter Noble' in *The Complete Works of Walter Savage Landor* Volume IV, edited by T. Earle Welby (New York: Barnes & Noble and London: Methuen 1969), pp. 102–9, p. 102. The dialogue appeared in *Imaginary Conversations*, 1824. Succeeding references given in text.

9 Robert Southey, *Sir Thomas More or Colloquies on the Progress and Prospects of Society* (London: 1831 second edition), Volume I (of 2), p. 27. Succeeding references given in text. Southey's book is integrated into a political overview by Marilyn Butler in her book, *Romantics, Rebels and Reactionaries* (Oxford: Oxford University Press 1981), Chapter 8. Butler also provides a map of poetic responses to *The Excursion* (pp. 140–1).

The Hind and the Panther: arguing with authority

> The Nation is in too high a Ferment, for me to expect either fair War, or even so much as fair Quarter from a Reader of the opposite Party. All Men are engag'd either on this side or that: and tho' Conscience is the common Word, which is given by both, yet if a Writer fall among Enemies, and cannot give the Marks of Their Conscience, he is knock'd down before the Reasons of his own are heard.
>
> (John Dryden, 'To The Reader' Before *The Hind and the Panther*)

One historical context of the seventeenth century is the role of reason in religious conflicts. Fundamental divisions between Roman Catholicism and the Church of England arose from this opposition: was the position of a true church based on an interpretation of the scriptures, which would, by its very nature, be a reasoned interpretation of holy text? Or was the position of a true church based on an original dispensation, signified in the voice of Christ, which had been delivered since that time by succeeding generations of his ministers in the true church, and which was enshrined in its traditions, beyond the scope of reason? The Church of England maintained a position based on the individually reasoned interpretation of scripture; the Roman Catholic Church took its position from an original source maintained through tradition. This is the distinction that appears in Dryden's *Hind and the Panther*, from which its argument develops and proceeds, an argument entangled in motives and threats, the elucidation of which constitute much of the narrative development. By the time he wrote this poem, Dryden was a Catholic, having previously been an adherent of the Church of England. In general, he now maintained the Catholic position and promoted the Catholic point of view. It is therefore profoundly significant for the role of reason in general, and its status at that time, that Dryden should have chosen to embrace reason, and reasoned argument by writing *The Hind and the Panther*, and broaching the religious differences of those times, since the case for his opponents rested on reason, and his own case on an inspiration whose origins could only be reached through a continuity enshrined in the traditions of the Roman Catholic Church.

There were, at that time, already literary precedents for testing the effect of the split between the churches. Thomas Hobbes, in his *Dialogue . . . Of the Common Laws* questioned, on this basis, the nature of heresy at that time, in the section 'Of Heresie':

> **Lawyer:** In the Preamble of the Statute of the 2nd, Hen. 4. Cap. 15. Heresie is laid down, as a Preaching or Writing of such Doctrine, as is contrary to the determination of Holy Church.
>
> **Philosopher:** Then it is Heresie at this day to Preach, or Write against Worshipping of Saints, or the Infallibility of the Church of *Rome*, or any other determination of the same Church. For Holy-Church, at that time, was understood to be the Church of *Rome*, and now with us the Holy-Church I understand to be the Church of *England*.[1]

The issue of reason arises quickly, when the talk focuses on the fate of the original heretic:

> **Philosopher:** By what Law then was he burned?
>
> **Lawyer:** By the Common-Law.
>
> **Philosopher:** What's that? It is not Custom; for before the time of Henry the 4th, there was no such Custom in England . . . . And if you will say he was burn't by the Law of Reason, you must tell me how there can be Proportion between Doctrine and Burning. (pp. 130–1)

What proportion indeed . . .?

The importance of reason and original inspiration is focused elsewhere in *A Friendly Debate Between A Conformist And A Non-Conformist* (1668, 3rd edition 1669). There is a pointed comparison to be made with Dryden's work, for the author, Simon Patrick, was an Anglican who subsequently became Bishop of Ely. Yet, dealing with the same matter as Dryden, his argumentative dialogue gives considerable effect to another opposition to the Anglican viewpoint on interpretation. But here the opponent is a dissenting non-conformist, the very type whom Dryden's poem will place beyond the pale of such exchange:

> **Conformist:** But, pray tell me, how shall we understand the Gospel, by our Reason, or by something else?
>
> **Non-Conformist:** By the Spirit.[2]

This preference for 'Spirit' over reason will not do for the Anglican, who protests:

> **Conformist:** . . . My Question is this, Doth the Spirit shew us any new thing, which is not the conclusion of the Reasonings and Discourses in our minds about the Sense of Scripture? (p. 7)

Differences in the importance given to reasoned interpretation are clear from the start, and the non-conformist proceeds to a direct assault on the Anglican position:

> **Non-Conformist:** I see one shall not want rational discourse at your Church (as you call it:) but methinks I never found that life and power in your Ministry which I have in ours.
> **Conformist:** I told you before, that I find nothing so powerful as the Christian Doctrine rationally handled. (pp. 14–15)

The Anglican conformist repeatedly attempts to bring the argument back onto his own ground:

> **Conformist:** Now I appeal to any man that reads the Gospel, whether this be not the very design of it, to teach us to live soberly, righteously, and godlily. . . .
> **Non-Conformist:** For all this, I think it were better if Jesus Christ were more preached.
> **Conformist:** . . . Doth not he preach Jesus Christ that preaches his Doctrine? If you doubt of it, you shall have scripture enough to prove it.
> **Non-Conformist:** But I mean that the Love of Jesus Christ to poor Souls should be more preached. (p. 145)

Significantly, Simon Patrick embarked on this long dialogue without much hope of a successful settlement in the end:

> **Non-Conformist:** Truly, Neighbour as long as you live well, I shall always desire to maintain a Familiarity with you, though you be not of my mind; believing that you are Christian, though of another way. And I hope you will do the like with me.
> **Conformist:** I assured you of it before. But let me enter this proviso, that you talk no more about matters of Religion; for unless you be so changed by this Discourse, we disagree so much, that it will be irksome to us both. (p. 239)

The final reflection is on argument itself.

Some of this pessimism over the outcome of religious argument is shared by a French Catholic, Malebranche, in a dialogue whose English version of 1695 was called *Christian Conferences: Demonstrating the Truth of the Christian Religion and Morality*. Aristarchus, a re-convert to Christian faith, is dismayed to find that he cannot convert others so easily:

> **Aristarchus:** 'Tis something strange, Theodorus, that a Man can't convince others of the same thing that he himself is fully convinced of; for it appears to me, that all men ought to see the same things.
>
> **Theodorus:** If all men were equally attentive to inward truth, they would all equally see the same things; but your Friend is not like you, he is taken up with a multitude of things, and his pride has now for many years kept him unconversant even with himself. . . [3]

Dryden, whose Church occupied a vulnerable position at the time, was profoundly sensitive to this dilemma – that argument seemed not to have the power to settle religious dispute – but he envisaged the dilemma as arising from *threats to argument* itself, and in *The Hind and the Panther* he accounted for them. In that poem, he resolved that such threats arise broadly from undeclared self-interest in debate on values, or from group interest, or factional interest, which loads an argument on theoretical – or religious – issues. He arrived therefore at a rhetorical analysis which contributes in a major way to understanding *bad faith* in argument, which is highly relevant to the conception of ideological dispute in our day. His awareness of the perils of argument paralleled his sense of the desperate need for argument, and gave to his poem a painful tension. In the end, though he himself had a particular point of view, he resisted frustration and disappointment to explore a broader view of argument and its possibilities. From these *The Hind and the Panther* never finally departed.

Dryden's poem *The Hind and the Panther* shows us why the problems of argument remain inexhaustible. To read Dryden's poem for its understanding of argument is to recognise afresh the questions which make the disciplines of arguing both essential and inconclusive. *The Hind and the Panther* connects the insoluble problems of argument with their human and historical interest. It presents two points of view, as they existed in the seventeenth Century: Catholic and Protestant. But in its handling of that particular interaction, it lights on problems of argument, which are also general. The poem is a fable in three parts. The first part introduces the dispute, and the two characters who personify the Catholic and Protestant cause: the Catholic Hind, the Protestant Panther. The argument between their views of faith is put forward by the poem's narrative voice: a dialogue between the two characters is implicit. In Parts II and III, Hind and Panther explicitly take up the argument and dispute with each other.

Most of the poem's issues are general differences between

Catholicism and Protestantism: transubstantiation and faith; biblical interpretation; the nature of traditional authority. In the poem, as elsewhere, the Catholic viewpoint requires the acceptance of the actual fact of the presence of Christ in the communion – whatever the senses say, and therefore implies the limiting of the evidence of the senses in some contexts. The Catholic viewpoint places traditional authority above the private interpretation of the biblical text, and the Protestant viewpoint prefers text before tradition. The poem is centrally about this question of tradition and interpretation of texts. Out of the terrible conflict of sixteenth and seventeenth century European history, comes a process of such delicacy that it almost eludes formulation. The problem is that we do not associate such conflicts with much delicacy – so that one may be tempted to regard the process as mere embellishment, and proceed to extract the familiar positions in their simple forms.

When he wrote the poem, Dryden had recently converted to Catholicism. Furthermore, the poet was also the Poet Laureate – to the Catholic King, James II. James had been working since his accession in 1685 to overcome obstacles which kept Catholics out of public positions – and by the spring of 1687, when the poem appeared, there was general tension, as Parliament resisted these efforts. Another year would bring the end of the story – or of the episode – with the arrival of William of Orange and the 'Glorious Revolution' of 1688. *The Hind and the Panther* is part of a suspended moment, before that ending, when the balance is still unclear. The story of *The Hind and the Panther* can be told in many ways. If enclosed in a larger narrative of the period, then the poem can be told as a desperate attempt to produce a moderate Catholic position by a man aware of the dangers brewing. Or the poem becomes a courageous affirmation of changed faith; or a more doubtful concession to political necessity – or to some degree, both courage and caution. But *The Hind and the Panther* also contains a story of argument itself – a profound story of what happens when argument is – in every sense – difficult. Yet the story of difficult arguing is another way to envisage the meaning of good argument – of what good argument may mean under stress, even with the possibility of violence. Inevitably, that story leaves us with questions which are larger than any answers we choose to select . . .

Issues and voices

The argument between the Hind and the Panther recognises the features of an arguable world, and ultimately a fine balance beyond which good argument cannot go without dangers that bring into question the usefulness of argument, though the poem remains committed to that usefulness throughout. Yet there are voices of truth in *The Hind and the Panther*. First, the unidentified voice of Part I speaks for an authority which the poem recognises:

> God thus asserted: man is to believe
> Beyond what sense and reason can conceive.
> And for mysterious things of faith rely
> On the Proponent, heav'ns authority. (Part I, ll. 118–21)

'Heav'ns authority', passes down from God to his intermediary, the Son, to the Catholic Church. The Hind embodies this pure spirit, and remains 'the unspotted Hind'. The Panther who is an Anglican, becomes 'spotted', though the 'fairest . . . of the spotted kind' (l. 328), who represent deviations from that original line.

The Hind is introduced as: 'A milk white *Hind*, immortal and unchang'd' (Part I, l. 1). The Hind's essence is homogeneous and single. Mixing dilutes the essence:

> Not so her young, for their unequal line
> Was Heroe's make, half-humane, half-divine. (Part I, ll. 9–10)

The Hind is a pure essence, and when this is mixed with 'Heroe's' nature the result is not synthesis but dilution. So a further dilution gives:

> The Panther sure the noblest, next the Hind,
> And fairest creature of the spotted kind; (Part I, ll. 327–8)

Beyond that mixture – and preceding it in the emphatic text – a great press of creatures emerges by further adulteration; the Wolfe, the Bear, the Boar; all with claims to the true faith.[4] Eventually we shall get:

> A slimy-born and sun-begotten Tribe:
> Who, far from steeples and their sacred sound,
> In fields their sullen conventicles found:
> These gross, half-animated lumps I leave; (Part I, ll. 311–14)

There is a decline from 'half-divine' to 'half-animated'; by mixing, we pass from something which is pure to something which is half as fine to something which is barely alive at all:

> So drossy, so divisible are They,
> As wou'd but serve pure bodies for allay: (Part I, ll.319–20)

To be 'divisible' is to be corruptible. Corruptibility points us back towards the 'milk white' of the original entity: in the *origins* of a belief you can discover value. If the case reaches back to the beginning which is the Source of truth, then we should believe in it; if it arises as a corruption of that origin, then we should distrust it. Yet the pure origin itself exists within the realm of argument, and not outside. What seems to be an answer to the problem – recognising truth in origins – begins the processes of arguing. We soon discover other voices with different standards for judging the truth. The poem cannot exclude those voices, which is why the world is arguable. Instead of exclusion, we find exploration.

One of the dominant counter-claims to the inheritance of an original truth is the claim to rely upon *perception* and *experience* in seeking the truth. Perception from experience is the ground of judgement and not origins. The narrative resists that view:

> Can I believe eternal God could lye
> Disguis'd in mortal mold and infancy?
> That the great maker of the world could dye?
> And after that trust my imperfect sense
> Which calls in question his omnipotence?
> Can I my reason to my faith compell,
> And shall my sight, and touch, and taste rebell? (Part I, ll. 80–6)

No one can easily reconcile 'sight, and touch, and taste' with belief in an all-powerful and benevolent deity, for we experience things which contradict such belief. Yet if 'reason' is reconcilable with faith, can we not bring our senses, too, into line with the requirements of original faith?[5]

The *other* voice which proposes that sense determine truth is more and more audible, so that the poem's world is more emphatically arguable. A good argument – as the main voice for origins seems to have – is not an *unarguable* authority:

'Tis urg'd again that faith did first commence
By miracles, which are appeals to sense,
And thence concluded that our sense must be
The motive still of credibility. (Part I, ll. 106–9)

If faith used to appeal to the senses, then why should sense no longer provide the criterion of belief? Ironically, the case for 'sense' lays claim to origins:

For latter ages must on former wait,
And what began belief, must propagate. (Part I, ll. 110–11)

Even the poem's own criterion of origins is contestable; the other side which endorses sense may try to repossess the logic of origins. As a result, the main voice becomes a *replying* voice, by acknowledging that there is a case to answer. The rhythm suggests a dialogue before we have named adversaries in debate:

But winnow well this thought, and you shall find,
'Tis light as chaff that flies before the wind. (Part I, ll. 112–13)

The reply begins by calling us to judgement of the case for the senses – and then asks a question about the first miracles:

Were all those wonders wrought by pow'r divine
As means or ends of some more deep design? (Part I, ll. 114–15)

The question leads to a further response:

Most sure as means, whose end was this alone,
To prove the god-head of th' eternal Son. (Part I, ll. 116–17)

Miracles were never an end in themselves, the case runs, therefore we misunderstand the origins of faith if we identify them with such palpable signs as sensible miracles. Behind the perceptible signs is an idea, an idea which precedes both human sense and human thought:

God thus asserted: man is to believe
Beyond what sense and reason can conceive. (Part I, ll. 118–19)

Authority is articulated from the outset as part of an argumentative strategy, a strategy which presupposes there will be opposition and voices contrary to authority. God's assertion implies an arguable world in which sense has differing contexts.

'Sense' is still far from exhausted as a possible criterion for judgement. When 'sense' has been previously mooted as a criterion on which to base the truth, it there referred to the senses of sight, smell and touch or to common sense associated with them: but it next reappears as the sense derived from *textual interpretation*. Can texts support a stronger 'sense' than experience provides?[6] The poem's voice argues that it is the Protestant churches that have relied on texts for their point of view, and to rely upon the understanding of texts is to render every dispute endless, because the sense of every text is endlessly disputable. In the specific instance of the Protestant churches, texts have been taken to justify reforming the original institutions of the Church, but the criterion of the text is dangerous in this view:

> If she reform by Text, even that's as plain
> For her own Rebels to reform again. (Part I, ll. 460–1)

If we expect our interpretations of texts to settle arguments, then arguing can come to no significant conclusions. This is particularly true of biblical texts. Other interpreters will make the same criterion offered by the text serve different purposes, so that what seems a general standard for adopting truth will be merely a pretext for different preferences. The case is explicit:

> As long as words a diff'rent sense will bear,
> And each may be his own Interpreter,
> Our ai'ry faith will no foundation find: (Part I, ll. 462–4)

'Bear' advances the argument on two fronts: words give birth to diverse interpretations and, conversely, words tolerate the expression of different views. Either way, the 'sense' of words is no more secure than the evidence of perceptions or the assumptions of everyday judgement.[a]

The poem is making a specific claim – that origins are the trustworthy criterion and that 'sense' is a delusive standard. But the claim also implies a general idea: the criteria by which the truth may be known are arguable and the selection of criteria is itself part of the dialogue. There is nothing weak about the claim on behalf of origins – on the contrary, the poem commits itself strongly. But, for Dryden,

[a]In *Truth and Method*, Gadamer recognises that the study of interpretation derives partly from rhetoric (pp. 19–29). Interpreters are always involved in exchanges with different views from their own, whether the views of the text being interpreted (pp. 345–51) or of other interpreters (pp. 325–41). Dryden's poem explores the relation of interpretation to argument in a more critical way.

such commitment is only possible within a dialogue. Criteria for such commitment are themselves arguable. Different views about the origin of truth are possible and even essential. To be arguable does not mean that different views are even, or equally worthwhile, but there is a difference between such *unequal arguability* and a single point of view. For Dryden's poem, such final statements of the truth are linguistically inconceivable: the word becomes arguable every time we discuss it. Such arguability is not merely metaphysical; it is the result of the language we use as we experience it, and not of any more nebulous assumptions. Language is always subject to interpretation.

The main voice pursues its implied opponents and their trust in interpreting texts. What authority has a church which concedes *first* place to its documents:

> How can she censure, or what crime pretend,
> But Scripture may be constru'd to defend? (Part I, ll. 481–2)

These terms – 'crime', 'defend' – imply an analogy between theological and legal arguments. Protestantism, the voice argues, expects the *statutes* to make the judgements for the court. But the text is no arbiter, since different sides can contest its sense. The text is *intrinsically* contestable. Where the hopeful might rely upon interpreters of *goodwill* to see the text in acceptable ways, Dryden considers the prospect of interpreters with trickier motives. Even as the poem argues for authority – the authority of origins – we can feel how *difficult* any authority will be to maintain.

A method for ending argument

Claims are often made that different views can be synthesised: so differences end, along with the tensions they cause. If the opposing views can merge in one truth, a *method* may be found for resolving arguments generally. We could take the contestants in turn and create a new whole from their cases to replace conflict. The poem's voice suggests that the Anglican church embodies the synthetic hope. The differences in question concern the eucharist:

> In doubtfull points betwixt her diff'ring friends,
> Where one for substance, one for sign contends,
> Their contradicting terms she strives to join, (Part I, ll. 410–12)

One party has argued that the eucharist involves actual transformation of bread into the body of Christ ('substance'), whereas another party sees the ceremony in symbolic terms ('for sign').[7] Method takes these opposed ideas and 'strives to join' them into a new unity. The words undermine the hope that striving will lead to success:: 'doubtfull . . . diff'ring . . . contends . . . contradicting' all come before the attempt 'to join'. The possibility of synthesis between 'contradicting terms' is delusive. No enduring 'join' is made. One might call such false resolutions 'pseudo-dialectic': if dialectic implies true synthesis achieved by uniting opposites, then pseudo-dialectic is false method, a technique for putting together opposites that are still separate and separable.[b] Differing views and voices are implicit in 'contradicting terms'. Dryden has here located a profound problem at the centre of traditions of thinking about argument. He is challenging the assumption that there are set techniques for resolving argument.

The poem needed to dispose of facile technique for a pseudo-dialectical resolution because otherwise there would have been an easy escape from argument about the precedence of the two Churches. The debate about criteria for belief is significant because, in the poem's view, synthetic method provides no way out of the conflict between the Churches and their doctrines. Real differences must be weighed with authentic judgements, which in turn depend upon strong criteria – and so we return to origins as a criterion for the evaluation of truth.

Authority, equality and argument

The argument of Part I already implies a dialogue: the main case for truth presupposes rivals for authority, and the relation between them is inescapable and critical. In Part II, the main case is made in the *voice* of the Hind and the rival case becomes the voice of the Panther. The Panther begins with a history of recent disputes between her own

[b]Juan Luis Vives – the sixteenth-century Spanish rhetorician – proposes the term 'pseudodialectic' in his criticism of current modes of disputation (Juan Luis Vives, *Against The Pseudodialecticians*, ed. and trans. by Rita Guerlac, Dordrecht: Reidel 1979). Vives is particularly critical of the inventing of methods and rules which lead to the distortion of the familiar meanings of words. The true dialectician, by contrast, 'does not fashion and transmit a new meaning of language' (p. 79). The poem is here criticising a similar tendency to ignore the 'old and familiar meaning' (p. 79), and substitute techniques of manipulation and synthesis.

Protestant church and the Catholic church of the Hind – and specifically in the context of plots against the Catholics:

> Dame, said the *Panther*, times are mended well
> Since late among the *Philistines* you fell,
> The toils were pitched, a spacious tract of ground
> With expert hunts-men was encompass'd round; (Part II, ll. 1–4)

The Catholic church – which the Hind partly represents – has come through a period of prosecution, disenfranchisement and worse. Only recently has the 'Lion-King' of England, James II, extended his favour and protection to Catholics. The Panther gibes at the Hind for being a lucky survivor of careful persecution. (Not only is the poem's recognised truth disputable, but its advocate is characterised to begin with by her opponent in the dispute.) The Hind responds from the situation portrayed by the Panther, and draws the Panther into the same predicament:

> As I remember, said the sober *Hind*,
> These toils were for your own dear self design'd,
> As well as me; . . . (Part II, ll. 18–20)

The times of plots and traps were – says the Hind – no safer for the Anglican Panther. Part II has begun with an exchange to underwrite the dialogue with characters: *the voices characterise each other*.[8]

Civil war and its aftermath has engendered danger and hatred between rivals for authority. But which authority is right? The dialogue between Panther and Hind turns to the issue of authority, the subject of the implicit disagreement in Part I. The Panther mocks what she assumes is the Hind's Catholic claim: 'I fain wou'd see /That wond'rous wight infallibility' (Part II, ll. 64–5). The Hind responds with a counter-challenge: that her Anglican rival's claims to authority are themselves unfounded:

> But mark how sandy is your own pretence,
> Who setting Councils, Pope, and Church aside,
> Are ev'ry man his own presuming guide. (Part II, ll. 105–7)

The Hind argues that 'every man' has a desperate need for self-assurance, and that the meaning of the biblical text is vulnerable to this need. Needy interpreters will compel the arguable script to satisfy them, and yet Protestantism has no other criterion of truth apart from biblical interpretation:

The sacred books, you say, are full and plain,
And ev'ry needfull point of truth contain:
All who can read, Interpreters may be:
Thus though your sev'ral churches disagree,
Yet ev'ry Saint has to himself alone
The secret of this Philosophick stone. (Part II, ll. 108–13)

Every position conceivable from the text is open to challenge; and each individual uses the text to justify himself or herself, desperately. All interpreters need be justified to themselves alone. There is a wonderful contradiction between the absolute authority of each saint, and the conflicts between them all. The Panther does not notice – says the Hind – how difficult it is to resolve the disagreements which ensue:

These principles your jarring sects unite,
When diff'ring Doctours and disciples fight. (Part II, ll. 114–15)

Principles taken to unify groups in fact divide them. The half-joke is that people mistake disagreement for agreement.

The Panther defends her grounding in texts, when they are interpreted rightly by her method:

No, said the *Panther*, for in that I view,
When your tradition's forg'd, and when 'tis true.
I set 'em by the rule, and as they square
Or deviate from undoubted doctrine there
This Oral fiction, that old Faith declare. (Part II, ll. 176–80)

Confronted by the Panther's contrast between her own textual truth and the Hind's 'oral fiction', the Hind substitutes 'tradition' for 'oral fiction', in a vision of past continuity and of present dangers:

The Council steer'd it seems a diff'rent course,[9]
They try'd the Scripture by tradition's force;
But you tradition by the Scripture try;
Pursu'd, by Sects, from this to that you fly,
Nor dare on one foundation to rely.
The word is then depos'd, and in this view,
You rule the Scripture, not the Scripture you. (Part II, ll. 181–7)

Her Church had a tradition which enabled it to interpret Scripture and judge what is true. In her whole address, the Hind shows how deeply she values the arguing process itself; yet she is acutely aware of the risks that reversals in the process of arguing will spin endlessly back and forth, until the process is self-consuming. The Hind then pursues her adversary's thought to what she sees as its implied low point: 'Thus all disputes for ever must depend' (Part II, l. 202) We wait for what the outcomes of these disputes 'depend' on – and nothing follows. 'Depend' turns round to mean just a sense of waiting, groundlessness looms. She then advances towards her own position:

> Thus all disputes for ever must depend;
> For no dumb rule can controversies end. (Part II, ll. 202–3)

However unsatisfactory this outcome, or lack of outcome, which follows from disputing, no 'rule' could ever settle disputes.[10] (This takes us back to the failure of syntheses and methods for aborting disagreement, and also to the delusive choice of 'sense' as a criterion of believability.) If there were a 'rule', we could dispense with argument. But then she adds 'dumb' to 'rule': what is wrong with the rule is partly rigidity and partly that it is *unspeaking*. Both the 'sense' of texts and the 'sense' of perceptions are 'dumb' rules: they are silent, and so they depend on interpreters. Speech has important consequences.

The Hind has picked up some weakness in the Panther's insistence that, instead of 'oral fiction', she 'set 'em by the rule'. One reason why the rule offers finality is because it comes from text. Because it has been written as opposed to spoken. It is writing which helps such a rule appear complete – writing as opposed to speech. Writing has a spurious finality. Since it is not possible to force the text to defend itself, either from errors or objections, texts are *seen* as authoritative – in reality they are just the reverse:

> Thus when you said tradition must be try'd
> By Sacred Writ, whose sense your selves decide,
> You said no more, but that your selves must be
> The judges of the Scripture sense, not we. (Part II, ll. 204–7)

And again:

> At least 'tis proved against your argument,
> The rule is far from plain, where all dissent. (Part II, ll. 210–11)

Putting it in writing offers only a false hope of transcending contention.

The Panther asks caustically: 'If not by Scriptures how can we be sure /. . . what tradition's pure?' (Part II, ll. 212–3) In reply, the Hind envisages a line of voices, passing on truth from age to age:

> Before the Word was written, said the *Hind*:
> Our saviour preach'd his Faith to humane kind;
> From his Apostles the first age receiv'd
> Eternal truth, and what they taught, believ'd.
> Thus by tradition faith was planted first,
> Succeeding flocks succeeding Pastours nurs'd. (Part II, ll. 305–10)

Arguing is a sequence of voices that is potentially endless; so is tradition: another sequence of voices carries the tradition which is also endless. The voices of tradition are harmonious, rather than differing, but the two lineages are analogous. Indeed the two structures *imply* each other: each represents a way of using language. Truth is *like* differing, because both truth and difference arise in the endless play of our voices. The truth can only establish its nature by contrast with the *other* side of that endlessness: argument.

Even within the harmony of an inherited tradition, there are possible variations. Inherited truth is not a *single* voice, but a sequence of voices in harmony. The Hind's 'tradition' is not static or monovocal, but a precise *analogy* to the stream of differing voices: dynamic, polyvocal and allowing for different positions of consciousness in time and space. Furthermore, the tradition *separates* the generations which convey it vocally as well as connecting them. Above all, *when we recognise that tradition is passed through the generations, we realise that the original source is not directly accessible*. There is a subtle mixture of assurance and elusiveness about the vision of an inherited tradition:

> Thus faith was e'er the written word appear'd,
> And men believ'd, not what they read, but heard. (Part II, ll. 323–4)

True authority can only reside in the original, speaking voice: the pure sound of that voice gave it authority. Many different views about the text generate obscurity:

> For this obscurity could heav'n provide
> More prudently than by a living guide,
> As doubts arose, the difference to decide?
> A guide was therefore needfull, therefore made, (Part II, ll. 346–9)

There is a continuous process in which 'doubts' multiply, in endless 'difference'. Without some authoritative voice, there is no way out of 'the difference'. The differing *makes* such an authority necessary: 'therefore needfull, therefore made'. The Hind has criticised the 'dumb rule' of texts, but she acknowledges *some* place for rule:

> Nor wou'd I thence the word no rule infer,
> But none without the church interpreter.
> Because, as I have urg'd before, 'tis mute,
> And is it self the subject of dispute. (Part II, ll. 357–60)

The 'word' of writing is important, once tradition validates it.

In the Hind's view, the human responsibility for resolving the process of differing must rest with connective *institutions*. The problem remains, where does the institution get its own authority?

The Panther has a subtle reply:

> Suppose, (the fair Apostate said,) I grant,
> The faithfull flock some living guide should want,
> Your arguments an endless chase persue:
> Produce this vaunted Leader to our view,
> This mighty *Moyses* of the chosen crew. (Part II, ll. 389–93)

The Hind responds quickly:

> The Dame, who saw her fainting foe retir'd,
> With force renew'd, to victory aspir'd;
> (And looking upward to her kindred sky,
> As once our Saviour own'd his Deity,
> Pronounc'd his words – *she whom ye seek am I*. (Part II, ll. 394–8)

The claim to represent the original authority is not quite easy: these are '*his* words' still, even though the Hind is repeating them.[11] The later voice can never merge finally with the original authority.

> Nor less amaz'd this voice the *Panther* heard,
> Than were those *Jews* to hear a god declar'd. (Part II, ll. 399–400)

The parallel implies a gap: 'this voice' is not *exactly* the earlier voice. Her voice *is* an authenticated echo, but not the original sound of truth. In a discourse which was less committed to arguing, the Hind's claim to authority would, nevertheless, be final. But the Hind needs to establish the parallel claims of her Church:

> For that which must direct the whole, must be
> Bound in one bond of faith and unity:
> But all your sev'ral churches disagree. (Part II, ll. 451–3)

These institutions perpetuate the conflicts which have given rise to them. The problem of difference between other institutions is the same as the problem between ordinary individuals in dispute:

What one can plead, the rest can plead as well;
For amongst equals lies no last appeal, (Part II, ll. 470–1)

For the Hind, there must be an authority to match the contest of differing voices. But the lines can also serve as an intense vision of the *equalising* force of those differing voices. And here is the crux. The Hind presents this equalising force of many differing individual voices as a problem. For others, that equal power of many voices may be the proper outcome of difference. Equality of utterance is important to those who differ.[c] So we understand the need for concentrating authority (in the Hind's view) and also the other possibility, of sharing authority. The poem never blurs the alternatives at issue:

Then, granting that unerring guide we want,
That such there is you stand oblig'd to grant:
Our Saviour else were wanting to supply
Our needs . . . (Part II, ll. 479–82)

On one side is the need for an 'unerring guide' as the process is otherwise insoluble.[12] On another side, we might be at *home* 'amongst equals' – though the Hind makes that condition alien to what she perceives to be our deeper need for authoritative direction to the truth.

The Hind follows her idea of centralised authority:

One is the church, and must be to be true:
One central principle of unity.
As undivided, so from errours free. (Part II, ll. 529–31)

[c]This view has been most forcefully put, recently, by Habermas; earlier versions can be found in sophistic thinking about law, where each of the parties has an equal say and giving each of the parties an equal say becomes the way of assuring a proper resolution. Habermas envisages 'the structures of an ideal speech situation immunized against repression and inequality in a special way. . .' (*The Theory of Communicative Action*, Volume One, translated by Thomas McCarthy, London: Heinemann 1984, p. 26).

Even the empire of Britain does not contain a more significant authority. The Church gives us 'The Gospel sound diffus'd from Pole to Pole' (Part II, l. 552). Whereas Britain's new empire parodies the diffusion of truth, exporting convicted felons instead:

> Thieves, Pandars, Palliards, sins of ev'ry sort,
> Those are the manufactures we export; (Part II, ll. 563–4)

The Church *is* an empire, but her growth is different from ordinary empire-building. The Hind needs to justify the institution by comparison with rivals or usurpers.

* * *

The Hind leads the Panther to 'her lonely cell' (l. 663), and the world turns strange with an almost bloody nightfall:

> The Western borders were with crimson spread,
> The moon descending look'd all flaming red, (Part II, ll. 668–9)

The poem recognises the Hind as the true voice, but there is no other place for that voice than the arguable world, which encompasses her round with a gesture that may promise redemption or prophesy murder.

There is no final answer at the end of the long exchange on the nature of tradition and the embodiment of authority – only the prospect of a further exchange in a world where being at home is difficult. But has the Hind won the first encounter? The Panther accepts the invitation to the Hind's cell which may mark some alteration in their relationship – at least she is wise to prefer the cell to the night, and 'took her friendly hostess at her word' (l. 656). But she may simply have no alternative: 'since she had to deal /With many foes' (Part II, ll. 693–4) *Has* the Panther even softened towards the Hind and her conception of the authority which she embodies? We cannot be sure; certainly, the Panther does not change her views and join the other side. The problem is that the Hind has only carried the day in terms of her own criterion for believing – and which criterion to adopt is precisely the issue of the argument. The poem endorses her criterion: origins *are* the only true measure of truth and the Hind personifies those origins – but nothing *compels* the Panther to agree. Even if her battle on behalf of texts is defeated there are two weaknesses in the Hind's position. Why should the argument about *origins* not be as endless as the dispute about texts? And, secondly, if the Hind represents the true voice, why are her words part of a written text? The arguable world is larger than the Hind's criteria, and the poem remains in the arguable world. Every reading implies several contexts. One context of the poem must be the historical struggle for power between Protestant and Catholic churches. The struggle was not (yet) resolved: we do not (yet) know whether the Hind of the Fable will return to power. The lion-king has allowed her back to the common pool; the huntsmen who hunted her have withdrawn. But neither Hind nor Panther know whether they are on the winning side, in the *historical* sense.

The sphere of interest

Part III takes its cue from the history, rather than from the case for authority. The Hind gives 'a full review' (l. 39) of their shared past[13]:

> what the *Panther* suffer'd for her sake.
> Her lost esteem, her truth, her loyal care,
> Her faith unshaken to an exil'd Heir, (Part III, ll. 40–2)

Both churches have endured great hardship. But the Panther's response takes the exchange another way, a darker way altogether than reconciliation:

> You, like the gawdy fly, your wings display,
> And sip the sweets, and bask in your great Patron's day. (Part III, ll. 66–7)

There is a specific, historical fibre in this accusation: the 'great Patron', the Catholic King James II, is here thought to favour the Catholic church. This partiality raises the suggestion that the Hind's position as the sole purveyor of the true faith is suspect. Her doctrines incite material favour: they serve, in other words, an undeclared interest. Confrontations do indeed commonly raise the accusation of corrupt motives. But if motives for holding a point of view are not to be trusted, all positions in a debate are undermined. The narrative brings us the Panther's accusation that the Hind is seeking Royal patronage, and the Hind's reaction:

> This heard, the *Matron* was not slow to find
> What sort of malady had seiz'd her mind; (Part III, ll. 68–9)

The Panther's 'malady' is also corrupt motivation: 'Ambition, int'rest, pride without control' (Part III, l. 72). But this is precisely the *Panther's* claim against the Hind. True, the poem endorses one voice against the other; but we can still observe the symmetry of the accusations, spoken or as yet unspoken.

Dryden's arguers are passing from argument over doctrine to mutual accusation. No judge appears to weight their mutual accusations. The only evidence is what they have to say against each other. The Hind insists that she has not exploited favour for material gain: 'My crying sins are not of luxury' (Part III, l. 115). But this claim to disinterestedness only produces from the Panther the rejoinder:

> I never grudged, whate're my foes report,
> Your flaunting fortune in the *Lyon's* court,
> You have your day, or you are much bely'd,
> But I am always on the suff'ring side: (Part III, ll. 135–8)

The Hind tries again and again 'the Lyon buyes no Converts' (Part III, l. 225) she says,[14] but her motives for disputing over doctrine remain suspect. She also retaliates with sharper accusations, directing them at the 'sons' (l. 144) of the Panther and then adding:

> And, but I blush your honesty to blot,
> Pray God you prove 'em lawfully begot: (Part III, ll. 163–4)

The Panther's sons are wolfish, threatening the very monarchy from which the Anglican Panther draws her power. But in the realm of accusation, others can always reply in kind; the Panther declares that the Hind has welcomed people: 'Allur'd with gain' (Part III, l. 198). Furthermore, the Panther adds, these false converts undermine genuine argument, since they do not give their true reasons:

> Bare lyes with bold assertions they can face,
> But dint of argument is out of place. (Part III, ll. 199–200)

The poem *has* endorsed the Hind – yet endorsement cannot prevent the exchange from following the symmetry of allegation and counter-allegation. Each side accuses the other of treachery and resists the other's right to debate – the Panther is diseased by 'ambition', the Hind is represented by 'bold assertions' from followers who lie. We are a long way from the Hind's case for an 'unerring guide', and her claim: 'She whom ye seek am I.'

Finally, the Hind is driven to survey the context of accusation, instead of denying the charges against herself:

What wonder is't that black detraction thrives,
The Homicide of names is less than lives;
And yet the perjur'd murtherer survives. (Part III, ll. 258–60)

Where black detraction destroys a person's good name, the arguing process will degenerate. The historical darkness thickens; the murderers of kings still live from the time of Charles I and the Civil War, everyone is suspect. In an atmosphere of mistrust, there is no way out from suspicion and calumny, no way from personal doubt to the issues of the argument. Does there come a point where the exchange is too distorted by personal suspicion for it to be useful? This question is a source for some of the most painful reflections on argument.[d] The poem continues to entrust its thinking to the disputing process; but we are made painfully aware of the risks that emerge from disagreement, risks of spreading poison instead of discovering truth. Once suspicion begins, there is no end to the risk. Violence looms in the background. The untrustworthy party may have to be eliminated.

The Hind is drawn deeper into making charges, including one of plagiarism against the Panther concerning a treatise claimed by the Protestants:

A Treatise of Humility is found.
. . .
The fam'd original through Spain is known,
Rodriguez work, my celebrated son,
Which yours, by ill-translating made his own,
Conceal'd its author, and usurp'd the name,
The basest and ignoblest theft of fame. (Part III, ll. 329,332–6)

[d]Walton (*Informal Logic*, Chapter 6) reflects sombrely upon 'Personal Attack in argumentation': he categorises as 'argumentum ad hominem', 'the kind of argument that criticizes the arguer rather than his argument. Basically, it is a personal attack on an arguer that brings the individual's personal circumstances, trustworthiness or character into question' (p. 134). Walton concedes that such attacks may constitute valid arguments, but warns that even so 'personal attack is inherently dangerous in argument'. He does suggest: 'One legitimate function of the argument against the person may be to shift the burden of proof in dialogue back on to an attacker' (p. 147). So indeed the Hind resolves . . . and we can grasp from the whole story how *history* itself drives the exchange in this dangerous direction.

Debate becomes rancour; on either side there is a sense of injury, each greater than the other. The Hind protests:

> Be judge your self, if int'rest may prevail,
> Which motives, yours or mine, will turn the scale. (Part III, ll. 384–5)

To have 'motives' is to be potentially corrupt. The whole tenor has fallen: the earlier discussion was about grounds of believability, now the issue is what different parties stand to gain from the beliefs they profess. It is the Hind who recognises the significance of this change: 'When int'rest fortifies an argument /Weak reason serves to gain the wills assent' (Part III, ll. 397–8) Any major account of what happens when voices differ needs to recognise that there is such a thing as a bad argument when personal advantage may affect what people profess. The process through which the truth must be asserted may be a channel of avarice. The key term for the sphere which the poem has been exploring and is about to explore further is 'interest'. The exchange has entered upon that area which modern theory speaks of as 'ideological', the area where ideas and interests interact. The poem is working towards a recognition that this interaction *may* be positive in the end, though interest often corrupts.

The previous exchange ended with two responses to endless 'dif-f'ring': the choice of an 'unerring guide', which is preferred in the Poem's terms, or the right to an opinion 'amongst equals'. But will either response survive the mutual accusation? Truth is not above the ideological fray – at least in the sense that truth may be charged with serving interests, just as the enemies of truth serve special interests. The designated true voice will need to master the skills of ideological conflict, of the forensic contest which no independent judge exists to arbitrate.[e]

At the centre of Part III, the Hind and the Panther swap their own fables within Dryden's fable. There is a profound relationship between the way in which they put their cases obliquely in the form of

[e]By contrast, C. Perelman and L. Olbrechts-Tyteca draw on a tradition deriving from Plato to propose that genuine argument is incompatible with such contests. They propose the notion of a 'universal audience' as the embodiment of disinterested judgement to which proper cases should address themselves (*The New Rhetoric*, trans. J. Wilkinson and P. Weaver, Notre Dame: Notre Dame University Press, 1969). To adapt Walton's more flexible approach, what we see in this episode is a mixing of quarrel, forensic debate and negotiation – none is either legitimate or illegitimate inherently, but the brew is volatile.

fables, and the fact that interest has become the issue. Obliqueness is essential to keep the channels open, once accusations of bad faith are being bandied about. If these parties are to continue talking, they must find a less direct way of conveying their accusations. And – in its whole continuing commitment – Part III demonstrates that it *is* possible to continue the exchange even through the reciprocal accusation of bad faith.

Naturally, if people tell fables about animals, then animals tell fables about birds. The Panther tells a fable about the swallow who, together with her kind, enjoys the summer 'as man's familiar guest', till the first signs of autumn provide auguries of winter:

> When prudence warn'd her to remove betimes
> And seek a better heav'n, and warmer clymes. (Part III, ll. 443–6)

And so the swallows turn south, but on their way their flight is interrupted by fears, which are encouraged and fanned by a Martyn:

> A church-begot and church-believing bird;
> Of little body, but of lofty mind,
> And much a dunce, as *Martyns* are by kind,
> Yet often quoted Cannon-laws and *Code*,
> And Fathers which he never understood, (Part III, ll. 462–6)

There is a disagreement among the swallows, for some can see the folly of giving in to such fears and breaking their journey South, and give contrary advice:

> Th' advice was true, but fear had seiz'd the most,
> And all good counsel is on cowards lost. (Part III, ll. 523–4)

Fear of the unknown world and sloth lead the swallows to follow the advice of the corrupt martyn-priest who advises staying. The Panther's fable here has a double point: one is that Catholics take their security too much for granted, instead of perhaps leaving England; the other point is that debates may be imperfect. Debates may be governed by 'fears' and by misconceived self-interest: short-term views may rule out long-term prudence.

The threat intensifies.[f] The swallows stay. With luck, the Martyn's advice is partly made good, and they survive the winter, with cells and refectories and large provisions prepared. Spring comes and they enjoy another summer. But now their numbers increase beyond their capacity to cope. So some must be planted abroad, and the entire flock sets off to guide the new young in the direction of the colonies. The flight is not properly organised, time is wasted, and the entire flock is swept up in terrible conditions on a moonless night:

> The joyless morning late arose, and found
> A dreadfull desolation reign a-round,
> Some buried in the Snow, some frozen to the ground:
> The rest were struggling still with death, and lay
> The *Crows* and *Ravens* rights, an undefended prey; (Part III, ll. 622–6)

There is a terrific gusto to the Panther's description of the swallows' massacre, a gusto which turns to menace.[15] Not surprisingly, the Hind is preoccupied by that aspect of the fable and objects: 'But through your parable I plainly see /The bloudy laws, the crowds barbarity:' (Part III, ll. 657–8). It is particularly hard for those who, like the Hind, entrust the truth to the exchange of voices that argument may mask a predilection for force and that this same exchange may pass into violence. But the Panther slyly reassures the Hind – *she* would take no part in any 'barbarity' against the current powers that be:

> My sons wou'd all support the regal side,
> Though heav'n forbid the cause by battel should be try'd. (Part III, ll. 668–9)

Hypocrisy follows menace: *others* might attack the crown because it favoured Catholics. . . . The Hind's reaction brings in to focus the practice of the whole poem:

[f]Walton remarks that 'one must be careful, in some cases, to distinguish between a threat and a warning' (*Informal Logic*, p. 96). The Panther's warning indeed turns here into a threat – and so enters the area of 'appeals to force' (p. 96). Walton regards such 'appeals' as dangerous though *sometimes* necessary – he particularly denounces, though, the appeal to force which seeks to foreclose a dialogue, to end the critical exchange. Habermas legislates even more strongly that true argumentation, 'excludes all force – whether it arises from within the process of reaching understanding itself or influences it from the outside – except the force of the better argument . . .'. (*Theory of Communicative Action*, p. 25). The Hind needs to live – and debate – in a different world, which such an ideal may help to present by contrast.

The Matron answer'd with a loud Amen,
And thus pursu'd her argument agen. (Part III, ll. 670–1)

Outside the contest of ideas, there is nothing creative; however unpromising the Panther's performance, it is necessary to respond with arguments creatively. Interest *may* corrupt the use of words, but that leaves the hope that words may still be the ends of argument in themselves. Can *menace* be kept at bay or edged back from the exchange of words? Now it is not 'interest' which is the problem, nor even deception – but threat. . . .

Ultimately, the Hind is going to have to resort in turn to fable, to its peculiar combination of the oblique and the direct, obliqueness of reference and directness of feeling. But first, she re-explores what has happened to the exchange itself. In Part I, over-easy synthesis was exposed as a false technique; now, by Part III, over-easy insult is the equivalent problem, and this problem, of facile repudiation, is what the Hind seeks to engage. First she defends the lion-King as 'studious of our common good' (l. 675). Then she analyses the laws which exclude Catholics from public offices. The Panther claims she disapproves of this restriction though the Hind is doubtful:

But smile to think how innocent you stand
Arm'd by a weapon put into your hand. (Part III, ll. 700–1)

Her arguments succeed in maintaining the exchanges, for the Panther *has* to make a counter-claim:

My gracious Sov'reign wou'd my vote implore:
I owe him much, but owe my conscience more. (Part III, ll. 784–5)

The King hopes the Anglicans will support a repeal of the laws restricting Catholics and dissenters. Of course, the Panther declares, she is not hostile to the repeal, although her 'conscience' could not tolerate such latitude. Now the Hind can pursue the truth behind this mask of reasoning:

Immortal pow'rs the term of conscience know,
But int'rest is her name with men below. (Part III, ll. 823–4)

Once the Panther is back in the justifying mode, the Hind can challenge her terms, even question her good faith – but always *responsively*, never in an exclusionary vein. Argument has been raised to a higher level.[g]

To try and re-establish a basis for further negotiations and a proper dispute, the poem introduces us to a key word, 'trust':

> Well, said the Panther, I believe him (the King) just,
> And yet –
> And yet, 'Tis because you must,
> You would be trusted, but you would not trust. (Part III, ll. 884–6)

An agency which undermines its opponents by casting doubt upon their motives, arouses the same suspicion. There is a kind of darkness here:

> The Matron woo'd her kindness to the last,
> But cou'd not win; . . . (Part III, ll. 892–3)

In the end, assent is an act of the will. We cannot presume to change the will of another, however eloquent we may be. Again, the Hind pursues the exchange in the darkest possible perspective. Yet, for the pursuance of truth through arguments, another criterion has emerged: trust, the antithesis of menace.

The Hind's parable now follows and the emphasis is upon imperfect and corrupt ways of exchanging views, and not upon an ideal exchange. In this respect there is a significant symmetry between the two parables. Each arguer is haunted, or animated, by an image of the corruptness of disputation. The Hind's fable envisages a good knight or 'Master' (l. 1058) on whose lands are two breeds of birds: the natural fowl – a humble and deprived species, 'banish'd' by law 'from the farms' (l. 1068) – and a vicious breed of unconfined pigeons, who have given up the tougher demands of their religious observance, and are jealous of the humble fare that goes to the fowl. At a 'grave Conseill' of pigeons, 'one more mature in Folly than the rest' advises them to import a buzzard, a 'potent bird of prey', to keep down the numbers of the fowl (l. 1108–15). The appearance of the buzzard focuses the issues, since 'Interest in all his Actions was discern'd' (Part III, l. 1149). The Buzzard personifies the quality which is posing the

[g]The modern theory of ideology has become a negative counterpart to theories of argument. J. Thompson (*Studies in The Theory of Ideology*, Cambridge: Polity Press 1984) considers large areas of communication are ideological, where communication deceives and is a manipulation on behalf of hidden interests. The poem implies that a distinction between threat and honest exchange is more important than the distinction between 'ideology' and 'non-ideology', if the latter distinction is feasible.

problem: 'interest'. The Hind's fable constructs the most negative version of ideology in modern terms. First, there is a narrow version of 'interest'; then there is the *deceiving* use of persuasive powers: 'False Fears their Leaders fail'd not to suggest' (Part III, l. 1205). In the story, argument is descending into ideology at its most negative, yet the words belong to the same Hind who in Part II herself entrusted the truth to dispute. The truth must be persuasive; but this is far from meaning that all strong persuasion is the truth. What follows this negative ideology is violence:

> 'Tis true, the *Pigeons*, and their Prince Elect
> Were short of Pow'r their purpose to effect:
> But with their Quills, did all the hurt they cou'd,
> And cuff'd the tender *Chickens* from their food: (Part III, ll. 1221–4)

Throughout, *The Hind and the Panther* has been alerting us to all the negative possibilities of the very process to which it is creatively committed: argument. Now acrimonious counsel has led to vicious action – but the outcome is not what was intended, for the Master sees what is happening:

> Concluding well within his Kingly Breast,
> His Fowl of Nature too unjustly were opprest,
> He therefore makes all Birds of ev'ry Sect
> Free of his Farm, with promise to respect
> Their sev'ral Kinds alike, . . . (Part III, ll. 1242–6)

Restrictions are repealed. In this newfound freedom, Arts and Wealth flourish, while the doves 'sunk in credit, decreas'd in Pow'r'. Quarrelsome and schismatic as they are, their end is in sight. Inevitably, when their good Lord dies, the Buzzard will feed off them, they will feed off each other and their kind will be destroyed.

But the key point is the closeness of the creative and the destructive in argument's nature. The Hind does not discard 'interest' but rescues it in a vision underwritten by reason and feeling at their largest;each individual must recognise the true interest of others as 'Combin'd in common Int'rest with his own' (Part III, l. 1254) The very term, 'interest', which has undermined arguing throughout Part III, recovers positive connotations at the last.[h] The Hind's fable becomes a type

[h]Habermas in his *Theory of Communicative Action* makes an analogous contrast between 'immediate interests' (p. 19), which corrupt exchange, and 'the claim to express . . . an interest *common to all* . . . and thus to deserve general recognition'.

of good argument: not the dismissal of interest, but the defining of 'the common int'rest'.[16] The antidote to corrupt ideology is not absolute purity, but a more generous ideology, one which recognises that diverse interests are connected. There are better and worse ways of pursuing argument: mean ways and generous ways. The nature of argument and its place in human affairs needs to be understood; the uses of argument advocated, the dangers considered. Arguing is arguable, but the argument needs to be pursued.[17]

The Hind and the Panther: further commentary and references

Text of *The Hind and the Panther* used is: *The Poems and Fables of John Dryden*, ed. James Kinsley (Oxford: Oxford University Press 1970).

1 Thomas Hobbes, *A Dialogue Between a Philosopher and a Student of the Common Laws of England*, edited by J. Cropsey (Chicago: University of Chicago Press 1971), p. 122–3. The dialogue was published in 1681, though composed earlier. Succeeding references given in text.

2 Simon Patrick, *A Friendly Debate Between A Conformist and A Non-Conformist* (The Third Edition, London 1669; Imprimatur Nov.7 1668), p. 7. Succeeding references given in text.

3 The author was given as 'F. Malebranche', that is 'Father', though the writer is now known as Nicolas Malebranche: 'F. Malebranche', *Christian Conferences: Demonstrating The Truth of the Christian Religion and Morality* (London 1695), 'Dialogue VI', p. 105.

4 To tell the story of *The Hind and the Panther* in terms of specific controversies requires detailed interpreting of these beasts – and of their other contexts. Sanford Budick gives the fullest account of sources for the choice of animals in his *Dryden and The Abyss of Light* (New Haven: Yale University Press 1970). His most important point is that there is no single source story capable of explaining all the references. Among his most tempting identifications is that of the Panther with a beast from the Book of Daniel: 'After this I beheld, and lo another, like a leopard . . .' (p. 199). He also uncovers a source for the Hind in sixteenth and seventeenth century interpretations of Daniel, where the same Hebrew word stands for beauty, virtue and the roe or hind (p. 212). Earl Miner in *Dryden's Poetry* (Bloomington: Indiana University Press 1967) connects the animals with 'sacred zoographies' which were partly scientific and partly symbolic in their approach. For instance, one such work termed the hind 'timerous' and the panther 'very crafty and subtle' (p. 162, pp. 164–5). Miner also shows how each of the dubious or wicked beasts can represent a type of heresy, from a Catholic point of view – the main types being larger than any contemporary manifestation (pp. 197–9). On the other hand, Myers contends that the animals should be seen in political terms, rather than primarily as theological positions – in his study of 'Politics in The Hind and the Panther' (*Essays in Criticism* 19 (1969) pp.19–33). The overwhelming impression is that though the identities may seem simple, they are not easy to fix finally and comprehensively in all respects. (The poem's accounts develop from I, l. 1–61 and again from l.150 to the Panther's appearance at l.326.)

5 The passage from ll. 62–159 can be seen as a 'confessio', a declaration of the poet's new conversion to Catholicism – as in Miner (*op.cit.* pp. 146–7). Such interpretation then concentrates on further references to 'My thoughtless youth' (l. 72) and follows the discussion of the senses fully through to the defence of the Catholic doctrine of transubstantiation and the real presence of Christ in the Host (ll. 92–3). That defence is also politically significant, because this belief was precisely the one which prevented Catholics from passing the 'test' established in 1672 to keep them from holding public office. Dryden had already made another public commitment in 1686 in his *Defence of the Papers Written by the Late King* . . ., where he defended Charles II who had died a Catholic – see for instance, G. Douglas Atkins, *The Faith of John Dryden* (Lexington, Kentucky 1980, p. 130). For present purposes, the important point is the opening up of the question of criteria for deciding what is believable. In this context, it is interesting to note that the famous declaration about the Host in communion is itself a question:

Can they who say the Host should be descry'd
By sense, define a body glorify'd?

We never lose the sense of an argument between different positions, so that confession seems a rather narrow term.

6 The word 'sense' is a problem for all attempts to tell stories of *The Hind and the Panther*. Victor H. Hamm explores the ways in which the poem echoes contemporary debates between Catholic and Protestant theologians, in his article 'Dryden's *The Hind and the Panther* and Roman Catholic Apologetics' (*PMLA* 83 (1968) pp.400–15). 'Sense' appears in the role of perception and worldly understanding – as in 'the greatest assurance that Sense can give me' – and in the role of interpretive achievement – as in 'the sense of Holy Scriptures' (p. 408 and p. 411). Other such echoes include a Protestant use of 'Motives of Credibility' (p. 407). Hamm's story of echoes is a helpful counterpart to a story of the process of argument – insofar as he suggests a context of subtle and rich debates between Catholic and Protestant writers. Perhaps the poem has done more justice to the flow of these arguments than more monological ways of presenting history.

7 Budick (*op.cit.* pp. 223–6) traces the term 'substance' both to textual controversy, where it refers to the main point of a text, and to the communion, where it refers to the real presence of Christ in the Host – though the passage seems more interested in mimicking the way the Panther's party of Anglicanism might make the meanings of such a word seem to vanish, as if by magic.

8 As well as seeing these lines as a prelude to exchange, it is possible to trace current tensions. The reference is to the incident of 'the Popish Plot', also handled by Dryden from a different perspective in his poem *Absalom and Achitophel*. In 1679, there were menacing claims of a conspiracy of Catholic parties under Charles II – and a flurry of pamphlets from 1679–82 explored charge and counter-charge, with claims that the supposed evidence was itself a plot. A larger narrative of Dryden's poetry and conspiracy theories emerges in Steven N. Zwicker's *Politics and Language in Dryden's Poetry* (Princeton: Princeton University Press 1984). His account then interweaves this moment in the poem: 'The Panther raises the issue of cowardice, and the lines evoke the plight and behaviour of English Catholics during the Popish Plot . . .' (p. 139). The

Hind replies with counter-accusations – first that the Panther was equally at risk, and then that she was hardly heroic. The detail of the counter-charge leads to references to the legislation under which Catholics were subject to an exclusionary test – 'The Test' (l. 30). Zwicker's story follows the 'counter-offensive', an attack on the Panther's advocacy of the 'Test Act'. The present story gains instead the sense of reciprocal characterisation as a starting point to an encounter.

9 The Hind shifts her case between the authority of 'Councils, Pope and Church', to adopt her own phrase from earlier. The most famous of the Church councils was the Council of Trent, whose authority appears in contemporary debates (Budick, *op.cit.* p. 220). Miner (*op.cit.* pp. 187–8) relates this indeterminacy to the 'good reason that there was at the time no authoritative Roman decision whether infallibility resided: 1) in the Pope; 2) in General Councils; 3) in the Pope and General Councils . . .'. Zwicker (*op.cit.* pp. 144–5) makes a version which is characteristically witty: 'The analysis of infallibility is conducted in a language and results in a position crucially reminiscent of the balanced construction of English legal tradition . . . civic authority resides in the combination of king and parliament, ecclesiastical authority resides in Pope and council.'

10 These passages are also rich in potential for stories where *The Hind and the Panther* replays contemporary controversies. Atkins (*op.cit.* p. 119) cites a Catholic work of 1675 called *Reason Regulated*: 'Apostolical Tradition, not written Books, etc is . . . the true, and certain rule of faith.' Hamm (*op.cit.* p. 407) traces the word 'rule' to the Protestant Stillingfleet: 'there must be a certain Rule of Faith supposed to have sufficient Authority to decide controversies without any dependence upon the church . . .'. But it is noticeable that 'rule' also appears in the Catholic passage of *Reason Regulated*. In relation to the present story, the poem can be said to have spun its own process of argument using some of the contested concepts of the time. But the emphasis here is not on the echoes so much as on the replacement of what emerges in Hamm and Atkins as a somewhat cumbersome contest by a most delicate and economical interplay. The comparison could suggest an idealising creativity with regard to the whole argument as much as a tactical intervention.

11 Such moments have necessarily incited interpretation. How are we to reconcile the animal fable aspect of the poem with such declarations which seem to break the allegory? And there have been others – for instance, amidst the ideas, we hear of the Panther's 'glowing eye-balls glitt'ring in the dark' (l. 223). Budick (*op.cit.* pp. 164–70) surveys the many mockers, including some sharp parodists. Miner suggests that any story of the poem will need to recognise it as a 'discontinuous' allegory (*op.cit.* pp. 146–7). David Hopkins in his *John Dryden* (Cambridge: Cambridge University Press 1986) gives a classical perspective on the poet's playing with such inconsistency, which is shown to be recognisable from Ovid's poetry. Hopkins argues that such playing enables Dryden 'to tease his readers out of complacent or fixed attitudes' in *The Hind and the Panther* (p. 101). It could also be said that the poem displays the power of argument as a process to incorporate diverse elements – without merely merging them all into a single system.

12 The 'guide' is the church as inheritor of Christ's message on earth – 'unerring' linking again to the issue of infallibility. It might be thought that 'unerring' was a hard term to contain in a story about argument and the arguable world. But it is precisely the sense of profound arguability which gives rise to the concept. Moreover, the idea itself stays profoundly within the debate. Another way to put the effect is in the more biographical terms of John F. Leonard:

> Dryden's sceptical, individualist disposition in matters of the mind was always as strong as his respect for royal authority. . . . Indeed the acceptance of an 'unerring guide' for the mind does not come across in the poem as an easy step to take. (Leonard, 'The Character of Dryden's Hind' in *Southern Review* 15 (1982) pp. 291–305, p. 296)

Atkins (*op.cit.* p. 135) points out how systematically Dryden is reversing the terms of his earlier poem, *Religio Laici*, written in 1682 from a Protestant perspective. The turn-around reuses many of the same ideas – so that the Protestant poem asserts of the bible that 'God wou'd not leave mankind without a way' (l. 296). Such a procedure is not calculated to make the Hind's path smooth – the story suggests a poet who seems as concerned to re-explore a whole disagreement as to resolve it in either case. Harold Love in his article on 'Dryden's Rationale of Paradox' (*ELH* 51 (1984) pp. 297–313, p. 298) credits the poet with a 'particular mode of intellectual pluralism' which depends upon 'invoking irreconcilable systems of explanation'. The whole of the argument contains its strongest cases, rather than the other way around – to connect these appealing biographies with the story in progress.

13 It is very possible to make this renewal of the exchange part of a political story for the times. Zwicker (*op.cit.* p. 128) notes the fact that it seemed clear by 1687 that: 'The King had abandoned efforts at a parliamentary repeal of the Test Acts and Penal laws . . .', and had moved towards other methods of admitting Catholics to posts in the army and public services. In such a perspective, the invitation could plausibly represent an idea of continued dialogue, however unappealing the prospect. Such a political parable corresponds richly to the general story of patience in argument – patience both tactical and ethical. Budick (*op.cit.* pp. 181–90) tells the story in very different terms by invoking the ancient legend of Saint Chad, which features a symbolic stag and also a dialogue between hermit and guest. Perhaps the poem's power to create an arguable world depends partly upon this mixing of perspectives and elements – we can never identify a fixed vantage-point from which to view the whole in static terms.

14 There is no difficulty in applying the idea to Dryden himself, in need of defence for his own conversion. Atkins (*op.cit.* p. 15) dates Dryden's own conversion in late 1685 or early 1686, James II having succeeded to the throne in 1685. A reading concerned with this story needs then to develop (ll. 235–97), where the Hind speaks of 'my sons accus'd' (l. 235). Miner regards these lines as a confessional intervention parallel to the passage of Book I (*op.cit.* pp. 146–7). But it is equally true that the exchange is not interrupted in its rhythm of forensic accusation and defence.

15 For an interpreter telling a story of the poem's political bearing on the times, the Panther's fable is at once apt and elusive. Zwicker points a double application: 'The Panther's fable . . . is, first of all, a device to frighten the Hind, to suggest that if Catholics take advantage of the false spring of James's reign, they will end up dead in the snow . . . the poet himself might also be using this nasty fable as a way of indirectly criticizing James's submission to Father Petre, a character mercilessly ridiculed in the figure of the martin . . .' (*op.cit.* p. 151). Leonard points a prophetic moral, since William was indeed to arrive in 1688: 'The swallows should be preparing for winter: in other words, for the succession of the Protestant king' (*op.cit.* p. 292). The prophetic applications also make the point that the fables presuppose a time before such endings were certain – a time when the history of kingship is itself arguable not only in terms of rights and judgments, but in terms of predictions too.

16 There is a particular crux in this fable as regards the tale of Dryden trying to keep pace with events. On 4 April 1687, King James issued a Declaration for Liberty of Conscience, or Declaration of Indulgence – releasing both Catholics and dissenters from the restraints of the test. In his Preface, Dryden remarks that 'About a fortnight before I had finish'd it, His Majesties Declaration for Liberty of Conscience came abroad . . .'. The fable seems to incorporate this event in its freeing of the farm to the various birds, assuming, as Zwicker interprets, that: 'James is the master of the farm; the lineal estates are England, Scotland, and Ireland; the pigeons alias doves are Anglican clergy; and the domestic poultry are Roman Catholic clergy' (*op.cit.* p. 156), or perhaps the birds are not so clearly clergy as more general representatives. The Buzzard emerges as William of Orange himself, already a potential threat to James, and also as 'Gilbert Burnet, an Anglican clergyman with whom Dryden had longstanding quarrels'. But there is a problem, in these terms, about the ending of the fable, and so about its implications. It is after the generous farmer's intervention that the buzzard destroys the pigeons. Interpretation finds another place to make the story in different ways. Myers (*op.cit.* p. 30) finds that the two fables with their murderous endings point the political moral in darkest shades: 'Just as the Declaration signals the final breakdown of relations between the King and his Anglican Parliament, so the Third Part of The Hind and the Panther indicates the end of Dryden's own political hopes.' Zwicker (p. 157) finds a more assertive conclusion, which is also more playful: 'That the fable predicts the Anglican demise is clear, but the details are not. Their meaning is difficult to fix, and the uncertainty turns the Hind's fable into a proper example of mysterious writ.' Equally, the arguability of the fable makes for a true ending to the whole process of the argument – an ending which refuses to transform the arguable world into a place of answers in a single voice, unopposable by any others.

17 At the very end, the Hind and the Panther retire to rest. The Panther has no simple response to the Hind's fable. Not surprisingly, she cannot 'blame . . . nor commend' (l. 1290). But the Hind has her sleep waited on by 'Ten thousand Angels . . . With glorious Visions of her future state'. Zwicker poignantly rounds his tale by turning round that 'future': 'But I suspect that on the night of May 27, 1687, ten thousand angels with glorious visions of his future state did not wait upon the poet' (*op.cit.* p. 158). The urge to retell the stories is compelling – and Zwicker's open horizons of history are complementary to the concept of an arguable world.

After the Book of Job: the hope of good argument

> . . . and come foorth, furnished with the best arguments that thou canst bring, . . . Theodore Beza, *Job Expounded*
>
> (Cambridge ?1589: commentary on 38.3)

In many versions, the Book of Job is mysterious – though its mystery is far more vivid than most plainness could ever be. The real problem for interpreters is to find questions which are worthy of being addressed to such a work, since only our questions will survive such an encounter. Suffering, tragedy, hope, justice: each becomes the beginning of a question to put to the Book of Job. Argument can also lead us to questions which are worth asking of such a text – and questions which must indeed connect with those others. What, we may ask of Job, is the nature and the meaning of the good argument? What, by comparison, are the sources of bad arguing?

Recreated by Robert Gordis's twentieth century translation[1] – the Book of Job begins to tell the great story when Satan argues with God:

> Then the Lord said to Satan,
> 'Have you noticed My servant Job?
> For there is no one on the earth like him:
>   a man blameless and upright,
>   fearing God and avoiding evil.'
> But Satan answered the Lord saying,
> 'Is it for nothing that Job has been fearing God?
> Have You not safely hedged him in,
>   and his house, and all he owns on every side?
> You have blessed the work of his hands
>   and his possessions have increased in the land.
> But put forth Your hand and touch whatever he owns
>   and he will surely curse You to Your face!' (1.8–11)

In a way, they are arguing about the compromised nature of goodness: God seeing goodness in Job, Satan seeing only the utility of goodness. To Satan, Job is making use of goodness, and may be making use of God, too, to achieve his wordly happiness and success. Job is rich and happy – he possesses many oxen, sheep and slaves, properties and children – until the argument which Satan picks with God; – but once man has become the subject of dispute, his happiness is threatened. God hands Satan power to torment Job, total power, apart from the power to hurt his body itself. Through Satan's intervention – which belies the rational humour of his voice – all the oxen, all the sheep and slaves, all the camels and other property, all the children are lost: the blessings disappear, consumed by various disasters.

The argument between God and Satan seems simple: a challenge and a test. Proof of goodness should be forthcoming. God seems to win the argument with Satan, and win it easily:

> Then Job arose and rent his robe and shaved his head, and fell upon the earth and worshipped. And he said,
> 'Naked I came from my mother's womb,
> naked shall I return.
> The Lord gave, and the Lord has taken away.
> Blessed be the name of the Lord.' (1.21)

The nineteenth-century philosopher Kierkegaard celebrated the fact that Job begins with 'the Lord gave' and only then declares that 'the Lord has taken away'.[2] In suffering, Job still sees the whole picture. He still recognises the benevolence of God, he sees it as part of an equitable situation, which includes loss. From Gordis's version, the effect is that God becomes almost complacent as the integrity of Job is reaffirmed:

> He still holds fast to his integrity
> though you incited Me against him
> to destroy him without cause. (2.3)

But Satan argues back – the proof that has been provided of Job's goodness is partial:

> But put forth Your hand
> and touch his own flesh and bones
> and he will surely curse You to Your face. (2.5)

God grants the request: Satan's case for Job's mutability remains an *arguable* case, however suspect his motives.

The story begins in heaven with an argument, and an argument not easily resolved by proof. The arguing then passes from heaven to earth, where Job's attitude hardens. Three friends visit Job, who sits suffering on his ash heap. Eliphaz, Bildad and Zophar 'come to condole with him and comfort him' (2.11). Job is famous for resisting their consolations. They defend the ways of God: their consolation for Job is that divine justice is responsible for his suffering, as it is for all human suffering – and in their view divine justice is never arbitrary: Job has brought down divine justice on himself. Job refuses to accept the justification – he insists that he is innocent, he has never done anything which deserves such punishment, and he condemns a world in which such injustices occur. Yet when the Lord does speak and he speaks from the whirlwind at the end of the book,[3] he responds strangely to this argument between Job and his would-be consolers:

> . . . the Lord said to Eliphaz the Temanite, 'My anger is kindled against you and against your two friends, for you have not spoken the truth about Me as has my servant Job. Now then, take seven bulls and seven rams, and go to My servant Job, and offer them as a burnt offering for yourselves. My servant Job must intercede for you, for only to him will I show favour and not expose you to disgrace for not speaking the truth about Me as did My servant Job.' (42.7–8)

Only Job's views about his innocence have made the exchange with his friends bearable to the Lord – only Job's good arguing has made the whole exchange a worthwhile argument to the Lord. Yet God hardly accepts Job's point of view:

> Then the Lord answered Job out of the whirlwind, saying,
> Who is this that darkens My plan
> by words without knowledge? (38.1–2)

And poor Bildad the Shuhite was so sure he understood God's way and was so determined to defend God's justice! As he thought of it:

> Does God pervert justice?
> Does the Almighty pervert the right? (8.3)

By contrast, Job has been scathing about the divine plan:

> It is all one – I say –
> the blameless and the wicked He destroys alike. (9.22)

How can God see *Job's* critical perspective as a good argument, and condemn Bildad's view which was so conciliatory towards him?[4]

* * *

God cannot simply win the argument with Satan: that is one enigma of arguing, an enigma with which the Book of Job begins its story. The end of the story creates a second enigma: why is Job the source of good arguing, and not his friends who defended divine justice? Such enigmas lure us on towards interpretation. The theme of this interpretation is the ideal of good argument and the practice of corrupt argument, a practice first represented by Satan whose motives are as carnal as his reasoning is cool. Job becomes the person who keeps alive – and is kept alive by – a hope of good arguing; the three friends become a complex representation of bad faith in argument.

Yet these friends arrive to hear Job's great lamentation.[5] He cries out:

> Why did I not die in the womb?
>   Or perish as I came forth from it? (3.11)

And it is they – or the first of them, Eliphaz – who seem to speak with human care. Their problem will be to console Job yet to defend divine justice, which they will need to justify after such an outcry against the order of things. Eliphaz starts to engage Job politely:

> If one tried a word with you, would you be offended?[6]
>   Yet who can refrain from speaking? (4.2)

Eliphaz leaves the question of judgement for later, merely remarking on what he takes to be a general truth:

> Indeed, misfortune does not come forth from the ground,
>   nor does evil sprout from the earth.
> It is man who gives birth to evil,
>   as surely as the sparks fly upward. (5.6–7)

In response, Job acknowledges that suffering may distort his perspective, though the acknowledgement is already double-edged:

> If indeed my anguish were weighed
>   and all my calamity placed in the scales,
> it would be heavier than the sand of the sea –
>   therefore I may have spoken rashly. (6.2–3)

Suffering – he concedes – perhaps distorts his view of God: but he is already complaining *against* the suffering God has permitted (caused). He begins to treat the friends as adversarial arguers rather than as the consolers they pretend to be:

> How forceful are true words!
> But what can your argument demonstrate? (6.25–6)

Even here Job hints at an ideal of true argument, though he discerns only falsity around him. His own words may be bitter, but he speaks without duplicity, without double motives, with no attempt to appear better than he is:

> Therefore I will not restrain my speech;
> I will speak out in the agony of my spirit; (7.11)

The roles take shape: though the friends defend God, they address their case with mixed motives or worse; though Job sometimes – not always – utters bitterness, he does so with a sense of what true argument would be, and with a respect for words themselves as the medium of the whole experience.

Bildad then tries his defence of divine justice, answering his own question: 'Does God pervert justice?' (8.3) with pat finality: 'Indeed, God will not spurn the blameless man,' (8.20). But the friends' way of arguing is beginning to give them away. The friends stop being so polite:

> Then Bildad the Shuhite answered, saying,
> How long will you mouth such notions
> and the words of your mouth be a mighty wind? (8.1–2)

> Zophar the Naamathite answered, saying,
> Shall a multitude of words go unanswered
> and a man full of talk appear in the right?
> Your rantings force men to silence; (11.1–3)

This dismissal shows ill-will – instead of confronting the other view, Job's view, the 'friends' exclude Job from the exchange altogether by dismissing his right to speak. For such people, only those views are allowed into play which already correspond with their ideas. We have already seen that the Lord Himself treats opposing views very differently from the way the friends do: it is because God has responded to Satan's perspective – however dubiously motivated –

that the story has evolved. If God *had* reacted to differences like Bildad and Zophar, then the world would be simpler, but the simplicity would have excluded the human story altogether. The arguable space is the human space; and, by narrowing this space, the friends are negating the rationale for their presence in the story. If arguments were not worth having, God would have silenced Satan and that would have been that! In an arguable world, we cannot dismiss other arguers so easily. Job is *not* so dismissive of the opposing view as are his friends:

> Then Job answered and said,
> I surely know that it is so,
> when you say, 'How can a man be just before God?' (9.1–2)

Job may contest the easy justification of things, but he argues in a way which suggests a deeper sense of value, the value of argument itself. For Job, the exchange is real.

There is a close connection between having ideal hopes and complaining about corrupt realities. Job feels that the universe is denying his need for a good argument:

> How then can I answer Him,
> choosing my words with Him?
> For even if I am right, I cannot respond,
> but must make supplication to my opponent.
> If I called Him, would He answer me? (9.14–16)

The ideal is patent: 'choosing my words with Him', but how could such an ideal be realised? Job only says 'even if I am right': he desires the chance to argue, for how can the universe be what it should be unless it offers a clear opportunity for him to be *sure* that he is *not* right?

Here is someone who knows that the universe is a place which needs argument – a place where simple gestures of exclusion are bound to betray weakness, though they seem like strength. The others dismiss Job altogether; even when heated, he implies ironies which are far less sweeping than dismissal against his antagonists:

> Then Job answered, saying,
> No doubt you are the people that count,
> and with you all wisdom will die!
> Yet I have a mind as well as you;
> I am not inferior to you.[7] (12.1–3)

The friends claim that they are absolutely superior to Job; he only claims to be equal to them.[a] If God allows Satan his say, we can recognise, then must people not do the same and hear each other's cases? Job claims no more than the whole structure of the text implies – whereas the friends make far larger claims to rightness and righteousness.

Job's hope still becomes more precise:

> What you know, I know too;
>   I am not inferior to you.
> But I wish to speak to the Almighty;
>   I desire to argue my case with God. (13.2–3)[8]

Job is not claiming to be right, he is claiming that the world is arguable enough for him to be given a chance to make his case. He adds that arguing on behalf of God can still be false arguing:

> Will you show partiality toward Him;
>   is it for God that you are arguing? (13.8)

Job has an intense consciousness of arguing, a consciousness born of the hope of good argument and the corresponding despair of bad arguments. Those who put their strongest hopes in arguing are most critical when argument is abused. Since he desires to argue his case with God, he is very offended by human ill-will masquerading as good argument. Why should the friends refuse Job a fair exchange with them, when Job feels entitled to an exchange even with God himself?

Job presents a vision of the good argument, both in the sense of *his* case and in the sense of a whole exchange – for the two senses are inseparable:

> Now, if I could prepare my case,
>   I know that I would be vindicated.
> But if God says, 'Who dares to argue with Me?'
>   then I must perish in silence.
> Spare me two things only
>   and I shall not need to hide from Your face:

[a]In his study of *Social Justice And The Liberal State* (New Haven: Yale University Press 1980, p. 15), Bruce Ackerman proposes a 'neutrality' rule for valid exchanges: 'Neutrality forbids me from saying that I'm any better than you are; it doesn't prevent me from saying that I'm at least as good.' This is the rule of 'Equal Respect', precisely what the friends are denying to Job, and what he is bravely demanding.

remove Your hand from me,
  and let not the dread of You terrify me;
Then You may call and I shall respond,
  or I shall speak, and You answer me. (13.18–22)

Job will produce a prepared case – his own good argument. But he can only develop that case in the context of a good argument in the larger sense, the sense which includes both sides. A good exchange cannot begin if one side refuses the right of the other side 'to argue with Me' – yet that is what the friends are doing. (We have already seen that God is prepared to bear the arguments of others.) Job sees intensely how a good argument might fail: *force and fear would suppress the good argument.*[b] When Job is beyond fear and beyond pain, then the good argument will be possible for him. The hope is real, painfully real: 'You may call and I shall respond . . . or I shall speak, and You answer me.' Job's hope of good argument is born out of his anguish, and also out of his critique of bad arguing such as his friends offer. But the hope also reflects Job's consciousness of his own value, not as an exceptional person but as one who is 'not inferior' to anyone else, except God. And even God might concede an equality in arguing, if nowhere else. For Job, the hope of good arguing is a hope of equality, equality asserted with other people and even requested from God.

The hope of good arguing contrasts with the fading of other hopes:

But as a mountain falls and crumbles
  and a rock is moved from its place,
as waters wear away stones
  and a torrent washes away the earth's soil,
  so do You destroy man's hope. (14.18–19)

[b]Habermas counterposes true argument to threat and force: 'Participants in argumentation have to presuppose in general that the structure of their communication . . . excludes all force . . . except the force of the better argument (and thus it also excludes, on their part, all motives except that of a co-operative search for truth)' (*The Theory of Communicative Action*, p. 25). Job's story suggests that motives cannot quite be reduced to disinterested aims and corrupt goals. Job is committed, intensely so – yet his arguing is still good arguing in the way he responds to other voices and seeks further hearings. Habermas (p. 41) does indeed recognise 'a therapeutic dialogue' in psychotherapy, where 'it is by no means the case that all motives except that of co-operatively seeking the truth are put out of play': but Job's context is less sympathetic, though the result may still become therapeutic!

* * *

Job lives in hope of a good argument. He is almost an embodiment of our hopes of good arguing – hopes which agony has intensified, since he is still the man who began:

> I have no ease, no peace, no rest.
> What has come is agony. (3.26)

The friends may seem righteous in the content of their arguments; but their motives are contradictory, and their tactics exclusionary. We have already had hints of another flaw, a flaw which becomes ever more damaging to these doubtful consolers. The friends also show argumentative bad faith by using *circular* arguments. They insist that Job must be guilty, because he is suffering – since the guilty suffer. Zophar perhaps begins the process by using a hypothetical mode, when he tells Job: 'if there be iniquity in your hand, put it away;' (11.14). Now Eliphaz makes a more sinister move by arguing that Job's own arguments that he is wronged are evidence of guilt.[9] If he were innocent, he would not need to argue that God is unjust:

> It is your guilt that teaches your mouth
> and makes you choose crafty speech.
> Your mouth condemns you, not I: (15.5–6)

The innocent would never argue against the justice of this world; Job must be guilty, since he is arguing against God's dispositions. But Job is only arguing in order to maintain his innocence. The circle closes when Eliphaz declares:

> He [the wicked man] will live in devastated cities
> in houses no one inhabits,
> that are destined to be heaps of ruins.
> He will not be rich; his substance will not endure,
> nor will his wealth remain long upon the earth. (15.28–9)

Job feels the circle closing. But he does not merely object to the unfair tactic – he *diagnoses* the trick by which he is being put in the wrong:

> He has shriveled me up –
> this has been the testimony against me!
> My leanness has risen up against me –
> this has been the evidence against me! (16.8)

When Job responds, we realise how limited is the arguing of his friends: his irony implies a higher standard of argument. For Job, true arguing should not move in circles, and certainly not such vicious circles.[c] But Bildad is unimpressed:

> Bildad the Shuhite answered, saying,
> How long will you go hunting for words?
> Acquire understanding and then we can speak. (18.1–2)

The friends dismiss Job's criticism of their circular arguments. We are gaining a full view of the arguments of bad faith. But Job remains in good faith. Whereas the others set Job's words aside, he takes up what they have said and uses their dismissals – by a technique of internal quotation celebrated by Robert Gordis and illuminated by his translation of the book:

> Then Job answered, saying,
> How long will you torment me
> and crush me with your words?
> It is now ten times that you have insulted me
> and have not been ashamed to abuse me.
> Even if it be true that I have erred,
> the error remains with me. (19.1–4)

Job reincorporates *their* dismissals into *his* arguing. Job is always responsive to the other side, however caustic his responses may become. His voice moves by way of half-recognitions: 'even if it be true . . .', as against dismissals or closed circlings. Whether Job's views are right or not, we can find in his arguing an idea of argument itself being a constructive process. If the friends' views are true, the more pity it is that their arguing is false to those views: and it is Job who reveals that falsity.

It is a man in agony who diagnoses the circularity of the arguments against him; it is a man in agony who responds to dismissal by including the other side's words in his own argument. All the more because he is so intensely partisan, Job's arguing includes dialogue:

[c]The classical *Rhetorica ad Herennium* rejects arguments where 'a Reason . . . appears to be presented . . . but says precisely the same as was said in the proposition . . .' (II 24) in the *Ad Herennium*, ed. and trans. H. Caplan (London: Heinemann 1964). For a contemporary view of circular arguments, see Walton *Informal Logic*, particularly (p. 22): 'The fallacy of arguing in a circle . . . occurs when the conclusion to be proved by an arguer is already presupposed by his premises.' The story of Job suggests that circularity may be more dangerous, not only a logical flaw but a technique of oppression.

When you say, 'How shall we persecute him,
since the root of the matter must be found in me?'
I answer, 'Be afraid of the sword,
for yours are crimes deserving the sword,
and you will learn that there is a judgement.' (19.28–9)

Job's voice lives in the exchange, because his voice is already an exchange of different perspectives. Job believes that he is right and the others are wrong; but he recognises that his belief exists in the context of another view, their counter-view, however false that view may seem to him. Job inhabits an arguable world – if he is mistaken, he is at least mistaken about the right *kind* of world, the world in which he lives. But even if the friends are right, they are being right about the wrong *kind* of world – a world which does not exist, an unarguable world. Theirs is a 'truth' which is false to the nature of the world. The nature of that world has been introduced to us from the first encounter between God and Satan in heaven. Arguments cannot be ended easily; to use even the truth to halt an argument is to make the truth false to the world, for in that world all truth exists in relation to its arguable opposite.

But Zophar is indifferent. He continues to close the spiteful circle:

The wealth he [the wicked man] has swallowed he must spew forth;
from his stomach God will drive it out.
He will suck the poison of asps;
the tongue of the viper will kill him.
He will never see the rivers of oil,
the streams of honey and milk. (20.15–17)

To Zophar, it is still clear that Job is suffering because he is wicked – and the more he argues, the more wicked he must be, and so the more his suffering must be justified and the greater it will be. If Job is patient, he is patient as an arguer:

If you say,
'Where is the house of the nobleman,
and where is the dwelling of the wicked?'
Why not ask the passers-by –
you cannot deny their evidence! (21.28–9)

The others have claimed that the wicked are punished in this world; conversely, the virtuous are rewarded. Job replies that 'the nobleman' may be as evil as anyone else, and that the wicked may flourish on all sides. But he still argues by way of *their* view: 'if you say . . .'. He puts their view in a question, and then he counters it with a question that becomes an exclamation. Furthermore, Job does not simply state his own views – he refers the friends to the 'evidence' of strangers. Job inhabits a world of many voices. Job argues by *including* the other side's views – whereas they attempt to exclude his voice.

* * *

The friends have tried to dismiss Job from the exchange; they have tried to close their circular arguments around him; next they resort to impugning his motives:

> Since you cannot see through darkness
> or when a flood of waters covers you,
> you thought,
> 'Indeed God is in the lofty heavens,
> and see the topmost stars, how high they are!'
> So you said,
> 'What does God know?' (22.11–13)

Eliphaz is implying that Job is dishonest. Job has claimed he is blameless and has given no cause for punishment – Eliphaz insists that Job is aware of his guilt, but has hoped to conceal his wrongdoings from God. Eliphaz comes close to insisting that Job *wants* to suffer:

> If you return to the Almighty, you will be rebuilt;
> if you remove iniquity from your tent, (22.23)

Anyone can be redeemed, and redemption saves us from suffering. Therefore, those who suffer do so voluntarily, they are refusing to be redeemed. According to Eliphaz, Job is suffering because he refuses to be redeemed. Therefore, in his suffering, he is not an object for sympathy. The crucial point is that Eliphaz is undermining Job's right to argue his case: he is not a fit person to do so, his position is not what it seems to be, he is not straightforward. This is a subtle slander on Job. The friends become a concentrated representation of argumentative bad faith – dismissiveness, logical traps, the impugning of motives, and slander. Furthermore, they are merely reciting their dogmas, rather than responding to Job's views in this particular exchange. The story is powerful not because Job resists his friends' views , but because he resists in the name of *good* arguing:

Oh that I knew where to find Him,
  that I could come to His dwelling!
I would lay my case before Him,
  and my mouth would not lack for arguments. (23.3–4)

The more corrupt the friends become in their *way* of arguing, the more intensely Job longs for a different kind of exchange, an exchange where the audience would recognise his many arguments. Again, the good arguing which Job desires is both the whole process of a proper argument and the presentation of his own case – the two are inseparable in his mind. As the present scene darkens, Job's vision of good arguing brightens. In such an argument:

I would learn what He would answer me
  and understand what He would say to me.
Would He contend with me merely through His great power?
  No, He would surely pay heed to me,
  for it would be an upright man arguing with Him, (23.5–7)

Job longs to put his own case, but he longs as strongly to hear the case against him being put properly. Nothing could be more moving than such good faith in the process of argument itself . . . . Job adds that God would surely treat him as an equal participant as far as the exchange was concerned. God will allow the arguing process to make man his equal, for the time in which argument is necessary. Job then glimpses an exchange where the other would *not* impugn his motives, 'for it would be an upright man arguing . . .'. Job can imagine putting his own case, but his imagination is far more generous than just to desire to speak eloquently on his own behalf. Around the image of his own case, Job imagines a whole relationship, an ideal relationship in arguing. The more corrupt are our present exchanges, the more vividly we may glimpse the dimensions of the ideal exchange. Only at the end of his imagined scene does Job supply the verdict: 'and I would be acquitted by my Judge for all time'[d] (23.7). Job believes God would find him innocent – and this trust is a trust in the ideal argument, as well as in his own blameless life. When Job imagines his

[d]Job's situation parallels Aristotle's definition of a human situation: '. . . all, up to a certain point, endeavour to criticize or uphold an argument, to defend themselves or to accuse'. (*Rhetoric* Ii) The striking analogy is with the twofold activity of criticism and defence (or affirmation and justification).

own self-justification, he imagines a mode of discourse, a relationship and a process.

We approach closer to the enigma of good arguing. What is this hope in arguing which brightens whereas all other hopes darken? What is this ideal which thrives out of a critique of corrupt reality? No simple answer is available, but the importance of the ideal is manifest: even heaven itself refuses to contravene true arguing. Ironically, it is because God accepts argument that Job suffers in the first place. The enigma intensifies. If God were against argument or argued unfairly, he would have stopped Satan in his tracks: then Job would have been safe and happy. So argument has undone Job: and yet it is argument he seeks. God *is* a fair arguer in the Book of Job, which is why Job must suffer. Yet Job must put his own hope in good arguing, for all other hopes have faded. The hope of good arguing is a difficult hope, and a hope beset with ironies in an endlessly arguable world.

The world of the Book of Job is an arguable world. Wherever one voice speaks, another voice can reply from a different perspective. The perspectives differ in value, even in truth, but the world permits the contradictions to evolve towards some other goal, an unknown goal. The world becomes more problematic as the book explores more arguments. Job insists that in our world there is no moral basis for good and bad fortune:

> The oppressed go about naked, without clothes,
> and are hungry as they carry the sheaves.
> Mid the sinner's olive trees they press out oil,
> and suffer thirst as they tread the wine vats. (34.10–11)

Experience does not bear out the idea that the universe is just, evenly and continuously just. There is a case to answer against the universe, against its rightness and fairness and justice, a case based on human experience. The book refuses to set arguing above experience – the arguments from experience must be heard. Logic is not enough to ensure a good argument. In other words, the good argument will need to be accessible to human experience, and that means it will reflect the *contradictions* in the human perspective. If there is an end to arguing, the answers found in the end will not be simple.

But Bildad can only repeat formulae – he cannot respond to the living process. His voice is tightly clenched around the same weapons as ever:

How then can man be just before God
  and how can one born of a woman be clean? (25.4)

Job's reply seems to encompass his conduct *in* the exchange as much as his life beforehand: 'My righteousness I have held fast,' (27.6). Now Zophar is left to spin his circle around some generalised sinner:

He goes to bed rich, but never more –
  When he opens his eyes, his wealth is gone. (27.19)

And so there must be a change: the cycles of this argument are done, the roles played.

Job's voice gives way briefly to a kind of philosophical song or Hymn to Wisdom:

But Wisdom, where may she be found,
  and where is the place of Understanding? (28.12)[10]

When the book gives us a Hymn to Wisdom, the refrain is a question. Questions are central to the arguable world. Wisdom lies in a question, and not an answer. Therefore, when Job comes to 'sum up' his defence, his summary takes the form of questions:

Have I ever concealed my transgressions like Adam,
  hiding my sin in my bosom
because I stood in fear of the crowd
  and the contempt of the masses terrified me –
  so that I kept silence and did not go out of doors? (31.33–4)

It is the question which unloosens the good argument. Questions must be respected. Satan asked: 'Is it for nothing that Job has been fearing God?' God did not deny Satan an answer. In the arguable world, even God accepts that questions are necessary. Indeed the arguable world begins *when* God accepts a necessary question. Job is sure that he has 'concealed' nothing, yet he puts his certainty into an interrogative form which allows for the possibility that he has concealed something. In other words, Job is certain insofar as *he* would answer the question in his way; but the question-form implies that others might answer in *their* way. What courage to see one's own self-justification can be questioned, however certain one may be of the answer . . . . Job's has the courage needed to live in an arguable world.

* * *

When the friends fall silent, finally silent, two other voices answer Job. First there is a human voice – an angry and committed voice:

It is the spirit of God that has made me,
  and the breath of the Almighty that gives me life.
If you can, answer me;
  prepare for the contest, take your stand.
Behold, I am equal with you in God's presence;
  I, too, have been moulded from clay.
Surely, no dread of *me* will terrify you;
  my pressure will not be heavy upon you. (33.4–7)

Elihu has appeared, a younger man who has listened to the whole encounter. Elihu does not dismiss Job from the exchange. On the contrary, he claims for himself a status *equal* with Job, and no more. In other words, Elihu offers Job his good argument here upon earth, here and now.[11] There is no need to wait for God before embarking upon the good argument which is Job's human hope. Job has insisted that in the good argument God would neither frighten nor oppress him: Elihu insists that he will be fair and offer Job the freedom to argue. Indeed, Elihu echoes Job's own claim, 'I am not inferior to you.' Is Job using the hope of arguing with God to avoid a good exchange upon earth?

Elihu is as full of dialogue as Job has been:

Behold, in this you are wrong – I shall answer you
  when you declare, 'God is stronger than man.' (33.12)

Elihu is a good arguer in Job's own sense of good arguing. Elihu is opposed to Job, but his is a voice in better faith than Job has heard previously, and it is Job's patience and persistence which have gained him a fairer opportunity to argue. Patience and persistence are important requirements for the good argument, and so is courage. Indeed Elihu has acknowledged that he is intervening because Job has been so impressive by comparison with his friends:

I paid attention to you,
and lo, there was no one to refute Job –
  no one among you to answer his words.

Beware lest you say, 'We have attained wisdom,
but only God can rebut him, not man!' (32.12–13)

Elihu accuses the friends of claiming 'wisdom' as a way of avoiding argument, rather than as a means to good arguing. Elihu is criticising the notion of *unarguing* wisdom. His own wisdom is the very reverse of unarguing – it is an intervention in a particular argument at a particular point. Elihu shares Job's spirit of responsiveness in argument. The hope of good arguing is in recreating the exchange from within.

Elihu returns the argument to the idea that God must be just. But he defends divine justice in a new way:

In truth, God will not act wickedly;
the Almighty will not pervert justice.
Who entrusted the earth to Him,
and gave Him charge over the whole world?
If He should withdraw His spirit
and gather His breath to Himself,
all living things would perish
and man would return to the dust. (34.12–15)

God is just in the sense that he sustains all life, a justice which surpasses human capacities. His is not the justice of a human law court, but the justice of creation itself. Elihu uses questions and hypotheses; he challenges and he speculates.

Elihu is as rich in arguments as Job has been, a richness which is another characteristic of good arguing in this story. The friends tended to repeat one point which showed that Job had done wrong because he is being punished. Elihu finds many different points. He makes arguing creative, rather than circular. For instance, Elihu takes up the link between suffering and sin, the link which was central to the friends' conception of Job's punishment; but for Elihu suffering is a warning against sin, rather than a punishment for past misdeeds: 'Now beware, lest you be seduced by your wealth' (36.18). Further, Elihu adds a different kind of argument, an argument from creativity:

He draws up the drops of water,
and rain is distilled from His mist,
which the clouds pour down
and shower upon all men. (36.27–8)

A good arguer expands the exchange: his argument from creativity is larger than any other argument so far advanced for God in the Book. Creation is all-inclusive: God's deeds fall 'upon all men'. According to Elihu, Job is wrong because he takes it for granted that so many different individuals *exist*, and then asks whether God treats them justly: without God's justice in creating all no one would exist in the first place. Creativity is just in the sense of being inclusive. Creativity is just in the sense that it has *given* everyone the right to exist. We are now confronting the power of good arguing. The idea of 'good argument' must include both the exchange and the individual case, for without the exchange there would *be no* new case. Elihu's view is a good argument – better than the friends' attempts at argument and probably equal to Job's own vision, because of its equivalent effect on the scope of the whole exchange.

Elihu continues to address Job, and his address is responsive to Job's own vistas of negation:

> Hear this, O Job,
> Stop and observe the wonders of God. (37.14)

Only when Elihu has created his good argument, does the Book give us the Lord speaking 'out of the whirlwind':

> Then the Lord answered Job out of the whirlwind, saying,
> Who is this that darkens My plan
> by words without knowledge? (38.1–2)

It is as if God cannot speak until the human exchange has advanced towards good arguing, from bad faith towards good arguing. Elihu's good argument – the argument from creativity – almost seems to summon up the speech of the Lord out of the whirlwind. Yet surely such authority as issues from this speech will be final? The answer is 'yes and no':

> Gird up your loins like a man;
> I will question you, and you may inform Me. (38.3)

Martin Buber has argued that the Book of Job explores different conceptions of God – from the just God to the God of creativity.[12] The arguments certainly seem to follow such a sequence of conceptions. At the same time, as Buber also suggests, we consistently return to the God of dialogue, the God of the arguable world. Such a God must allow Satan his case; and such a God will respond to Job by asking questions, and challenging the man to reply. The Lord of the whirlwind almost echoes Job's hope of good arguing;

> Then You may call and I shall respond,
> Or I shall speak and You answer me. (13.22)

When Job justified himself, he uttered his certainty of being right as a question: 'have I ever concealed my transgressions . . .?' The Lord too can entrust *His* certainty to questions:

> Have you entered the storehouses of snow,
> have you seen the storehouses of the hail,
> which I have reserved for the time of trouble,
> for the day of battle and war?
> In what way are the air currents scattered
> and is the east wind spread upon the earth? (38.22–4)

From the whirlwind we hear again the argument from creativity: can Job – or any man – measure the extent of the creativity which sustains the universe?[13] If not, how can Job judge particular events within the creative scheme and say that they are good or bad, just or unjust? The voice redoubles the questioning:

> Do you know the time when the mountain goats give birth,
> and do you watch the travail of the hinds?
> Can you number the months they fulfil,
> and do you know the time that they give birth,
> when they crouch, bring forth their offspring,
> and are delivered of their young? (39.1–3)

God does not defend his judgements of the guilty and innocent, not directly; instead, He argues more expansively or generously from creation as a whole. How can you judge the particular moves in a process unless you understand the scope of the whole movement?

The speech from the whirlwind responds to Job's hope of good arguing, to Job's case against the universe, to the friends' conception of justice, and to Elihu's larger arguments from the nature of creation. Yet an enigma remains: we cannot say *exactly* how the human exchange relates to the arguments from creation. The enigma raises the effect of generosity. How can an exchange that began in personal 'anguish' end with the argument of universal creativity? How can an exchange which endured so much ill-will end by creating rich perspectives which were nowhere to be seen at the beginning? *Why* is God a God of dialogue, a God of good arguing? We have no answers to these questions, and that lack of answers is part of what sustains the last defence of the universe.

The effectiveness of the book remains one of good argument:

(The Lord answered Job, saying,)
Can he who argues with the Almighty instruct Him?
Can he who reproves God answer all this? (40.1–2)

We recall Job fearing that God would say to him, 'Who dares to argue with me?' But the God of good arguing puts a question about argument, a question which is far more open to response than the mere threat which Job feared in his darkest moment. Nevertheless, the question is conclusive, as the ironic structure of the sequel makes clear:

Job answered the Lord, saying,
Behold, I am of small account; how can I answer You? (40.4)

The answer is that there is no answer. Nonetheless, the speaker of the whirlwind continues to ask:

Gird up your loins like a man;
I will ask you, and do you inform Me. (40.7)

A whole world is implicit in the new questions, the endless possibilities of both experience and inquiry:

Can you seize Leviathan with a net
or press down his tongue with a cord? (40.25)[14]

Job responds by replaying the previous dialogue, a method which he used earlier to deal with the friends and which now celebrates the response – however overwhelming – of the whirlwind:

You have said,
'Who is it this that hides My plan without knowledge?'
Indeed, I have spoken without understanding,
of things too wonderful for me which I did not grasp.
You have said,
'Hear, and I will speak;
I will ask you, and do you inform me.' (42.3–4)

The last words to echo in Job's responsive dialogue are: 'I will ask you, and do you inform me.' It is the invitation to exchange which finally holds sway, at least in the response of Job. Job asked for the ideal exchange, and he asked in good faith: therefore, when he receives the response, he is responsive in turn – even if the outcome is not what he expected.

Yet, mysteriously, the verdict seems to be as Job hoped: ' "My servant Job must intercede for you, for only to him will I show favor . . . ." ' (42.8). Job hoped that the good argument with God would lead to the right verdict, in his view a verdict supporting his innocence:

> Now, if I could prepare my case,
> I know that I would be vindicated. (13.18)

Job does appear to be vindicated, but not in the way which he expected. He seems to concede that God has the better arguments, but God in turn concedes that Job has had better arguments than the friends, to one of whom – Eliphaz – he says: ' "My anger is kindled against you and against your two friends, for you have not spoken the truth about Me as has my servant Job" ' (42.7). Job has not out-argued God, but he *has* out-argued the friends. God's truth gives rise to a better argument than Job's truth, but Job's truth gives rise to a better argument than the friends can manage. The arguable world has a mysterious structure, a structure which allows a perspective to be the truth of one exchange, and to be out-argued by another truth in a different exchange. The absolutes of truth and falsehood co-exist *with the relativities of good argument*. Arguments – both exchanges and cases – must be seen in their contexts, though all contexts are not equal.

The God of dialogue blesses Job:

> So the Lord blessed the end of Job's life more than his beginning. He had fourteen thousand sheep, six thousand camels, a thousand yoke of oxen, and a thousand she asses. He also had fourteen sons and three daughters. (42.12–13)

Job's patient arguing ends in renewal, and the renewal is greater than the original condition. It is almost as if the arguing process had been therapeutic. God lets the argument unfold, both the argument with Satan and the arguments on earth. Suffering is bound up with these unfolding processes of exchange. Yet out of exchange, there comes renewal, generous renewal:

> After this, Job lived a hundred and forty years and saw his sons, and his sons sons', four generations. So Job died, an old man, satisfied with life. (42.16–17)

Arguing is connected with suffering; arguing is a source of hope; arguing is therapeutic. The enigma can only be explored, never resolved.

* * *

There is great potential for the story of Job and good argument in the version by Robert Gordis, because this version brings out different voices and their ways of addressing each other. In the King James bible of 1611, the Authorised Version of English tradition, the same voices are recognisable but the sound is subtly different. When Gordis makes Eliphaz a man who is darkly polite ('. . . would you be offended?'), the King James text has a voice which anticipates the issue of suffering: 'If we assay to commune with thee, wilt thou be grieved?'(4.2). Gordis makes Zophar dismiss Job for talking nonsense ('Your rantings force men to silence'); King James' Zophar is eager to contradict Job: 'Should thy lies make men hold their peace?' (11.3). The comparisons do not reveal a systematic difference between the modern Jewish responses and the seventeenth century Christian work – the differences are themselves various. But we can trace afresh just how subtle a thing is bad faith in arguing. Job's voice can also sound different. Gordis shows Job hoping to be granted a debate with God: 'I desire to argue my case with God' (13.2). The King James text suggests that Job is aspiring even to change the judge's mind: 'I desire to reason with God.' Job is hoping for good argument – but good argument means slightly different things – the freedom to put a view, or the success in persuading an audience.

Elsewhere, the King James text attributes words to a different voice from the modern version. It would be inappropriate to arbitrate. But the distinctions are enriching. In Gordis' moving lines, Job envisages the dark possibility that the deity may not allow equal arguing: 'But if God says, "Who dares to argue with me?" ' (13.9). The King James text gives the whole assertion to Job, who thereby proclaims that he is confident and sincere in seeking justification by argument: 'Who is it that will plead with me?' Another pertinent variation affects that great image of Job having been 'shrivelled' by suffering. In Gordis, Job is ironically recycling the logic of the other side, to establish that their case is circular and in bad faith:

> He has shrivelled me up –
> this has been the testimony against me (16.8)

But in the other text, Job is addressing God and lamenting his fate: 'And thou has filled me with wrinkles, which is a witness against me'. Here Job turns aside from the debate with the friends, appealing instead towards the ear – and the voice – of God. Good argument is an idea which includes fine shadings as well as intense feelings.

No story of Job excludes other stories. One story from this endless source has a transforming impact on the idea of good argument, on the question – what is a good argument? And on the inseparable counterpart, what are bad or corrupt arguments? What makes the essential difference between the good argument and bad arguing? We can be the questions' rich inheritors, though not the recipients of answers.

The argumentative imagination

The Book of Job is a work of the argumentative imagination; so desperate are its arguments, and so vividly are they transcribed by the imagination, that the work throws light on the whole nature of the argumentative imagination and its place in literature. In such a work, as in *The Excursion*, and the parable of *The Hind and the Panther*, human predicaments are explored through the way in which people argue the case for their beliefs. Their predicaments – the situation in which they find themselves – are visionary; the characters are transformed by vision – but the matter of the arguments is human experience. And in those situations, as in other great imaginative literature, qualities of character are thrown into sharp focus. Job conducts a fraught argument against terrifying odds, amidst the entanglements thrown by by his 'friends' in ill faith: his demeanour under duress adds a painful tension to the story, and demands a *heroic* character. The stress on character, as a requirement for good argument, was known also to Plato, and embodied in his conception of Socrates – and in the traditions of Socrates. In Mill's version of *The Gorgias*, Socrates meets up with a devious character called Callicles who does not contradict himself because he does not acknowledge logic and truth; he is intent upon maintaining his own position at all costs, and has no interest in the better argument. Socrates accepts his intervention as he would:

> . . . one of those touchstones with which they try the purity of gold, that I might try my soul by it, and if it stood the test, I might know that I am as I should be, and need no further test . . .[15]

Endurance and consistency: this is how Martin Buber values those qualities in Socrates and his determination to maintain dialogue to the end:

> But how lovely and how fitting the sound of the lively and impressive *I* of Socrates! It is the *I* of endless dialogue, and the air of dialogue is wafted around it in all its journeys, before the judges and in the last hour in prison. This *I* lived continually in the relation with man which is bodied forth in dialogue. It never ceased to believe in the reality of men, and went out to meet them. So it took its stand with them in reality, and reality forsakes it no more. Its very loneliness can never be forsaken . . . very loneliness can never be forsakenness . . .[16]

Along with the question of character, the imaginative dialogue raises the question of *identity*. Job's identity is threatened by loss, by the change in his fortunes, and particularly by the change in his status as a favourite of God. Here the work of Johnson in rhetoric raises a profound question:

> If identities are lost through acts of negation, they are also acquired thereby, and the restoration of what has been denied cannot be accomplished through simple affirmation. (*A World of Difference*, p. 4)

Job has been excluded from the situation which affirmed his own identity, he has been almost effaced as the character he was considered to be – *but* his argument persists, and is carried on through the voice of that excluded person. For it is the effaced voice, or almost effaced voice, which preserves most animatedly the whole criterion of good argument. In that parable, argument belongs to the outsiders, it is their inalienable right – as it is in life – to renegotiate their way back into society's affairs through argument.

Imagination highlights another aspect of argument: its intrinsic narrative connections; for it is evident in the Book of Job, as it is in the other texts examined, that arguments are not abstract entities merely – they are embroiled with human affairs and identities, with desire, need and hope and the obstacles to them. Argument has a beginning in human motivations and runs its course, driven by hope of success, through impediments and frustrations, to a conclusion, or some point which appears to be a conclusion, which may not at all be what was hoped for, or predicted, and may not even lie along the course which the argument set out to take, a course which, in the case of literature, is charted by the text. This is the narrative course, and it is intrinsic to the argument as it develops in literature – intrinsic to the four texts examined here, as argument extends through them and is inseparable from them.

Insofar as the work is literature, The Book of Job dealt with here is also a translation. Some aspects of translation are considered in the next chapter, on the *Bhagavad Gita*, but here the translation of Job is considered as a literary entity in its own right, which has passed through the argumentative imagination, and tells us something about the argumentative imagination, and about literature. No limiting significance is given therefore to the fact that the text under consideration is a translation, and the fidelity of the translation to the original is not called into question. However the visionary claims of the translator, Robert Gordis, are considerable, and his has been throughout an interpretive vision through which has reappeared the argumentative imagination of the Book of Job.

The Book of Job: further commentary and references

1 Robert Gordis, *The Book of God and Man: A Study of Job* (Chicago: University of Chicago Press 1965). In his review of 'Current Trends in the Study of the Book of Job' in W. E. Aufrecht (ed.) *Studies in the Book of Job* (Wilfred Laurier University Press 1985, pp. 1–27, p. 5), Ronald J. Williams emphasizes how 'well received' Gordis' version and view has been, not that it has settled anything of course! David Daiches in an essay on 'The Book of Job' collected with his volume *More Literary* Essays (Edinburgh: Oliver and Boyd 1968, pp. 268–74) acknowledges Gordis's translation as 'impressive and illuminating' (p. 274), which indeed it is . . . .

2 Collected in Nahum Glatzer, *The Dimensions of Job*: 'A Study and Selected Readings' (New York: Schocken Books 1969, pp. 253–68, p. 254).

3 The text itself is contested in several places. Williams (*op.cit.* p. 12) gives the 'scholarly consensus' as: (1) Prose Prologue, ch.l–2; (2) Dialogue, ch.3–27; (3) Wisdom Hymn, ch.28; (4) Job's monologue, ch.29–31; (5) Elihu speeches, ch.32–7; (6) Yahweh speeches with Job's responses, ch.38.1–42.6; (7) Prose Epilogue, ch.42.7–17. Some interpreters see the Elihu or the whirlwind passages as later additions, most see the dialogue as incomplete or disarranged. As Williams recognises, it is nonetheless appropriate for literary criticism to deal with the text as given.

4 David Clines formulates the problem differently, by 'Deconstructing the Book of Job' in M. Warner (ed.) *The Bible As Rhetoric* (London: Routledge 1990, pp. 65–80). Clines contends that the work is a 'confrontation of philosophies' between a theory of retribution and a denial of such logic. His point is that the denial by Job seems stronger than the friends' defence; yet the very end of the story seems to restore a logic of reward and punishment. Clines sees the contradiction as untying the work – whereas the present approach is to tell the story in a way which makes possible sense of the tension. Glatzer (*op.cit.* p. 287) argues – over-sweepingly – that traditions of interpretation have tried to avoid confronting the true power of Job's case against the way the world appears in the central exchanges with the friends. But he delivers a philosophical solution: 'The aim of the Book of Job was to refute certain notions of retribution . . .'.

5 Perhaps another reason why the Book has so demanded interpretation is that the first view of Job the patient is hard to apply consistently to the whole story. Though Job still recognises his God and turns to the deity in appeal, the agonies he experiences also create other voices for Job, voices which question the order of the world, and even seem to reject that world. The arguing Job of the present chapter is an alternative to other rich traditions of the complaining Job. For a reading which treats the complaining and especially the sarcastic Job with a different emphasis, see Edwin Good 'Job: The Irony of Reconciliation' (Chapter 7 of his book on *Irony in the Old Testament*, Sheffield: Almond Press 1981, pp. 196–240). Much depends upon the selection of passages – as in all interpretation: other approaches have found great riches in the lamentations themselves, as isolated utterances. W. A. Irwin contends amidst a complex study of verse form ('Poetic Structure in the Dialogue of Job', in the *Journal of Near Eastern Studies* 5 (1946) pp. 26–39, p. 33) that through the whole process which starts in lamentation and continues as debate, 'Job experienced the cathartic effect of self-expression'. Gordis's *commentary* gives us his sense of Job as moral visionary who (*op.cit.* p. 86) 'proceeds to discover a new faith – forged in the crucible of his undeserved suffering'.

6 Dr A. Benisch's mid-Victorian *Jewish School and Family Bible* (London 1851–61) has a distinctive touch along similar lines: 'If we attempt a word with thee, wilt thou find it tiresome?' This moment bears out James Barr's general view of the dynamic of the Book of Job ('The Book of Job and its Modern Interpreters', in *The Bulletin of The John Rylands Library* 54 (1971–2) pp. 28–46, p. 41): 'If a story is to be good, it has to move in some way, and much of the movement in the book of Job seems to come from the entry of new persons and the passage from one speech to another.'

7 An even stronger formulation is found by the text of the 'Thomas Matthew' Bible of 1549 (a text in fact based on Tyndale, see F. F. Bruce, *History of the Bible in English* 3rd ed., Guildford: Lutterworth Press 1979): 'But I have understanding as well as ye, I am no lesse than ye,' declares Job there. It is the negative assertion of equal right which is so moving and so demands recognition, which it does not (yet) receive from the other side.

8 In his powerful *Job Expounded* (Cambridge ? 1589), the scholar and biographer of Calvin, Theodore Beza (de Bèze) elaborates on Job's behalf: 'Put the case therefore, that I am to deale not with these men, but with thee, and that this whole matter is to be debated between us.' The longing for proper exchange is palpable in these lines of a text, whose dedication to Queen Elizabeth notes 'From Geneva, besieged by the Duke of Saxony'. Gordis's commentary emphasises the stress in his version on 'a free and fair confrontation' (*op.cit.* p. 284).

9 In his eloquent essay, 'A Dissertation on the Design and Argumentation of the Book of Job', the eighteenth-century clergyman William Worthington remarks pointedly on: 'The Conduct of Job's Friends; which is so strange and unaccountable that it is very difficult to reconcile it with that Character in the View it commonly appears in. Their seeming uncharitableness and Inhumanity, their Acrimony, virulence, unjust Censure, and pertinacious obstinacy, . . . looks as if they came with a Design to mock and insult, and not as they professed, to mourn with, and comfort him' (William Worthington, *An Essay on the Scheme and Conduct . . . of Man's Redemption . . . To which is annexed A Dissertation . . .*, London 1743, p. 477). The intensity of this moment also supports the tragic interpretation espoused by, among others, Richard B. Sewell: 'This method of the Poet's – sustained tension throughout the thrust-and-parry of ideas, the balancing of points of view in the challenge-and-response of argument – is the inner logic or dialectic, of the tragic form as it appears in fully developed drama' ('The Book of Job' collected in Paul S. Sanders (ed.) *Twentieth Century Interpretations of the Book of Job*, Englewood Cliffs, N. J.: Prentice Hall 1968, pp. 21–35, p. 25).

10 Williams (*op.cit.* p. 12) records the consensus that this Hymn is an interruption of Job's speeches, separating his final reply in the debates from a last monologue before the situation is transformed by other voices. The Book of Job is sometimes classified as 'Wisdom literature', and linked with Babylonian as well as Jewish traditions in this respect. The point is contested. Gordis resists the connection with other traditions; Williams points to 'the near Eastern matrix from which the Book of Job emerges' (p. 6). In any case, Northrop Frye in his account of the Book of Job (*The Great Code*: 'The Bible and Literature', London: Ark Paperbacks 1983, p. 197) suggests that wisdom literature cannot contain the whole of Job, in any tradition.

11 Theodore Beza (*op.cit.*) produces a compelling extension, making Elihu into a model rhetorician, willing always to encounter the opposing voice: 'but if there be anie thing, whereat thou wilt take exception, it shall be free for thee, without all feare and regarde, to turn the same backe againe upon mee, whatsoever it bee, or in what manner or order thou thinkest best.' Such a response almost seems to anticipate John Stuart Mill's *On Liberty* in the intensity of its respect for the controversial testing of ideas between free participants! Another commentary, *The Book of Job Paraphrased* by Simon Patrick, Lord Bishop of Ely (London 1697, p. 150) makes Elihu more combative but also has his voice echoing Job's affirming of his equal right to an argument with the friends: 'Look upon me, the Combate is not unequal'. Gordis sees Elihu as introducing a new philosophy of nature into the dispute, a philosophy pointing towards the voice from the whirlwind (*op.cit.* p. 286). But H. H. Rowley in 'The Book of Job and its meaning' (*The Bulletin of the John Rylands Library* 41 (1958–9) pp. 167–207, p. 173) questions the integrity of the text at this point: 'Elihu appears, and speaks, and vanishes.

No notice is taken of him by Job or by God, . . .'. Like other views, the present response derives from the structure as given, but perspectives such as Rowley offers here are important because they remind us of the limits of all coherence-making when the text is so richly problematic.

12 Martin Buber on the Book of Job is collected in Glatzer (*op.cit.* pp. 56–65). Buber distinguishes four concepts of the deity, of which the last is 'the voice of Him who answers' (p. 63).

13 Fr R. A. F. Mackenzie in his essay on 'The Purpose of the Yahweh Speeches in the Book of Job' (*Biblica* 40 (1959) pp. 435–45) gives a witty interpretation of the questions that takes us in another direction. Mackenzie recognises that the questions offered to Job 'do not seem to answer the questions that have been raised' previously (p. 436). He argues (p. 441) that God is 'pretending to believe that such criticism and challenge as Job has uttered can come only from a rival God.' Hence the tone is ironic. The important link with the present story is the need to take the question form seriously. Another account which does so is that by Frye (*op.cit.* p. 196), who argues that the major achievement is to avoid suggesting 'a God who was glibly ready to explain it all'. Bishop Simon Patrick (*op.cit.* p. 189) conjures a fine moment out of the space between the two speeches from the God in the whirlwind: 'After a short silence, to see what Job would reply to this long Discourse, the Lord proceeded . . .'.

14 The interpretations of these speeches are particularly rich and diverse. Williams (*op.cit.* p. 26) defines the problem:

> whether a later addition or an integral part of the original poem, the Yahweh Speeches have usually been thought to have as their aim the evocation of the omnipotence and transcendence of the Deity. In the opinion of some scholars their effect would then be merely to browbeat the sufferer into abject submission. The tendency of recent criticism is to understand the significance of the divine confrontation with Job on a much deeper level.

Dale Patrick and Allen Scult, in their *Rhetoric and Biblical Interpretation* (Sheffield: Almond Press 1990, pp. 81–102) put this issue of interpretation in ethical terms: 'A God who overwhelmed Job by his deity, rather than convincing him of his worthiness, would not elicit our respect' (p. 102). They also give a challenging outline of the interpretive ideal: 'For Job to be the best work it can be, YHWH's addresses should affirm his right to protest and find fault with his rule of the world, yet convince Job that YHWH is worthy of praise for his just and merciful deeds' (p. 96).

15 John Stuart Mill, *Four Dialogues of Plato: Translated and with Notes by John Stuart Mill*, edited by Ruth Borchardt (London: Watts and Co. 1946), 'The Gorgias' pp. 107–1, p. 138. The version first appeared in the *Monthly Repository*, 1834–5.

16 Martin Buber, *I and Thou*, trans. by Ronald Gregor Smith (Edinburgh: T. and T. Clark Ltd 1958, 2nd ed.), p. 89.

After the *Bhagavad Gita*: good argument as creative mystery

> not an aphoristic work, but a great religious poem . . . .
> Gandhi on the *Gita*, from the collection of his writings, *Gita The Mother* (Lahore 1946–7)

Therapeutic arguments

> I who once composed with eager zest
> Am driven by grief to shelter in sad songs; [1]

Boethius, the imprisoned poet, is in despair. Dame Philosophy seeks to remove this terrible oppression of mind. What follows between them is an argument in which his point of view is pitted against her attempts to cure him of his despair. True, philosophy has the lion's share. Furthermore, much of the time the poet expresses agreement. But the whole work is structured by his initial outlook, which initiates the dialogue with strong arguments:

> Grief has not so dulled my wits in all this as to make me complain that the wicked have piled up their crimes against virtue; but what does fill me with wonder is that they have brought their hopes to fruition. (Book II, p. 44)

What is there to be said about grief, and the causes of grief, which can ameliorate its devastating effect? Dame Philosophy proceeds like this:

> What I want to say is a paradox and so I am hardly able to put it into words. For bad fortune, I think, is more use to a man than good fortune. Good fortune always seems to bring happiness, but deceives you with her tricks, whereas bad fortune is always truthful because by changing she shows her true fickleness. (Book II, p. 76)

Like some modern psychoanalysts, in her attempts to cope with unhappiness, she introduces views that give a new vision of life. Her ultimate argument is that the poet has failed to understand his world:

> It is because you men are in no position to contemplate this order that everything seems confused and upset. But it is no less true that everything has its own position which directs it towards the good and so governs it. (Book IV, p. 137)

The therapeutic process moves, by critical argument, towards new understanding.

Translations such as those of Boethius and Job make connections: they transfer, through those connections, something from one place, and one time, to another place and time. They may retain, in this transfer, some connection with their original context, its ambience, some of its logic and motivations, even perhaps its physical reality and values – and some of its original meaning may come with it. The meanings which it had to the writer, or early audience, are altered by losing some of the circumstances that impacted on the writer, some of the social and psychological conditions of the time, which are beyond historical recall. The act of translation is also enhancing: creative and re-creative. Different translations give different impressions of the text on which they are based through a selection of new words incorporating new meanings. And, further than that, where translation from the past is concerned, as with the *Gita*, the translation connects previous experience with a contemporary situation in which the original will be *read* differently.

Meanings will adhere to the reading, which are drawn *out of* the context into which the translation *has arrived*. That is the case with Boethius, and with the *Gita*, too: for in our time the therapeutic argument has become a technical strand in literary theory, and therapeutic argument is a deeply rooted practice in psychoanalysis and psychotherapy, some aspects of which are considered further in the conclusion to this chapter. Gandhi had this to say of the *Gita* in 1927:

> It [the *Bhagavad Gita*] has afforded me invaluable help in my moments of gloom. I have read almost all the English translations of it, . . .[2]

Gandhi himself found other sources which impacted on the meaning of the *Gita* for him, and helped him to see its meaning in a broader way:

> But the New Testament produced a different impression, especially the Sermon on the Mount which went straight to my heart. I compared it with the *Gita*. (p. 77)

Further connections that affected Gandhi's conception of the Gita shaped his whole outlook in which political and religious elements were fused:

> My young mind tried to unify the teachings of the *Gita*, *The Light of Asia* and the Sermon on the Mount. That renunciation was the highest form of religion appealed to me greatly.
>
> This reading whetted my appetite for studying the lives of other religious teachers. A friend recommended Carlyle's *Heroes and Hero-Worship*. I read the chapter on the hero as a prophet and learnt of the Prophet's greatness and bravery and austere living. (p. 78)

This Gandhian sense of interconnectedness between great human themes is itself incorporated into Mascaro's translation and his whole response to the *Gita*.

After the *Bhagavad Gita*: a story of interconnections

The *Bhagavad Gita* is 'the song of the adorable lord' or of the 'blessed lord'. The original work was composed in Sanskrit, possibly between 400BC and 200AD. The text consists of complex stanzaic verse, through which proceeds a sustained dialogue between two speakers, with occasional narrative comments particularly at the beginning and the ending. One voice belongs to Arjuna, one of the heroes of the Hindu epic called *The Mahabharata*. The other voice, which has much the larger part, is the voice of Krishna, a complex and difficult figure with many different meanings. In the context of the episode presented by the *Gita*, Krishna is Arjuna's charioteer, but he is also a supreme authority and later emerges as 'a manifestation of the Supreme Deity'. The exchange springs from a particular situation, and then through Krishna's responses to problems posed by Arjuna – posed to and not against authority – there unfolds a view of how to live rightly and a vision of the universe. The essay which follows treats English versions in the spirit proposed by Gandhi in the comment at the chapter opening.[3]

There have been many attempts to realise versions of the *Gita* in English, beginning with Sir Charles Wilkins in 1785. These responses across language and context are fascinating and diverse as texts in themselves, and as variations on certain shared material. The main purpose of this essay is to tell a rich and revealing story of good argument which one of these texts can make possible – not to assess the relation between translation and original. Indeed the *Gita* is part of a transformative influence which has in any case altered the language with which the translations are realised. Successive translations of the *Gita* participate in the diffusion of some important terms and concepts, such as 'yoga', 'karma-yoga', and the theory of reincarnation along judgemental lines. These concepts have several different lives – within the history of Hinduism[4] and again as more general influences. From Wilkins onwards, translators have made difficult compromises as to how far to seek paraphrases in English for such terms, and how far to introduce some echo of the Sanskrit into their response. These choices are in turn altered as the resources and associations change.

This story of good argument takes its text from Juan Mascaro's modern version of, or – perhaps better – response to, the *Gita*.[5] Mascaro's work is powerful in its own terms, but it is probably particularly important not to confuse this power with any simple transmission of an original (as indeed with the King James bible . . .): some other responses are considered after the main story, and there is reference to other texts and commentary in notes where it seems helpful – though only to keep an awareness of the range of possibilities in the margin. Mascaro's text enables the telling of a tale of good argument with a distinct emphasis. From his text, we can make out a dynamic process by which creativity absorbs and develops from initial negations and subsequent problems.

* * *

The *Bhagavad Gita* is structured as a dialogue – between Arjuna and Krishna – within a dialogue – between the blind king, called Dhritarashtra and Sanjaya. The framing exchange intervenes only briefly at the start, where the king inquires of Sanjaya for news of a battle between his sons and the sons of his dead brother, Pandu – among which latter Arjuna is numbered.[6] Sanjaya conjures a scene where two great armies confront each other: the great warriors of the world are present. The storyteller himself is amazed by the tale:

> And King Drupada and the sons of his daughter Draupadi; and Saubhadra, the heroic son of Arjuna, sounded from all sides their conch-shells of war.
>
> At that fearful sound the earth and the heavens trembled, and also trembled the hearts of Duryodhana and his warriors. (1, 18–19)

But Arjuna drives his chariot in between the armies, Arjuna greatest of all the warriors:

> Then Arjuna saw in both armies fathers, grandfathers, sons, grandsons; fathers of wives, uncles, masters; brothers, companions and friends.
>
> When Arjuna saw his kinsmen face to face in both lines of battle, he was overcome by grief and despair . . . (1,26–8)

The moment is complex. The story makes it clear that the two sides are not equivalent, not *morally* equal: Arjuna and his allies represent good, and their enemies are evil. But there is an irony about these forces of good and evil, as Arjuna recognises:

> Even if they, with minds overcome by greed, see no evil in the destruction of a family, see no sin in the treachery to friends;
>
> Shall we not, who see the evil of destruction, shall we not refrain from this terrible deed? (1,38–9)

The evil army have no ethical dilemmas and no hesitation about fighting and destroying. But Arjuna – the hero of the true – is bound to be conscious there is a problem in making war, precisely *because* he represents goodness. The crisis is acute and profound. Will the forces of virtue be weakened by consciousness of the evil of destruction, weakened by the terrible deeds required to preserve goodness? Here is the sense of an arguable world in which everything, even the preservation of good, has two sides to it, which are arguable.

Will evil triumph over good because Arjuna inhabits an arguable world? Is it the fate of the virtuous to find the world arguable and so to be indecisive, when the wicked have no doubts and no inhibitions? Arjuna has terrible doubts:

> Better for me indeed if the sons of Dhrita-rashtra, with arms in hand, found me unarmed, unresisting, and killed me in the struggle of war. (1,46)

Is virtue an impossible contradiction? Does virtue bring with it contradictions in an arguable world that lessen the value of virtue?

The story does not proceed to the battle; instead, the *Bhagavad Gita* tells of the intervention on the scene of Krishna, and the argument between Arjuna and Krishna on the necessity for war, and what this involves in terms of man's nature and existence. What we have, then, is a dialogue of ideas, not a battle story:

> Then arose the Spirit of Krishna and spoke to Arjuna, his friend, who with eyes filled with tears, thus had sunk into despair and grief. (2,1)

At first, Krishna delivers a simple message of encouragement:

> Strong men know not despair, Arjuna, for this wins neither heaven nor earth.
>
> Fall not into degrading weakness, for this becomes not a man who is a man. Throw off this ignoble discouragement, and arise like a fire that burns all before it. (2,2–3)

But encouragement is not enough to cure Arjuna of despair. On the contrary, he responds by justifying the *reasons* for his dejection:

> . . . Shall I kill with my arrows my grandfather's brother, great Bhishma? Shall my arrows in battle slay Drona, my teacher?
>
> Shall I kill my own masters who, though greedy of my kingdom, are yet my sacred teachers? . . .
>
> And we know not whether their victory or ours be better for us. . . .
>
> In the dark night of my soul I feel desolation. In my self-pity I see not the way of righteousness. I am thy disciple, come to thee in supplication: be a light unto me on the path of my duty. (2,4–7)

Arjuna points to the contradictions which have aroused his despair: if he wins, he loses; if he kills the other side, he kills his own people. Although Arjuna resists Krishna and a disagreement between them becomes inevitable, he resists Krishna with goodwill: 'I am thy disciple . . .'. Good faith is a prior condition for good arguing – and on good arguing, depends the hope of virtue.[a]

Only a good argument can turn virtue from inhibitions which are a source of despair to effective action. Can Krishna produce a good argument? In fact, Krishna can produce far more than one good argument: he responds to Arjuna's appeal by generating half a dozen arguments. First, Krishna argues that no one is ever killed, in the sense that no one is finally destroyed; all are reborn from death to another life:

[a]Habermas gives the credit of high rationality to 'one who is capable of letting himself be enlightened about his irrationality' (*Theory of Communicative Action*, p. 21). Such indeed is this Arjuna – for otherwise there could be no exchange.

> When a man knows him as never-born, everlasting, never-changing, beyond all destruction, how can that man kill a man, or cause another to kill? (2,21)

Krishna's first argument is that all are reborn from death to another life.[7] He links this argument on to a second claim – the claim that life is a procession of inevitable moments:

> For all things born in truth must die, and out of death in truth comes life. Face to face with what must be, cease thou from sorrow. (2,27)

Life is a cycle, and cycles are closed. The argument from inevitability leads to a third claim, the argument from duty: 'Think thou also of thy duty and do not waver' (2,31). And the argument for war from duty shades into a fourth contention, the case from honour:

> Men will tell of thy dishonour both now and in times to come. And to a man who is in honour, dishonour is more than death. (2,34)

Each claim is distinct, but the claims are also continuous: from rebirth after death to the inevitability of what happens, from inevitability to duty, and from duty to the requirements of honour and the horror of dishonour. The good argument is expansive, like creation itself. It develops continually, to become larger and more varied, and thus more vital. It never finishes at any point, but is always prepared to negotiate fresh challenges, as these arise from the endless nature of experience. It is never final, never finished, never totally self-contained. It is on-going, like life itself, because it is the nature of good argument to correspond with the conditions of life itself. The good argument is creative. The claims that Krishna has made so far metamorphose seamlessly into other claims. The language of Juan Macscaro's translation may perhaps be criticised for being too recognisably 'poetic' – but it conveys a *rhythm*, which is the rhythm of arguing, a rhythmic contention, and the good argument is the most vital rhythm within the exchange.

Krishna pauses to stress his authority:

> This is the wisdom of Sankhya – the vision of the Eternal. Hear now the wisdom of Yoga, path of the Eternal and freedom from bondage.[8] (2,39)

No sooner has Krishna ended his first cycle of arguments, than he begins a second cycle. Now he contends that *action* is necessary, and justifies action. So far he has argued that virtue must not be inert; now he makes the positive case that action is right, when we understand action in the right way:

> No step is lost on this path, and no dangers are found. And even a little progress is freedom from fear. (2,40)

If Arjuna acts rightly, he will be achieving *self*-advancement, which is a new kind of claim for action. Previously, Krishna's arguments depended on the nature of the world. Now he perceives through action the prospect of self-advancement. But not *all* action is justified: 'Set thy heart upon thy work, but never on its reward' (2,47). Krishna is now arguing about *motives*. The argument has moved inwards, towards the internal life of the active agent. Therefore, Krishna ends with subjectivity:

> When thy mind leaves behind its dark forest of delusion, thou shalt go beyond the scriptures of times past and still to come.[9] (2,52)

Krishna is generous, in the way that good arguing is generous: asked for his perspective on war against evil, he gives not one reason for this battle, but multiple reasons, which have diverse feelings associated with them. Yet the multiplicity of reasons is always coherent. We feel as if the individual arguments grow out of a larger structure, and that this larger argument remains enigmatic. The paradox is that Krishna is lucid and explanatory, and yet his words are finally mysterious. What is the source of such richness? How is it possible to be both lucid and mysterious at the same time? Indeed Arjuna responds to the enigma:

> How is the man of tranquil wisdom, who abides in divine contemplation? What are his words? What is his silence? What is his work? (2,54)

Where does humanity find access to such arguments? Previous chapters related arguments about the value of hope and the need to be involved in life and activity, and these arguments turned on the nature of God and faith. Now, in the *Bhagavad Gita*, we have a justification for action which arises from a source that is as inaccessible as Wordsworth's God; an authority that is as fundamental as Dryden's God. Here are arguments which appeal to a source beyond human understanding. Where is the silence from which such eloquence must arise? What is the character which can mediate between that silence and that eloquence? Good arguing becomes an enigma, explicitly.

Krishna responds to questions about the source of this enigma with a riddle:

> In the dark night of all beings awakes to light the tranquil man. But what is day to other beings is night for the sage who sees. (2,69)

Krishna does not try to smooth the way to understanding the mystery of what is both lucid and mysterious. The path to understanding is *difficult*, and the words must be difficult. In these difficulties therefore, Arjuna is soon back with his problem about action and renewing his sense of contradiction:

> If thy thought is that vision is greater than action, why dost thy enjoin upon me the terrible action of war?
>
> My mind is in confusion because in thy words I find contradictions. Tell me in truth therefore by what path may I attain the Supreme. (3,1–2)

A contradiction has emerged in Krishna's case for action, because there is something in the nature of wisdom which is opposed to action: wisdom requires vision and perception; vision and perception are best served by tranquillity, calm and thoughtfulness. Arjuna responds argumentatively, in the sense that he uncovers contradictions in Krishna's ideas. He presents these contradictions to Krishna to have them resolved, it is true, but the appeal grows out of a potential critique of Krishna's views. In other words, Arjuna develops a criticism and then inverts it to make a supplication for help. He implies a trust in Krishna's ability to respond to criticism – as if someone *else*, not Krishna, might be less sympathetic when contradictions in his views are pointed out. Arjuna is not such a good arguer as Krishna: he cannot *create* such cycles of good arguments; but Arjuna is able to bring out contradictions in such a way as to arouse constructive responses. And his trust is rewarded. Krishna responds:

> Not by refraining from action does man attain freedom from action. Not by mere renunciation does he attain supreme perfection. (3,4)

Krishna is responsive, but he is able to respond so precisely because Arjuna has prepared the way. His response is *inclusive*. Arjuna has posed the problem in terms of 'vision' and 'action': if vision is better than action, then why act at all? Krishna glances towards 'freedom from action' – thus acknowledging the challenge – but he includes that acknowledgement within a larger idea – 'not by refraining from action . . .'. Action is not the goal – but only through action can the goal be attained. He redoubles the response: 'Action is greater than inaction: perform therefore thy task in life' (3,8). Arjuna's 'contradictions' are illusory: there is no polarity between action and vision – both action and vision can be positive forces, in contrast with mere inertia, negative 'inaction'. Krishna is always willing to give reasons, and his reasons lead on to other reasons, in a process which carries emotion alongside. Krishna's willingness to *give* arguments is the precise complement of Arjuna's capacity to invite a response. The good argument depends on the meeting of these two agents: the one who invites and the one who responds. Together, Arjuna and Krishna compose an ideal of generous exchange.

Arjuna responds to Krishna not by simply assenting, but by asking a question. The question implies a possible objection, though the objection is tactfully oblique:

> What power is it, Krishna, that drives man to act sinfully, even unwillingly, as if powerlessly? (3,36)

If action is so necessary, why does some action become wrong, harmful, sinful? The good argument – the whole exchange – manages to incorporate that objection as a perspective on action, yet in terms of pure goodwill, it is also an invitation to respond.[b] What would be an obstacle to further discussion becomes instead a resource for developing the theme. Krishna can draw upon the new question to expound further arguments:

> It is greedy desire and wrath, born of passion, the great evil, the sum of destruction: this is the enemy of the soul. (3,37)

We are coming to understand the meaning of the two armies with which the story began: the evil forces against which Arjuna is opposed are the powers of passion, 'greedy desire and wrath'. They are the enemies of the Soul. A Ghandian interpretation may emerge here. Ghandi's disciple, Vinoba Bhave, interprets the direction taken by the exchange between Arjuna and Krishna using a title added to the first

[b]Habermas celebrates 'the behaviour of a person who is both willing and able to free himself from illusions' (*Theory of Communicative Action*, p. 20–1). Arjuna here demonstrates how such 'behaviour' might be represented in full exchange – for the problems which he poses incite Krishna to dissolve the very illusions which are so threatening at the start, and which indeed take long to clear.

chapter at a later date, as 'the yogi [path] of despondency'. He argues that if Arjuna had not been in despair to start with, Krishna would have no opportunity to develop the arguments which lead towards a higher state of understanding. Without despondency, there would be no access to wisdom. If we ask, how does despondency lead us towards wisdom, the answer must be: by way of good argument.[10] That answer is also an enigma, since good argument is generous in a way that we cannot easily explain or understand. What are the sources of such generosity? How is it that Arjuna – the one who invites – and Krishna – the good arguer – are so perfectly consonant? We sense a higher order in the nature of argument and its development and correspondence, and a higher order from which wisdom proceeds.

Every challenge dovetails perfectly with a response in the good argument, against a background of goodwill. The fit between them makes the challenges almost seem to be anticipations of the arguments which they arouse.[c] But it is important that the challenges are also real – Arjuna's interventions are strong in relation to what precedes them, they have to do with his deeply felt anxiety about acting wrongly – and acting wrongly to defend what is right. And his interventions make way for the better accounts that follow.

* * *

Krishna: I revealed this everlasting Yoga to Vivasvan, the sun, the father of light. He in turn revealed it to Manu, his son, the father of man. . . .

Arjuna: Thy birth was after the birth of the sun: the birth of the sun was before thine. What is the meaning of thy words: 'I revealed this Yoga to Vivasvan'?

Krishna: I have been born many times, Arjuna, and many times hast thou been born. But I remember my past lives, and thou hast forgotten thine. (4,1; 4,4–5)[11]

[c]Such rhythm is also evoked by Gadamer when he defines the general process of 'play', of which true exchange is in his view a special instance: 'If we examine how the word "play" is used and concentrate on its so-called transferred meanings we find talk of the play of light, the play of the waves, ... In each case what is intended is the to-and-fro movement . . . .' (*Truth and Method*, p. 93). Clearly the conception of 'argument' is being expanded by the inclusion of such harmonious rhythms, both in Gadamer's theory of interpretation and in this response to a particular vision.

Arjuna prompts Krishna's ideas to unfold and in this unfolding locates the problem of right action and wisdom by locating the problems in the earlier stages of their development. Krishna recognises that the sun does come before him, but at the same time he comes before the sun – the process is cyclical. The cycle of rebirth was the first argument advanced to justify Arjuna's killing of his enemies: no one ever dies, finally dies. Now the same idea of rebirth returns at a higher level: explaining the lineage of wisdom itself. One idea can reappear in another form: in defence of action; or in defence of a claim to wisdom. We feel that the same material is being expanded from different points of view, points of view towards which opposition turns the material in the dynamic of the exchange. We also gain a stronger sense of the form of Krishna's arguing. When Arjuna introduces his contradictions, contradictions between doing and not doing, Krishna does not eliminate the contradictions. Instead, he includes both sides of the contradiction which troubles Arjuna in a larger argument:

> **Arjuna**
> Renunciation is praised by thee, Krishna, and then the Yoga of holy work. Of these two, tell me in truth, which is the higher path?
>
> **Krishna**
> Both renunciation and holy work are a path to the Supreme; but better than surrender of work is the Yoga of holy work. (5,1–2)

Arjuna no longer presents Krishna with a simple contradiction between the values of activity and inactivity; instead, he suggests that ideas about them are diverging along opposing paths. He wants a decision as to *which* path should be followed: renunciation of activity or holy work? Krishna replies that the two paths are one way, from a higher point of view: 'a path to the Supreme'. Only then, will Krishna declare that one of the alternatives may be preferable. The word 'argument' is still necessary to describe what Krishna does, because he carries on giving reasons, reasons with a deep feeling behind them – though the feeling is mysterious:

> But renunciation, Arjuna, is difficult to attain without Yoga of work. . . .
>
> No work stains a man who is pure, . . . (5,6–7)[12]

Why is the way of holy work preferable to complete renunciation of worldly activity? The first reason is that 'renunciation' is impossible without such work; the second reason is that true work is itself an ideal. Krishna embraces the problems – in the generous embrace of good arguments. We begin to understand his discourse as a kind of embrace – an embrace which is at once secure and liberating. We can observe these powers in a good argument, though we can never finally explain them. We do not know why the universe is so ordered that the good argument can draw upon plentiful reasons.

Yet the problems are almost as plentiful as the responses they produce. Arjuna accepts the oneness of the two ideas, from a *higher* point of view, but for *him*, in his worldly nature, a further problem appears:

> Thou hast told me of a Yoga of constant oneness, O Krishna, of a communion which is ever one. But, Krishna, the mind is inconstant: in its restlessness I cannot find rest.
>
> The mind is restless, Krishna, impetuous, self-willed, hard to train: to master the mind seems as difficult as to master the mighty winds. (6,33–4)

Arjuna has presented a contradiction between ideal and reality, between theory and personal experience. Everything that Krishna has said may be true, with the truth of higher theory, yet human experience may not bear out such wisdom. Will Krishna now dismiss the argument from experience as irrelevant? Will the transcendent become separated from the human perspective? On the contrary: the form of the good argument always embraces the problem, and here the problem is human experience itself. Krishna turns towards Arjuna's difficulty, and not away from the crux of his problem:

> The mind is indeed restless, Arjuna: it is indeed hard to train. But by constant practice and by freedom from passion the mind in truth can be trained.
>
> While the mind is not in harmony, this divine communion is hard to attain; but the man whose mind is in harmony attains it, if he knows and if he strives. (6,35–6)

Krishna begins by *accepting*: Arjuna is right, human experience does not easily lead to wisdom. But instead of leaving it at that, Krishna then produces two further arguments to accommodate wisdom with human experience. First, he insists that there are ways of developing human experience towards the ideal of harmony. Second, he explains that the disarranged mind will see harmony as a far more difficult objective than necessary. In other words, disturbed subjectivity both creates the problem of inaccessible wisdom and prevents us seeing that a cure is possible. At the same time, Krishna accepts that there is such a thing as disturbed subjectivity, and that the disturbance has real impacts in terms of perspective. In his argument we feel the embrace of larger claims and the reasons for them, an embrace which closes round Arjuna's problem and opens up new possibilities for him. The closer the argument applies to the situation in which Arjuna finds himself, the greater is the possibility of liberating him from the situation. This sense of simultaneous closure and liberation is perhaps the most profound enigma in the exchange. The therapeutic possibilities have analogies with the Wanderer's method of drawing the Solitary into the exchange by offering him, through the means of argument, a way out of his pessimism and inactivity.

Krishna is trying to persuade Arjuna – to persuade the hero out of despair. The goal is therapeutic, since the persuasion would end by transforming Arjuna back to health, and not merely by changing his views. Both stories show how difficult a task is the therapy of good argument. Krishna and Arjuna are complementary as participants in a good argument, and even then the cure is far off, and often deferred. Krishna has argued that 'the mind in truth can be trained'; he has embraced Arjuna's point that 'the mind is restless' and moved on to a more inclusive argument for progress, an argument for harmony which includes man's restless nature. Immediately, Arjuna has a new problem. Again, he offers the problem as an appeal, even though the appeal is implicitly a challenge:

> And if a man strives and fails and reaches not the End of Yoga, for his mind is not in Yoga; and yet this man has faith, what is his end, O Krishna?
>
> Far from earth and far from heaven, wandering in the pathless winds, does he vanish like a cloud into air, not having found the path of God? (6,37–8)

If you say that the mind can rise above confusion to a higher perspective, are you condemning those who cannot advance to this condition? Would such a judgement be just? Is there not a near-contradiction: is the hope of betterment not a cause for fear? Is there just enough scope in Krishna's solution for man to be condemned? Arjuna turns the crisis into an invitation to respond:

> Be a light in my darkness, Krishna: be thou unto me a Light. Who can solve this doubt but thee? (6,39)

Krishna begins his answer from the idea of the cycle of lives again, the cycle which was his first argument against Arjuna's dejection:

> Neither in this world nor in the world to come does ever this man pass away; for the man who does the good, my son, never treads the path of death.
>
> He dwells for innumerable years in the heaven of those who did good; and then this man who failed in Yoga is born again in the house of the good and the great. (6,40–1)

First, judgement is never final, because there are always lives to come in which the judgement may be reversed. But more than that: a good try in one life ensures a better life in the next cycle, at least a better starting-point in that life. Krishna embraces the idea that a man may fail, and returns that counter-argument to the side of hope. The exchange between Arjuna and Krishna takes a long effort, a slow movement towards the therapeutic goal. Good arguing is no short-cut to wisdom and healthy living – on the contrary, the way of good argument is a patient way.

* * *

The balance of the dialogue shifts: Arjuna's questions contain less challenge as the exchange advances towards the goal. Instead, Arjuna is eliciting information. For instance, Krishna (7,29–30) identifies an elect who 'know Brahman' and 'know Atman'. Arjuna responds:

> Who is Brahman? Who is Atman? . . .
>
> **Krishna:** Brahman is the Supreme, the Eternal. Atman is his Spirit in man. . . . (8,1; 8,3)[13]

Krishna's voice gives the whole momentum to the work. Yet the first half of the story remains essential to Krishna's point of view: without the challenges and appeals from Arjuna, there would have been no opportunity for the voice of authority to emerge, embracing as it does so, man's contradictions in one authoritative account. Furthermore, Krishna *still* works by embracing contradiction, in an embrace which produces truth from the contradiction:

> Thus through my nature I bring forth all creation, and this rolls round in the circles of time.
> But I am not bound by this vast work of creation. I am and I watch the drama of works. (9,8–9)

Krishna is the creator: but is he not therefore confined within creation? He both is and is not confined to creation: for he is also the observer of creation. We have a continuing sense that there could be contradictions, if Krishna had not anticipated and included the difficulties; Arjuna takes on the role of affirmation, but his affirmations are still more than mere gestures of assent:

> I have faith in all thy words, because these words are words of truth, and neither the gods in heaven nor the demons in hell can grasp thy infinite vastness. (10,14)

Arjuna draws our attention to the fact of 'words', the words in which he has faith: he is being persuaded by utterances, and not merely by meanings or presences. *The therapy is in communication, not simply in revelation*. Indeed, Arjuna would like the exchange to become a revelation: 'For ever in meditation, how shall I ever know thee?' (10,17). Arjuna begins to resemble Job, insofar as he longs to apprehend the presence:

> I have heard thy words of truth, but my soul is yearning to see: to see thy form as God of this all. (11,3)

Sanjaya, the narrator of the *Bhagavad Gita*, tells us that the appeal is granted: Krishna appears to Arjuna as 'The Infinite Divinity' (11,11). The divine form now corresponds closely to an outcome of Plato's dialectic – division and diversity reappear under the heading of unity. Authority has emerged:

> And Arjuna saw in that radiance the whole universe in its variety, standing in a vast unity . . . (11,13)[14]

The important point is that presence reveals itself only *after* the arguing process: the same logic as applies in Job.

Argument comes *before* revelation. Furthermore, revelation turns back into argument. When Krishna has appeared as diversity in unity, he re-appears in a different guise. Arjuna responds to this new presence: 'Who art thou in this form of terror?' (11,31). The answer takes us back to the start of the exchange in which Arjuna hesitated to destroy his enemies. Krishna declares that:

> I am all-powerful Time which destroys all things, and I have come here to slay these men. Even if thou dost not fight, all the warriors facing thee shall die.
>
> Arise therefore! Win thy glory, conquer thine enemies, and enjoy thy kingdom. Through the fate of their Karma I have doomed them to die: be thou merely the means of my work. (11,32–3)

We return to the argument that Arjuna should destroy his enemies, since Krishna has doomed them whether Arjuna engages them or not. The revelation of Krishna's nature becomes part of the exchange between Krishna and Arjuna.

Krishna has revealed himself twice: as creation and as terror. He then transforms the double revelation into a vision, a vision of Brahman:

> He is ONE in all, but it seems as if he were many. He supports all beings: from him comes destruction, and from him comes creation. (13,16)

Furthermore, the idea of Brahman is again part of the good argument, it is the inclusive argument. The same outcome includes both destruction and creation with their opposing natures. The good argument is inclusive in the sense that it includes the case to which it is opposed. The good argument does not eliminate or destroy ideas to which it is opposed; nor does it turn away from them, nor avoid them. It acknowledges them within the form that it takes. The good argument forms round opposition, so that areas of opposition can still be identified from it, within its structure. The ideas to which an argument is opposed have a living source in the reactions and problems of people; those problems, like those people, will not disappear, and their own justification arises from within the endless, interlinked complexity of life. The good argument respects difference and opposition, and within the form that it takes, opposition retains a vital presence. Opposition is included within the good argument; it is in that sense that the good argument is said to be inclusive. It is also infinitely *patient*. The patience continues even after revelation, and even after Arjuna seems to have been cured. We are again encountering the endless fertility of the good argument, which is also the voice of truth as the story comes to its close.

Krishna has connected creation and destruction; the idea becomes realised visually:

> There is a tree, the tree of Transmigration, the Asvattha tree everlasting. Its roots are above in the Highest, and its branches are here below. Its leaves are sacred songs, and he who knows them knows the Vedas.
>
> Its branches spread from earth to heaven, and the powers of nature give them life. . . .
>
> Men do not see the changing form of that tree, nor its beginning, nor its end, nor where its roots are. But let the wise see, and with the strong sword of dispassion let him cut this strong-rooted tree, and seek that path wherefrom those who go never return. (15,1–4)[15]

Krishna conveys the infinite scope of creativity: 'the powers of nature' which give life. But he then adds that we need to take 'the strong sword of dispassion' and 'cut this strong-rooted tree'. Again, we are returning to the image of strong action, action which leads beyond action and the meaning of action which includes its opposite. All the claims and arguments are coming together. Creation and destruction go together – and from the destruction will come a new order of being. The destruction is not wanton, nor malicious: on the contrary, the destruction is transformative. (Here once more, the Ghandian reading is relevant: the field of battle lies within the individual in the first instance and it is from opposing forces within us that new revitalising possibilities emerge.) The voice has celebrated creativity, and then celebrates the moment of action which reaches beyond creation – returning in the process to the argument for Arjuna to arise against his enemies, who are perhaps the forces of worldly attachment. The whole account becomes, in turn, a celebration: a celebration of the infinite diversity of the good argument which is the voice of truth.

But surely the voice of truth should stand outside all argument? On the contrary, Krishna recognises the arguable world – for the arguable world is part of his truth:

> Evil men know not what should be done or what should not be done. Purity is not in their hearts, nor good conduct nor truth.
>
> They say: 'This world has no truth, no moral foundation, no God. There is no law of creation: what is the cause of birth but lust?' (16,7–8)

These men are wrong – yet they have a voice in the scheme of things: lust does indeed lead to birth. But they are wrong to infer there is *no* truth. The world is arguable, but the world is not arguable in the sense that there is no truth. There is an argument between the true vision and another way of seeing what happens. It is part of the true vision to recognise that this argument is inevitable. Therefore, Krishna continues to propound the truth *as* a good argument. Truth is contained *in* a dialogue. His voice is itself a dialogue. Indeed, he puts the other side, the nature of destruction and the case against truth, far more directly than Arjuna – who only hinted at possible objections to the accepting view and proffered contradictions to be resolved. Krishna recognises that everything he has said is reversible. He has shown a world informed by divine creation, and leading outwards to a higher level. But another voice can declare that 'there is no law of creation' and that the only cause of 'birth' is 'lust'. The other voice comes close to the heart of the matter:

> 'I have slain that enemy, and others also shall I slay. I am a lord, I enjoy life, I am successful, powerful and happy.' (16,14)

So the enemies of truth declare: they have reasons for their conduct, powerful reasons. Why do they kill? Because killing makes them 'successful, powerful and happy'. But the exchange began when Arjuna refused to kill his enemies: so Krishna is bringing in an additional complexity. He has been arguing that Arjuna must fight – but now he recognises that others will fight eagerly! Perhaps Arjuna's opponents will fight, to enjoy life, to be powerful and happy. The difference between the two sides is one of motivation:

> Three are the gates to this hell, the death of the soul: the gate of lust, the gate of wrath, and the gate of greed. Let a man shun the three.
>
> When a man is free from these three doors of darkness, he does what is good for his soul, and then he enters the Path Supreme. (16,21–2)

The views of the wicked are wrong, because they have the wrong motives. Arjuna's action will be the antithesis of their energies – because his actions will be motivated to escape what their actions seek to attain. After revelation, and when authority is clear, Krishna's words still move *through* the arguable world.

Indeed, Krishna seems to become more attuned to dialogue as the end approaches:

> Some say that there should be renunciation of action – since action disturbs contemplation; but others say that works of sacrifice, gift and self-harmony should not be renounced.
>
> Hear my truth about the surrender of works, Arjuna. Surrender, o best of men, is of three kinds.
>
> Works of sacrifice, gift, and self-harmony should not be abandoned, but should indeed be performed; for these are works of purification.
>
> But even these works, Arjuna, should be done in the freedom of a pure offering, and without expectation of a reward. This is my final word. (18,3–6)

* * *

Krishna begins the final chapter by recognising that people have different views, even about salvation. He moves back through the acceptance of each view: that action should be renounced and that some works are essential. His answer is that works done rightly become renunciations because there is nothing to be expected from doing them, nothing that the doer will gain from them. Krishna still moves through the arguable world, to truth as the good argument – which is the more conclusive argument. He then turns back to the starting-point:

> And that steadiness whereby a fool does not surrender laziness, fear, self-pity, depression and lust, is indeed a steadiness of darkness. (18,35)

We began with 'despair and grief' (2,1); the whole exchange is designed to be curative. When, at the end of the exchange, we return to 'self-pity, depression' – it is not to the righteous depression of Arjuna but to the more usual condition. Krishna places the exchange in the context of the wider problem of man's foolishness. He then responds to human depression, which is 'a steadiness of darkness'. The implications are not harsh, but therapeutic:

> Hear now, great Arjuna, of the three kinds of pleasure. There is the pleasure of following that right path which leads to the end of all pain. What seems at first a cup of sorrow is found in the end immortal wine. That pleasure is pure: it is the joy which arises from a clear vision of the Spirit. (18,36–7)

Krishna responds to the 'steadiness of darkness' with a vision of 'pleasure' – and of justified pleasure. But his vision of pleasure *includes* the possibility of some darkness: 'a cup of sorrow is found in the end immortal wine'. It is not necessary to read the darkness as the end of all light. On the contrary, the darkness may be the other side of a brighter light. Krishna contrasts that particular relation between pleasure and pain with its inversion:

> But the pleasure which comes from the craving of the senses with the objects of their desire, which seems at first a drink of sweetness but is found in the end a cup of poison, is the pleasure of passion, impure.
>
> And that pleasure which both in the beginning and in the end is only a delusion of the soul, which comes from the dullness of sleep, laziness or carelessness, is the pleasure of darkness. (18,38–9)

The prospect of pleasure stands against 'a steadiness of darkness' – but then other kinds of pleasure must also be recognised, pleasures which lead back to the darkness.[16] The good argument curves around contradictions, here the contradictions of pleasure and darkness. And in the centre, Krishna is still concentrating on the initial problem, the problem of curing Arjuna of dejection. The good arguer is infinitely patient, as patient as the world is complex. His patience is the other side of the world's complexity. The therapeutic moment approaches:

> Hast thou heard these words, Arjuna, in the silent communion of thy soul? Has the darkness of thy delusion been dispelled by thine inner Light? (18,72)

Krishna is still emphasising 'these words' – the enterprise is persuasive, even if it includes moments of revelation through vision. Nothing replaces 'these words'. Furthermore, in the end, the persuasive enterprise depends not upon the persuader but upon the persuaded: 'Hast thou *heard* these words . . .'. The whole enterprise is 'other-centred'. What matters is the perspective of the other side of the words of the good argument, which may even be the words of truth. And, crucially, the cure, when it comes, will be achieved 'by *thine* inner Light': all that words of wisdom can do is to arouse capacities present within the recipient, within the other. The site of the cure is internal. Krishna does not confuse his own arguments with the actual achievement of the cure.[d] Those arguments may be the preconditions for cure, but they are not the goal itself. Here, then, is the strange humility of the good argument, even when it is – or sees itself as – the argument of truth. This humility is the last enigma. There is always a gap between the closing of the argument – the case – and the fulfilment of the whole process – the argument in the larger sense. Arjuna crosses the gap:

> By thy grace I remember my Light, and now gone is my delusion. My doubts are no more, my faith is firm; and now I can say 'Thy will be done'. (18,73)

Arjuna reaffirms the point: 'by thy grace' he has recovered his light. It is his own light – 'my light' – that he has recovered. The exchange does not reduce Arjuna's autonomy, but rather makes him more conscious of that autonomy as a creative force. The good argument leaves Arjuna more independent than he was before the exchange. Yet that independence mysteriously derives from the authority of the convincing argument.

The narrator, Sanjaya, closes the account by recalling us to a sense of dialogue:

[d]Gadamer suggests that it is false and harmful to assume 'a mutually exclusive antithesis between authority and reason' (*Truth and Method*, p. 246). He distinguishes between 'blind obedience', which would indeed imply a 'concept of authority . . . diametrically opposed to reason and freedom' (p. 248), and true authority, which

> rests on recognition and hence an act of reason itself which, aware of its own limitations, accepts that others have better understanding. (p. 248)

Arjuna's response to Krishna has affinities with such a conception. The way in which he continues to formulate questions implies a capacity analogous to Gadamer's 'act of reason' – and likewise he uses that act to seek confirmation, rather than to hope for victory. The most useful aspect of the comparison is Gadamer's distinction between any such recognitions and 'blind obedience' – and it is this distinction which is being implied by keeping the term 'good argument' active when the relation is one of acceptance and aid. The point is not to show that Arjuna and Krishna are at odds, but rather to develop a sense of argument which can include this relation of appeal and creativity. Raghavachar in his reworking of the classical commentary of Ramanuja (p. 203), celebrates the whole process from the perspective of the ending in terms which bring out the power of this work as a story of good argument, not in a competitive sense of argument but in the sense of a certain fundamental freedom without which authority is merely the facade of tyranny:

> Arjuna is asked to consider the entire teaching critically and choose his course of conduct according to his desire. It signifies an invitation to critical inquiry as opposed to the imposition of a dogma not to be questioned.

> Thus I heard these words of glory between Arjuna and the God of all, and they fill my soul with awe and wonder. (18,74)

We have heard 'words of glory between . . .' – an exchange, and never a monologue. The triumph is a triumph of exchange:

> I remember, O king, I remember the words of holy wonder between Krishna and Arjuna, and again and again my soul feels joy. (18,76)

We do recall revelation, but in the context of the exchange:

> And I remember, I ever remember, that vision of glory of the God of all, and again and again joy fills my soul.
>
> Wherever is Krishna, the End of Yoga, wherever is Arjuna who masters the bow, there is beauty and victory, and joy and all righteousness. This is my faith. (18,77–8, The End)

From the single 'vision', we return to the double vision: 'Wherever is Krishna . . . wherever is Arjuna . . .'. We need the two parts of the whole exchange. The form of the good argument bears witness to our deepest need.

* * *

A reading of the *Gita* in Mascaro's version gives us this inescapable sense of necessary process. We end with the good argument as indeed something of a creative mystery, though also a human experience. Other versions give different inflections. The first text in English, by Wilkins,[17] does not provide a strong ground for elaborating Krishna's response in substance. But we can make out a relationship, and how it unfolds in this crisis, particularly in terms of Arjuna's reactions. This Arjuna too continues to express reverence for Krishna, and to appeal for his guidance. And he also remarks upon what seems to him to be possible inconsistencies, doing so with an extra edge by comparison with Mascaro:

> If, according to thy opinion, the use of the understanding be superior to the practice of deeds, why then dost thou urge me to engage in an undertaking so dreadful as this? (3,1–2)

The tension comes through the words, particularly through the emphasis of 'dreadful', where Mascaro has 'the terrible action of war'. We, therefore, feel all the more strongly the tone of appeal, rather than of rejection or challenge in a hostile spirit.

We can make out in Wilkins' Arjuna a subtle attitude towards authority. Arjuna speaks in recognition of Krishna's authority: yet he incorporates a critical touch in his responses to the advice, and we feel that with even more sharpness than in Mascaro. The purpose of such criticism is, of course, not to undermine the authority, but, on the contrary, to gain confirmation. Wilkins gives us an Arjuna who is at once desperate and trusting when confronted by complex ideas:

> Thou, as it were, confoundest my reason with a mixture of sentiments; wherefore, choose one amongst them, by which I may obtain happiness, and explain it unto me. (3,1–2)

There is no challenge to Krishna's authority – on the contrary, the whole exchange presupposes that authority. Yet Arjuna appeals for answers in terms which involve a sense of desperation which might have been more adversarial. Mascaro gives 'My mind is in confusion' for 'Thou . . . confoundest my reason' – and by comparison, Wilkins' Arjuna is almost resentful, or could easily have been resentful were he not also reverential. That striking 'mixture of sentiments' corresponds to '. . . in thy words I find contradictions'. Mascaro's Arjuna makes it easier for Krishna to respond by offering him the term 'contradictions'; Wilkins has the more awkward 'mixture'. From Mascaro, we receive the impact of a whole process, where negation encounters the generous creativity of response. Wilkins suggests another shading, where the negation is a touch more desperate.

Another pertinent comparison arises between the versions of the final perspective after the main dialogue. The Mascaro version gives Sanjaya confirming the experience of 'these words of glory between Arjuna and the God of all . . .'. In Wilkins' version, we have an even stronger sense of the power of exchange:

> In this manner I have been an ear-witness of the astonishing and miraculous conversation that hath passed . . . As, o mighty Prince, I recollect again and again this holy and wonderful dialogue of Kreeshna and Arjuna. (18,74)

Given Arjuna's more desperate tones at times, perhaps this ending provides a correspondingly heightened affirmation of the encounter.

Wilkins gives us more of a romantic drama than the sustained process of subtle interplay and response in the modern account. But other responses can move the work further than Mascaro in the direction of a great system, a system which Krishna is applying in the particular exchange with philosophical clarity. In Edgerton's realisation,[18] with its philosophical precision, Krishna's theories have a geometric beauty, though there is no audible voice. Krishna propounds for Arjuna his generous cycle of arguments at the start. This time, though much stays the same, there is perhaps less sense of movement, and instead a number of distinctions are clearer. Krishna explains the illusory power of 'the opposites', categories which apply only to the world conceived in terms of material nature, or 'the Strands'. He then can advise:

> Be thou free from the three Strands, Arjuna,
> Free from the pairs [of opposites] . . . (2,45)

Mascaro makes one of his more awkward compromises by keeping 'gunas' for the 'strands' and then giving: 'Be in truth eternal, beyond earthly opposites'. Yet by his economy Mascaro does sustain the process – where Edgerton clarifies the particular theory. Mascaro conveys a mysterious sympathy, where Edgerton gives a crystalline system being applied.

When Krishna returns to the definition of enlightenment and right action, Edgerton lucidly develops the theme of the opposites:

> Content with getting what comes by chance,
> Passed beyond the pairs [of opposites], free from jealousy,
> Indifferent to success and failure,
> Even acting, he is not bound. (4,22)

Therefore, when Krishna comes to reveal His divine being to Arjuna, the Edgerton version uses verse structure to draw attention to the transcending of what would otherwise be opposites:

> Both the goodly odor in earth,
> And brilliance in fire am I,
> Life in all beings,
> And austerity in ascetics am I. (7,9)

Here in the world are two spirits,
  The perishable, and the imperishable;
The perishable is all beings;
  The imperishable is called the immovable.

But there is a higher spirit other [than this],
  Called the Supreme Soul; (15,16–17)

This Krishna is more methodical, less creative in the process itself than using the exchange to introduce systematic distinctions. These two dimensions are not contrary, but different. This is not the place to arbitrate claims to express an original. Here it is proper instead to observe how rich a source of stories of good arguing is the poetic vision of the *Bhagavad Gita* unfolding through the diverse responses in English.

Argument, difference and therapeutic exchange

Argument comprehends a dimension of potential *harmony*: a conception of argument that is very different from those which associate arguing with dissonance. Arjuna's questions are appeals for help, for arguments against his own despair. He does not reject Krishna's intervention; he longs for it. Nevertheless such intervention is only possible because there is a *difference* between life as Arjuna perceives it, and the world as Krishna conceives it. Their relations are not precisely those that govern many arguments, for Krishna's authority is never in question. But Arjuna has difficulty in fathoming Krishna's point of view, and this maintains a gap between them. Argument crosses the gap, and reduces it: it is an argument, an exchange with and of different and opposed viewpoints, but it is harmonious, the most harmonious possible instance of such an exchange.

Underlying such exchanges is a will to accept, rather than a drive to challenge. Habermas puts particular emphasis on this will to receive enlightenment and places the connection between argument and therapy in a psychoanalytic setting:

> Freud examined the relevant type of argumentation in his model of the therapeutic dialogue between analyst and patient. In the analytic dialogue the roles are asymmetrically distributed; the analyst and the patient do not

> behave like proponent and opponent. (*The Theory of Communicative Action*, I p. 21)

However, some qualifications must be introduced about psychotherapy as therapeutic *argument*, and these qualifications also apply in the later stages of Krishna's exchange with Arjuna, and perhaps even to the whole nature of therapeutic interaction. The element of argument peters out *eventually*, as a conversion comes into sight. At some point it shades into a monologue in which interpretations are not opposed, though their therapeutic intention remains clear. In his introduction to the *Interpretation of Dialogue*, Tullio Maranhao refers to

> the exemplary attitude of a dialogue leader. This central speaker appears in every manifestation of represented dialogue and can be illustrated by the Socratic philosopher, the psychoanalyst, or the main character in the novel.[19]

Without accepting that a dialogue leader appears in 'every' dialogue, the proposition does focus the question: when is a dialogue leader not leading a dialogue any longer. A later essay in the same volume proposes eventually:

> Thus psychoanalysis can be regarded as dogmatic and as imposing its principles of text adequacy on the patient's semi-literate skills.[20]

But even here, according to Sven Daelmans and Tullio Maranhao, there is still a gap of difference between therapist and client which maintains a difference:

> However, neither Freud nor his followers ever insisted that the patient should learn the words of the story that best describes his illness.

At the end of the *Gita*, Krishna still asks whether Arjuna has 'heard these words'. Authority need not remain insular, a self-imposing view: the words of authority must reach the recipient and it is to the recipient's true understanding that they are directed. Arjuna remains an essential part of the exchange, in this last sense, a potential point of divergence even if only by way of non-understanding.

The *Bhagavad Gita*: further commentary and references

1 Boethius, *The Consolation of Philosophy*, trans. by V. E. Watts (Harmondsworth: Penguin 1969), I p. 35. Succeeding references given in text.

2 M. K. Gandhi, *An Autobiography or The Story of My Experiments with Truth*, trans. from the original Gujarati by Mahadev Desai (Harmondsworth: Penguin 1982), p. 76. Succeeding references given in the text.

3 The versions of the titles come respectively from Eric J. Sharpe, *The Universal Gita: Western Images of the Bhagavadgita* (London: Duckworth 1985, p. xv) and Franklin Edgerton, *The Bhagavad Gita: Translated and Interpreted* (Cambridge Mass.: Harvard University Press 1972, p. 105). The dating is given by Sharpe (p. xvi), with the important proviso that such estimates have been made by Western scholars on philological grounds. The definition of Krishna's complex divinity is by Edgerton (p. 105). Any study which focuses on the life of this work in English versions begins from Sharpe's overall account of the range of Western responses.

4 Hinduism is an essential context although some interpreters have regarded the name as retrospective only in relation to the *Gita*. For instance, Swami Vivekananda argued in his *Thoughts On The Gita* (Calcutta, Advaita Ashram 1974, 8th impression p. 18): 'It is the most curious fact that the disciples and descendants of Krishna have no name for their religion, although foreigners call it Hinduism or Brahminism.' The view comes from a lecture originally given in California, April 1 1900. Swami Vivekananda is regarded by S. S. Raghavachar in his scholarly study *Sri Ramanuja On The Gita* (Mangalore: Ramakrishna Ashram 1969, p. iii) as one of the four great authorities of modern times on the *Gita* – the others being Tilak, Gandhi and Sri Aurobindo. It is important to recognise that such views also belong to the political development of modern India, as indeed does the *Gita* itself.

5 *The Bhagavad Gita*, Translated by Juan Mascaro (Harmondsworth: Penguin 1962). Many readers will observe the affinity with T. S. Eliot's *Four Quartets*. Sharpe (*op.cit.* pp. 132–5) sees Eliot as a major influence within the influence of this work – and, I think, Mascaro does make of Eliot's intervening presence a creative resource, rather than an inhibiting model.

6 In the *Mahabharata*, there are two brothers who are both kings – Dhrita-rashtra and Pandu. Dhrita-rashtra has one-hundred sons; Pandu has five sons, including Arjuna. The sons of Dhrita-rashtra are mainly wicked, the others are virtuous. Pandu dies and leaves his sons in the care of his blind brother. Rivalries ensue. The five sons of Pandu – the Pandavas – flee into the forest. But Arjuna wins the hand of the daughter of another king, Drupada, and Krishna too becomes the ally of the Pandavas. After the wicked party refuse any land to the virtuous party, a great battle is prepared. It is news of this battle which the blind king requests at the beginning. Sources consulted here include: G. A. Feuerstein, *Introduction to The Bhagavad-Gita: Its Philosophy and Cultural Setting* (London: Rider 1974), of which Chapter 4 is on 'The Mahabharata'; Swami Vivekananda (*op.cit.* p. 48) refers the setting to a suggestive struggle for 'the empire of

India'; S. S. Raghavachar (*op.cit.* p. 1) notes that the classical commentary of Ramanuja finds an allegory here: 'Ramanuja comments that his (the king's) blindness was not merely physical . . .'.

7 Raghavachar (*op.cit.* p. 8) comments that 'He (Krishna) gives him (Arjuna) what is needed, which may well be in excess of what he explicitly seeks.' The answer is far larger than the terms of the request. Raghavachar responds to another problem which is implicit here and later: 'That the philosophical dialogue on the battlefield at the moment of action is too extensive is an unimaginative charge . . . Such a voluminous and lengthy struggle . . . affords plenty of scope for conferences, deliberations and consultations.'

8 Edgerton (*op.cit.* pp. 165–6) explains in relation to the term 'yoga': 'The word which I translate "discipline" is yoga . . . The word yoga is unfortunately a very fluid one . . .'. Edgerton adds that the 'discipline' is first and foremost 'a discipline of action' (karma-yoga). The discipline of action is the way of reconciling the need to perform certain acts with the hope of escaping from the limits of action: 'Action characterised by indifference is the central principle.' Whatever the prevalent assumptions in some Western commonplaces about 'the east', the emphasis of the *Gita* is not on passive acceptance, but rather on how to act rightly. In this passage, the 'discipline of action' is also being distinguished from a path of knowledge, the Sankhya or 'reason method'. This conjunction is one of the most complex in the *Gita.* An enlightening essay on 'Sankhya and Yoga' by Sri Aurobindo appears in that author's *Essays on the Gita* (Pondicherry: Aurobindo Ashram 1966, pp. 61–72). Aurobindo presents the Sankhya and the Yoga as two different traditions being connected by Krishna in a new way: 'The Sankhya is also a Yoga, but it proceeds by knowledge; it starts, that is to say, by intellectual discrimination and analysis . . . Yoga, on the other hand, proceeds by works . . .' (p. 63). In other words, the passage signals a transition from the more philosophical approach to a more practical emphasis, a transition which others might see as a contradiction but which Krishna presents as a continuity.

9 These scriptures are the ancient works called Vedas, the main collection being the Rig Veda or Vedic hymns. See Edgerton (*op.cit.* p. 111).

10 Gandhi (in the collection of his writings, *Gita The Mother* 4th ed. (Lahore 1946–7) p. 14) gives an interpretation in terms of other paths which the work takes 'instead of teaching the rules of physical warfare'. He also interprets the battle itself as a moral symbol: 'I felt that it was not a historical work but that under the guise of physical warfare, it described the duel that perpetually went on in the hearts of mankind and that physical warfare was brought in really to make the description of the initial duel more alluring.' Vinoba Bhave's ideas are developed along these lines in his *Talks on the Gita* (London: Macmillan 1960), of which 'The Yogi of Despondency' is Chapter One. Bhave concentrates on mental states, the avoidance indeed of this 'wrath' being even more important than actual physical behaviour: 'it is possible to be non-violent in externals, and yet in fact be filled with violence' (p. 50).

11 Aurobindo (*op.cit.*, Essay XV 'The Possibility and Purpose of Avatarhood', p. 131) gives a context:

> Krishna has disclosed in passing that this was the ancient and original Yoga, which he gave to Vivasvan, the sun-god, Vivasvan gave it to Manu, the father of man, Manu gave it to Ikshvaku, head of the Solar line, and so it came down from royal sage to royal sage till it was lost in the great lapse of time, and is now renewed for Arjuna . . . .

The passage, Aurobindo argues, raises the problem of the complex nature of Krishna. Arjuna 'asks how the Sun-God, one of the first born of beings, ancestor of the Solar dynasty, could have received the Yoga from the man Krishna who is only now born into the world . . .'. In his reply, Krishna explains the idea of rebirth anew, but he is more significantly 'declaring his concealed Godhead'. ('Avatarhood' is the concept of the descent of the deity into human form.) Raghavachar (*op.cit.* p. 48) gives a slightly different emphasis in recounting the classical commentary of Ramanuja: 'Ramanuja explains that Arjuna is aware of the fact that Sri Krisna is an incarnation of the Supreme Deity but does not comprehend the nature of the incarnation . . . .'

12 Aurobindo (*op.cit.* Essay 24 'The Gist of Karmayoga', p. 227) interprets this theory of work in terms of a practice of spiritual yoga:

> This upward transference of our centre of being . . . with a resultant change in the whole spirit and motive of our action, the action often remaining precisely the same in its outward appearances, makes the gist of the Gita's karmayoga . . . Make the work you have to do here your means of inner spiritual rebirth . . . .

Gandhi (*op.cit.* p. 15) stresses that what is to be renounced is 'fruits of action', not action itself.

13 Raghavachar (*op.cit.* p. 93) comments on this transition from the end of chapter 7 to the start of chapter 8: 'The conclusion arouses the questions which Arjuna puts in the beginning of the next chapter . . . . The questions seem to be invited by the very brevity of this conclusion and the use of a set of technical terms . . . .' The terms themselves are rich in potential for interpretation, even after Krishna has explained. Raghavachar interprets: 'By Brahman in this context is to be understood the imperishable spiritual principle in man' (p. 94). Aurobindo (*op.cit.* Essay III of second series, p. 265) has a different perspective:

> By that Brahman . . . the Gita intends, it appears, the immutable self-existence which is the highest self-expression of the Divine and on whose inalienable eternity all the rest, all that moves and evolves, is founded. By adhyatna (Atman in Mascaro) it means . . . the spiritual way and law of being of the soul in the supreme nature.

Edgerton (*op.cit.* pp. 116–9) puts the term 'brahman' in the context of earlier traditions of the Vedic texts. He sees the term as a focus for different developments at the centre of Hindu thought and belief.

14 Raghavachar (*op.cit.* p. 124) reads the vision thus: 'The central scene of this chapter is the self-revelation of Sri Krisna to Arjuna in His divine and all inclusive form.'

15 Raghavachar (*op.cit.* pp. 165–6) expounds an interpretation of this vision:

> The world in which the bound soul moves from birth to birth in its career of evil and suffering is pictured as the Aswatta tree. Its roots are above and its branches hang downwards. The significance of this is that it is a creation of the creator God . . . and all other beings fashioned by him are of lower levels of creation. This tree is fairly permanent, for it exists as an unbroken stream of existence, till the rise of enlightenment from which comes non-attachment . . . This tree, which is deep-rooted as well as many-rooted, must be cut down by the weapon of non-attachment . . .

16 The three kinds of 'pleasure' correspond to a threefold structure which has played a part in the whole conception. Edgerton (*op.cit.* p. 141) explains: 'The variety of material nature . . . is composed of three elements called gunas, that is, "threads, strands", or "qualities": namely, sattva, "goodness, purity"; rajas, "passion, activity"; and tamas, "darkness, dullness, inactivity".' The acceptable happiness – that which grows – belongs to the first of these three strands: sattva or goodness. The other two forms of happiness – those which decay or become poisonous – belong to the other two strands. See also Raghavachar (*op.cit.* p. 193): '. . . happiness is the supreme end of all endeavour. Hence three kinds of happiness are also to be distinguished. That happiness which becomes increasingly enjoyable through continuous experience and which puts an end to the sufferings of human bondage, is Sattwic.'

17 Charles Wilkins, *The Bhagvat-Geeta* (1785), facsimile with introduction by George Hendrick (Gainsville, Florida 1959). Sharpe (*op.cit.* pp. 3–14) sets Wilkins' endeavour in the context of the East India Company for which he worked. Sharpe argues (p. 10) that this text 'was to exercise enormous influence on the mind of Europe and America'.

18 Edgerton's translation first appeared in 1944, and was offered then by him as a direct comparison with a poetic recreation, by the Victorian Sir Edwin Arnold.

19 Tullio Maranhao (ed.) *The Interpretation of Dialogue* (Chicago: The University of Chicago Press 1990), p. 14.

20 Sven Daelemans and Tullio Maranhao, 'Psychoanalytic Dialogue and the Dialogical Principle' in *The Interpretation of Dialogue*, pp. 219–41, pp. 234–5.

Argument and the argumentative imagination: contemporary contexts

Dialogism

Bakhtin exemplifies a very narrow view of argument, when proposing

> the narrow understanding of dialogism as argument, polemics, or parody. These are the externally most obvious, but crude, forms of dialogism.[1]

A primary aim of this book is to rescue argument from such restrictive definitions. True, many arguments are crude, but the process of arguing is alive with other possibilities. These possibilities can make great stories, stories which carry the reader's attention forwards as effectively as any action. These are arguments worth imagining fully. Bakhtin can even reduce the status of human encounters, actual or imagined, in the realm of dialogue:

> But dialogic relations, of course, do not in any way coincide with relations among rejoinders in real dialogue – they are much broader, more diverse, and more complex. (p. 124)

'Rejoinders in real dialogue' are the nuts and bolts of argument in the imagination, where the stories of argument are engendered.

Bakhtin pushes argument to the margins of dialogue. He also finds little or no place for *poetry* in dialogue:

> In genres that are poetic in the narrow sense, the natural dialogization of the word is not put put to artistic use . . .[2]

Bakhtin's definitions find only a limited place in dialogue for argument, encounters and poetry. In the four readings of this book, argument, encounters and poetry are intimately connected. Heightened language substantiates the outcomes of heightened imagining in fervent encounters that intensify argument in the mind of the reader. By comparison with the intense involvements encountered in this book, Bakhtin's central instances may seem depleted:

> Two juxtaposed utterances belonging to different people who know nothing about one another if they only slightly converge on one and the same subject (idea), inevitably enter into dialogic relations with one another.

> They come into contact with another on the territory of a common theme, a common idea.[3]

This oblique interplay of voices seems insubstantial, and is even less substantial when compared with encounters between people – so Bakhtin *has* to reduce the significance of such direct encounters.

Bakhtin has another theory which could counter the significance of argumentative dialogue in my four texts, a theory of covert monologue. According to that idea, exchanges might be weighted, weighted in a way that represents a single point of view. In his words:

> Monologized creative consciousness frequently joins and personifies others' words, others' voices that have become anonymous, in special symbols: 'the voice of life itself,' 'the voice of nature,' . . . .[4]

It could be argued that some of the voices in these stories had taken over the words of others in the same text. But the whole drive of the narrative is against that perspective. The Solitary, for instance, has a viewpoint which is not simply part of some overarching monologue. His viewpoint is intrinsic to his own life and personality, and is inseparable from his own story. Are such stories to be lost sight of in a viewpoint that proceeds through neat definitions?

Bakhtin's exclusive definitions and classifications obscure fundamental insights that are valuable and that are integral to this study:

> There can be no such thing as an isolated utterance. It always presupposes utterances that precede and follow it.[5]

Utterances *connect*, that is the principle propounded. The four stories realise such a principle of interconnected utterances intensely; they take that principle to its imaginative consequence. Bakhtin uses this insight of connected utterances in different ways. Sometimes, he generalises it almost to vanishing point:

> No one utterance can be either the first or the last. Each is only a link in the chain, and none can be studied outside this chain. (p. 136)

But, if a rule applies equally to all utterances how does it function in practice? Hence an over-elaborate set of definitions is required to provide against occasions which test the absolute generalisation. On the other hand, Bakhtin sometimes applies his insight more pragmatically:

> Active agreement/disagreement (if it is not dogmatically predetermined) stimulates and deepens understanding, makes the other's word more resilient and true to itself, and precludes mutual dissolution and confusion. (p. 142)

Here different voices are connected with a dynamic exchange that is unstable and unpredictable. This undetermined dynamic is basic to the stories in this book. Bakhtin can be overwhelming in his response to the exchange of different voices:

> Dialogue and dialectics. Take a dialogue and remove the voices (the partitioning of voices), remove the intonations (emotional and individualizing ones), carve out abstract concepts and judgments from living words and responses, cram everything into one abstract consciousness – and that's how you get dialectics. (p. 147)

What counts here is the central image of *living* voices in dynamic relations, rather than the peripheral play of definition and exclusion. Could the boundaries ever be so clear? But still, Bakhtin brings to life the idea of exchange by connecting exchange with a whole vision of language as dialogue. If at times the language-as-dialogue threatens to dissolve the dialogue-as-exchange, at other times the whole force of the theory can reinvigorate the encounter of different voices, real and imagined.

Rhetorical criticism

'The argumentative imagination' also fits into a context of contemporary thought which is based on a literary revival of rhetorical theory. Aristotle makes competing voices fundamental to rhetoric; fundamental, too, to rhetoric are the speakers whose voices are heard. As the introduction noted, Barbara Johnson recreates deconstruction in the terms of such a rhetoric, when she asserts that: 'deconstruction focuses on the functioning of claim-making and claim-subverting structures within texts'.[6]

Johnson means that there are central claims in all texts, and the *same* texts contain marginalised resistances to the claims being made in them. Her concept supports the present approach in a fundamental way, for it points up the fact that in interpreting a script it is necessary to hear *all* the voices in it. And further – assumptions about which is the main voice should not prevent us from diligently listening for others. In many cases, Johnson might ask other questions about the texts in this study, and that would draw from them different stories. But her approach uncovers analogous problems, because it concentrates on different voices. One effect of doing so is to forestall a quick resolution to the reading. She also considers what implications a slow appraisal and suspended judgement have for political action:

> Yet how can the plea for slowness, for the suspension of decision, for the questioning of knowledge, ever function as anything other than a refusal to intervene? . . . Yet if undecidability is politically suspect, it is so not only to the left, but also to the right. (p. 30)

Johnson is not advocating compromise: she is talking about sustained attention to the difficult combinations of voices in a text. My readings do not meet Johnson's criteria in a definitive way. But there are close convergences between stories of argument, and her vision of interwoven, contrasted meanings.

Reading a poem by Baudelaire, Johnson concludes that: 'it can only demystify metaphor by participating in it' (p. 105). *Participation* is the important concept here, a further factor which prevents a single-minded resolution of an argument, or imaginative argument, including a resolution by an interpreter. Even Krishna cannot transform Arjuna without participating in an exchange which involves suspending judgement on the outcome. In other words, Johnson also expects rhetoric to do something other than neutrally register different voices in narrative terms. An outcome of the story is not to be reached by judiciously weighing up the words used in an argument by differing voices. The Panther is not a mere formula of words that states a hostile position, but, on the contrary, a substantial presence in the story of an argument. Job is not just an excluded voice transforming the process of exchange. Arjuna is not just an initial position to which Krishna's thoughts can be addressed. These texts contain more than the terms in which arguments are exchanged. My readings are a *process* of interpretation and of participation that proceeds until it reaches the stories which I have told, stories which indeed do *not* constitute demystifications. The emphasis on process leaves the interpretations available. Other stories can be found in the texts. Those found in this book are not final and definitive. And the texts considered are not 'a complete set of stories'. They are not 'a canon of arguments'. The hope is to evoke other stories from the same texts, and stories from other sources. For instance, in this book, Anna Barbauld's dialogues offer a perspective on *The Excursion*: but *The Excursion* could be used to throw light on her dialogues and, of course, would be read differently in doing so. It is worthwhile to tell stories of argument: it is not necessary to tell a particular set of stories. And it is not necessary to find the same story in the same context, or tell it in the same way.

Johnson recognises that a story resists a single, whole interpretation, and yet seems to invite it through its ending:

> The search for wholeness, oneness, universality, and totalization can nevertheless never be put to rest. However rich, healthy, or lucid fragmentation and division may be, narrative seems to have trouble resting content with it, as though a story could not recognize its own end as anything other than a moment of totalization – even when what is totalized is loss. (p. 164)

In this book, each story in some ways invites a unified interpretation and also resists it; and the same may be said about the book as a whole: there are temptations to offer a single whole interpretation that covers all four stories. But local meanings adhere to each story in its own environment. From each story, something is to be gained – not the same thing for each occasion, or for each reader.

Rhetorical philosophies

Another modern rhetorician considers the problem of wholeness in another way:

> Relativism is got by the fragmentation of either drama or dialectic. That is, if you isolate any one agent in a drama, or any one advocate in a dialogue, and see the whole in terms of his position alone, you have the purely relativistic . . . . For relativism sees everything in but one set of terms – and since there are endless other terms in which things could be seen, the irony of the monologue that makes everything in its image would be in this ratio: the greater the *absolutism* of the statements, the greater the *subjectivity* and *relativity* in the position of the agent making the statements.[7]

Burke reverses the common assumption that relativism applies within a complex situation, where many voices are heard. For him, relativism operates meaningfully in the single situation with a homogeneous character, on the basis that relative comparisons are only natural between associated elements of an integral situation. In that case, judgements of a relative kind are appropriate within a single scheme when there is scope for seeing the elements in the same perspective. For Burke, therefore, it is the *single* voice that introduces relativism, all *other* voices being excluded are left outside the perspective altogether. Such a perspective in which only a single voice is heard would represent a small part of the whole story. One agent, with one voice, cannot be a whole story. And it is necessary to perceive whole stories, and use them, so that they enter into exchanges with other whole stories, particularly with contrasting stories. Burke elaborates on his criterion for a whole story. He offers a 'pentad of terms', the basis of his grammar of motives, a grid of act, agent, scene, agency and purpose. It is not necessary here to fill out this project: as with Bakhtin, the approach adopted in this book benefits from some central illumination in Burke's work and proceeds along a path that is heading in the same direction as he takes, guided by rhetorical indications. An approach is bound to be rhetorical if it tells whole stories of arguments, even if the terms used to tell those stories do not belong to a specific rhetorical system. Thus, proceeding in this direction, he employs his term 'dramatism': 'dramatism, which treats of human motives in the terms of verbal action' (p. 33).

The stories in this book do indeed represent human motives in verbal action, motives that correlate people's arguments with their lives, hopes and fears. As Burke and Johnson insist, rhetoric is a search, a search for meaning in oppositions. Searching, it looks and finds the meaning to interpret: there is no end to the search, its activities do not end when it reaches a final conclusion. The search is at the heart of rhetoric.

One way of seeing this book is that it attempts to interpret four works without 'fragmentation of either drama or dialectic', so that other stories can be told in response. The interaction of those stories could form other arguments in turn. The aim is not simply to 'convert' argument into story – but to foster an interplay *between* story and argument, a sequence without a final outcome, an interaction that goes on.

The stories have referred to Habermas, and his views have an important place in this context. He proposes criteria for an *ideal argument*, a proposition which aligns very naturally with the Wanderer's hopes and attitude, and might seem to proceed inevitably from the good argument and the better argument. But the four stories point up the limitations in this view of argument: for can an ideal argument, such as Habermas proposes, have sufficient purchase upon the specific instances of arguing? How does the ideal vision fit the instances which give rise to the notion that there can be an ideal? What is the relationship between emergent truth and the process of exchange? What connection exists between the process of exchange and the truth which is sought in it? The four imagined arguments have a direct bearing on such questions. In those four instances, narrative and argument were inextricably bound together. But Habermas's ideal makes one specific requirement, to separate argument from narrative. This indeed is what he does. He condemns any blurring of the distinction as constituting merely: 'the no man's land between argumentation, narration, and fiction'.[8]

In his study, *The Philosophical Discourse of Modernity*, Habermas scrutinises the defenders of myth, such as Heidegger, and to myth he counterposes rational argument. By counterposing argument to myth, he ultimately paves the way for a separation between argument itself and narrative, if narrative is a descendent of myth:

> The event of Being can only be meditively experienced and presented narratively, but not argumentatively retrieved and explained. (p. 152)

Habermas takes for granted that argument and narrative are contrary to each other: then he defends argument against the claims of narrative. Narrative offers a world where:

> *To contradict*, to negate, now has only the sense of '*wanting to be different*'. (p. 124)

'Wanting to be different' reduces narrative to a matter of will and motive, not of 'validity claims in general' (p. 124). But the four readings connect argument and narrative in an organic way and suggest that argument and narrative are not antithetical, as Habermas has it. In the argumentative imagination, argument is also narrative – the argument emerges from the narrative, and the narrative is part of the argument – and those narratives, in turn, become grounds for further arguments.

A central idea round which Habermas's ideal argument coheres is:

> the model of unconstrained consensus formation in a communication community standing under cooperative constraints. (p. 295)

Such co-operation, such unconstrained consensus, implies a criticism of everyday life with its messy entanglements; but he fails to recognise that without story-telling, his ideal cannot connect with the world. Even the ideal of argument needs narrative, to connect it with what happens in the world.

The separation that Habermas has made between argument and narrative has unforeseen consequences: waiting in the wings is someone who will pounce upon these separated elements in an attempt to demolish them. Jean-François Lyotard has fabricated a powerful weapon for the purpose – *The Differend*:

> As distinguished from a litigation, a differend would be a case of conflict, between (at least) two parties, that cannot be equitably resolved for lack of a rule of judgment applicable to both arguments.[9]

In Lyotard's stories, opposing parties cannot even begin a meaningful exchange. Every voice has its own world: 'There are as many universes as there are phrases' (p. 76). Lyotard draws together all these stories in the idea of 'incommensurability', the idea that there is no rule for arbitrating between different perspectives. He even suggests that 'incommensurability' applies to the relationship between questions and propositions of different types. If one speaker asks questions, and another party makes propositions or urges rules, then there can be no significant encounter:

> Incommensurability, in the sense of heterogeneity of phrase regimens and of the impossibility of subjecting them to a single law . . . also marks the relation between either cognitives or prescriptives and interrogatives . . . . (p. 128)

Yet Lyotard's own repertoire of stories is tiny. *The Differend* repeats a single storyline as if it were the only possible story of argument. Every time different views arise, the storyline is the same: because there is no universal rule, there can be no development at all. But within the scheme, a contradiction arises:

> Why these encounters between phrases of heterogeneous regimen? Differends are born, you say, from these encounters. Can't these contacts be avoided? – That's impossible, contact is necessary. (p. 29)

Ultimately Lyotard is only interested in *absolute* resolutions, resolutions achieved by applying a fixed rule. But arguments can develop their own dynamic, a dynamic which belongs to the exchange itself, to the *particular* encounter. Underlying Lyotard's one story, there is an assumption about the motives of people arguing. Lyotard's participants are indifferent to truth:

> What you are calling bad will, etc., is the name that you give to the fact that the opponent does not have a stake in establishing reality, that he does not accept the rules for forming and validating cognitives, that his goal is not to convince. (p. 19)

For Habermas, ideal arguments depend on participants being motivated purely by the search for truth; Lyotard's opponents are not interested in 'establishing reality'. Between them, Habermas and Lyotard have an insufficient vocabulary for discussing the motives of participants in argument. If not pure, corrupt or indifferent; if not ideal, impossible. But there are as many more stories of argument as there are motives for arguing.

Without the argumentative imagination, a theory of argument lacks a repertoire of stories. Each theory is likely to turn on a 'representative anecdote', to adopt a term from Kenneth Burke.[10] Hans-Georg Gadamer is interested in the character of the person who seeks understanding through argument. Such a person appears in the *The Excursion* as the Wanderer, and Gadamer believes that such a person will seek knowledge in a particular way:

> Only a person who has questions can have knowledge, but questions include the antitheses of yes and no, of being like this and being like that.[11]

Gadamer recreates argument as:

> the process of question and answer, giving and taking, talking at cross purposes and seeing each other's point, . . . (p. 331)

Both Gadamer and Habermas are searching for a balanced exchange, but Gadamer believes that Habermas underestimates the role of tradition in supporting true exchanges. Gadamer, too, is conscious of the rhetorical influence on his own thinking, referring to 'the old topica', which

> is the art of finding arguments and serves to develop the sense of what is convincing, which works instinctively and ex-tempore and for this very reason cannot be replaced by science. (p. 21)

In Lyotard's story, there are never any motives to support a true exchange; in Gadamer's story, antithetical voices are brought to order by a shared respect deriving from a supportive tradition. When we juxtapose these theories, it seems ever clearer that each tells a significant story, but not the only story of argument. Each of these rhetorical stories intersects along some lines taken by the four main stories in this book – but they never overlap them along their length completely. Mascaro's *Bhagavad Gita*, for instance, tells a story of therapeutic exchange which interacts with Habermas's story of therapeutic exchange, and it also connects with another story that Gadamer tells about argument and authority. But the *Gita* is never accounted for by either story.

We need to recognise how *many* stories of argument can be told, and how many ways there are of telling them. Theories of argument have brought rhetoric to bear on one chosen pattern of events. But we can also connect rhetoric with the different fact, the fact of diversity. But the connection with narrative will only be sustained if we preserve the other criterion: the telling of *whole* stories. What is required is a range of complete stories, rather than an array of fragments. To engage with the complete story, Habermas uses informal logic, in an attempt to mediate between his ideal argument and specific instances. The basis of informal logic is the idea that arguments have contexts, and that contexts differ. For Habermas these contexts are primarily intellectual disciplines: theoretical discourse, practical discourse, aesthetic criticism, therapeutic critique and explicative discourse.[12]

Other informal logics focus more on social contexts, and ways of behaving. Douglas Walton distinguishes such contexts as quarrels, debates, negotiations and educational discussions.[13] Walton then analyses stories of arguments in terms of contexts:

> If a group of students and faculty were having an informal discussion, it might be quite reasonable to include arguments on tuition fees with those on library hours. In some ways, the two issues could be connected. But if a

> meeting is called on the topic of a specific proposal to extend library hours, the issue is purposely defined very narrowly, . . . (p. 72)

Some of Walton's examples have a bearing on *The Excursion* and on *The Hind and the Panther*. But the argumentative imagination makes us experience the intensity of argument and the ambiguities it throws up as great tensions, and informal logic necessarily regards such issues in a detached way that relieves them of much of their quality:

> Moreover, many arguments on controversial issues, for example in politics and religion, may quite rightly be based on passionate conviction. (p. 83)

There is no contradiction between informal logic and the way stories are dealt with in this text – there could be an interesting exchange, given the difference in tonality – but the argumentative imagination widens our sense of what is involved in a *whole* story of argument.

Hannah Arendt suggests that we live in 'dark times' if there is no hope of illumination through argumentative exchange. The inhabitants of such times naturally seek to

> avoid disputes and try as far as possible to deal only with people with whom they cannot come into conflict.[14]

Arendt turns too easily from such dark times to an idealised past, claiming that:

> the public realm has lost the power of illumination which was originally part of its very nature. (p. 4)

In fact, there is much contemporary thought which makes an intense effort to uphold argument, and is full of critical reflection on arguments which tries to find support for arguing. Her ideal is as vulnerable to other stories as Habermas's not-yet-realised paradigm. But through her own courage, and the perception of courage in others, she encourages us to hang on, and keep searching for stories of argument. She praises Karl Jaspers for nurturing the exchange of voices by having

> the patience to linger over a matter under discussion, and above all the ability to lure what is otherwise passed over in silence into the area of discourse, to make it worth talking about. (p. 78)

We need these other stories not as rigid ideals by which to disparage our own voices, nor as a comparative indication of failure to set against our own successes. Other stories raise other questions. There will always be other questions. There will always be other stories.

Argument and the argumentative imagination: references

1 M. M. Bakhtin, *Speech Genres and Other Late Essays*, 'The Problem of the Text', p. 121. Succeeding references given in text.

2 M. M. Bakhtin, *The Dialogic Imagination*, 'Discourse in the Novel', p. 285.

3 M. M. Bakhtin, *Speech Genres*, 'The Problem of the Text', pp. 114–15.

4 M. M. Bakhtin, *Speech Genres*, 'Methodology for the Human Sciences', p. 163.

5 M. M. Bakhtin, *Speech Genres*, 'From Notes Made in 1970–1', p. 136. Succeeding references given in text.

6 B. Johnson, *A World of Difference*, p. 17. Succeeding references given in text.

7 Kenneth Burke, *A Grammar of Motives*, p. 512. Succeeding references given in text.

8 Jurgen Habermas, *The Philosophical Discourse of Modernity*, trans. by Frederick Lawrence (Cambridge: Polity Press in assoc. with Basil Blackwell, translation copyright Massachussetts Institute of Technology, 1987), p. 302. Succeeding references given in text.

9 Jean-François Lyotard, *The Differend: Phrases in Dispute*, trans. by Georges Van Den Abbeele (Manchester: Manchester University Press, copyright the University of Minnesota, 1988), p. xi. Succeeding references given in text.

10 Kenneth Burke, *A Grammar of Motives*, p. 59.

11 Hans-Georg Gadamer, *Truth and Method*, p. 328. Succeeding references given in text.

12 Jurgen Habermas, *The Theory of Communicative Action* I, p. 23.

13 Douglas N. Walton, *Informal Logic*, p. 10 for a typology of contexts. Succeeding references given in text.

14 Hannah Arendt, *Men in Dark Times* (San Diego: Harcourt Brace Jovanovich 1955), p. 30. Succeeding references given in text. (Passages cited are from chapters in translation by Clara and Richard Wilson.)

Index